AF522328

Contemporary Political Philosophy

Contemporary Political Philosophy

Dr. Ashok Purohit

RANDOM PUBLICATIONS
NEW DELHI (INDIA)

Contemporary Political Philosophy

ISBN 978-93-5111-653-0

Published in 2015 in India by

RANDOM PUBLICATIONS

4376-A/4B, Gali Murari Lal, Ansari Road
New Delhi-110 002
Phone : +9111-43580356, 011-23289044, 011-43142548
e-mail: sales@randompublications.com, info@randompublications.com, randomexports@gmail.com

Reprinted 2025

Type Setting by : Friends Media, Delhi-110089
Digitally Printed at : Replika Press Pvt. Ltd.

Preface

Political philosophy is the study of topics such as politics, liberty, justice, property, rights, law, and the enforcement of a legal code by authority: what they are, why (or even if) they are needed, what, if anything, makes a government legitimate, what rights and freedoms it should protect and why, what form it should take and why, what the law is, and what duties citizens owe to a legitimate government, if any, and when it may be legitimately overthrown, if ever. In a vernacular sense, the term "political philosophy" often refers to a general view, or specific ethic, political belief or attitude, about politics that does not necessarily belong to the technical discipline of philosophy. In short, political philosophy is the activity, as with all philosophy, whereby the conceptual apparatus behind such concepts as aforementioned are analyzed, in their history, intent, evolution and the like.

Political philosophy is the normative study of government, relationships between individuals and communities, rights and justice. Depending on the philosopher, it can be entangled with metaphysics, ethics or economics. Pretty much every ideology that ever existed has its roots in political philosophy, making it hard to separate the analytical and normative branches of the discipline.

Even within a political community, there may be sharp disagreements about the role and purpose of government. Some want an active, involved government, seeing legal and political institutions as the means to solve our most pressing problems, and to help bring about peace, equality, justice, happiness, and to protect individual liberty. Others want a more minimal government, motivated, perhaps, by some of the disastrous political experiments of the 20th Century, and the thought that political power is often just a step away from tyranny. In many cases, these disagreements arise out of deep philosophical disagreements.

The aim of the book is to put researchers engaged in different areas of research on a common platform so as to be benefited by the current state of knowledge in the field of this subject.

I would like to thank my team for standing beside me throughout my career and writing this book. My special thanks go to "Random Publications" who have published the book.

– Dr. Ashok Purohit

Contents

1

Political Philosophy

Political philosophy is the study of such topics as liberty, justice, property, rights, law, and the enforcement of a legal code by authority: what they are, why they are needed, what makes a government legitimate, what rights and freedoms it should protect and why, what form it should take and why, what the law is, and what duties citizens owe to a legitimate government, if any, and when it may be legitimately overthrown—if ever. In a vernacular sense, the term 'political philosophy' often refers to a general view, or specific ethic, political belief or attitude, about politics that does not necessarily belong to the technical discipline of philosophy. Political philosophy can also be understood by analysing it through the perspectives of metaphysics, epistemology and axiology thereby unearthing the ultimate reality side, the knowledge or methodical side and the value aspects of politics. Then it gives insights into the various aspects of the origin of the state, its institutions and laws.

METHODOLOGY

Methodology can be:

- "The analysis of the principles of methods, rules, and postulates employed by a discipline".
- "The systematic study of methods that are, can be, or have been applied within a discipline".
- Is the study or description of methods.

Method can be defined as as a systematic and orderly procedure or process for attaining some objective. A methodology is instantiated and materialized by a set of methods, techniques and tools.

A tool is any instrument or apparatus that is necessary to the performance of some task. A methodology does not describe specific methods; nevertheless it does specify several processes that need to be followed. These processes constitute a generic framework. They may be broken down in sub-processes, they may be combined, or their sequence may change. However, any task exercise must carry out these processes in one form or another. Methodology may be a description of process, or may be expanded to include a philosophically coherent collection of theories, concepts or ideas as they relate to a particular discipline or field of enquiry.

Methodology may refer to nothing more than a simple set of methods or procedures, or it may refer to the rationale and the philosophical assumptions that underlie a particular study relative to the scientific method. For example, scholarly literature often includes a part on the methodology of the researchers.

POLITICAL SOCIOLOGY

Political sociology is the study of the relations between state and society. The discipline draws on comparative history to analyse socio-political trends. A typical research question in this area might be: "Why do so few American citizens choose to vote?" The field developed from the work of Max Weber, Barrington Moore, Jr., and Moisey Ostrogorsky.

THEORY

There are four main areas of research focus in contemporary political sociology:

- The socio-political formation of the modern state.
- "Who rules"? How social inequality between groups influences politics.
- How public personalities, social movements and trends outside of the formal institutions of political power affect politics.
- Power relationships within and between social groups. Contemporary theorists include Robert A. Dahl, Seymour Martin Lipset, Theda Skocpol, Luc Boltanski and Nicos Poulantzas.

Political sociology looks at how major social trends can affect the political process, as well as exploring how various social forces work together to change political policies. Political sociologists apply several theories to substantive issues. Three major theoretical frameworks are pluralism, elite or managerial theory and class analysis which overlaps with Marxist analysis. Pluralism sees politics primarily as a contest among competing interest groups. Elite or managerial theory is sometimes called a state-centred approach. It explains what the state does by looking at constraints from organizational structure, semi-autonomous state managers, and interests that arise from the state as a unique, power concentrating organization. A leading representative is Theda Skocpol.

Social class theory analysis emphasizes the political power of capitalist elites. The theory emerged from Marxism in the 1850s based primarily on the premise of economic exploitation of one class by another. It split into two parts: one is the power structure or instrumentalist approach, another is the structuralist approach. The power structure approach focuses on Who Rules? and its most well-known representative is G. William Domhoff. The structuralist approach emphasizes how the very way a capitalist economy operates only allows and encourages the state to do some things but not others. Its best known representative was Nicos Poulantzas. Important innovations in the field come from the French Pragmatism and particularly from the Political and Moral Sociology elaborated by Luc Boltanski and Laurent Thévenot. Political sociology also concerns the play of power and personality, for instance, the impact of globalization upon identity: "The fragmentation and pluralization of values and life-styles, with the growth of mass media and consumerism and decline of stable occupations and communities, all means that previously taken for granted social identities have become politicized."

PSEPHOLOGY

Psephology is that branch of political science which deals with the study and statistical analysis of elections. Psephology uses historical precinct voting data, public opinion polls, campaign finance information and similar statistical data. The term was coined in the United Kingdom in 1952 by historian R.B. McCallum to describe the scientific analysis of past elections. In Britain the term occasionally appears in scholarly literature. Psephology also has various applications specifically in analyzing the results of election returns for current indicators, as opposed to predictive purposes. For instance, the Gallagher Index measures the disproportionality of an election. Notable psephologists include Australians Antony Green and Malcolm Mackerras; and Americans Michael Barone.

HISTORY

ANCIENT

Ancient China

Chinese political philosophy dates back to the Spring and Autumn Period, specifically with Confucius in the 6th century BC. Chinese political philosophy developed as a response to the social and political breakdown of the country characteristic of the Spring and Autumn Period and the Warring States period. The major philosophies during the period, Confucianism, Legalism, Mohism, Agrarianism and Taoism, each had a political aspect to their philosophical schools. Philosophers such as Confucius, Mencius, and Mozi, focused on political unity and political stability as the basis of their political philosophies. Confucianism advocated a hierarchical, meritocratic government based on empathy, loyalty, and interpersonal relationships. Legalism advocated a highly authoritarian government based on draconian punishments and laws. Mohism advocated a communal, decentralised government centered on frugality and ascetism.

The Agrarians advocated a peasant utopian communalism and egalitarianism. Taoism advocated a proto-anarchism. Legalism was the dominant political philosophy of the Qin Dynasty, but was replaced by State Confucianism in the Han Dynasty. Prior to China's adoption of communism, State Confucianism remained the dominant political philosophy of China up to the 20th century.

Ancient Greece

Western political philosophy originates in the philosophy of ancient Greece, where political philosophy begins with Plato's *Republic* in the 4th century BC. Ancient Greece was dominated by city-states, which experimented with various forms of political organisation, grouped by Plato into four categories: timocracy, tyranny, democracy and oligarchy. One of the first, extremely important classical works of political philosophy is Plato's *Republic*, which was followed by Aristotle's Nichomachean Ethics and Politics.

Roman political philosophy was influenced by the Stoics, including the Roman statesman Cicero.

Ancient Indian Subcontinent and Hindu Philosophy

Indian political philosophy evolved in the ancient times, and created well organised and mature institutions of state.

There was a clear distinction between:

- Nation and state
- Religion and state.

The Hindu states used constitutions which evolved over time and were based on:

- Political and legal treatises
- Prevalent social institutions.

The institutions of state were broadly divided into governance, administration, defence, law and order. Mantranga or the principal governing body consists of the King, Prime Minister, Commander in chief of army, Chief Priest of the King. Prime Minister heads the committee of ministers along with head of executive (Maha Amatya). Chanakya is a well known political philosopher regarded as among the greatest of all times. His treatise Arthashastra not only was a great ancient text but as recent as Niccolò Machiavelli. reflect his views. Chanukya in his political treatise Arthashastra of 4th Century BC makes comprehensive accounting of the science of politics for a wise ruler, policies for foreign affairs and wars, system of spy state and surveillance and economic stability of the state. However Chanakya himself quotes several authorities like Brihaspati,Ushanas, Prachetasa Manu, Parasara, Ambi and mentions himself as a descendant of a long lineage of political philosophers with his father Chanaka being his immediate predecessor. Sukra Neeti sara is another treatise of ancient Indian political philosophy which is still extant. An example of constitution of ancient India is the Manusmrti or Laws of Manu

MEDIEVAL CHRISTIANITY

Saint Augustine

The early Christian philosophy of Augustine of Hippo was heavily influenced by Plato. The main change that Christian thought brought was to moderate the Stoicism and theory of justice of the Roman world, and emphasize the role of the state in applying mercy as a moral example. Augustine also preached that one was not a member of his or her city, but was either a citizen of the City of God (Civitas Dei) or the City of Man (Civitas Terrena). Augustine's *City of God* is an influential work of this period that refuted the thesis, after the First Sack of Rome, that the Christian view could be realised on Earth at all - a view many Christian Romans held.

Saint Thomas Aquinas

In political philosophy, Aquinas is most meticulous when dealing with varieties of law. According to Aquinas, there are four different kinds of laws:

1. God's cosmic law
2. God's scriptural law
3. Natural law or rules of conduct universally applicable within reason
4. Human law or specific rules applicable to specific circumstances.

ISLAMIC GOLDEN AGE

Mutazilite vs Asharite

The rise of Islam, based on both the Qur'an and the prophet Muhammad strongly altered the power balances and perceptions of origin of power in the Mediterranean region. Early Islamic philosophy emphasized an inexorable link between science and religion, and the process of ijtihad to find truth - in effect *all* philosophy was "political" as it had real implications for governance. This view was challenged by the "rationalist" Mutazilite philosophers, who held a more Hellenic view, reason above revelation, and as such are known to modern scholars as the first speculative theologians of Islam; they were supported by a secular aristocracy who sought freedom of action independent of the Caliphate. By the late ancient period, however, the "traditionalist" Asharite view of Islam had in general triumphed. According to the Asharites, reason must be subordinate to the Quran and the Sunna. Islamic political philosophy, was, indeed, rooted in the very sources of Islam, *i.e.* the Qur'an and the Sunnah, the words and practices of Muhammad - thus making it essentially theocratic. However, in the Western thought, it is generally supposed that it was a specific area peculiar merely to the great philosophers of Islam:

- al-Kindi (Alkindus),
- al-Farabi (Abunaser),

- Ibn Sina (Avicenna),
- Ibn Bajjah (Avempace),
- Ibn Rushd (Averroes), and
- Ibn Khaldun.

The political conceptions of Islam such as kudrah (power), sultan, ummah, cemaa (obligation)-and even the "core" terms of the Qur'an, *i.e.* ibadah, din (religion), rab (master) and ilah- is taken as the basis of an analysis. Hence, not only the ideas of the Muslim political philosophers but also many other jurists and ulama posed political ideas and theories. For example, the ideas of the Khawarij in the very early years of Islamic history on Khilafa and Ummah, or that of Shia Islam on the concept of Imamah are considered proofs of political thought. The clashes between the Ehl-i Sunna and Shia in the 7th and 8th centuries had a genuine political character.

Ibn Khaldun

The 14th century Arab scholar Ibn Khaldun is considered one of the greatest political theorists. The British philosopher-anthropologist Ernest Gellner considered Ibn Khaldun's definition of government, "...an institution which prevents injustice other than such as it commits itself," the best in the history of political theory. For Ibn Khaldun, government should be restrained to a minimum for as a necessary evil, it is the constraint of men by other men.

MEDIEVAL EUROPE

Medieval political philosophy in Europe was heavily influenced by Christian thinking. It had much in common with the Mutazalite Islamic thinking in that the Roman Catholics though subordinating philosophy to theology did not subject reason to revelation but in the case of contradictions, subordinated reason to faith as the Asharite of Islam.

The Scholastics by combining the philosophy of Aristotle with the Christianity of St. Augustine emphasized the potential harmony inherent in reason and revelation. Perhaps the most influential political philosopher of medieval Europe was St. Thomas Aquinas who helped reintroduce Aristotle's works, which had only been transmitted to Catholic Europe through Muslim Spain, along with the commentaries of Averroes.

Aquinas's use of them set the agenda, for scholastic political philosophy dominated European thought for centuries even unto the Renaissance. Medieval political philosophers, such as Aquinas in *Summa Theologica*, developed the idea that a king who is a tyrant is no king at all and could be overthrown. Magna Carta, viewed by many as a cornerstone of Anglo-American political liberty, explicitly proposes the right to revolt against the ruler for justice sake. Other documents similar to Magna Carta are found in other European countries such as Spain and Hungary.

EUROPEAN RENAISSANCE

During the Renaissance secular political philosophy began to emerge after about a century of theological political thought in Europe. While the Middle Ages did see secular politics in practice under the rule of the Holy Roman Empire, the academic field was wholly scholastic and therefore Christian in nature.

Niccolò Machiavelli

One of the most influential works during this burgeoning period was Niccolò Machiavelli's *The Prince*, written between 1511–12 and published in 1532, after Machiavelli's death. That work, as well as *The Discourses*, a rigourous analysis of the classical period, did much to influence modern political thought in the West. A minority (including Jean-Jacques Rousseau) could interpret The Prince as a satire meant to be given to the Medici after their recapture of Florence and their subsequent expulsion of Machiavelli from Florence. Though the work was written for the di Medici family in order to perhaps influence them to free him from exile, Machiavelli supported the Republic of Florence rather than the oligarchy of the di Medici family.

At any rate, Machiavelli presents a pragmatic and somewhat consequentialist view of politics, whereby good and evil are mere means used to bring about an end, *i.e.* the secure and powerful state. Thomas Hobbes, well known for his theory of the social contract, goes on to expand this view at the start of the 17th century during the English Renaissance. Although neither Machiavelli nor Hobbes believed in the divine right of kings, they both believed in the inherent selfishness of the individual. It was necessarily this belief that led them to adopt a strong central power as the only means of preventing the disintegration of the social order.

John Locke

John Locke in particular exemplified this new age of political theory with his work *Two Treatises of Government*. In it Locke proposes a state of nature theory that directly complements his conception of how political development occurs and how it can be founded through contractual obligation. Locke stood to refute Sir Robert Filmer's paternally founded political theory in favour of a natural system based on nature in a particular given system. The theory of the divine right of kings became a passing fancy, exposed to the type of ridicule with which John Locke treated it. Unlike Machiavelli and Hobbes but like Aquinas, Locke would accept Aristotle's dictum that man seeks to be happy in a state of social harmony as a social animal. Unlike Aquinas's preponderant view on the salvation of the soul from original sin, Locke believes man's mind comes into this world as tabula rasa. For Locke, knowledge is neither innate, revealed nor based on authority but subject to uncertainty tempered by reason, tolerance and moderation. According to Locke, an absolute ruler as proposed by Hobbes is unnecessary, for natural law is based on reason and seeking peace and survival for man.

EUROPEAN AGE OF ENLIGHTENMENT

During the Enlightenment period, new theories about what the human was and is and about the definition of reality and the way it was perceived, along with the discovery of other societies in the Americas, and the changing needs of political societies (especially in the wake of the English Civil War, the American Revolution and the French Revolution) led to new questions and insights by such thinkers as Thomas Hobbes, John Locke, Montesquieu and Jean-Jacques Rousseau. These theorists were driven by two basic questions: one, by what right or need do people form states; and two, what the best form for a state could be. These fundamental questions involved a conceptual distinction between the concepts of "state" and "government." It was decided that "state" would refer to a set of enduring institutions through which power would be distributed and its use justified. The term "government" would refer to a specific group of people who occupied the institutions of the state, and create the laws and ordinances by which the people, themselves included, would be bound.

This conceptual distinction continues to operate in political science, although some political scientists, philosophers, historians and cultural anthropologists have argued that most political action in any given society occurs outside of its state, and that there are societies that are not organised into states that nevertheless must be considered in political terms. As long as the concept of natural order was not introduced, the social sciences could not evolve independently of theistic thinking. Since the cultural revolution of the 17th century in England, which spread to France and the rest of Europe, society has been considered subject to natural laws akin to the physical world. Political and economic relations were drastically influenced by these theories as the concept of the guild was subordinated to the theory of free trade, and Roman Catholic dominance of theology was increasingly challenged by Protestant churches subordinate to each nation-state, which also (in a fashion the Roman Catholic Church often decried angrily) preached in the vulgar or native language of each region. However, the enlightenment was an outright attack on religion, particularly Christianity.

The publication of Denis Diderot's and Jean d'Alembert's *Encyclopédie ou Dictionnaire raisonné des sciences, des arts et des métiers* marked the crowning intellectual achievement of the epoch. The most outspoken critic of the church in France was François Marie Arouet de Voltaire, a representative figure of the enlightenment. After Voltaire, religion would never be the same again in France. In the Ottoman Empire, these ideological reforms did not take place and these views did not integrate into common thought until much later. As well, there was no spread of this doctrine within the New World and the advanced civilizations of the Aztec, Maya, Inca, Mohican, Delaware, Huron and especially the Iroquois. The Iroquois philosophy in particular gave much to Christian thought of the time and in many cases actually inspired some of the institutions adopted in the United States: for example, Benjamin Franklin was a great admirer of some of the methods of the Iroquois Confederacy, and much of early American literature emphasized the political philosophy of the natives.

INDUSTRIALISATION AND THE MODERN ERA

Karl Marx and his critique of capitalism—developed with Friedrich Engels—was, alongside liberalism and fascism, one of the defining ideological movements of the Twentieth Century. The industrial revolution produced a parallel revolution in political thought. Urbanisation and capitalism greatly reshaped society.

During this same period, the socialist movement began to form. In the mid-19th century, Marxism was developed, and socialism in general gained increasing popular support, mostly from the urban working class. Without breaking entirely from the past, Marx established principles that would be used by future revolutionaries of the 20th century namely Vladimir Lenin, Mao Zedong, Ho Chi Minh, and Fidel Castro. Though Hegel's philosophy of history is similar to Immanuel Kant's, and Karl Marx's theory of revolution towards the common good is partly based on Kant's view of history—Marx is said to have declared that on the whole, he was just trying to straighten out G. W.F.

Hegel who was actually upside down. Unlike Marx who believed in historical materialism, Hegel believed in the *Phenomenology of Spirit*. Be that as it may, by the late 19th century, socialism and trade unions were established members of the political landscape. In addition, the various branches of anarchism, with thinkers such as Mikhail Bakunin, Pierre-Joseph Proudhon or Peter Kropotkin, and syndicalism also gained some prominence.

In the Anglo-American world, anti-imperialism and pluralism began gaining currency at the turn of the 20th century. World War I was a watershed event in human history. The Russian Revolution of 1917 (and similar, albeit less successful, revolutions in many other European countries) brought communism - and in particular the political theory of Leninism, but also on a smaller level Luxemburgism (gradually) - on the world stage. At the same time, social democratic parties won elections and formed governments for the first time, often as a result of the introduction of universal suffrage. However, a group of central European economists led by Austrians Ludwig von Mises and Friedrich Hayek identified the collectivist underpinnings to the various new socialist and fascist doctrines of government power as being different brands of political totalitarianism.

CONTEMPORARY POLITICAL PHILOSOPHY

From the end of World War II until 1971, when John Rawls published *A Theory of Justice*, political philosophy declined in the Anglo-American academic world, as analytic philosophers expressed skepticism about the possibility that normative judgements had cognitive content, and political science turned towards statistical methods and behaviouralism. In continental Europe, on the other hand, the postwar decades saw a huge blossoming of political philosophy, with Marxism dominating the field. This was the time of Jean-Paul Sartre and Louis Althusser, and the victories of Mao Zedong in China and Fidel Castro in Cuba, as well as the events of May 1968 led to increased interest in revolutionary ideology, especially by the New Left. A number of continental European émigrés to Britain and the United States—including Hannah Arendt, Karl Popper, Friedrich Hayek, Leo Strauss, Isaiah Berlin, Eric Voegelin and Judith Shklar—encouraged continued study in political philosophy in the Anglo-American world, but in the 1950s and 1960s they and their students remained at odds with the analytic establishment.

Communism remained an important focus especially during the 1950s and 1960s. Colonialism and racism were important issues that arose. In general, there was a marked trend towards a pragmatic approach to political issues, rather than a philosophical one. Much academic debate regarded one or both of two pragmatic topics: how (or whether) to apply utilitarianism to problems of political policy, or how (or whether) to apply economic models (such as rational choice theory) to political issues. The rise of feminism, LGBT social movements and the end of colonial rule and of the political exclusion of such minorities as African Americans and sexual minorities in the developed world has led to feminist, postcolonial, and multicultural thought becoming significant. This led to a challenge to the social contract by philosophers Charles W. Mills in his book *The Racial Contract* and Carole Patemen in her book *The Sexual Contract* that the social contract excluded persons of colour and women respectively.

In Anglo-American academic political philosophy, the publication of John Rawls's *A Theory of Justice* in 1971 is considered a milestone. Rawls used a thought experiment, the original position, in which representative parties choose principles of justice for the basic structure of society from behind a veil of ignorance. Rawls also offered a criticism of utilitarian approaches to questions of political justice. Robert Nozick's 1974 book *Anarchy, State, and Utopia*, which won a National Book Award, responded to Rawls from a libertarian perspective and gained academic respectability for libertarian viewpoints. Contemporaneously with the rise of analytic ethics in Anglo-American thought, in Europe several new lines of philosophy directed at critique of existing societies arose between the 1950s and 1980s. Most of these took elements of Marxist economic analysis, but combined them with a more cultural or ideological emphasis.

Out of the Frankfurt School, thinkers like Herbert Marcuse, Theodor W. Adorno, Max Horkheimer, and Jürgen Habermas combined Marxian and Freudian perspectives. Along somewhat different lines, a number of other continental thinkers—still largely influenced by Marxism—put new emphases on structuralism and on a "return to Hegel". Within the (post-) structuralist line (though mostly not taking that label) are thinkers such as Gilles Deleuze, Michel Foucault, Claude Lefort, and Jean Baudrillard. The Situationists were more influenced by Hegel; Guy Debord, in particular, moved a Marxist analysis of commodity fetishism to the realm of consumption, and looked at the relation between consumerism and dominant ideology formation. Another debate developed around the (distinct) criticisms of liberal political theory made by Michael Sandel and Charles Taylor. The liberal-communitarian debate is often considered valuable for generating a new set of philosophical problems, rather than a profound and illuminating clash of perspectives. There is fruitful interaction between political philosophers and international relations theorists. The rise of globalisation has created the need for an international normative framework, and political theory has moved to fill the gap. One of the most prominent subjects in recent political philosophy has been the theory of deliberative democracy. The seminal work is by Jurgen Habermas in Germany but the most extensive literature has been in English, led by theorists such as Jane Mansbridge, Joshua Cohen, Amy Gutmann and Dennis Thompson.

INFLUENTIAL POLITICAL PHILOSOPHERS

A larger list of political philosophers is intended to be closer to exhaustive. Listed below are some of the most canonical or important thinkers, and especially philosophers whose central focus was in political philosophy and/or who are good representatives of a particular school of thought.

- *Aristotle:* Wrote his *Politics* as an extension of his *Nicomachean Ethics*. Notable for the theories that humans are social animals, and that the polis (Ancient Greek city state) existed to bring about the good life appropriate to such animals. His political theory is based upon an ethics of perfectionism (as is Marx's, on some readings).
- *Murray Rothbard:* The central theorist of anarcho-capitalism and an Austrian School economist.
- *Thomas Aquinas:* In synthesizing Christian theology and Peripatetic (Aristotelian) teaching, Aquinas contends that God's gift of higher reason—manifest in human law by way of the divine virtues—gives way to the assembly of righteous government.
- *Mikhail Bakunin:* After Pierre Joseph Proudhon, Bakunin became the most important political philosopher of anarchism. His specific version of anarchism is called collectivist anarchism.
- *Jeremy Bentham:* The first thinker to analyse social justice in terms

of maximization of aggregate individual benefits. Founded the philosophical/ethical school of thought known as utilitarianism.

- *Isaiah Berlin:* Developed the distinction between positive and negative liberty
- *Edmund Burke:* Irish member of the British parliament, Burke is credited with the creation of conservative thought. Burke's Reflections on the Revolution in France is the most popular of his writings where he denounced the French revolution. Burke was one of the biggest supporters of the American Revolution.
- *Confucius:* The first thinker to relate ethics to the political order.
- *William E. Connolly:* Helped introduce postmodern philosophy into political theory, and promoted new theories of pluralism and agonistic democracy.
- *John Dewey:* Co-founder of pragmatism and analysed the essential role of education in the maintenance of democratic government.
- *Han Feizi:* The major figure of the Chinese Fajia (Legalist) school, advocated government that adhered to laws and a strict method of administration.
- *Michel Foucault:* Critiqued the modern conception of power on the basis of the prison complex and other prohibitive institutions, such as those that designate sexuality, madness and knowledge as the roots of their infrastructure, a critique that demonstrated that subjection is the power formation of subjects in any linguistic forum and that revolution cannot just be thought as the reversal of power between classes.
- *Antonio Gramsci:* Instigated the concept of *hegemony*. Argued that the state and the ruling class uses culture and ideology to gain the consent of the classes it rules over.
- *Thomas Hill Green:* Modern liberal thinker and early supporter of positive freedom.
- *Jürgen Habermas:* Contemporary democratic theorist and sociologist. He has pioneered such concepts as the public sphere, communicative action, and deliberative democracy. His early work was heavily influenced by the Frankfurt School.
- *Friedrich Hayek:* He argued that central planning was inefficient because members of central bodies could not know enough to match the preferences of consumers and workers with existing conditions. Hayek further argued that central economic planning - a mainstay of socialism - would lead to a "total" state with dangerous power. He advocated free-market capitalism in which the main role of the state is to maintain the rule of law and let spontaneous order develop.
- *G. W. F. Hegel:* Emphasized the "cunning" of history, arguing that it

followed a rational trajectory, even while embodying seemingly irrational forces; influenced Marx, Kierkegaard, Nietzsche, and Oakeshott.

- *Thomas Hobbes:* Generally considered to have first articulated how the concept of a social contract that justifies the actions of rulers (even where contrary to the individual desires of governed citizens), can be reconciled with a conception of sovereignty.
- *John Locke:* Like Hobbes, described a social contract theory based on citizens' fundamental rights in the state of nature. He departed from Hobbes in that, based on the assumption of a society in which moral values are independent of governmental authority and widely shared, he argued for a government with power limited to the protection of personal property. His arguments may have been deeply influential to the formation of the United States Constitution.
- *David Hume:* Hume criticized the social contract theory of John Locke and others as resting on a myth of some actual agreement. Hume was a realist in recognising the role of force to forge the existence of states and that consent of the governed was merely hypothetical. He also introduced the concept of utility, later picked up on and developed by Jeremy Bentham.
- *Thomas Jefferson:* Politician and political theorist during the American Enlightenment. Expanded on the philosophy of Thomas Paine by instrumenting republicanism in the United States. Most famous for the United States Declaration of Independence.
- *Immanuel Kant:* Argued that participation in civil society is undertaken not for self-preservation, as per Thomas Hobbes, but as a moral duty. First modern thinker who fully analysed structure and meaning of obligation. Argued that an international organisation was needed to preserve world peace.
- *Peter Kropotkin:* One of the classic anarchist thinkers and the most influential theorist of anarcho-communism
- *Niccolò Machiavelli:* First systematic analyses of:
  - How consent of a populace is negotiated between and among rulers rather than simply a naturalistic (or theological) given of the structure of society;
  - Precursor to the concept of ideology in articulating the epistemological structure of commands and law.
- *James Madison:* American politician and protege of Jefferson considered to be "Father of the Constitution" and "Father of the Bill of Rights" of the United States. As a political theorist, he believed in separation of powers and proposed a comprehensive set of checks and balances that are necessary to protect the rights of an individual from the tyranny of the majority.

- *Herbert Marcuse:* Called the father of the new left. One of the principal thinkers within the Frankfurt School, and generally important in efforts to fuse the thought of Sigmund Freud and Karl Marx. Introduced the concept of *repressive desublimation*, in which social control can operate not only by direct control, but also by manipulation of desire. His work Eros and Civilization and notion of a non-repressive society was influential on the 1960s and its counter-cultural social movements.
- *Karl Marx:* In large part, added the historical dimension to an understanding of society, culture and economics. Created the concept of *ideology* in the sense of (true or false) beliefs that shape and control social actions. Analysed the fundamental nature of class as a mechanism of governance and social interaction. Profoundly influenced world politics with his theory of communism.
- *Mencius:* One of the most important thinkers in the Confucian school, he is the first theorist to make a coherent argument for an obligation of rulers to the ruled.
- *John Stuart Mill:* A utilitarian, and the person who named the system; he goes further than Bentham by laying the foundation for liberal democratic thought in general and modern, as opposed to classical, liberalism in particular. Articulated the place of individual liberty in an otherwise utilitarian framework.
- *Baron de Montesquieu:* Analysed protection of the people by a "balance of powers" in the divisions of a state.
- *Mozi:* Eponymous founder of the Mohist school, advocated a form of consequentialism.
- *Robert Nozick:* Criticized Rawls, and argued for libertarianism, by appeal to a hypothetical history of the state and of property.
- *Thomas Paine:* Enlightenment writer who defended liberal democracy, the American Revolution, and French Revolution in Common Sense and The Rights of Man.
- *Plato:* Along with his mentor, Socrates, and his student, Aristotle, Plato helped to lay the foundations of Western philosophy and science.
- *Pierre-Joseph Proudhon:* Commonly considered the father of modern anarchism, specifically mutualism.
- Ayn Rand – The creator of the philosophy of Objectivism
- *John Rawls:* Revitalised the study of normative political philosophy in Anglo-American universities with his 1971 book A Theory of Justice, which uses a version of social contract theory to answer fundamental questions about justice and to criticise utilitarianism.
- *Jean-Jacques Rousseau:* Analysed the social contract as an expression of the general will, and controversially argued in favour of absolute democracy where the people at large would act as sovereign.

- *Carl Schmitt:* German political theorist, tied to the Nazis, who developed the concepts of the Friend/Enemy Distinction and the State of exception. Though his most influential books were written in the 1920s, he continued to write prolifically until his death (in academic quasi-exile) in 1985. He heavily influenced 20th century political philosophy both within the Frankfurt School and among others as diverse as Jacques Derrida, Hannah Arendt, and Giorgio Agamben.
- *Adam Smith:* Often said to have founded modern economics; explained emergence of economic benefits from the self-interested behaviour ("the invisible hand") of artisans and traders. While praising its efficiency, Smith also expressed concern about the effects of industrial labour (*e.g.* repetitive activity) on workers. His work on moral sentiments sought to explain social bonds outside the economic sphere.
- *Socrates:* Widely considered the founder of Western political philosophy, via his spoken influence on Athenian contemporaries; since Socrates never wrote anything, much of what we know about him and his teachings comes through his most famous student, Plato.
- *Baruch Spinoza:* Set forth the first analysis of *rational egoism*, in which the rational interest of self is conformance with pure reason. To Spinoza's thinking, in a society in which each individual is guided of reason, political authority would be superfluous.
- *Max Stirner:* Important thinker within anarchism and the main representative of the anarchist current known as individualist anarchism
- *Leo Strauss:* Famously rejected modernity, mostly on the grounds of what he perceived to be modern political philosophy's excessive self-sufficiency of reason and flawed philosophical grounds for moral and political normativity. He argued instead we should return to pre-modern thinkers for answers to contemporary issues. His philosophy was influential on the formation of Neo-Conservativism, and a number of his students later were members of the Bush administration.
- *Henry David Thoreau:* Influential American thinker on such diverse later political positions and topics such as pacifism, anarchism, environmentalism and civil disobedience who influenced later important political activists such as Martin Luther King, Mahatma Gandhi and Leo Tolstoy.
- *François-Marie Arouet (Voltaire):* French Enlightenment writer, poet, and philosopher famous for his advocacy of civil liberties, including freedom of religion and free trade.
- *Bernard Williams:* A British moral philosopher whose posthumously published work on political philosophy 'In the Beginning was the Deed'

has been seen - along with the works of Raymond Geuss - as a key foundational work on Political Realism.

MEANING OF POLITICAL SCIENCE

Political Science is that part of social science which deals with the foundations of the *state* and the principles of the *government*. According to J W Garner, "Politics begins and ends with the state." Similarly, R G Gettel wrote that Politics is the "study of the state in the past, present and future". Harold J Laski stated in the same vein that the study of Politics concerns itself with the life of men and women in relation to organized state. Thus as a social science, Political Science deals with those aspects of individuals in society which relate to their activities and organizations devoted to seeking of power, resolution of conflicts and all these, within an overall framework of the rule and law as laid down by the state.

CHANGING MEANING OF POLITICAL SCIENCE

The term Politics is derived from the Greek word *polis* which means city-state. That is why many commentators, as you saw, rightly define Politics in terms of the state or government.

However, this definition does not exhaust the meaning of Politics. Politics also deals with *power*. Harold D. Lasswell and Abraham Kaplan define Political Science as "the study of shaping and sharing of power". In a word, *Politics deals with both state and power*. However, the power that Political Science deals with is, more often than not, the legitimate power. Since science is the systematic study of any phenomenon through observation and experiment, it follows that Political Science studies the state and power in all their aspects. You will learn more about the state and power later in this lesson. Political Science deals with both empirical facts and normative issues. Facts are in the domain of "what is" and value preferences are in the domain of "what should be." For example, if somebody says India is a parliamentary democracy, he or she is making a statement of empirical fact.

This is what India today actually is. But if she or he were to make a statement like the one that India should switch over to presidential form of democracy, the statement would be a normative one.

Political Science is not satisfied with describing the state of affairs, it wants to change or improve upon them. Empirical statements are true or false by virtue of what observation shows to be the case. Evaluative statements are ethical/moral imperatives, which are often said not to be true or false in any sense at all. Formal statements are true or false by virtue of the meanings of their constituent terms alone. Political Philosophy deals with formal statements. Political Science deals with empirical statements and also evaluates the existing political institutions, practices and focuses on how to improve them.

GROWTH OF THE DISCIPLINE OF POLITICAL SCIENCE

Systematic study of Politics started with the Greeks in the fourth century BC. Philosophers like Plato and Aristotle used it in the most comprehensive sense. Aristotle called Politics a "master science". For him, it comprised of not only the institutions of state or government but also family, property and other social institutions. Politics, for the Greeks, was an allencompassing activity. The ancient Greek view about Political Science was mainly *ethical*. In contrast, the ancient Romans considered the *legal* aspect of Politics more important for their governance. During the Middle Ages, Political Science became a branch of religious order of the Church. Political authority was, then, subordinated to the authority of the Church. As the state grew in size and became more complex, Political Science acquired a realistic and secular approach. After the Industrial Revolution, the role of the State, which was limited to maintenance of law and order and providing defence against external aggression, underwent considerable changes with the emergence of the new economic system called capitalism. In the twentieth century, after the Second World War, the 'behavioural approach' offered a new dimension of Political Science.

The behavioural movement in American Political Science in the 1950s and the 1960s placed a lot of emphasis on the 'science' part of Politics. It wanted to model Politics after the methods followed by natural sciences like Physics, Botany, etc. The behaviouralists built theory inductively from empirical propositions. Those who follow inductive method would come to the conclusion after study, observation and experiment. For example, when some behaviouralists saw African-Americans of the southern United States of America voted for the Democratic Party of the United States, they came to the conclusion that the African-Americans do vote for the Democrats. This behavioural approach shifted the focus of its study from political institutions and structures to their functions.

It placed stress on political activity and the behaviour of men and women who control these institutions. It replaced the study of ideas by the study of facts, evidence and behaviour. It considered political activity manifested in behaviour as the true subject of Political Science. A political activity may be in the form of an individual contesting an election.

It may be the activity of a group seeking the adoption of a particular policy in its favour by the government. As different people pursue different interests, such activities tend to generate disagreement, competition and conflict. But the distinctive quality of Politics is that it includes *physical coercion* or *force* by the government. It may and usually does involve the persuasive influence and effort of the government to resolve conflicts through its balanced policy decisions. Politics is also viewed as a process whereby individuals, groups or communities seek to achieve their specific but conflicting goals. Politics, as the process, seeks to allocate resources authoritatively. Politics, as the study of structures, institutions, processes and activities, recognizes the possibility of the use of power. The Marxist approach, which is derived from the writings of the nineteenth century German philosopher Karl Marx, views Politics as a study of irreconcilable conflicts between the two classes 'haves' and the 'have-nots'; in other words, the exploiters and the exploited.

The emancipation of the have-nots will come only through a revolution which would put an end to the institution of private property, thus changing the class society to the classless society. But Politics, as against the Marxist view, has another view also, the liberal view, according to which Politics is considered as an as effort for conciliation and accommodation to bring about rule of order and Justice. Incidentally, the Marxist view of politics comes as a reaction to the liberal view of politics.

HISTORY OF POLITICAL SCIENCE

Political science as a separate field is a relatively late arrival in terms of social sciences. However, the term "political science" was not always distinguished from political philosophy, and the modern discipline has a clear set of antecedents including also moral philosophy, political economy, political theology, history, and other fields concerned with normative determinations of what ought to be and with deducing the characteristics and functions of the ideal state.

The antecedents of Western politics can be traced back to the Socratic political philosophers, Plato (427–347 BC), Xenophon (c. 430–354 BC), and Aristotle ("The Father of Political Science") (384–322 BC).

These authors, in such works as *The Republic* and *Laws* by Plato, and *The Politics* and *Nicomachean Ethics* by Aristotle, analyzed political systems philosophically, going beyond earlier Greek poetic and historical reflections which can be found in the works of epic poets like Homer and Hesiod, historians like Herodotus and Thucydides, and dramatists such as Sophocles, Aristophanes, and Euripides.

THE RISE AND FALL OF THE ROMAN EMPIRE

During the height of the Roman Empire, famous historians such as Polybius, Livy and Plutarch documented the rise of the Roman Republic, and the organization and histories of other nations, while statesmen like Julius Caesar, Cicero and others provided us with examples of the politics of the republic and Rome's empire and wars. The study of politics during this age was oriented towards understanding history, understanding methods of governing, and describing the operation of governments. Nearly a thousand years elapsed, from the foundation of the city of Rome in 753 BC to the fall of the Roman Empire or the beginning of the Middle Ages.

In the interim, there is a manifest translation of Hellenic culture into the Roman sphere. The Greek gods become Romans and Greek philosophy in one way or another turns into Roman law, *e.g.* Stoicism. The Stoic was committed to preserving proper hierarchical roles and duties in the state so that the state as a whole would remain stable. Among the best known Roman Stoics were philosopher Seneca and the emperor Marcus Aurelius. Seneca, a wealthy Roman patrician, is often criticized by some modern commentators for failing to adequately live by his own precepts. The Meditations of Marcus Aurelius, on the other hand, can be best thought of as the philosophical reflections of an emperor divided between his philosophical aspirations and the duty he felt to defend the Roman Empire from its external enemies through his various military campaigns. According to Polybius, Roman institutions were the backbone of the empire but Roman law is the medulla.

THE MIDDLE AGES

With the fall of the Western Roman Empire, there arose a more diffuse arena for political studies. The rise of monotheism and, particularly for the Western tradition, Christianity, brought to light a new space for politics and political action. Works such as Augustine of Hippo's *The City of God* synthesized current philosophies and political traditions with those of Christianity, redefining the borders between what was religious and what was political. During the Middle Ages, the study of politics was widespread in the churches and courts. Most of the political questions surrounding the relationship between church and state were clarified and contested in this period. The Arabs lost sight of Aristotle's political science but continued to study Plato's *Republic* which became the basic text of Judeo-Islamic political philosophy as in the works of Alfarabi and Averroes; this did not happen in the Christian world, where Aristotle's *Politics* was translated in the 13th century and became the basic text as in the works of Saint Thomas Aquinas.

INDIAN SUB-CONTINENT

In ancient India, the antecedents of politics can be traced back to the *Rig-Veda*, *Samhitas*, *Brahmanas*, the Mahabharata and Buddhist *Pali Canon*. Chanakya (c. 350–275 BC) was a political thinker in Takshashila. Chanakya wrote the *Arthashastra*, a treatise on political thought, economics and social order. It discusses monetary and fiscal policies, welfare, international relations, and war strategies in detail, among other topics. The Manusmriti, dated to about two centuries after the time of Chanakya is another important Indian political treatise.

EAST ASIA

Ancient China was home to several competing schools of political thought, most of which arose in the Spring and Autumn Period. These included Mohism (a utilitarian philosophy), Taoism, Legalism (a school of thought based on the supremacy of the state), and Confucianism. Eventually, a modified form of Confucianism (heavily infused with elements of Legalism) became the dominant political philosophy in China during the Imperial Period. This form of Confucianism also deeply influenced and were expounded upon by scholars in Korea and Japan.

WEST ASIA

In Persia, works such as the Rubaiyat of Omar Khayyam and Epic of Kings by Ferdowsi provided evidence of political analysis, while the Middle Eastern Aristotelians such as Avicenna and later Maimonides and Averroes, continued Aristotle's tradition of analysis and empiricism, writing commentaries on Aristotle's works. Averroe did not have at hand a text of Aristotle's *Politics*, so he wrote a commentary on Plato's *Republic* instead.

THE RENAISSANCE

During the Italian Renaissance, Niccolò Machiavelli established the emphasis of modern political science on direct empirical observation of political institutions and actors. Machiavelli was also a realist, arguing that even evil means should be considered if they help to create and preserve a glorious regime. Machiavelli therefore also argues against the use of idealistic models in politics, and has been described as the father of the "politics model" of political science. Later, the expansion of the scientific paradigm during the Enlightenment further pushed the study of politics beyond normative determinations.

THE ENLIGHTENMENT

Like Machiavelli, Thomas Hobbes, well known for his theory of the social contract, believed that a strong central power, such as a monarchy, was necessary to rule the innate selfishness of the individual but neither of them believed in the divine right of kings. John Locke, on the other hand, who gave us Two Treatises of Government and who did not believe in the divine right of kings either, sided with Aquinas and stood against both Machiavelli and Hobbes by accepting Aristotle's dictum that man seeks to be happy in a state of social harmony as a social animal. Unlike Aquinas' preponderant view on the salvation of the soul from original sin, Locke believed man comes into this world with a mind that is basically a tabula rasa. According to Locke, an absolute ruler as proposed by Hobbes is unnecessary, for natural law is based on reason and equality, seeking peace and survival for man.

Religion would no longer play a dominant role in politics. There would be separation of church and state. Principles similar to those that dominated the material sciences could be applied to society as a whole, originating the social sciences. Politics could be studied in a laboratory as it were, the social milieu. In 1787, Alexander Hamilton wrote: "...The science of politics like most other sciences has received great improvement." (*The Federalist Papers* Number 9 and 51). Both the marquis d'Argenson and the abbé de Saint-Pierre described politics as a science; d'Argenson was a philosopher and de Saint-Pierre an allied reformer of the enlightenment.

Other important figures in American politics who participated in the Enlightenment were Benjamin Franklin and Thomas Jefferson.

MODERN POLITICAL SCIENCE

Because political science is essentially a study of human behaviour, in all aspects of politics, observations in controlled environments are often challenging to reproduce or duplicate, though experimental methods are increasingly common. Citing this difficulty, former American Political Science Association President Lawrence Lowell once said "We are limited by the impossibility of experiment. Politics is an observational, not an experimental science." Because of this, political scientists have historically observed political elites, institutions, and individual or group behaviour in order to identify patterns, draw generalizations, and build theories of politics.

Like all social sciences, political science faces the difficulty of observing human actors that can only be partially observed and who have the capacity for making conscious choices unlike other subjects such as non-human organisms in biology or inanimate objects as in physics. Despite the complexities, contemporary political science has progressed by adopting a variety of methods and theoretical approaches to understanding politics and methodological pluralism is a defining feature of contemporary political science.

The advent of political science as a university discipline was marked by the creation of university departments and chairs with the title of political science arising in the late 19th century. In fact, the designation "political scientist" is typically reserved for those with a doctorate in the field. Integrating political studies of the past into a unified discipline is ongoing, and the history of political science has provided a rich field for the growth of both normative and positive political science, with each part of the discipline sharing some historical predecessors. The American Political Science Association was founded in 1903 and the American Political Science Review was founded in 1906 in an effort to distinguish the study of politics from economics and other social phenomena.

BEHAVIOURAL REVOLUTION AND NEW INSTITUTIONALISM

In the 1950s and the 1960s, a behavioural revolution stressing the systematic and rigorously scientific study of individual and group behaviour swept the discipline. A focus on studying political behaviour, rather than institutions or interpretation of legal texts, characterized early behavioural political science, including work by Robert Dahl, Philip Converse, and in the collaboration between sociologist Paul Lazarsfeld and public opinion scholar Bernard Berelson. The late 1960s and early 1970s witnessed a takeoff in the use of deductive, game theoretic formal modeling techniques aimed at generating a more analytical corpus of knowledge in the discipline.

This period saw a surge of research that borrowed theory and methods from economics to study political institutions, such as the United States Congress, as well as political behaviour, such as voting. William H. Riker and his colleagues and students at the University of Rochester were the main proponents of this shift. Criticisms of the use of this rational choice theorizing has been widespread, even among political scientists who adopt quantitative methods.

This trend towards formalization has continued and accelerated, even as the behaviouralist revolution has subsided. At the same time, because of the interdependence of all social life, political science also moved towards a closer working relationship with other disciplines, especially sociology, economics, history, anthropology, psychology, public administration, law, and statistics without losing its own identity.

Increasingly, political scientists have used the scientific method to create an intellectual discipline involving quantitative research methods, as well as the generation of formal economics-style models of politics to derive testable hypotheses followed by empirical verification. Over the past generations, the discipline placed an increasing emphasis on relevance and the use of new approaches to increase scientific knowledge in the field and provide explanations for empirical outcomes.

Kenneth R. Mladenka, a political scientist at Texas AandM University, was among the academics that proceeded to bring acceptance of the newer urban studies component of the discipline. In the 1970s and 1980s, he found that urban scholars were not as prominent on the editorial boards of the major political science journals, and that traditional scholars, called empiricists, regard most urban research, dependent on case studies, paradigms, qualitative analysis, and theoretical perspectives, as less reliable than the traditional emphasis of the discipline. The urban scholars such as Mladenka stress "local settings where global, national, and voting behaviour outcomes happen at street level and where day-to-day lives are affected."

RECENT DEVELOPMENTS

In 2000, the Perestroika Movement in political science was introduced as a reaction against what supporters of the movement called the mathematicization of political science. Those who identified with the movement argued for a plurality of methodologies and approaches in political science and for more relevance of the discipline to those outside of it.

DISTINCTION BETWEEN POLITICAL SCIENCE AND POLITICS

The terms 'Political Science' and 'Politics' are often used interchangeably. However, the distinction between the two needs to be understood. Some scholars define Politics to be "the science and art of government." But this is only a part of the total explanation of the subject of Political Science. Now-a-days the term Politics is used to mean the problems of the citizens interacting with the instrument of political power in one form or the other. Sometimes, Politics was and still is used as the technique of compromise or the method to capture power and retain it.

According to many political scientists, the study of Political Science comprises theory of the state, concept of sovereign power, forms and functions of government, making and execution of laws, elections, political parities, rights and duties of citizens, policy functions and study of welfare activities of the State and government. There is another aspect of Politics that needs to be emphasised. Politics, many a time, implies practical politics.

Practising politics is different from studying it. Practical politics includes actual formation of government, the working of government, administration, laws and legislation. It also includes international politics including matters such as peace and war, international trade and economic order, protection of rights, etc. All these also comprise the subject matter of the study of Politics. While the knowledge of Political Science as a discipline is acquired through study, the skill of practical politics is acquired through politicking or manipulations and craftiness or by exploiting caste and regional loyalties and religious sentiments. Practical politics is often described as the 'dirty game' and a 'corrupting' process in the common people's mind.

But we find that there are hardly any human groupings or societies, which are free from 'politics' and hardly any individual who does not know the implications of the "game of politics". Practical Politics also has many positive aspects. In this era of welfare state many positive programmes such as removal of untouchability, land reforms, release of bonded labourers, prohibition of trafficking in human beings and *begar*, introduction of minimum wages, employment generation programmes, empowerment of the other backward classes are all examples of positive aspects of practical politics. 'Politics' refers to the process of actual happenings in society and in institutions, which Political Science refers to its understand in a systematic manner.

PUBLIC ADMINISTRATION

Public administration is a "field of enquiry with a diverse scope", of which the "fundamental goal...is to advance management and policies so that government can function." Some of the various definitions which have been offered for the term are: "the management of public programmes"; the "translation of politics into the reality that citizens see every day"; and "the study of government decision making, the analysis of the policies themselves, the various inputs that have produced them, and the inputs necessary to produce alternative policies."

Public administration is "centrally concerned with the organization of government policies and programmes as well as the behaviour of officials formally responsible for their conduct". Many unelected public servants can be considered to be public administrators, including police officers, municipal budget analysts, HR benefits administrators, city managers, Census analysts, and cabinet secretaries. Public administrators are public servants working in public departments and agencies, at all levels of government. In the US, civil servants and academics such as Woodrow Wilson promoted American civil service reform in the 1880s, moving public administration into academia.

However, "until the mid-20th century and the dissemination of the German sociologist Max Weber's theory of bureaucracy" there was not "much interest in a theory of public administration." The field is multi-disciplinary in character; one of the various proposals for public administration's sub-fields sets out five pillars, including human resources, organizational theory, policy analysis and statistics, budgeting, and ethics.

LOCAL GOVERNMENT

Local government refers collectively to administrative authorities over areas that are smaller than a state. The term is used to contrast with offices at nation-state level, which are referred to as the central government, national government, or federal government. 'Local government' only acts within powers delegated to it by legislation or directives of the higher level of government and each country has some kind of local government which will differ from those of other countries. In primitive societies the lowest level of local government is the village headman or tribal chief. Federal states such as the United States have two levels of government above the local level: the governments of the fifty states and the federal national government whose relations are governed by the constitution of the United States. Local government in the United States originated in the colonial period and has been modified since then: the highest level of local government is at county level.

In modern nations, local governments usually have some of the same kind of powers as national governments do. They usually have some power to raise taxes, though these may be limited by central legislation. The question of Municipal Autonomy—which powers the local government has, or should have, and why—is a key question of public administration and governance. The institutions of local government vary greatly between countries, and even where similar arrangements exist, the terminology often varies. Common names for local government entities include state, province, region, department, county, prefecture, district, city, township, town, borough, parish, municipality, shire and village. However all these names are often used informally in different countries and local government is the legal part of central government.

LOCAL GOVERNMENT IN INDIA

In India the local government is the third level of government apart from the State and Central governments. There are two types of Local Government in operation: Panchayats in rural areas and Municipalities in urban areas. The Panchayats are a linked-system of local bodies with Village Panchayats, Panchayat Samities at the intermediate level, and district panchayats.

The rural panchayats created in around 1959 were based on the soviet model of tiering with hierarchical control to undertake mainly agency tasks of the states through earmarked funding, with limited civic tasks financed from assigned land revenue and local surcharge thereon. This resulted in overlapping functional jurisdiction and a mismatch of functions and taxes among the three tiers. The urban municipalities, created during the colonial days of mid-19th century, survived the 'socialist' experiment and retained their separate character as their English counterparts.

In 1991, through two identical constitutional amendments, one for the Panchayats and the other for the Municipalities, a number of changes were introduced to strengthen local governments in India ensure regularity of their election every five years and limiting their period of super session or dissolution to six months, three sets of local local governments for the Panchayats and the Municipalities, reservation of seats and chairpersons for women and scheduled castes and tribes, creation of independent state selection commission, state finance commission linked with the central finance commission, and planning committees at the districts and metropolitan areas. In addition, these amendments have indicated guidelines for the states to empower the local governments through increased devolution of functions and taxes to them–these are not been followed-up by the states. However, the CFCs have been allocating discretionary grants for local governments passed through the states. One lacuna in the existing arrangement is that the Panchayats do not have a statutorily delegated list of functions on which its revenues could be spent; this has created problems of financing their own activities from their own revenues or through general grants from the CFC-SFC arrangements. Panchayats act mostly as agencies for implementing their erstwhile soviet plan schemes and projects on cost reimbursement that do not have any maintenance component for transferred completed works. The major national parties are committed to improve the effectiveness of the Panchayats through further central action to remedy the situation.

SCOPE OF POLITICAL SCIENCE

Here we shall learn about the scope of Political Science in terms of role of the State, functions of government and its relationship with citizens.

ROLE OF THE STATE

The term 'State' in its modern sense was first used by Machiavelli, the Italian statesman. The study of the State has since remained the focal point for the political scientists. The State consists of four elements. These are:

- The people;
- The territory on which they live;
- The government to rule and regulate the lives of the people and
- Sovereignty, which implies unrestricted authority to take decisions and manage its own affairs.

You will read in detail about these four elements in the second lesson. The role and nature of the State have been interpreted differently. Modern western liberal thinking, about which you will study more in the fourth lesson, arose with the commerial Revolution in Western Europe in the sixteenth century and became prominent with the Industrial Revolution in the eighteenth century. These Revolutions brought into focus a new economic system called capitalism.

The social group consisting of traders, merchants and businessmen and later the industrialists was the major beneficiary of this system. The liberals emphasized that the consent of the people is the true basis of the state. Early liberal thinkers also considered the state as a 'necessary evil'- an evil but necessary for the purpose of protecting the individual from the external and internal enemies. According to this view, that government is the best which governs the least. In other words, the state should be a 'police state' and hence a limited one. It should also be limited in a different sense: as John Locke, the famous English liberal philosopher of the seventeenth century, said it is there to protect the individual's natural right to life, liberty and property. By contrast, the Marxist view, about which you will study more in the fourth lesson, does not consider the State as an impartial institution.

It asserts that, throughout the centuries, the state has been a tool in the hands of the "haves" for exploiting and dominating the "have-nots." In the future classless society like the communist society, the state would "wither away,". In Gandhian view, the State would justify its existence, by acting as a "trustee" of the people. It should help the poorest and the weakest one.

It should restore to him or her, a control over his or her own life and destiny. The Welfare State, which slowly emerged during the 1930s, tries to promote the well being of its citizens, especially the poor, the needy, the unemployed and the aged. It is now generally agreed that the Welfare State exists to promote common good. So the functions of the state have increased manifold. Power refers to the ability of one person affecting the attitudes or action of another. I have power over you if I can make you do what you would not have done otherwise. But power is not always exercised openly. It can be exercised in unseen way, as in controlling the agenda. However, power can be best exercised when I can convince you about what is good/bad for you.

To that extent, my power over you would be complete. And this dominance would always go unchallenged. By power of the government, we think of the different aspects of government. We think of ministers who have departments under them for the exercise of power over the area of their domains. There is the bureaucracy and the enormous structure of governmental administration, which has power over us. It can control our lives in various ways by making, administering and implementing laws. Here, one thing is to be noted. Power does not lie only in the highly publicized areas of social life, like government, administration, elections, etc.

It also exists in small institutions like family etc.Many feminists are of the opinion that inside the private world of family man exercises power or dominance over woman. Hence, it is very aptly said, "even the personal is political." Another thing to be noticed is that there is a distinction between legitimate and illegitimate power. There can be power, which is considered right or proper, while another may be improper. A dacoit's power over me is very real, because if I do not comply with his wishes, I might lose my life or limb. But it is not proper power as is generally understood. Contrary to it the power that the government's representatives, policemen or judges exercise over me is proper power. The dacoit's power is illegitimate power while the government's is legitimate. And the power of constitutional authorities over me is called authority. Authority contains the two ideas of power and legitimacy. Authority is that form of power which is legitimate. It is power plus ligitimacy.

CITIZENS AND GOVERNMENT

The government is the most important instrument of the State through which the latter realizes its objectives. Through its three organs i.e; the Legislature, the Executive and the Judiciary, it makes laws and rules, implements them, maintains peace and order in the Individual and the State country and resolves clashes of interests. It also tries to ensure territorial integrity or unity of the country. Modern democratic governments perform many other functions for the development and welfare of citizens and the society, as a whole.

This is especially so in a developing country like ours. The relationship between citizens and the government is reciprocal. The citizens are members of the State. The state recognizes certain rights of the citizens and in turn expects certain duties from them. So far as the rights of the citizens are concerned, they can be divided into three: civil, political and social. CIVIL

RIGHTS are those rights which are necessary for the freedom/ liberty of the individual. They include the right to life and personal liberty, right to freedom of speech, expression and thought, right to own property, right to enter into contract, right to equality before law and equal protection by law. Equality before law means absence of special privileges; equal protection of laws implies equals should be treated equally.

POLITICAL RIGHTS include the right to vote and the right to contest election. SOCIAL RIGHTS include the right to some degrees of economic welfare and security and the right to live the life of a civilized being according to standards prevailing in the society. It is the primary duty of the citizens to pay taxes to the government. They should cooperate with the government and abide by the laws and rules; should help in preventing diseases by immunization and by keeping neighbourhood clean.

They should have small families to help the government check the population growth. They should preserve public property, help in catching and punishing anti-social and anti-national elements. Further, the citizens of different castes, religions, languages and regions should solve their problems by understanding and agreement and not by violent means. In this way, a lot of resources, energy and time of the government can be saved for constructive purposes.

LIBERTY

The term liberty is derived form the Latin word *liber* meaning free. Thus liberty means freedom. Freedom is of paramount importance for the development of an individual's personality. Historically speaking, the term liberty was initially defined as absence of all restraints on an individual. This is known as the negative concept of liberty.

Early liberalism championed negative liberty. John Stuart Mill, the nineteenth century English political philosopher, described, "Restraint as an evil". Mill was especially worried about the restraints coming from the state and society.

However, since individuals live together in a society, complete absence of restraints would be neither possible nor desirable. Further, differentiating between the self-regarding and other-regarding action is not always possible. It has been very aptly said that your liberty to swing your arm ends there where my nose begins.

For liberty to be enjoyed by everyone, it should have reasonable restraints. This is the concept of positive liberty. This concept further means freedom to be a master of one's own self. Harold J Laski supported this concept. Freedoms are opportunities which history has shown to be essential to the development of personality. The freedom of many requires restraint of law on the freedom of some. Later liberals supported the positive liberty.

Safeguards of Liberty

Declaration of rights of the individuals in the Constitution is considered as an important safeguard of liberty. This way the government can be prevented from encroaching upon the freedoms of the people. Impartial judiciary is rightly called the watchdog of liberty. Without it the liberty of the individuals would be meaningless. Decentralization of powers is another important safeguard of liberty. History is witness to the fact that concentration of power has very often led to despotism. Separation of powers, *i.e.* the executive, the legislature and the judiciary being separate, is a great ally of liberty. Montesquieu said, "Power should be a check on power."

Rule of law or equality in the eyes of the law is also an important safeguard of liberty. This is the bulwark against discrimination based on caste, class, colour, creed, etc. A large measure of social justice or diffusion of social and economic privileges is a prerequisite for liberty. If privileges become the prerogative of the select few, then effective liberty would be denied to a vast majority. A well-knit party system is also indispensable for the preservation of liberty. All these institutional safeguards are inadequate to preserve liberty if the citizens themselves do not possess the proud spirit to preserve it. People should always be on their toes to ensure that their liberty is not encroached upon. Eternal vigilance, it has been rightly said, is the price of liberty.

PUBLIC LAW

Public law is a theory of law governing the relationship between individuals and the state. Under this theory, constitutional law, administrative law and criminal law are sub-divisions of public law. This theory is at odds with the concept of constitutional law, which requires all laws to be specifically enabled, and thereby sub-divisions, of a constitution. Generally speaking, private law is the area of law in a society that affects the relationships between individuals or groups without the intervention of the state or government. In many cases the public/private law distinction is confounded by laws that regulate private relations while having been passed by legislative enactment. In some cases these public statutes are known as laws of public order, as private individuals do not have the right to break them and any attempt to circumvent such laws is void as against public policy.

AREAS OF PUBLIC LAW

- Constitutional law deals with the relationship between the state and individual, and the relationships between different branches of the state, such as the executive, the legislative and the judiciary. In most legal systems, these relationships are specified within a written constitutional document. However, in the United Kingdom of Great Britain and Northern Ireland, due to historical and political reasons there does not exist one supreme, entrenched written document. The UK has an unwritten constitution—the constitution of this state is usually found in statutes, such as the Magna Carta, the Petition of Right, the Bill of Rights, The Act of Settlement 1700 and the Parliament Act 1911 and Parliament Act, 1949. The constitution is also found in case-law, such as the historical decision in Entick v. Carrington 19 St Tr 1030, and the landmark decision of M v. Home Office 1 AC 377; QB 270. Due to the lack of a written constitution, the idea of the legislative supremacy of Parliament and the rule of law play an important role in the constitution. Despite all this, in reality, much of the constitution is a political phenomenon, rather than a legal one.

- Administrative law refers to the body of law which regulates bureaucratic managerial procedures and defines the powers of administrative agencies. These laws are enforced by the executive branch of a government rather than the judicial or legislative branches. This body of law regulates international trade, manufacturing, pollution, taxation, and the like. This is sometimes seen as a subcategory of civil law and sometimes seen as public law as it deals with regulation and public institutions.
- Criminal law involves the state imposing sanctions for defined crimes committed by individuals or businesses, so that society can achieve its brand of justice and a peaceable social order. This differs from civil law in that civil actions are disputes between two parties that are not of significant public concern.

2

State and Political Philosophy

INTRODUCTION

The term 'state' is central to the study of political science. But it is wrongly used as synonym for nation, society, government etc. The term 'state' is also used as state management, State aid and so on.

Also as the states of Indian union or the fifty states that make the United States of America. But in political science, we use this term differently; it has a more specific meaning.

Some of the definitions of the concept of state are as follows:

- "The state is the politically organized people of a definite territory"- Bluntschli
- State is "a community of persons, more or less numerous, permanently occupying a definite portion of territory, independent, or nearly so, of external control, and possessing an organized government to which the great body of inhabitants render habitual obedience."- Garner
- State is "a territorial society divided into governments and subjects, whether individuals or associations of individuals, whose relationships are determined by the exercise of this supreme coercive power."- Laski
- State "is a people organized for law within a definite territory".- Woodrow Wilson
- "The State is a concept of political science, and a moral reality which exists where a number of people, living on a definite territory, are unified under a government which in internal matters is the organ of expressing their sovereignty, and in external matters is independent of other governments."- Gilchrist

Human beings are social animals and cannot live alone. When people live together, they fulfil their socials needs. But everybody is not good and kind. There are all sorts of men and women, who exhibit various emotions such as pride, jealousy, greed, selfishness and so on. As per Burke, "Society requires not only the passions of individuals should be subjected, but that even in the mass and body as in the individuals the inclination of men individual and the State should be thwarted, their will controlled and their passions brought into subjection." The best is to control human perversity through means of political authority.

Therefore people are bound by rules of common behaviour. If these are broken then they can be punished. Society fulfils people's need for companionship; the state solves the problem created by this companionship. The state exists for the sake of good life. It is an essential and natural institution and as Aristotle said, "The State comes into existence originating in the bare needs of life and continues its existence for the sake of good life." It is only within a state that an individual can rise to his or her ability.

If there is no authority, no organisation and no rules, then society cannot be held together. The state has existed where human beings have lived in an organized society. The structure of the state has evolved gradually over a long period of time, from a simple to a complex organization that we have today. The essence of state is in its monopoly of coercive power. It has a right to demand obedience from the people. However, the Marxists believe that state is a class organization, which has been created by the propertied class to oppress and exploit the poor.

They refuse to believe that the state is a natural institution. To them the propertied class created the state and it has always belonged to them only. Thus, the state is just a means of exploitation. Therefore, they visualize a situation of classless society or communism in which there will not be any need of the state. State will, thus, wither away.

THE RISE AND DEVELOPMENT OF THE MODERN NATION STATE

This section examines the factors that gave rise to the nation states in Europe and studies the reasons because of which the nation state became the supreme form of the modern state. As regards the first question, the reasons for the rise of the nation state are also coincidentally the factors in the formation of Europe and vice-versa. The creation of nation states in Europe has contributed to the distinct identity that Europe has. The state system of Europe has exerted exceptional influence in the world beyond Europe, for European colonization has positively drawn the political map of the modern world.4 It is interesting, for a larger part of human history, human beings have lived without states but not without governments.

States are historical phenomena emerging under particular conditions changing and quite fluid, without actually being fixed. The pre-state political communities were enormously divergent—all the more so since they often developed out of each other, interacted with each other, conquered each other and merged with each other to produce infinite varied forms, most of them hybrid. It may be possible to classify these into

- Tribes without rulers
- Tribes with rulers, (chiefdoms) and
- City-states.

TRIBES WITHOUT RULERS

There were no states where human beings lived in hunting and gathering communities, small agrarian units and the regions inhabited by sparsely populated nomadic and semi-nomadic people. Even today anthropologists point out to communities that have no states, for example, the Jale Pale of the New Guinea highlands, the pastoral Anuak, Dinka, Masai and Nuer of the South Sudan, the M'dendeuile and Arusha of East Africa and some pre-Columbian Amerindian tribes in North and South America. In all these, government began and ended with the extended family, lineage or clan. None was superior except for men, elders, parents and no one was inferior except for women, young and children.

The kin defined social relations and its rights and obligations. Within the kin one's sex, age and marital status determined an individual's position. In the absence of institutional authority, except for what operated within an extended family, these societies were egalitarian and democratic. All adult males were equal. Public tasks were performed not by rulers and ruled but by leaders and followers. The absence of centralized authority also meant absence of permanent, specialized war-making armed forces or even popular militias. None of these societies had a system of rent, tribute or taxation that redistributed wealth, or a class of individuals with leisure. Institutional religion hardly played any role and every household chief was also his own priest. However, the priest did not have the right to command obedience, levy taxes, have an organized following to enforce their wishes and did not exercise command in war. Their methods were persuasion and mediation but not coercion.

CHIEFDOMS

These existed in many societies in Southeast, West and South Africa, as well as over Southeast Asia, Polynesia, Hawaii and New Zealand. History tells us of tribes that destroyed the Mycenean civilization and ruled Greece between 1000 and 750 BC. These tribes were the various Gothic, Frankish and other Germanic tribes as they were from the later centuries of the Roman empire and the Scandinavian tribes during the tenth century just before they became Christianized and turned towards more centralized forms of government. In chiefdoms, the chief had an elevated position over other people with the right to command them. This right claimed as divine became the basis of succession from father to son.

This led to frequent clashes and warfare. Most of these societies were polygamous. Women for their looks or their noble lineages were status symbols for their owners. Their labour was also a source of wealth. The natural result of polygyny was a large number of sons, candidates for succession when the time came, resulting in potential conflicts. Normally the chief's first or principal wife was descended from an eminent family and her offspring(s) enjoyed precedence over the rest.

Next to the chief, society was divided into two different layers or classes—privileged group, small and consisting of the chief's extended family, lineage or clan. They enjoyed special rights such as access to the chief, a higher compensation in case of injury or death and immunity from certain kinds of punishment that were considered degrading. They wore special insignia and clothing and in areas with moderate climate they were distinguished by tattoos. Their position in society depended exactly on their relationship to the chief. From these people the chief selected the provincial rulers and since they had some claim to succession they were rarely appointed to senior court positions.

Below the royal lineage or clan were the numerous class of commoners: such as the ancient Greek labourers or thetes, subject to different kinds of discrimination, such as, not being allowed to own cattle (the Hutu in Burundi and Rwanda), ride stallions (the bonders in pre-Christian Scandinavia), wear feather headgear (the Americas) or bear arms. In an event of injury or death they got very little compensation and their punishment was savage. They were not blood relations of the chief. In parts of Africa the chief and the commoners belonged to different ethnic groups and did not share the same customs or speak the same language. The commoners owed allegiance to the chief.

The chief had extensive powers especially in large territories he stood at the apex of a pyramid consisting of regional sub-chiefs. The chiefdoms became the first political entities to institute rent, tribute and taxation, forms of compulsory unilateral payments from the ruled to the rulers leading to concentration of wealth in the ruling few. The precise nature of the wealth paid depended on the resources made possible by the environment and also on custom. Everywhere it consisted of staple crop like rice and grain. There could be prestigious objects also, such as fine domestic animals, clothes in various forms and in some societies, women.

Some of the tributes paid to the chief's storehouses were directly by his tenants. The rest of the population made payments to the sub-chiefs who, having collected them, took their cut which was not fixed, and depended on how much they could get away without inviting the wrath of the chief and passed the rest on. Both the chiefs and sub-chiefs possessed additional sources of revenue originating in their right to exercise justice, such as fees, fines, the belongings of condemned persons and often bribes. There also existed some form of licensing system under which chiefs of all ranks demanded and received payment for granting their subjects certain privileges like the right to hold markets, engage in long-distance trade, go on raiding expeditions against other tribes (part of the booty went to the chief) and so on. In short, there was hardly any economic activity in which the chief was not involved and from which he did not get his share.

CITY STATES

These were overwhelmingly rural with a livelihood that was hunting, gathering, cattle-raising, fishing and agriculture practiced at the subsistence level. Most of these people were nomadic or semi-nomadic. There were three types of cities in the first, the majority were ruled by petty chiefs, known as lugal in ancient Middle East, wanax in the Mycenean world and kshatriya in India. This type differed from the chiefdoms, mainly by their more sophisticated administrative system and a more complex social structure.

The second type of cities were not independent communities but served as either capitals or as provincial centers like Mesopotamia in 235 BC, China from the time of the first imperial dynasties; India during the periods of centralized empire (320-185 BC, AD 320-500 and AD 1526-1707) and pre-Columbian Latin America. The third type comprised of self-governing cities that existed in pre-dynastic Mesopotamia confined to the Mediterranean littoral. Only in such self-governing cities were Greeks, Romans and possibly also Etruscans and Phoenicians (Carthage) able to come up with a new principle of government. The earliest important political organization was the polls or the city-state in Greece that began as a common association for the security and for the satisfaction of daily needs but gradually became the pivot around which all human activity—moral, intellectual, social, cultural, aesthetic and practical life revolved.

The Greek archipelago consisted of many islands among which Athens, Crete and Sparta were well-known. Mountainous terrain, valleys and rivers physically separated these islands. In spite of their territorial and political separateness, the Greeks shared cultural and social unity due to one language, common religious rituals and Olympic festivals. The Greeks never called themselves Greeks but Hellas.

Most of the city-states were small and compact in size and population. Athens between 750-550 BC had 40,000 square miles of territory and 40,000 citizens and 400,000 mixed population. The limit on size was important, for the Greeks were convinced that good order could be sustained any in small cohesive communities. It was both self-sufficient and self-governing. It was the cradle to the ideas of democracy, constitutional government and the due process of law, which were transmitted through Rome to the modern Europe. Rome also put into practice the Stoic idea of a universal society and the need for a uniform system of law.

A number of textbooks, case books and codes of law were devised by a group of trained lawyers at the level of theory and for practical use of officials. The Romans established a system of jurisprudence as a system of general rules by which actions could be classified clearly with definitions. Gaius, Paulus and Ulpian's treatises were systematic delineations of constitutional and political institutions. In order to unify the divergent peoples within the empire, to deal with the colonies it had conquered, to deal with aliens, to advance the idea of common citizenship and to settle commercial cases with foreign traders a system of law was needed and that was provided by the formulation of a law of nations (jus gentium). This worked alongside the Stoic law of nature (jus naturale), the law common to all nations and the law common to all human beings.

Roman lawyers also attempted to distinguish between public law—in essence constitutional law—and private law that which concerned private individuals and the institution of private property. Approximately sixteen hundred years ago, Roman Empire under Theodosius I (379-95) was the last sole ruler and that split after his death in to Western and Eastern Roman Empires. In comparison to the East the western side of the Empire sustained recurring attacks and thus became weak. In AD 410, the city of Rome was attacked by roaming Germanic tribes and fell in 476 AD following the dethroning of the last Roman Emperor of the West. The Eastern portion was economically safer than the West because the export trade in spices and other commodities continued through the Middle Ages until the Islamic Ottoman Empire challenged it in 1453.

The centuries following the disintegration of the Roman Empire saw no another imperial power in Europe, which continued to be ravaged by wars. The political map continued to be drawn and redrawn, as was evident from the presence of five hundred, more or less independent political units, with ill-defined boundaries in the late fifteenth century. This process continued till 1900. Five types of states can be distinguished since the fall of Rome in the fifth century:

1. Traditional tribute-taking empires;
2. System of divided authority characterized by feudal relations, city-states and urban alliances, with the Church (Papacy) playing a leading role from eighth to sixteenth centuries;
3. The polity of estates from the fourteenth to sixteenth centuries;
4. Absolutist states from fifteenth to eighteenth centuries and
5. Modern nation-states with constitutional, liberal democratic or single party polities locked progressively into a system of nation states.

EMPIRES

Imperial systems or empires of varying sizes and grandeur have dominated the history of states over the centuries. Some, such as Rome and China retained institutional forms for considerable period of time. Empires have sustained themselves through focus on coercive means and the ability to make money and through accumulation and when this ability decreased, they disintegrated.

All empires were expansionists, which was the main cause for their development. Empires having long distance trading routes met their economic requirements through the exaction of tribute that sustained the emperor, his administrative and military apparatuses. Paradoxically, in spite of being powerful, their administrative authority was limited since they lacked the institutions, organizations, personnel and information to provide for regular administration in their territories.

Most empires contained a plethora of communities that were culturally diverse and heterogeneous. Ruling rather than governing, was intrinsic to empires for their dominance in social and geographical space was restrictive. The polities of empires busied themselves with conflicts and intrigue within dominant groups and classes and within local urban centres; beyond that use of military force was to knit peoples and territories together.

FEUDALISM

Feudalism was a political system with an overlapping and divided authority. It took different forms between eighth and fourteenth centuries. Its distinguishing feature was a 'network of interlocking ties and obligations with system of rule fragmented into many small autonomous parts'. Political power was local and personal in nature producing a 'social world of overlapping claims and powers'. There was no one ruler or state sovereign in the sense of being supreme over a given territory and people. War was frequent and tensions endemic.

The early roots of feudalism date back to the remnants of the Roman Empire and to the militaristic culture and institutions of Germanic tribal peoples. There was a special relationship between a ruler or lord or king generally recognized or 'nominated' by followers on the basis of his military and strategic skills. The warriors swore faithfulness and obeisance to their lord and secured in return protection and privileges.

In the late seventh century rulers bestowed vassals with the rights of land, later called feudum in the hope of securing continued loyalty, military service and flows of income. As a consequence, a hierarchy of lord, vassal and peasants, distinguished by a great chain of relations and obligations as major vassals sub-contracted parts of their lands to others. The vast majority of people were at the bottom of the hierarchy but they constituted the subject of a political relationship. While the feudal kings were primus inter pares or first among equals they, with the exception of England and France, had diverse privileges and duties that included the need to consult and negotiate with the most powerful lords or barons, when taxes or armies were to be raised. The autonomous military capability that the lord was expected to maintain was for supporting their kings but this provided them with an independent power base which they at times used to promote their own interests. While some political forces pushed for centralization other sought local autonomy, thus, leading to disintegrative tendencies. In medieval Europe, agriculture was the basis of the feudal economy and its surplus were diverted for competing claims and the one that succeeded, constituted a basis to create and sustain political power. The complex network of kingdoms, principalities, duchies and other centres of power was challenged by the emergence of alternative powers in the towns and cities that depended on trade, manufacture and high capital accumulation.

Different social and political structures emerged as independent centres like Florence, Venice and Sienna in Italy. Europe in the Middle Ages meant 'Christendom' securing overarching unity from the Holy Roman Empire and the Papacy. The Holy Roman Empire existed in some form from the eighth to the early nineteenth century. Under the patronage of the Catholic Church, the Empire represented an attempt at its zenith, to unite and centralize the fragmented power centres of western Christendom into a politically unified Christian empire.

Countries from Germany to Spain and from northern France to Italy federated under the Empire. However, the complex power structures of feudal Europe, on the one hand, and the Catholic Church, on the other, circumscribed the actual secular power of the Empire. The Catholic Church was the main rival power to the medieval feudal and city networks and the Church, throughout the Middle Age, subordinated the secular to spiritual authority. It emphasized that Good lay. in the submission to God's will. In the absence of any theoretical alternative to the theocratic positions of Pope and Holy Roman Empire, this order was described as the order of 'international Christian society'.

It was first Christian, regarding God as the arbiter of disputes and conflicts with reference to religious doctrine and was coated with presumptions about the universal nature of human community. The rise of national states and Reformation gave rise to the idea of the modern state that challenged western Christendom. Its basis was prepared by the development of a new form of political identity—national identity.

THE POLITY OF ESTATES

This can be traced to the crisis within feudalism that is understood to have begun around 1300. The decline of feudalism began with the emergence of new concepts and ideas, for example, the claims of different social groups or estates to political prerogatives, specifically to rights of representation. Though these were extensions of existing feudal relations they had some distinctive and new qualities. In the first place, in the polity of estates the rulers present themselves primarily not as feudal superiors, but as the holders of higher, public prerogatives of non—and often pre-feudal origins, surrounded by the halo of a higher majesty; often imparted by means of sacred ceremonies.

In the second place, the counterpart to the ruler is typically represented not by individuals but by constituted bodies of various kinds: local assemblies of aristocrats, cities, ecclesiastical bodies, corporate associations. Taken singly, each of these bodies—the 'estates' represents a different collective entity: a region's noblemen of a given rank, the residents of a town, the faithful of a parish or the practitioners of a trade. Taken together, these bodies claim to represent a wider, more abstract, territorial entity—country, Land, terra, pays—which, they assert, the ruler is entitled to rule only to the extent that he upholds its distinctive customs and serve its interests. In turn, however, these interests are largely identified with those of the estates; and even the customs of the country or the region in question have as their major components the different claims of the various estates.

Thus, the ruler can rule legitimately only to the extent thar periodically he convenes the estates of a given region or of the whole territory into a constituted, public gathering. In these situations the rulers had to deal with estates and estates, had to deal with rulers resulting in the emergence of a variety of estate-based assemblies, parliaments, diets and councils which sought to legitimate and enjoy autonomous faculties of rule. The polity of estates meant dual power, the power split between rulers and estates, which did not last long.

It was threatened by the estates seeking more power and by the monarchy hoping to undermine the assemblies in order to centralize power in their own hands. With the loosening of feudal traditions and customs, notions like nature and limits of political authority, rights, law and obedience began to engage political theorists.

ABSOLUTIST STATES

From the fifteenth to the eighteenth centuries Europe had two types of regimes: the 'absolute' monarchies of France, Prussia, Austria, Spain, Sweden and Russia and 'constitutional' monarchies and republics in England and Holland. These two regimes differed in conceptual and institutional sense but some of these differences were more apparent than real.

Absolutism was made possible by the absorption of smaller and weaker political units into larger and stronger political systems; an invigourated ability to rule over a united territorial space; a tightened system of law and order enforced throughout a territory; the application of a 'more unitary, continuous, calculable and effective' rule by a single sovereign head; and the development of a relatively small number of states engaged in an 'open-ended, competitive, and risk-laden power struggle'.

The absolutist rulers claimed that they alone had the legitimate right of decision over state affairs as evident from the statement attributed to Louis XV, King of France from 1715 to 1774:

- In my person alone resides the sovereign power, and it is from me alone that the courts hold their existence and their authority. That... authority can only be exercised in my name... For it is to me exclusively that the legislative power belongs.... The whole public order emanates from me since I am its supreme guardian.... The rights and interests of the nation... are necessarily united with my own and can only rest in my hands.

The absolute king claimed to be the supreme source of human law although he justified his writ rule as being derived from the law of God, backed by the divine right theory. He stood at the pinnacle of a new system of rule that was progressively centralized and his sovereign authority to be supreme and indivisible. All qualities were visible in the rituals and routines of courtly life.

There were developments, six in all that are crucial to the history of state system: uniform system of rule within a territory, creation of new mechanisms of law-making and law-enforcement; the centralization of administrative power; extension of fiscal management; the formalization of relations among states through the development of diplomacy and diplomatic institutions and the introduction of a standing army. Absolutism accelerated the process of state-making that began to decrease social, economic and cultural disparity within states and expand the variation among them.

One reason for the expansion of state administrative power was because of its ability to collect and store information about its subjects and use that for supervising them. This meant the need to rely more on cooperative forms of social relations, for force alone could not be the basis of managing its affairs and sustaining its offices and activities. As a consequence there was an increased mutuality between the rulers and ruled, and since more reciprocity was involved there were more opportunities for subordinate groups to influence their rulers. Briefly absolutism encouraged the development of new forms and limits on state power—constitutionalism and for the eventual participation of powerful groups in the process of government itself.

Absolute regimes in comparison to ancient emperor were limited despotisms, for they were not the sole source of law, of coinages, weights and measures, of economic monopolies and could not impose compulsory cooperation. The absolutist ruler owned only his own estates and was weak in relation to powerful groups in society, for example, the nobility, merchants and urban bourgeoisie. Like its constitutional counterparts, the absolutist state tried to coordinate the activities of these groups and build up the state's infrastructural strength. A complex set of factors are responsible for the historical changes that changed medieval notion of politics.

Struggle between the monarch and barons over the domain of rightful authority; peasant rebellion against excessive taxes and weighing social obligations; the spread of trade, commerce and market relations; the prospering of Renaissance culture with renewed interest in classical political ideas that included Athenian democracy and Roman law; changes in technology particularly with regard to military skills; the consolidation of national monarchies particularly in England, France and Spain; religious conflicts and the challenge to Catholicism's universal claims and the struggle between the Church and State were all contributory factors. By the end of the seventeenth century, Europe was no longer a mosaic of states.

The claim of each state to supreme authority and control also meant the recognition of such a claim by other states as equally entitled to autonomy and respect within their own borders. In international context, sovereignty signified the independence of the state, namely an acknowledgement of its sole rights to jurisdiction over a particular group and territory, acceptance of a similar right of other states and equal rights to self-determination. In international relations, the principle of sovereign equality of all states was to become pre-eminent in the formal conduct of states with one another. With the emergence of international society, there also emerged international law as exemplified by the Westphalian5 model covering a period from 1648 to 1945 and its features are:

- The world consists of, and is divided by, sovereign states, which recognize no superior authority.
- The processes of law-making, the settlement of disputes and law-enforcement are largely in the hands of individual states subject to the logic of 'the competitive struggle for power'.
- Differences among states are often settled by force: the principle of effective power holds sway. Virtually no legal fetters exist to curb the resort to force; international legal standards afford minimal protection.
- This came about after the Peace of Westphalia of 1648 that brought to an end the Eighty-years was between Spain and the Dutch and the German phase of the Thirty-years war.
- Responsibility for cross-border, wrongful acts are a private matter concerning only those affected; no collective interest in compliance with international law is recognized.
- All states are regarded as equal before the law; legal rules do not take into account asymmetries of power.
- International law is oriented to the establishment of minimal rules of co-existence; the creation of enduring relationship among states and peoples is an aim only to the extent that it allows military objectives to be met.
- The minimization of impediments on state freedom is the 'collective' priority.

The era of absolutist states and its constitutional counterpart ushered in a new international order, which had a enduring and contradictory quality rich in implications: an increasingly integrated states system simultaneously endorsed the right of each state to autonomous and independent action. As a result the state were 'not subject to international moral requirements because they represent separate and discrete political orders with no common authority among them'. According to this model, the world comprises of separate political powers pursuing their own interests, and backed ultimately by their organization of coercive powers.

MODERN STATE

Absolutism, by concentrating political power in its own hands and in seeking to create a central system of rule, paved the way for a secular and national system of power. The English (1640-88) and French (1789) Revolutions marked the transition from absolutism to modern state with the following features of fixed territory, control of the means of violence, impersonal power structure and legitimacy. The nation-state or national state does not essentially mean that a state's people 'share a strong linguistic, religious and symbolic identity'. Though important, it is necessary to separate the nation-state from nationalism, 'What makes the "nation" integral to the nation-state...is not the existence of sentiments of nationalism but the unification of an administrative apparatus over precisely defined territorial boundaries'.

The modern state can be understood with reference to its forms: constitutional state, the liberal state, the liberal-democratic state and the single-party polity. Constitutionalism refers to explicit and/or implicit limits on political or state decision-making. These limits can be procedural as to how decisions and changes can be made or substantive preventing certain changes altogether. Constitutionalism stipulates the proper limits and forms of state action. An important doctrine in this context that emerged to become a central tenet of European liberalism was a state exists to safeguard the rights and liberties of citizens who are ultimately the best judges of their own interests.

The state's scope and practice have to be restrained to ensure the maximum possible freedom of every citizen. The liberal state is the effort to create a private space independent of the state and freeing the civil society—personal, family and business life—from unnecessary political interference and thereby limiting state's authority. The components of liberal state are constitutionalism, private property, the competitive market economy and the patriarchal family. The Western state, at first a liberal state becomes a liberal democratic state with the extension of franchise to the working class and women. The third type is the liberal representative democracy or a system of elected rulers who profess to represent the interests and views of the citizens within a framework of the rule of law. Election through two or multiparty system constitutes the life breath of representative governments. There is the one party or single party system that existed in erstwhile communist societies of East Europe and the Soviet Union and some Third world countries, on the basis that a single party can legitimately express the overall will of the society. The collapse of communism has ended the single party system. Even some third world countries, like Tanzania, have moved towards a multi-party system. An important factor in the emergence of the modern state is the capacity of the states to organize the means of coercion (armies, navies and other types of military might) and to deploy them when necessary. Modern states spend considerable amount of their finances in acquiring military equipment and technology. Another crucial factor in the creation of the democratic nation-state is nationalism.

The attempt to construct a national identity to bring people together within a framework of delimited territory gives the state a heightened power and status. National identity has been used to bring about mobilization and legitimacy though state-building and nationbuilding have never overlapped. In certain cases, nationalism has become a means to challenge the existing nation-state boundaries, *e.g.* Northern Ireland. The economic factor for the rise of the modern state is trade and commerce.

The main features of the modern states system—the centralization of political power, the expansion of administrative rule, the emergence of massed standing armies, the deployment of force—that exists in sixteenth century Europe in nascent form becomes part of the entire global system. It all began with the European states' capacity for overseas operations by means of naval and military force for purpose of long range navigation. The Spanish and Portuguese were the early explorers followed by the Dutch and the English. By the middle of the eighteenth century, English power was on the ascendancy and had become dominant by the nineteenth century, so much so that England, the first industrial power also became the first world power.

London became the centre of world trade and finance. The expansion of Europe across the globe, in turn, became a major source for expansion of state activity and efficiency. All the core organization types of modern society—the modern state, modern corporate enterprise and modern science— were shaped by it and benefited greatly from it. While European state systems developed and expanded non-European civilizations—the Chinese, Indian and Middle East progressively declined, and in this, capitalism played a crucial role with its origins in the sixteenth century. Capitalism penetrated and integrated the different and distant corners of the world, for its aspirations were never determined by national boundaries.

The earliest political units that could be properly called states were France, Spain, Portugal, Britain, the countries comprising the Holy Roman Empire (Germany, Italy, Balkans, Austria Hungary) and Scandinavia and the

Netherlands. This was in the seventeenth and eighteenth century occupying 1,450,000 square miles out of a global mass of 57, 000,0000. Wallerstein (1980) points out that capitalism from the beginning has been 'an affair of the world economy and not of nation states'. He distinguishes between two types of world systems that have existed historically: world-empires and world economies.

The former are political units characterized by imperial bureaucracies with substantial armies to exact tax and tribute from territorially dispersed populations, their capacity for success depend upon political and military achievements. World empires are inflexible and eventually displaced by the world economy that emerged in the sixteenth and seventeenth centuries because of its gargantuan appetite for endless accumulation of wealth. This world economy is an economic unit that crosses boundaries of any given state and any constraint is on the state and not on the process of economic expansion. Wallerstein divides the modern world system into three components: the core (initially the northwest and central Europe); the semi-periphery (the Mediterranean Zone) and the periphery (colonies).

Each zone of the world-economy is characterized, according to Wallerstein, by a particular kind of economic activity, state structure, class formation and mechanism of labour control. The world capitalist economy creates a new form of worldwide division of labour. While colonialism in its original form has practically disappeared. The world capitalist economy creates and reproduces massive imbalances of economic and political power among the different constituent areas. Initially the world capitalist economy took the form of expansion of market relations compelled by a growing need for raw materials and other factors of production. Capitalism invigourated this drive and was invigourated by it.

The development of capitalism can be explained partly due to the long-drawn changes in 'European' agriculture from as early as the twelfth century: changes resulting in part from the drainage and utilization of wet soils, which increased agricultural yields and created a sustainable surplus for trade. Connected to this was the establishment of long-distance trade routes in which the northern shores of the Mediterranean were initially prominent. A combination of agricultural and navigational opportunities helped invigourate the European economic dynamic and the constant competition for resources, territory and trade. Accordingly, the objectives of war gradually became more economic: military endeavour and conquest became more closely connected to the pursuit of economic advantage.

There was a direct connection between success of military conquest and the triumphant pursuit of economic gain. As capitalism developed and matured, the state gradually got more entangled with the interests of civil society partly for its own sake. To be able to pursue and implement policy of its choice it needed financial resources and for this reason it began to steadily coordinate the activities of the civil society. The other side of the process also meant that the civil society with its powerful groups and classes began to shape state action to suit their own interests.

Weber analyzes the relationship between modern capitalism and the emerging modern state. He points out that the Marxist analysis is based on a deficient understanding of the nature of the modern state and of the complexity of political life. The history of the state and the history of political struggle cannot in any way be reduced to class relations: the origins and functions of the state implies that it is far more than a 'superstructure' on an economic 'base'.

IDEAL STATE OF PLATO

Plato, was a Classical Greek philosopher, mathematician, student of Socrates, writer of philosophical dialogues, and founder of the Academy in Athens, the first institution of higher learning in the Western world. Along with his mentor, Socrates, and his student, Aristotle, Plato helped to lay the foundations of Western philosophy and science. In the famous words of A.N. Whitehead:

- The safest general characterization of the European philosophical tradition is that it consists of a series of footnotes to Plato. I do not mean the systematic scheme of thought which scholars have doubtfully extracted from his writings. I allude to the wealth of general ideas scattered through them.

Plato's sophistication as a writer is evident in his Socratic dialogues; thirty-six dialogues and thirteen letters have been ascribed to him. Plato's writings have been published in several fashions; this has led to several conventions regarding the naming and referencing of Plato's texts. Plato's dialogues have been used to teach a range of subjects, including philosophy, logic, ethics, rhetoric, and mathematics.

PHILOSOPHY OF PLATO

Recurrent Themes

Plato often discusses the father-son relationship and the "question" of whether a father's interest in his sons has much to do with how well his sons turn out. A boy in ancient Athens was socially located by his family identity, and Plato often refers to his characters in terms of their paternal and fraternal relationships. Socrates was not a family man, and saw himself as the son of his mother, who was apparently a midwife. A divine fatalist, Socrates mocks men who spent exorbitant fees on tutors and trainers for their sons, and repeatedly ventures the idea that good character is a gift from the gods. Crito reminds Socrates that orphans are at the mercy of chance, but Socrates is unconcerned. In the *Theaetetus*, he is found recruiting as a disciple a young man whose inheritance has been squandered. Socrates twice compares the relationship of the older man and his boy lover to the father-son relationship and in the *Phaedo*, Socrates' disciples, towards whom he displays more concern than his biological sons, say they will feel "fatherless" when he is gone.

In several dialogues, Socrates floats the idea that knowledge is a matter of recollection, and not of learning, observation, or study. He maintains this view somewhat at his own expense, because in many dialogues, Socrates complains of his forgetfulness. Socrates is often found arguing that knowledge is not empirical, and that it comes from divine insight. In many middle period dialogues, such as the *Phaedo*, *Republic* and *Phaedrus* Plato advocates a belief in the immortality of the soul, and several dialogues end with long speeches imagining the afterlife. More than one dialogue contrasts knowledge and opinion, perception and reality, nature and custom, and body and soul. Several dialogues tackle questions about art: Socrates says that poetry is inspired by the muses, and is not rational. He speaks approvingly of this, and other forms of divine madness in the *Phaedrus* and yet in the *Republic* wants to outlaw Homer's great poetry, and laughter as well. In *Ion*, Socrates gives no hint of the disapproval of Homer that he expresses in the *Republic*. The dialogue *Ion* suggests that Homer's *Iliad* functioned in the ancient Greek world as the Bible does today in the modern Christian world: as divinely inspired literature that can provide moral guidance, if only it can be properly interpreted.

On politics and art, religion and science, justice and medicine, virtue and vice, crime and punishment, pleasure and pain, rhetoric and rhapsody, human nature and sexuality, love and wisdom, Socrates and his company of disputants had something to say.

Metaphysics

"Platonism" is a term coined by scholars to refer to the intellectual consequences of denying, as Socrates often does, the reality of the material world. In several dialogues, most notably the Republic, Socrates inverts the common man's intuition about what is knowable and what is real. While most people take the objects of their senses to be real if anything is, Socrates is contemptuous of people who think that something has to be graspable in the hands to be real. In the *Theaetetus*, he says such people are "eu a-mousoi", an expression that means literally, "happily without the muses". In other words, such people live without the divine inspiration that gives him, and people like him, access to higher insights about reality.

Socrates's idea that reality is unavailable to those who use their senses is what puts him at odds with the common man, and with common sense. Socrates says that he who sees with his eyes is blind, and this idea is most famously captured in his allegory of the cave, and more explicitly in his description of the divided line. The allegory of the cave is a paradoxical analogy wherein Socrates argues that the invisible world is the most intelligible and that the visible world is the least knowable, and the most obscure. Socrates says in the *Republic* that people who take the sun-lit world of the senses to be good and real are living pitifully in a den of evil and ignorance. Socrates admits that few climb out of the den, or cave of ignorance, and those who do, not only have a terrible struggle to attain the heights, but when they go back down for a visit or to help other people up, they find themselves objects of scorn and ridicule.

According to Socrates, physical objects and physical events are "shadows" of their ideal or perfect forms, and exist only to the extent that they instantiate the perfect versions of themselves. Just as shadows are temporary, inconsequential epiphenomena produced by physical objects, physical objects are themselves fleeting phenomena caused by more substantial causes, the ideals of which they are mere instances. For example, Socrates thinks that perfect justice exists and his own trial would be a cheap copy of it. The allegory of the cave is intimately connected to his political ideology, that only people who have climbed out of the cave and cast their eyes on a vision of goodness are fit to rule. Socrates claims that the enlightened men of society must be forced from their divine contemplations and be compelled to run the city according to their lofty insights. Thus is born the idea of the "philosopher-king", the wise person who accepts the power thrust upon him by the people who are wise enough to choose a good master. This is the main thesis of Socrates in the *Republic*, that the most wisdom the masses can muster is the wise choice of a ruler.

The word metaphysics derives from the fact that Aristotle's musings about divine reality came after his lecture notes on his treatise on nature. The term is in fact applied to Aristotle's own teacher, and Plato's "metaphysics" is understood as Socrates' division of reality into the warring and irreconcilable domains of the material and the spiritual. The theory has been of incalculable influence in the history of Western philosophy and religion.

Theory of Forms

The Theory of Forms typically refers to the belief expressed by Socrates in some of Plato's dialogues, that the material world as it seems to us is not the real world, but only an image or copy of the real world. Socrates spoke of forms in formulating a solution to the problem of universals. The forms, according to Socrates, are roughly speaking archetypes or abstract representations of the many types of things, and properties we feel and see around us, that can only be perceived by reason. In other words, Socrates sometimes seems to recognise two worlds: the apparent world, which constantly changes, and an unchanging and unseen world of forms, which may be a cause of what is apparent.

Epistemology

Many have interpreted Plato as stating that knowledge is justified true belief, an influential view that informed future developments in modern analytic epistemology. This interpretation is based on a reading of the *Theaetetus* wherein Plato argues that belief is to be distinguished from knowledge on account of justification. Many years later, Edmund Gettier famously demonstrated the problems of the justified true belief account of knowledge. This interpretation, however, imports modern analytic and empiricist categories onto Plato himself and is better read on its own terms than as Plato's view.

Really, in the *Sophist*, *Statesman*, *Republic*, and the *Parmenides* Plato himself associates knowledge with the apprehension of unchanging Forms and their relationships to one another. More explicitly, Plato himself argues in the *Timaeus* that knowledge is always proportionate to the realm from which it is gained. In other words, if one derives one's account of something experientially, because the world of sense is in flux, the views therein attained will be mere opinions. And opinions are characterized by a lack of necessity and stability. On the other hand, if one derives one's account of something by way of the non-sensible forms, because these forms are unchanging, so too is the account derived from them. It is only in this sense that Plato uses the term "knowledge".

In the Meno, Socrates uses a geometrical example to expound Plato's view that knowledge in this latter sense is acquired by recollection. Socrates elicits a fact concerning a geometrical construction from a slave boy, who could not have otherwise known the fact. The knowledge must be present, Socrates concludes, in an eternal, non-experiential form.

The State

Plato's philosophical views had many societal implications, especially on the idea of an ideal state or government. There is some discrepancy between his early and later views. Some of the most famous doctrines are contained in the *Republic* during his middle period, as well as in the *Laws* and the *Statesman*. However, because Plato wrote dialogues, it is assumed that Socrates is often speaking for Plato. This assumption may not be true in all cases.

Plato, through the words of Socrates, asserts that societies have a tripartite class structure corresponding to the appetite/spirit/reason structure of the individual soul. The appetite/spirit/reason stand for different parts of the body. The body parts symbolize the castes of society.

- *Productive*, which represents the abdomen — the labourers, carpenters, plumbers, masons, merchants, farmers, ranchers, etc. These correspond to the "appetite" part of the soul.
- *Protective*, which represents the chest— those who are adventurous, strong and brave; in the armed forces. These correspond to the "spirit" part of the soul.
- *Governing*, which represents the head— those who are intelligent, rational, self-controlled, in love with wisdom, well suited to make

decisions for the community. These correspond to the "reason" part of the soul and are very few.

According to this model, the principles of Athenian democracy are rejected as only a few are fit to rule. Instead of rhetoric and persuasion, Plato says reason and wisdom should govern. As Plato puts it:

- "Until philosophers rule as kings or those who are now called kings and leading men genuinely and adequately philosophise, that is, until political power and philosophy entirely coincide, while the many natures who at present pursue either one exclusively are forcibly prevented from doing so, cities will have no rest from evils... nor, I think, will the human race."

Plato describes these "philosopher kings" as "those who love the sight of truth" and supports the idea with the analogy of a captain and his ship or a doctor and his medicine. According to him, sailing and health are not things that everyone is qualified to practice by nature. A large part of the *Republic* then addresses how the educational system should be set up to produce these philosopher kings.

However, it must be taken into account that the ideal city outlined in the *Republic* is qualified by Socrates as the ideal *luxurious* city, examined to determine how it is that injustice and justice grow in a city. According to Socrates, the "true" and "healthy" city is instead the one first outlined in book II of the *Republic*, 369c–372d, containing farmers, craftsmen, merchants, and wage-earners, but lacking the guardian class of philosopher-kings as well as delicacies such as "perfumed oils, incense, prostitutes, and pastries", in addition to paintings, gold, ivory, couches, a multitude of occupations such as poets and hunters, and war.

In addition, the ideal city is used as an image to illuminate the state of one's soul, or the will, reason, and desires combined in the human body. Socrates is attempting to make an image of a rightly ordered human, and then later goes on to describe the different kinds of humans that can be observed, from tyrants to lovers of money in various kinds of cities. The ideal city is not promoted, but only used to magnify the different kinds of individual humans and the state of their soul. However, the philosopher king image was used by many after Plato to justify their personal political beliefs. The philosophic soul according to Socrates has reason, will, and desires united in virtuous harmony. A philosopher has the moderate love for wisdom and the courage to act according to wisdom. Wisdom is knowledge about the Good or the right relations between all that exists.

Wherein it concerns states and rulers, Plato has made interesting arguments. For instance he asks which is better—a bad democracy or a country reigned by a tyrant. He argues that it is better to be ruled by a bad tyrant, than be a bad democracy This is emphasised within the *Republic* as Plato describes the event of mutiny onboard a ship. Plato suggests the ships crew to be in line with the democratic rule of many and the captain, although inhibited through ailments, the tyrant. Plato's description of this event is parallel to that of democracy within the state and the inherent problems that arise.

According to Plato, a state made up of different kinds of souls will, overall, decline from an aristocracy to a timocracy, then to an oligarchy, then to a democracy, and finally to tyranny.

Unwritten Doctrine

For a long time Plato's unwritten doctrine had been considered unworthy of attention. Most of the books on Plato seem to diminish its importance. Nevertheless the first important witness who mentions its existence is Aristotle, who in his *Physics* writes: "It is true, indeed, that the account he gives there of the participant is different from what he says in his so-called *unwritten teaching*." The term literally means *unwritten doctrine* and it stands for the most fundamental metaphysical teaching of Plato, which he disclosed only to his most trusted fellows and kept secret from the public.

The reason for not revealing it to everyone is partially discussed in Phaedrus where Plato criticizes the written transmission of knowledge as faulty, favouring instead the spoken logos: "he who has knowledge of the just and the good and beautiful... will not, when in earnest, write them in ink, sowing them through a pen with words, which cannot defend themselves by argument and cannot teach the truth effectually." The same argument is repeated in Plato's *Seventh Letter*: "every serious man in dealing with really serious subjects carefully avoids writing." In the same letter he writes: "I can certainly declare concerning all these writers who claim to know the subjects that I seriously study... there does not exist, nor will there ever exist, any treatise of mine dealing therewith." Such secrecy is necessary in order not "to expose them to unseemly and degrading treatment". It is however said that Plato once disclosed this knowledge to the public in his lecture *On the Good*, in which the Good is identified with the One, the fundamental ontological principle. The content of this lecture has been transmitted by several witnesses, among others Aristoxenus who describes the event in the following words: "Each came expecting to learn something about the things that are generally considered good for men, such as wealth, good health, physical strength, and altogether a kind of wonderful happiness. But when the mathematical demonstrations came, including numbers, geometrical figures and astronomy, and finally the statement Good is One seemed to them, I imagine, utterly unexpected and strange; hence some belittled the matter, while others rejected it."

Simplicius quotes Alexander of Aphrodisias who states that "according to Plato, the first principles of everything, including the Forms themselves are One and Indefinite Duality, which he called Large and Small... one might also learn this from Speusippus and Xenocrates and the others who were present at Plato's lecture on the Good"

Their account is in full agreement with Aristotle's description of Plato's metaphysical doctrine. In *Metaphysics* he writes: "Now since the Forms are the causes of everything else, he supposed that their elements are the elements of all things. Accordingly the material principle is the Great and Small, and the essence is the One, since the numbers are derived from the Great and Small by participation in the One". "From this account it is clear that he only employed two causes: that of the essence, and the material cause; for the Forms are the cause of the essence in everything else, and the One is the cause of it in the Forms. He also tells us what the material substrate is of which the Forms are predicated in the case of sensible things, and the One in that of the Forms - that it is this the duality, the Great and Small. Further, he assigned to these two elements respectively the causation of good and of evil".

The most important aspect of this interpretation of Plato's metaphysics is the continuity between his teaching and the neo-platonic interpretation of Plotinus or Ficino which has been considered erroneous by many but may in fact have been directly influenced by oral transmission of Plato's doctrine. A modern scholar who recognized the importance of the unwritten doctrine of Plato was Heinrich Gomperz who described it in his speech during the 7th International Congress of Philosophy in 1930

Dialectic

The role of dialectic in Plato's thought is contested but there are two main interpretations; a type of reasoning and a method of intuition. Simon Blackburn adopts the first, saying that Plato's dialectic is "the process of eliciting the truth by means of questions aimed at opening out what is already implicitly known, or at exposing the contradictions and muddles of an opponent's position." Karl Popper, on the other hand, claims that dialectic is the art of intuition for "visualising the divine originals, the Forms or Ideas, of unveiling the Great Mystery behind the common man's everyday world of appearances."

ARISTOTLE'S CLASSIFICATION OF STATE

Aristotle was a Greek philosopher and polymath, a student of Plato and teacher of Alexander the Great. His writings cover many subjects, including physics, metaphysics, poetry, theater, music, logic, rhetoric, linguistics, politics, government, ethics, biology, and zoology. Together with Plato and Socrates, Aristotle is one of the most important founding figures in Western philosophy. Aristotle's writings were the first to create a comprehensive system of Western philosophy, encompassing morality and aesthetics, logic and science, politics and metaphysics. Aristotle's views on the physical sciences profoundly shaped medieval scholarship, and their influence extended well into the Renaissance, although they were ultimately replaced by Newtonian physics. In the zoological sciences, some of his observations were confirmed to be accurate only in the 19th century. His works contain the earliest known formal study of logic, which was incorporated in the late 19th century into modern formal logic. In metaphysics, Aristotelianism had a profound influence on philosophical and theological thinking in the Islamic and Jewish traditions in the Middle Ages, and it continues to influence Christian theology, especially the scholastic tradition of the Catholic Church. His ethics, though always influential, gained renewed interest with the modern advent of virtue ethics. All aspects of Aristotle's philosophy continue to be the object of active academic study today. Though Aristotle wrote many elegant treatises and dialogues, it is thought that the majority of his writings are now lost and only about one-third of the original works have survived.

PRACTICAL PHILOSOPHY

Ethics

Aristotle considered ethics to be a practical rather than theoretical study, *i.e.*, one aimed at doing good rather than knowing for its own sake. He wrote several treatises on ethics, including most notably, the *Nicomachean Ethics*.

Aristotle taught that virtue has to do with the proper function of a thing. An eye is only a good eye in so much as it can see, because the proper function of an eye is sight. Aristotle reasoned that humans must have a function specific to humans, and that this function must be an activity of the *psuchç* in accordance with reason. Aristotle identified such an optimum activity of the soul as the aim of all human deliberate action, *eudaimonia*, generally translated as "happiness" or sometimes "well being". To have the potential of ever being happy in this way necessarily requires a good character often translated as moral virtue.

Aristotle taught that to achieve a virtuous and potentially happy character requires a first stage of having the fortune to be habituated not deliberately, but by teachers, and experience, leading to a later stage in which one consciously chooses to do the best things. When the best people come to live life this way their practical wisdom and their intellect can develop with each other towards the highest possible human virtue, the wisdom of an accomplished theoretical or speculative thinker, or in other words, a philosopher.

Politics

In addition to his works on ethics, which address the individual, Aristotle addressed the city in his work titled *Politics*. Aristotle considered the city to be a natural community. Moreover, he considered the city to be prior in importance to the family which in turn is prior to the individual, "for the whole must of necessity be prior to the part". He also famously stated that "man is by nature a political animal." Aristotle conceived of politics as being like an organism rather than like a machine, and as a collection of parts none of which can exist without the others. Aristotle's conception of the city is organic, and he is considered one of the first to conceive of the city in this manner.

The common modern understanding of a political community as a modern state is quite different to Aristotle's understanding. Although he was aware of the existence and potential of larger empires, the natural community according to Aristotle was the city which functions as a political "community" or "partnership". The aim of the city is not just to avoid injustice or for economic stability, but rather to allow at least some citizens the possibility to live a good life, and to perform beautiful acts: "The political partnership must be regarded, therefore, as being for the sake of noble actions, not for the sake of living together." This is distinguished from modern approaches, beginning with social contract theory, according to which individuals leave the state of nature because of "fear of violent death" or its "inconveniences."

Rhetoric and Poetics

Aristotle considered epic poetry, tragedy, comedy, dithyrambic poetry and music to be imitative, each varying in imitation by medium, object, and manner. For example, music imitates with the media of rhythm and harmony, whereas dance imitates with rhythm alone, and poetry with language. The forms also differ in their object of imitation. Comedy, for instance, is a dramatic imitation of men worse than average; whereas tragedy imitates men slightly better than average. Lastly, the forms differ in their manner of imitation – through narrative or character, through change or no change, and through drama or no drama. Aristotle believed that imitation is natural to mankind and constitutes one of mankind's advantages over animals.

While it is believed that Aristotle's *Poetics* comprised two books – one on comedy and one on tragedy – only the portion that focuses on tragedy has survived. Aristotle taught that tragedy is composed of six elements: plot-structure, character, style, spectacle, and lyric poetry. The characters in a tragedy are merely a means of driving the story; and the plot, not the characters, is the chief focus of tragedy. Tragedy is the imitation of action arousing pity and fear, and is meant to effect the catharsis of those same emotions. Aristotle concludes *Poetics* with a discussion on which, if either, is superior: epic or tragic mimesis. He suggests that because tragedy possesses all the attributes of an epic, possibly possesses additional attributes such as spectacle and music, is more unified, and achieves the aim of its mimesis in shorter scope, it can be considered superior to epic.

Aristotle was a keen systematic collector of riddles, folklore, and proverbs; he and his school had a special interest in the riddles of the Delphic Oracle and studied the fables of Aesop.

ARISTOTLE'S CLASSIFICATION OF STATES

No scientific classification of states is possible because all the slates are alike in as much as all are supposed to have population, territory ^ government and sovereignty.

All enjoy equal status in the eyes of inter-national law. As governments arc the only tangible manifestations of the existence of states the classification of governments is, in essence the classification of states. The government existed in the past and exists at present in various forms.

Monarchy, aristocracy and pure democracy are its old forms. In the present age, representative democracy is an accepted form. It is further distinguished as the parliamentary, presidential, unitary and federal types.

Aristotle, an ancient Greek philosopher, classified states on the basis of two principles:-

- In whom the sovereign powers are vested?
- Whether it is exercised for the good of the community or for the good of the ruler?

If the supreme power is vested in the hands of the one man and is exercised for the good of community, it is monarchy. If the power is exercised by the monarch for his self aggrandizement it becomes tyr-anny—a perverted form of monarchy.

If power is vested in the hands of a few and is exercised for the good of the community, it is aristocracy. If it is exercised for the good of the rulers, it becomes oligarchy—a perverted form of aristocracy. If power is vested in the hands of all citizens and is exercised for common good, it is polity. If the power is exercised by mobs and demagogues it becomes democracy—perverted form of polity. Aristotle's democracy is likely to surprise the modern man, but this surprise will disappear if one bears in mind that Aristotle used the term in a sense different from what we use today. What Aristotle called polity, we designate as democracy; what he named democracy, we call as mobocracy.

Cycle of State

Aristotle further believes that all the states go through a cycle of revolutions. The state began with the establishment of monarchy which was the virtuous rule of a single man. Though after some time such a virtuous man could no longer be produced yet the rule of one man remained and his power was maintained by force.

It was tyranny or despotism. It was replaced by aristocracy by means of a revolution. The spirit of aristocracy also began to degenerate and was replaced by oligarchy. By a popular uprising, oligarchy was turned into polity which soon degenerated into democracy, a sort of mob-rule. Out of darkness, then, again arises the supremely virtuous man, some Caesar who restores law and order. The cycle is completed and begins all over again.

DEFINITION OF POLITICS

Distorted form of Politics. When we try to understand the word 'polities' as common men, it appears before us in the form of practical politics or the art of administration. Its philosophical aspect disappears. Working of political parties, use of fair or foul means in elections, use of bureaucracy for selfish ends through corrupt means, etc., are included in politics. Not only this, now-a-days, there is more distorted form of politics which comes before us, we daily hear about politics of the family, politics of the mohalla, politics of the college, politics of the village etc.

All this implies that to achieve our aims by telling lies, by cheating and by dishonesty, is called politics. Conferences, processions, slogans, stribes and riots, are being accepted as parts of politics. In fact, it is the distorted form of politics. The Real Nature of Politics. Politics, as a study, is a very broad discipline. It is called a broad physical activity. In his book, 'An Introduction to Polities', Soltau says, "Politics is the concern of everybody with any sense of responsibility," because it is concerned with everybody.

So, nobody can avoid it in spite of the fact whether he has any interest in it or not. When some individuals search for the solution of a problem and take the help of mutual co-operation and struggle, politics comes into being. Because of this very reason, politics exists in every association, organisation-national and international. According to Herbert J. Spiro, Politics is the process by which communities of human beings deal with their problems. Thus, we see that many human problems are being solved out of the state and the associations concerned there with, political parties, pressure groups and elections etc., are such fields, the study of which is an important part of politics.

By Politics, L. Lipson means "a process of active controversy." By it he means that, in every society there are limited means for the fulfilment of the various necessities and every individual, group or organisation tries to achieve its aims by utilising these limited means. Therefore, because of the limitation of the means, struggle is inevitable. According to Lipson, this process of struggle goes on constantly. In politics, we study the process of solving problem is a constant struggle. In this connection, rise of struggle or clash is not enough. Politics comes into being when man becomes active in solving his problem, participation in politics, criticism of government. Discussion and getting the policy of the government amended through agitation as peasants, labourers and businessmen are the subject matter of politics. On the basis of the above given analysis it can be said that politics is a fundamental political activity with the help of which man solves his problems by using limited means.

POLITICS AS THE CONCILIATION OF INTERESTS

Politics has been termed as the means of establishing conciliation and coordination among different interests. We know that people living in the society have different desires and aspirations. In order to fulfil them numerous organisations, communities and institutions are formed. We see countless such institutions in economic, social, religions and cultural spheres. State is also a political institution/organisation but due to its prime importance it is the most powerful one among all the institutions. Man goes on trying always to fulfil his desires, aspirations and wants. In the course of fulfilling them it is natural to face opposition, confrontation and struggle. Thus there remains a continuous situation of struggle and confrontation between man and various institutions formed by him. Politics is the means of establishing rapport, coordination and conciliation among different interests created among individuals, communities and groups (classes).

As politics establishes conciliation after removing various confrontations and struggles, where there is politics there would be problems, confrontations, oppositions and struggles. In this way every walk of life is confronted with politics. Stephan L. Wasby has rightly said that it is generally said that politics will exist where there is a dispute. Where there is problems there is politics. Where there is no dispute, there is no situation of debate on problems and there is no question of the existence of politics. (Political Science—The Discipline and its Dimensions). Politics is such a process of removing confrontation and solving disputes and problems that goes on in every field of society without break.

- *Controversy should be within State limits:* Disputes may be of two types-one of individual or private disputes and the other of state limits. Individual disputes between husband and wife may be on what is to be prepared in the meals and to which park we have to go on strolling in the evening, what should be the cost of cloths to be purchased from the market? And in which institution/school children should be admitted. Such disputes do not come in the scope of state limits, hence they are out of our study. The other group of disputes are those disputes which come under the scope of state limits. If there is a dispute or controversy between husband and wife over the division of a property, its solution is possible only through politics or in other words through state. The subject matter of studies is the solution of such disputes and controversies which come under the scope of state.
- *Existence of Established Laws about Controversy:* It is also necessary to have established laws to settle these disputes or controversies. Such established laws are accepted by one and all. Both the parties should also be made confident that through laws framed by state we are capable of settling disputes and controversies.
- The state and politics will bring about unity and agreement in the society full of conflicts and disagreements. Man is a rational animal,

he bases his behaviour on criteria of good and bad or useful and useless. He is vigilant about his interests, and he is busy in the fulfilment of his various types of interests. In the society, there is clash of interests of the individuals. And, because of it, the conflicts and struggles among them are natural. Where, in a society there is disorder and lack of peace because of the conflict of interests, development is restricted and the individual interests also are not satisfied. The liberals hold that, in the society full of conflicts and differences, state and politics try to establish unity and agreement. They say that state is an instrument for establishing unity and agreement in the human society. Politics is the process through which unity and agreement are born. J.B. Miller has said that "The origin of politics lies in social diversity." By saying this, he meant that politics comes into being for removing the conflicts, differences and disagreements present in the society. The process in the instrument, *i.e.*, the state lessens the gulf between these interests. Thus, the liberals consider the state and politics as the means for developing a peaceful society minus conflicts. In this context, according to Maurice Duverger, two self-contradictory points of view come to the fore, regarding the aims of politics. The first point of view is that of the Communists. They say that the powerful men, who are in authority, to maintain their hold in the society and to achieve their interest, make use of politics. In their eyes, there is no good aim of politics. It is an instrument of the strong to maintain their domination over the weak. According to the other view, politics is an effort to bring about the rule of order and justice in which power guarantees the general interest and the common good against the pressures of private interest. The fact is, that in every society, the above given both the forms of politics, are active. On the one hand, the ruling class tries to use politics for the fulfilment of its interests and for making its authority permanent to dominate others, and, on the other hand, politics works as such an instrument with the help of which a definite social order is established and in which, the efforts are made to limit the individual interest for the satisfaction of the general interest. The liberals support the second aspect of politics.

- Politics is the process through which peaceful social change is possible. By studying the history of the political ideologies, it becomes clear that liberalism was a revolt against blind faith, traditionalism, conservatism and religious fundamentalism. It always supported the wise and reasonable ideas because liberalism has faith in the rationality of man. Therefore, it supported all those ideas and faiths, which may protect the interests of the rational man, and opposed those ideas which bind the man like animals to restrain them and because of which there may be no development of the human mind and intellect. Though there were revolutions in the U.S.A., U.K. and France against traditionalism and conservation, yet, in the modem times liberalism favours peaceful means of change against the violent revolutions. A violent revolution paves the way for another and it spoils the reasonableness of man and creates lack of peace. Therefore, it is an admitted fact in liberalism that social reforms should be introduced slowly. The mind of man should be prepared for it first. As soon as this consciousness develops, he will accept the social reforms and necessary changes. The communist thinkers allege that liberalism is in favour of status quo and say that they are traditionalist and liberal, and they are against progress, but we have seen that many capitalist countries and many developing countries are making progress in every sphere through the same process with the help of which social change can be brought by peaceful means. Being in accordance with human nature, the individuals accept them because the people are encouraged to accept them. Violence, domination and pressure are not used for spread of education, for the betterment of health, for scientific research, and for the removal of conservatism and had customs, but the concerned classes are educated for this purpose. Though liberalism is in favour of bringing changes peacefully, but it also supports the use force when the need arises. Army, police and judiciary are the symbols of its brute force, the use of which is allowed in special circumstances. The aim of the use of this force is to reform the criminal and to bring change in his life instead of punishing him. Therefore, army, police, judiciary and jails in the states are considered reformative institutions and not those with the aim of punishing them. In addition to it, in liberalism, the state is encouraged to play a positive role, *i.e.*, it is expected of state that it will create such circumstances in which, on the one hand, man's basic necessities may be easily fulfilled and, on the other, his talent may be developed.

- Politics is the means to govern Democracies. Democracy is such an administration in which there is very much scope of settling disputes and struggles. These situations are:
  - There is freedom of speech in the Democracy. Through this man is able to express his point of view fearlessly and without any hurdle. Due to freedom of speech ways and means can be found for the settlement or solution of various disputes.
  - Freedom to form Political Parties. Due to this freedom various

political parties are formed. These political parties provide opportunities to the common people to express their view point on the basis of open competition.

- Law formation by the Executive of the Country. In democracy the people's representatives make laws and the executive through these laws settle the disputes and struggles. If the executive works arbitrarily, the judiciary comes in between and settles the disputes between the people and the government, and protects the interests of the people. In this politics works for removing disputes and establishing conciliation in such countries which have democratic set-ups.
- Debate in Parliament. The democratic government's main characteristic feature is that the people's representatives find solutions to different problems through debate. Different parties express their views on every issue whether it is of minor value or the prime value. Through discussion there is every possibility to find solution to these problems, which is acceptable to one and all. There is a check on the power of the government and the common good comes to the fore.
- Important Role of pressure and Interest Groups. Every problem or dispute or controversy has several aspects. Different interest groups on the basis of interest work in the form of pressuregroups to further their interests. These interest groups by using different ways they try to make administrative decisions in their favour. There pressure groups in democracy help in decisionmaking and also help in finding the middle way through mutual discussions in place of disputes or confrontation. Many times when there is a situation of dispute or confrontation, even then these groups prove helpful in finding a peaceful way in place of dispute and confrontation.

There exist circumstances to solve problems through peaceful means in democracy. Sir Bernard Crick has said that in democratic society government/ administration is run through politics.

CRITICISM OF THE MARXIST VIEW OF POLITICS

Though, because of spread of communism, there is no dearth of writers who support Marxist view of politics, yet because of the defects in the Marxist ideology, there seem to be certain defects in the Marxist View of Politics. That is why, Marxist View has been critically discussed below.

- The individual-self is merged in the social-self. Idea of Marx about the individual has actually merged the individual-self with the social-self. The fact is that, in liberalism, society was so much neglected for the individual that some powerful persons of the society fully exploited others, but, on the other hand, because of discussion of the all-round development of the individual as a part of society in communism, free personality of the individual was lost. Perhaps, unknowingly, Marx like Hegel merged the self of the individual in the social self. Thus, it may be liberalism or communism, the class, owing the material resources and political power, uses the common man of the society as a means of the fulfilment of its interest. Marxists claim that politics is an instrument of development of the individual, but, practically, they use him for exploitation. This fact becomes clear by studying social set-up of those countries where dictatorship of the proletariat has been established.

- Material conditions are not the only basis of politics. Marx recognises man only in his economic capacity, and he thinks that the other aspects of his life depend only on material conditions. Religious, cultural, moral and other sentimental aspects of individual are influenced by his economic life and direction is provided by it. That is why, Marx has come to the conclusion that material conditions of man are the basis of politics. This point of view of Marx can not be accepted. It is a fact that material conditions influence politics, but these are not the sole basis. In addition to cultural, religious, spiritual and moral values, traditions and customs of a country also influence its political process. Marx admitted this fact in his later writings and admitted that only economic conditions are not believed to be the whole process of political development. Clarifying this fact, Fyodorov says, "Marxism- Leninism, however, does not consider that whole process of political development is only directly and indirectly dependent on production." Avineri also says that Marx, in his later writings, did not consider politics only as a reflection of the economic conditions. Thus, political process, as explained by Marx, seems to be defective in itself.
- Politics is not merely the study of class-struggle. Marx has divided the society into two mutually opposing classes, whose interests are always opposed to each other and they constantly go on struggling. In the present era, it can not be accepted that whole society is divided into two mutually opposite classes (capitalists and labourers). The fact is that every society is divided into various classes and those classes are not necessarily organised on economic basis. Some of these classes may be such that they have no economic basis and there is no condition of their being in struggle. Even between the capitalists and the labourers, as explained by Marx, these days, there is cooperation and not struggle because, needs of the labourers having

been fulfilled and the functions concerning their welfare having been performed, the difference between the labourers and capitalists, as discussed by Marx, do not seem to be working now. So, saying that politics is merely a study of class-struggle is not logical because that form of class-struggle does not seem to be working in the society.

- All political conflicts are not class-struggle. It is wrong to accept all political struggles as class conflicts. It may be possible, that there is a very important economic reason behind every political question, but it will not be reasonable to call them class-struggle. For example, in India, it is being demanded that right to vote should be giver at 18. But the arguments, being advanced for this demand, are more political and social than economic. If a young man of 18 can become an able, efficient and reliable soldier who shoulders the responsibility of defence of the country, why should he not be allowed to take part in the politics of the country? Similarly, a yong man of 18 is considered fit for handling the property as an adult person, how has he become unable to participate in the administration of the country? We do not see that between 18 years and 21 years' age, there is an economic class of the young men and they have a struggle with the ruling class. Now the youth aged 18 is permitted to cast votes or in other words he has been given adult franchise. The public of a country wants to establish democracy in place of monarchy or wants to establish presidential form of government in place of parliamentary government, the form of this struggle is political or social and not economic. Therefore, it is correct to say that every political struggle is not class-struggle. Economic conditions of the proletariat have improved in the capitalist society, Marx had said that, in a capitalist society, politics is an instrument for exploiting the labourers, and consequently, economic condition of the labourers will worsen but the study of social organisations of capitalist countries indicate that there capitalist class has made many changes and arrangements have been made for ameliorating economic and social conditions of the labourers and for the security of their lives, their health and education. Because of these arrangements, on the one hand, there is amelioration in the economic conditions of the labourers and, on the other hand, their professional efficiency has increased. It does not prove assertion of Karl Marx that politics will become the basis of economic exploitation in the capitalist countries.
- Politics also did not create consciousness for revolution. The countries, where communist revolutions have occurred, were not industrially advanced, as Marx had claimed. And, in modern times, no revolution has been brought by the labourers in the industrialised

countries. The fact is that because of fulfilment of economic, social and cultural demands and because of betterment in their condition, consciousness of class struggle did not develop in the labourers in capitalist countries. If any consciousness had developed it was for co-operation with the capitalists. It is correct that, sometimes, the labour class becomes ready for struggle with the capitalists, but it is not for establishing dictatorship of the proletariat, but for betterment of their economic conditions. So, it is clear that in the capitalist society, politics does not prepare ground for class struggle.

- The politics could not become a means to establish a new society. According to Marx, after the revolution, Politics will be utilised for destroying remnants of capitalism and to eradicate the traditions and moral values of capitalism and, out of it, such a society will be established, in which there is no place for class struggle. The whole of society will become one class in which there is no antagonism of economic classes. When we study those countries of the world, where dictatorship of the proletariat was established, according to the Marxists, *e.g.*, Russia and China. The conditions of dictatorship of the proletariat are still prevailing there. And there is no possibility in the near future, for the establishment of classless society there, which was the dream of a stateless society of Marx. By this, it can be concluded that with the help of politics, a classless society could not be established. In the countries like Russia and China, politics, even today is a means for the ruling class for getting hold of authority, and their society is still divided into two classes, *i.e.*, the rulers and the ruled.

3

Sovereignty and Political Authority

On the international level, sovereignty means independence, *i.e.*, non-interference by external powers in the internal affairs of another state. International norms are based on the principle of the sovereign equality of independent states; international law excludes interference and establishes universally-accepted rules. Thus, sovereignty is eminently rational, if not dialectical, since the sovereignty of a state depends not only on the autonomous will of its sovereign, but also on its standing *vis-a-vis* other sovereign states. From this perspective, one can say that the sovereignty of any single state is the logical consequence of the existence of several sovereign states.

It is thus a serious mistake to assume that sovereignty is possible only within the framework of the classic type of state, *i.e.*, a nation-state, as do representatives of the "realist" school, such as Alan James and F. H. Hinsley, or neo-Marxist theoreticians like Justin Rosenberg. One should not confuse the concepts of nation and state, which do not necessarily belong together, or assume that the concept of sovereignty was formulated clearly only in terms of the theory of the state. Closer to the truth is John Hoffman's assertion that "sovereignty has been an insoluble problem ever since it became associated with the state."

Even though a concept of sovereignty did not exist before the 16th century, it does not follow that the phenomenon did not exist in political reality, and that it could not have been conceptualized differently.

For example, Aristotle does not mention sovereignty, but the fact that he insists on the necessity for a supreme power shows that he was familiar with the idea, since any supreme power — *kuphian aphen* with the Greeks; *summum imperium* with the Romans — is sovereign by definition. Sovereignty is not related to any particular form of government or to any particular political organization; on the contrary, it is inherent in any form of political authority. The problem with sovereignty appeared at the end of the Middle Ages, when the question posed was no longer only about the best form of government or the limits of political authority, but about the relation between the government and the people, *i.e.*, the relation between ruler and ruled in a political community.

This is the question that Jean Bodin attempted to answer in *La Republique*, published in 1576. Bodin did not invent sovereignty, but he was the first to make a conceptual analysis of it and to propose a systematic formulation. He did not initiate this project by observing a real state, but by attempting to restore public order, which had been damaged by the religious wars, and by legitimating the emancipation of French kings from the Pope and the emperor. This is why Bodin's doctrine naturally constituted the ideology of territorial realms seeking to gain independence from the empire, and to transform the power that had obtained in royal dominance over feudal lords.

CONCEPT OF SOVEREIGNTY

The concept of sovereignty is one of the most complex in political science, with many definitions, some totally contradictory. Usually, sovereignty is defined in one of two ways. The first definition applies to supreme public power, which has the right and, in theory, the capacity to impose its authority in the last instance. The second definition refers to the holder of legitimate power, who is recognized to have authority. When national sovereignty is discussed, the first definition applies, and it refers in particular to independence, understood as the freedom of a collective entity to act. When popular sovereignty is discussed, the second definition applies, and sovereignty is associated with power and legitimacy.

DEFINITION AND TYPES

There exists perhaps no conception the meaning of which is more controversial than that of sovereignty. It is an indisputable fact that this conception, from the moment when it was introduced into political science until the present day, has never had a meaning which was universally agreed upon—Lassa Oppenheim, an authority on international law

ABSOLUTENESS

An important factor of sovereignty is its degree of absoluteness. A sovereign power has absolute sovereignty when it is not restricted by a constitution, by the laws of its predecessors, or by custom, and no areas of law or policy are reserved as being outside its control. International law; policies and actions of neighbouring states; cooperation and respect of the populace; means of enforcement; and resources to enact policy are factors that might limit sovereignty.

For example, parents are not guaranteed the right to decide some matters in the upbringing of their children independent of societal regulation, and municipalities do not have unlimited jurisdiction in local matters, thus neither parents nor municipalities have absolute sovereignty. Theorists have diverged over the desirability of increased absoluteness.

EXCLUSIVITY

A key element of sovereignty in a legalistic sense is that of exclusivity of jurisdiction. Specifically, the degree to which decisions made by a sovereign entity might be contradicted by another authority. International law, competing branches of government, and authorities reserved for subordinate entities represent legal infringements on exclusivity. Social institutions such as religious bodies, corporations, and competing political parties might represent de facto infringements on exclusivity.

DE JURE AND DE FACTO

De jure, or legal, sovereignty concerns the expressed and institutionally recognised right to exercise control over a territory.

De facto, or actual, sovereignty is concerned with whether control in fact exists. Cooperation and respect of the populace; control of resources in, or moved into, an area; means of enforcement and security; and ability to carry out various functions of state all represent measures of de facto sovereignty. When control is practised predominately by military or police force it is considered coercive sovereignty. It is generally held that sovereignty requires not only the legal right to exercise power, but the actual exercise of such power. Thus, de jure sovereignty without de facto sovereignty has limited recognition.

INTERNAL

Internal sovereignty is the relationship between a sovereign power and its own subjects. A central concern is legitimacy: by what right does a government exercise authority? Claims of legitimacy might refer to the divine right of kings or to a social contract.

With sovereignty meaning holding supreme, independent authority over a region or state, internal sovereignty refers to the internal affairs of the state and the location of supreme power within it. A state that has internal sovereignty is one with a government that has been elected by the people and has the popular legitimacy. Internal sovereignty examines the internal affairs of a state and how it operates. It is important to have strong internal sovereignty in relation to keeping order and peace. When you have weak internal sovereignty organization such as rebel groups will undermined the authority and disrupt the peace.

The presence of a strong authority allows you to keep agreement and enforce sanctions for the violation of laws. The ability for leadership to prevent these violations is a key variable in determining internal sovereignty. The lack of internal sovereignty can cause war in one of two ways, first, undermining the value of agreement by allowing costly violations and second requiring such large subsidies for implementation that they render war cheaper than peace. Leadership needs to be able to promise members, especially those like armies, police forces, or paramilitaries will abide by agreements. The presence of strong internal sovereignty allows a state to deter opposition groups in exchange for bargaining. It has been said that a more decentralized authority would be more efficient in keeping peace because the deal must please not only the leadership but also the opposition group. While the operations and affairs within a state are relative to the level of sovereignty within that state, there is still an argument between who should hold the authority in a sovereign state.

This argument between who should hold the authority within a sovereign state is called the traditional doctrine of public sovereignty. This discussion is between an internal sovereign or an authority of public sovereignty. An internal sovereign is a political body that possesses ultimate, final and independent authority; one whose decisions are binding upon all citizens, groups and institutions in society. Early thinkers believe sovereignty should be vested in the hands of a single person, a monarch. They believed the overriding merit of vesting sovereignty in a single individual was that sovereignty would therefore be indivisible; it would be expressed in a single voice that could claim final authority. An example of an internal sovereign or monarch is Louis XIV of France during the seventeenth century; Louis XIV claimed that he was the state. Jean-Jacques Rousseau rejected monarchial rule in favour of the other type of authority within a sovereign state, public sovereignty. Public Sovereignty is the belief that ultimate authority is vested in the people themselves, expressed in the idea of the general will. This means that the power is elected and supported by its members, the authority has a central goal of the good of the people in mind. The idea of public sovereignty has often been the basis for modern democratic theory.

Modern Internal Sovereignty: Within the modern governmental system we usually find internal sovereignty in states that have public sovereignty and rarely find it within a state controlled by an internal sovereign. A form of government that is a little different from both is the UK parliament system. From 1790-1859 it was argued that sovereignty in the UK was vested neither in the Crown nor in the people but in the "Monarch in Parliament". This is the origin of the doctrine of parliamentary sovereignty and is usually seen as the fundamental principle of the British constitution. With these principles of parliamentary sovereignty majority control can gain access to unlimited constitutional authority, creating what has been called 'elective dictatorship' or 'modern autocracy'. Public sovereignty in modern governments is a lot more common with examples like the USA, Canada, Australia and India where government is divided into different levels.

EXTERNAL

External sovereignty concerns the relationship between a sovereign power and other states. For example, the United Kingdom uses the following criterion when deciding under what conditions other states recognise a political entity as having sovereignty over some territory;

- "Sovereignty." A government which exercises de facto administrative control over a country and is not subordinate to any other government in that country is a foreign sovereign state -The Arantzazu Mendi, Strouds Judicial Dictionary

External sovereignty is connected with questions of international law, such as: when, if ever, is intervention by one country onto another's territory permissible?

Following the Thirty Years' War, a European religious conflict that embroiled much of the continent, the Peace of Westphalia in 1648 established the notion of territorial sovereignty as a norm of non-interference in the affairs of other nations, so-called Westphalian sovereignty, even though the actual treaty itself reaffirmed the multiple levels of sovereignty of the Holy Roman Empire. This resulted as a natural extension of the older principle of cuius regio, eius religio, leaving the Roman Catholic Church with little ability to interfere with the internal affairs of many European states. It is a myth, however, that the Treaties of Westphalia created a new European order of equal sovereign states.

In international law, sovereignty means that a government possesses full control over affairs within a territorial or geographical area or limit. Determining whether a specific entity is sovereign is not an exact science, but often a matter of diplomatic dispute. There is usually an expectation that both de jure and de facto sovereignty rest in the same organization at the place and time of concern. Foreign governments use varied criteria and political considerations when deciding whether or not to recognize the sovereignty of a state over a territory.

Sovereignty may be recognized even when the sovereign body possesses no territory or its territory is under partial or total occupation by another power. The Holy See was in this position between the annexation in 1870 of the Papal States by Italy and the signing of the Lateran Treaties in 1929, when it was recognized as sovereign by many states despite possessing no territory - a situation resolved when the Lateran Treaties granted the Holy See sovereignty over the Vatican City. Another case, sui generis, though often contested, is the Sovereign Military Order of Malta, the third sovereign entity inside Italian territory and the second inside the Italian capital, which is the last existing heir to one of several once militarily significant, crusader states of sovereign military orders. In 1607 its grand masters were also made Reichsfürst by the Holy Roman Emperor, granting them seats in the Reichstag, at the time the closest permanent equivalent to a UN-type general assembly; confirmed 1620). These sovereign rights never deposed, only the territories were lost. 100 modern states still maintain full diplomatic relations with the order and the UN awarded it observer status.

The governments-in-exile of many European states during the Second World War were regarded as sovereign despite their territories being under foreign occupation; their governance resumed as soon as the occupation had ended. The government of Kuwait was in a similar situation vis-à-vis the Iraqi occupation of its country during 1990-1991.

Commonly mistaken to be sovereign, the International Committee of the Red Cross, having been granted various degrees of special privileges and legal immunities in many countries, that in cases like Switzerland are considerable, which are described as amounting to de facto sovereignty, is a private organisation governed by Swiss law.

SHARED

Just as the office of head of state can be vested jointly in several persons within a state, the sovereign jurisdiction over a single political territory can be shared jointly by two or more consenting powers, notably in the forms of a condominium or a co-principality.

NATION-STATES

A community of people who claim the right of self-determination based on a common ethnicity, history and culture might seek to establish sovereignty over a region, thus creating a nation-state. Such nations are sometimes recognized as autonomous areas rather than as fully sovereign, independent states.

FEDERATIONS

In a federal system of government, sovereignty also refers to powers which a constituent state or republic possesses independently of the national government. In a confederation constituent entities retain the right to withdraw from the national body, but in a federation member states or republics do not hold that right. Controversy over states' rights contributed to the outbreak of the American Civil War. Eleven southern states in which slavery was legal declared their independence from the United States and formed the Confederate States of America. The position of the United States government was that this act was unconstitutional and that secession was not a right that the states possessed, and thus that the states were not sovereign entities.

HISTORY OF SOVEREIGNTY

Different cultures and governments have, understandably, had different ideas about sovereignty.

CLASSICAL

The Roman jurist Ulpian observed that:

- The imperium of the people is transferred to the Emperor,

- The Emperor is not bound by the law,
- The Emperor's word is law. Emperor is the law making and abiding force.

Ulpian was expressing the idea that the Emperor exercised a rather absolute form of sovereignty, although he did not use the term expressly. Ulpian's statements were known in medieval Europe, but sovereignty was not an important concept in medieval times. Medieval monarchs were not sovereign, at least not strongly so, because they were constrained by, and shared power with, their feudal aristocracy. Furthermore, both were strongly constrained by custom.

MEDIEVAL

Sovereignty existed during the Medieval Period as the de jure rights of nobility and royalty, and in the de facto capability of individuals to make their own choices in life.

Around c. 1380-1400, the issue of feminine sovereignty was addressed in Geoffrey Chaucer's Middle English collection of Canterbury Tales, specifically in The Wife of Bath's Tale.

A later English Arthurian romance, The Wedding of Sir Gawain and Dame Ragnell uses much of the same elements of the Wife of Bath's tale, yet changes the setting to the court of King Arthur and the Knights of the Round Table. The story revolves around the knight Sir Gawain granting to Dame Ragnell, his new bride, what is purported to be wanted most by women.

REFORMATION

Sovereignty reemerged as a concept in the late 16th century, a time when civil wars had created a craving for stronger central authority, when monarchs had begun to gather power into their own hands at the expense of the nobility, and the modern nation- state was emerging. Jean Bodin, partly in reaction to the chaos of the French wars of religion; and Thomas Hobbes, partly in reaction to the English Civil War, both presented theories of sovereignty calling for strong central authority in the form of absolute monarchy.

In his 1576 treatise 'Les Six Livres de la Rėpublique' Bodin argued that it is inherent in the nature of the state that sovereignty must be:

- *Absolute*: On this point he said that the sovereign must not be hedged in with obligations and conditions, must be able to legislate without his subjects' consent, must not be bound by the laws of his predecessors, and could not, because it is illogical, be bound by his own laws.
- *Perpetual*: Not temporarily delegated as to a strong leader in an emergency or to a state employee such as a magistrate. He held that sovereignty must be perpetual because anyone with the power to

enforce a time limit on the governing power must be above the governing power, which would be impossible if the governing power is absolute.

Bodin rejected the notion of transference of sovereignty from people to sovereign; natural law and divine law confer upon the sovereign the right to rule. And the sovereign is not above divine law or natural law. He is above only positive law, that is, laws made by humans.

The fact that the sovereign must obey divine and natural law imposes ethical constraints on him. Bodin also held that the lois royales, the fundamental laws of the French monarchy which regulated matters such as succession, are natural laws and are binding on the French sovereign. How divine and natural law could in practice be enforced on the sovereign is a problematic feature of Bodin's philosophy: any person capable of enforcing them on him would be above him.

Despite his commitment to absolutism, Bodin held some moderate opinions on how government should in practice be carried out. He held that although the sovereign is not obliged to, it is advisable for him, as a practical expedient, to convene a senate from whom he can obtain advice, to delegate some power to magistrates for the practical administration of the law, and to use the estates as a means of communicating with the people.

With his doctrine that sovereignty is conferred by divine law, Bodin predefined the scope of the divine right of kings.

AGE OF ENLIGHTENMENT

Hobbes, in Leviathan introduced an early version of the social contract theory, arguing that to overcome the 'nasty, brutish and short' quality of life without the cooperation of other human beings, people must join in a 'commonwealth' and submit to a 'Soveraigne Power' that is able to compel them to act in the common good. This expediency argument attracted many of the early proponents of sovereignty.

Hobbes deduced from the definition of sovereignty that it must be:

- *Absolute*: Because conditions could only be imposed on a sovereign if there were some outside arbitrator to determine when he had violated them, in which case the sovereign would not be the final authority.
- *Indivisible*: The sovereign is the only final authority in his territory; he does not share final authority with any other entity. Hobbes held this to be true because otherwise there would be no way of resolving a disagreement between the multiple authorities.

Hobbes' hypothesis that the ruler's sovereignty is contracted to him by the people in return for his maintaining their safety, led him to conclude that if the ruler fails to do this, the people are released from their obligation to obey him.

Bodin's and Hobbes's theories would decisively shape the concept of sovereignty, which we can find again in the social contract theories, for example, in Rousseau's definition of popular sovereignty, which only differs in that he considers the people to be the legitimate sovereign. Likewise, it is inalienable - Rousseau condemned the distinction between the origin and the exercise of sovereignty, a distinction upon which constitutional monarchy or representative democracy are founded. Niccolò Machiavelli, Thomas Hobbes, John Locke, and Montesquieu are also key figures in the unfolding of the concept of sovereignty.

The second book of Jean-Jacques Rousseau's *Du Contrat Social, ou Principes du droit politique* deals with sovereignty and its rights. Sovereignty, or the general will, is inalienable, for the will cannot be transmitted; it is indivisible, since it is essentially general; it is infallible and always right, determined and limited in its power by the common interest; it acts through laws. Law is the decision of the general will in regard to some object of common interest, but though the general will is always right and desires only good, its judgement is not always enlightened, and consequently does not always see wherein the common good lies; hence the necessity of the legislator. But the legislator has, of himself, no authority; he is only a guide who drafts and proposes laws, but the people alone has authority to make and impose them.

Rousseau, in his 1763 treatise *Of the Social Contrac*t argued, "the growth of the State giving the trustees of public authority more and means to abuse their power, the more the Government has to have force to contain the people, the more force the Sovereign should have in turn in order to contain the Government," with the understanding that the Sovereign is "a collective being of wonder" resulting from "the general will" of the people, and that "what any man, whoever he may be, orders on his own, is not a law"- and furthermore predicated on the assumption that the people have an unbiased means by which to ascertain the general will. Thus the legal maxim, "there is no law without a sovereign".

The 1789 French Revolution shifted the possession of sovereignty from the sovereign ruler to the nation and its people.

Carl Schmitt defined sovereignty as "the power to decide the state of exception", in an attempt, argues Giorgio Agamben, to counter Walter Benjamin's theory of violence as radically disjoint from law. Georges Bataille's heterodox conception of sovereignty, which may be said to be an "anti-sovereignty", also inspired many thinkers, such as Jacques Derrida, Agamben or Jean-Luc Nancy.

IDEOLOGIST OF TERRITORIAL REALMS OF JEAN BODIN

In *La République*, Bodin begins by reminding his readers that sovereignty, the foundation of his entire system, is a prerogative of authority, being itself one of the presuppositions of politics. Like the majority of the authors of his time, he asserts that a government is strong only when it is legitimate, and he emphasizes the fact that a government's actions always should be in accord with certain norms, which are determined by justice and reason. Nevertheless, he understands that such considerations do not suffice to clarify the idea of sovereign power. Thus, he asserts that the source of power lies in the law, and that the capacity to make and break laws belongs only to the sovereign: the power to legislate and to rule are identical.

The conclusion Bodin reaches is radical: since the prince is not subject to his own decisions or decrees, he is above the law. This formula was already the work of Roman jurists: "*Princeps legibus solutus*". Bodin writes: "Those who are sovereign must not be subject to the authority of anyone else.... This is why the law says that the prince must be excluded from the power of law.... The law of the prince depends exclusively upon his pure and sincere will." In this case, it is sovereign power that allows the prince to impose laws that do not apply to him, because the exercise of power does not oblige him to have the consent of his subjects — sovereignty is totally independent of the subjects on whom laws are imposed. Richelieu later would say that "the prince is the master of the formalities of law." Because of this legislative power, supreme authority had to be unique and absolute, which is why Bodin's definition of sovereignty is the "absolute and perpetual power of a republic," *i.e.*, this power is unlimited in the sphere of human affairs. Sovereignty is absolute in the sense that the sovereign is not subject to law; on the contrary, he may decree and annul laws at will.

Conversely, the ability to make laws requires sovereignty to be absolute, because the power to legislate is indivisible. The remainder of the political prerogatives of the sovereign are dependent upon this initial affirmation. One could say that the fundamental characteristic of sovereignty is that it grants to the prince, who is subject to his will alone, the power of not being tied to or dependent upon anyone. His power is not delegated, temporary, or accountable to anyone; if his power depended upon anyone but himself, either internally or externally, he would not have the power to make law.

He no longer would be sovereign. Thus, Bodin's sovereignty is totally exclusive: by giving the king the role of unique legislator, it grants the state an unlimited and original authority. Consequently, a sovereign state is defined as one whose prince does not depend on anyone but himself. This implies that a nation is formed within a state, and that it is identified with this state. For Bodin, a country might eventually be defined in terms of its history, its culture, its identity, or its morals, but, politically, what constitutes a state as such is its sovereignty: the absolute power that forms the republic as a political entity, unique and absolute. The state must be one and indivisible, because it represents the legislative monopoly of the sovereign. Local autonomies are allowed, but only if they do not constrain the authority of the prince.

Actually, they are always more limited. The state is a monad, while the prince is "separated from the people," *i.e.*, placed in an isolation bordering on solipsism. Obviously, this new theory of sovereignty was crucial. On the one hand, it dissociated civil from political society, a theme which became crucial at the start of the 18th century; on the other, it laid the foundation for the modern nation-state, which is characterized by the indivisibility and absoluteness of its power. With Bodin, political theory became modern.

For Bodin, sovereignty is inseparable from the idea of a political society that abolishes particular ties and loyalties, and bases itself on the ruins of concrete communities. Implicitly, the political bond already creates a governmental contract in which all mediations between the members of society and power are eliminated. This rupture between prepolitical communities and political society was adopted first by the absolute monarchy, and then by the nation-state. The state is defined primarily by its homogeneous character, and this homogeneity can be either natural or synthetic. In other words, given the implicit egalitarianism ensuing from the fact that the model is based on a direct and unconditional bond between ruler and ruled, Bodin's concept of sovereignty redefined "the people" as being uniquely composed of individuals, equally alienated from sovereign power.

DIVINE ABSOLUTISM BECOMES ROYAL ABSOLUTISM

It is not difficult to detect the religious foundations of Bodin's doctrine. Bodin's understanding of political power is merely a profane transposition of the absolute way God and the Pope exercise power over Christians, even though he denounces the medieval concept of power as merely a delegation of God's authority. For Bodin, the prince no longer is satisfied to hold power by "divine right." By granting himself the power to decree and annul laws, he acts like God. He forms a distinct entity, ruling the social body in the same way that God governs the cosmos.

Thus, the sovereign's absolute rectitude is nothing more than the transposition into the political sphere of the Cartesian God, who can do everything except desire evil. Surreptitiously, sovereignty became infallible.

In other words, Bodin makes sovereignty profane by taking it away from God, and then makes it again sacred in a profane form: he takes leave of God's monopolistic and absolute sovereignty and ends up with the monopolistic and absolute sovereignty of the state. All of modernity resides in this ambiguity: on the one hand, political power is secularized; on the other, the sovereign, now identified with the state, becomes a person granted quasi-divine political power.

This confirms Carl Schmitt's theory, according to which: "All significant concepts of the modern theory of the state are secularized theological concepts." It is important to note that Bodin's theory of sovereignty does not imply any particular type of regime. Bodin prefers monarchy, since power is naturally more concentrated, but he emphasizes that the exercise of sovereignty is equally compatible with aristocracy and democracy, although the danger of division of power is much greater. It is equally significant that the appearance of an indivisible sovereignty, excluding any limits or controls, was accompanied by the strong intervention of state jurists. The direct heir of 13th century legists, whose work allowed royalty to impose itself on feudal lords, Bodin identifies political power with the capacity to make laws.

However, he adds that the sovereign, although not bound by the laws he decrees, can still be bound by a contract, a treaty, or even by his subjects in what today is called a constitution. s Julien Freund notes: "This makes Bodin see sovereignty no longer only as a phenomenon of power, but also of right." And this is what allows certain liberals to claim to be followers of Bodin. The problem with sovereignty is differently posed with Thomas Hobbes.

While, in Bodin's theory, the idea of absolute sovereignty is oriented explicitly against feudal power, which implies granting the prince authority independent of his subjects' consent, for Hobbes, it results from a meditation on the destructive character of the "state of nature." As is well-known, Hobbes was the first to invoke a social contract based on the rationality of individuals. He says that individuals have decided to enter society and to place themselves under the authority of a prince in order to end the "war of all against all," which is characteristic of the "state of nature." Thus, Hobbes introduced the concept of the consent of the governed, but the conclusions he drew from this went even further than Bodin.

While Bodin maintains a certain duality between the sovereign and the people, Hobbes erases it completely. By entering society, individuals agree to give up entirely their sovereignty in favour of the prince, which is the opposite of Rousseau's social contract.

With Hobbes, the price of security is obedience; the people are fused within the sovereign, whose authority is assimilated with the individual wills. Thus, it could be said that the state "swallows" the people.

LIBERALS INVENT "ETHICAL" AND JURIDICAL SOVEREIGNTY

In principle, such an attempt is problematic from the very beginning, since law and politics are not one and the same. Thus, the concept of sovereignty can never be expressed entirely in juridical terms. On the one hand, and contrary to what is accepted today, what is morally right is not synonymous with what is politically desirable. On the other hand, the capacity to judge without appeal is useless without the capacity to *decide* without appeal and to apply what is decided, which law by itself cannot guarantee. As Julien Freund observes: "Law has a specific sphere and so does politics, and they do not coincide, which is why conflicts between them ensue.... No judicial system is able to abolish the ruler's original and arbitrary political will. This reasoning is sufficient in itself to answer definitively the question of the juridical character of sovereignty.... The juridical reason stems from procedure, not from power, *i.e.*, the 'sovereignty of the law' exists to legitimate power, not to constitute it." The liberal theory of the limitation of sovereignty by law — in effect, the sovereignty of law — usually is linked with the desire for a purely legal and rational administration of human affairs. Politics, which is considered to be inevitably dependent upon irrational and arbitrary "decisions," is disqualified, since the political sphere denies the autonomy and, thus, the essence of law.

The attempt to suppress sovereignty first with legislative power, then with law itself, turns out to be a "depolitization" of public life. Accordingly, the titular wielder of power is no more than an executor; in the worst case, merely a figurehead. The democratic sphere of the people's will can be ignored, since it contradicts the juridical and moral norms that are considered to be superior. In the field of international relations, the result was that it became impossible to recognize political equality among different national sovereignties, and to resolve international disputes collectively. This contradiction led, in turn, to the "right of intervention," which also pretends to limit political sovereignty by a legal norm and, ultimately, by "moral" values. For example, Daniel Cohn-Bendit and Zaki Laïdi have declared that "ethical sovereignty is a new way to think about sovereignty," and they have defined this new form as "the refusal to allow anyone to claim sovereignty for objectives contrary to basic freedoms and human rights."

Such a type of discourse, which is regularly used to justify "humanitarian wars," *i.e.*, military aggression pretending to be "just," immediately poses the question of who, besides sovereign states, should concretely limit political sovereignty. By definition, only those who have the means to do so can exercise the "right of intervention." But, then, law becomes subordinated to power, which contradicts the theory. Far from disappearing, political sovereignty becomes a privilege of those strong enough to enforce the law. Carl Schmitt is one of the strong critics of the liberal concept of sovereignty, in which the state is subordinated to law, and decision is reached exclusively through discussion, while public life is strictly separated from a largely depoliticized "private sphere." Schmitt demonstrates that this concept is fundamentally anti-democratic, first, because it tends to discourage wider participation in public life, and second, because it rejects democratic choices which might oppose current juridical and constitutional norms. Schmitt also asserts that legal sovereignty, based on a collection of norms and procedures, is, by definition, unable to indicate who should decide in a state of exception. Sovereignty then reverts to the problem of identifying the instance with the capacity to impose its will in a concrete situation — independently, even from law.

Since the state of exception most precisely reveals this instance, Schmitt concludes: "Sovereign is he who decides on the state of exception." This is a matter of who decides whether a state of exception *exists,* and who decides *in* this situation. As Freund concludes: "When the exception is not covered by rules or norms, an instance other than law is needed to decide what should be done. Those situations will always be present, especially because they are unpredictable." From a Schmittian viewpoint, it could be said that there is never an interruption or vacancy of sovereignty. When an instance ceases to be sovereign, another immediately takes its place. It is not necessarily a state instance, but always a higher one. This explains why the real sovereign is not always recognized or called "sovereign." Hegemony, exercised in a context of power and with effects often exterior to law, is also a form of sovereignty. Thus, sovereignty always exists in the real world. Abandoning the concept will not erase the reality, but only occlude it.

DIVIDED SOVEREIGNTY OF JOHANNES ALTHUSIUS

Bodin's concept of sovereignty successively inspired absolute monarchy, revolutionary Jacobinism, state nationalism, republican ideology, fascism and totalitarian regimes. This explains why today this view of sovereignty can be found within totally opposite political groups: "nationalistic" republicans and xenophobic nationalists, revolutionaries and counterrevolutionaries, and among both leftists and rightists. All these groups have in common an attachment to the notion of sovereignty and, above all, to the belief that sovereignty cannot be conceived of other than in Bodin's sense. However, the idea of sovereignty expressed by Johannes Althusius in his major work, *Politica methodice digesta*, is completely different. An adversary of Bodin, Althusius bases his argument on Aristotle when describing man as a social animal naturally inclined to mutual solidarity and reciprocity — what he calls communication of goods, services, and rights.

For Althusius, political science is a methodical description of the conditions of social life; he uses the word "symbiosis" to describe how it functions. Denouncing the idea of a self-sufficient individual, he argues that society is first, a relation among its members and second, based on a series of political and social pacts concluded successively from the bottom up by a multitude of autonomous, natural, and institutional associations both public and private: families and households, guilds and corporations, civil communities and secular bodies, towns and provinces, etc. These "consociations" coalesce in an order from the most simple to the most complex. On each level, individuals interact, not as isolated units, but as members of an already existing community, which never abandons the totality of its rights in favour of a larger society.

In this context, Althusius examines the notion of representation in a sense completely different from that of liberal thought: for Althusius, the social contract is not a unique act resulting from free individual wills, but, rather, an integrating alliance— a continuing process of "symbiotic" communication of individuals defined, above all, by their mutual belonging.

THE PEOPLE DELEGATE, BUT THEY DO NOT FORFEIT SOVEREIGNTY

Global society, which Althusius calls the "integral symbiotic community," is defined as an organization ascending from a plurality of communities founded on prior associations and multiple memberships, and disposing of overlapping powers. The political body is the result of this process of uniting communities, where each successive level draws its legitimacy and its capacity to act from the autonomy of the lower levels. The goal of public action is to specify the levels of mutual solidarity and the autonomy of the collective participants, whose consent is actualized and organized in an open dialectic of the general and the particular, the basic idea being "what concerns all must be approved by all". In this regard, one could speak of "an ascending system of "consecutive federalization" or a "consociative democracy". For Althusius, sovereignty or "majesty" belongs to the people in perpetuity. It cannot be prescribed, because it resides inalienably in the popular community, and because "there is no absolute personal power in a community."

The people can delegate it, but cannot forfeit it. "The right of majesty," writes Althusius, "cannot be ceded, abandoned, or alienated by its proprietors.... This right has been established by those who participate in this kingdom collectively, and by each of them individually. They are the ones who create it; without them, it could neither be established nor maintained. I have given politics the right of majesty, but I have attributed it to the kingdom, *i.e.*, to the republic or the people," says Althusius, adding that he "does not care about Bodin's clamour." Far from being separated from the people, sovereignty emanates from them. The prince derives his function only from the inalienable right of the people to govern themselves.

There is no other authority than that invested in the people — no authority in the form of the transfer of power from the people to the prince, but, rather, in the form of a delegation of power that the people never cease to possess intrinsically and substantially. In other words, the prince exercises his power under the control of the people, and he must use it for the common good, which remains his main goal. Thus, the prince does not govern society as if he were alienated from it or independent of it. He is not the proprietor, but the trustee of sovereignty: he possesses only the right of this sovereignty. This same idea can be found in Rousseau, but with a crucial difference: Rousseau admits *only* that, in terms of his theory of the general will, a fundamentally unitary and homogeneous society is based on the absolute denial of any "partial society," while Althusius' system is based on the participation and representation of all particular identities. Therefore, sovereignty is not absolute; on the contrary, it can be distributed and shared. Inspired both by the imperial model, ancient Germanic communal "freedoms," and the functioning of the common and cooperative associations of the old Hanseatic towns, Althusius concludes that, on each level of society, two series of organs are needed: one, representing the lower communities, which are established to retain the power that they may exercise concretely; the other, representing the upper level, whose attributions always are limited by the first.

Each lower level designates its rulers, who are also its representatives *vis-à-vis* the upper level, and the delegation of this power can be withdrawn at any time. Given the conditional nature of this delegation, the power of the upper level is always dependent upon the consent of the lower levels. The state is superior to each of the levels beneath it, but not to the unity of them all.

The prince, as already seen, exercises sovereign power through delegation based on a reciprocal pact, in which he is considered to be the representative of the people, while the people retain the power to delegate. The power of the prince is supreme, since he has the greatest authority, but this authority also is limited by the autonomy of the "consociations," which prevent him from infringing upon their own particular powers. The principle of sovereignty is preserved, but is subordinated to mutual consent.

THE INTERLACING OF LEVELS OF POWER

For Althusius, sovereignty is not synonymous with omnicompetent authority. It only represents the level of power with the greatest capacity to decide and to execute a given task. The sovereign cannot act willfully without being held accountable. He has more extensive power, but he can use it only for what it was granted. On each level, there is an "exchange of sovereignty," *i.e.*, a differentiation of instances, and a sharing of jurisdictions, which are arranged from the lowest to the highest. While Bodin's sovereignty is at once a pyramid and a circumference, with a surface oriented towards the center, Althusius' sovereignty is structured like a labyrinth and is based on the essential principle that "the vassal of my vassal is not my vassal," *i.e.*, it implies plurality, autonomy, and the interlacing of levels of power and authority.

Bodin's model has prevailed since the Treaty of Westphalia and it is precisely on this model that the nation-state, the most common political form of modernity, was constructed. One of the consequences of this evolution has been that those who wanted to reject this model, judging it to be implicitly totalitarian, but not having any other concept, often have been prone to reject any notion of sovereignty. This is the case with Jacques Maritain, for whom sovereignty cannot be conceived other than as a phenomenon that transcends the body politic absolutely, and that exercises its power independently of it, which is why he rejects it. Maritain writes: "Sovereignty is incompatible with democracy." Inapplicable with respect to the people and to the state, it implies that power is superimposed on the body politic and that it "absorbs" those who are governed. Thus, he concludes that: "The concepts of sovereignty and absolutism were forged together on the same anvil. They need to be banished together. Advocates of sovereignty today commit the same error as Maritain. They assume that a sovereignty that is shared, distributed, or limited, a sovereignty that is not allowed to develop into an unlimited, unconditional, and absolute power, does not merit the name, and they come to precisely the opposite conclusion. They say that they favour sovereignty, but one based on the same definition.

FEDERALISM AND SUBSIDIARITY

As Chantal Delsol has observed, in reality " today Bodin's sovereignty is only surface deep. In fact, it has neither a concrete existence nor a traceable legitimacy." The idea of the nation-state, which reigned in Europe from the Peace of Westphalia until the first half of the 20th century, is today reaching its end; two world wars have revealed its limits. The erosion from both the top and the bottom of the nation-state signifies the end of modernity; in political terms, the end of the Westphalian Age. Referring in conclusion to what has been called "Bodin's evil" should not be understood as an intention to renounce sovereignty, but, rather, to redefine it from a different prospective, one inspired by Althusius.

In the past, the Althusian type of sovereignty already inspired certain imperial or multinational constructs. Its traces can be found in Austro- Marxist theoreticians like Otto Bauer and Karl Renner, and supporters of a "federative state of nationalities," in which sovereignty is distributed between different levels of political life. But, today, federalism is particularly receptive to a notion of sovereignty closely associated with the principles of autonomy and subsidiarity. In the 1930s, Maritain favoured a federal Europe and called for substituting the "statolatry that reigns today" with recognition by states of "a relative autonomy, stronger than the one existing nowadays, to the smaller communities, existing inside the nation-states." A true key to Althusius' system, the principle of subsidiarity, requires that decisions be made on the lowest possible level by those who sustain the consequences of them most directly.

It implies that the smallest political units retain substantial autonomous jurisdictions, and that they be represented collectively on higher levels of power. Decentralization is not the issue. In decentralization, local power is given only the authority that the central power wants to grant it; this authority is only a delegation of this central power, which remains the substantial nucleus of politics in a strictly pyramidal structure of society. For subsidiarity, the reverse is true: local levels do not delegate power to higher levels; rather, they delegate responsibilities and tasks that they cannot perform themselves; they do not cede jurisictions that they cannot assume, since they resolve in their own way all the problems they can, and they sustain the consequences of their own decisions and choices. Thus, subsidiarity represents a sharing of sovereignty: each level of authority assumes the tasks that it can. One of the consequences is that each community must be able to decide independently what goods and services it wants to have, rather than having a standardized offer of goods and services imposed on it.

SOVEREIGNTY REINFORCED OF THOMAS HOBBES

Not only unbound by the reciprocity of contract, since he did not sign it, but, also, since his power is derived from the rational will of all, the sovereign has the right to require total obedience from everyone. Since his legitimacy stems from the fact that the members of society have forfeited their sovereignty voluntarily, he depends neither on persons nor situations, but stands on right and law. The people cannot oppose him since, not owing anything to anyone, he cannot be dispossessed of his authority. Better yet, he is the only one who retains the unlimited freedom of the state of nature.

His sovereignty is thus equally indivisible and absolute. As with Bodin, sovereignty for Hobbes is completely unitary and identified with the state; any division or fragmentation of power is considered to be the cause of instability and political separation. Fair enough, there is something paradoxical in this modern formulation of sovereignty. In fact, both Bodin and Hobbes distinguish between tyranny and sovereignty, but they are able to do so only because they specify the objective limits of sovereignty, even while defining it as indivisible and absolute. This limitation might reside in the prince's obligation to respect certain natural or divine laws, or in the finality of power or in the criteria of the legitimate exercise of power: for Bodin, it is the law; for Hobbes, it results from individual consent. This entirely unexpected theoretical conclusion emerges even from the dynamics of absolutism.

Another contradiction in Bodin stems from the fact that, to the extent that sovereignty constitutes an unlimited authority, the political community presumably constitutes the relation of ruler and ruled, despite the distinction between them, as it is precisely this relation that gives the prince the power to promulgate laws in a sovereign manner. In other words, the more autonomous the state, the more problematic the exercise of sovereignty. Conversely, if the public sphere has unlimited authority over the private sphere, the distinction between the two becomes relative. This contradiction creates a widening gap between state sovereignty and popular sovereignty.

THE FRENCH REVOLUTION: CONTINUITY AND NO RUPTURE

The French Revolution preserved the very content of the concept of sovereignty embodied in the absolute monarchy, and took credit for giving it back to the nation. Hence the difficulty for the republican tradition to reconcile the first two articles of the Declaration of Rights, which affirmed the pre-eminence of universal individual rights, with the third article, which decreed that the nation is the supreme authority: "The principle of sovereignty resides essentially in the nation; no body, no individual can exercise authority not emanating from it." The idea of absolute sovereignty not only remained constant from the *ancien régime* to the Revolution, but the revolutionary idea of the pre-eminence of national sovereignty was also stressed from the beginning of the movement, *i.e.*, prior to 1792 or 1793, and, thus, before the Jacobinist party came to power.

The key moment can be traced to the unilateral decision of the people in 1789 to initiate a process of verification of the mandates of the deputies, which launched the process of transformation of the general states into a national assembly, as well as the process leading to the political sovereignty of the deputies. A discussion arose concerning the question of whether the common people should be represented in a Popular Assembly or in a National Assembly. Siéyès' faction, which urged the communes to constitute a "National Assembly," opposed the Mirabeau faction, which proposed the name "Assembly of the People's Representatives." The rivalry between the two factions revealed a difficulty in defining the "nation."

Eventually, Siéyès' proposition was accepted, while Mirabeau's was rejected as harmful to the right of the nation. Siéyès considered the nation to be "a body of members, living under a common law," a rigorously homogeneous body, whose foundation is separated from any pre-political determination. It was to this body, and only to this body, that sovereignty should be returned: "The nation is before all, it is the origin of all. Its will is always legal, it is the law itself." On June 17, 1789, the name "National Assembly" was adopted, based on the assumption that the representation of the nation must be "one and indivisible." Since the general will was embodied in the legislative body, it followed that national representation *is* the nation.

From this moment on, sovereignty became an attribute of the nation and was transferred from the "the top" to the National Assembly. Thereafter, the "nation" corresponded to the space of the collective sovereignty incarnated in the National Assembly. Fundamentally, revolutionary sovereignty did not originate with the appearance of the electoral body, but simply represented a transfer of royal sovereignty: the nation was said to be sovereign, it was a *fait accompli*, and it acquired legitimacy even before the citizen statute was discussed. The 1791 Constitution went even further. It specified that "sovereignty is indivisible, inalienable, and imprescriptible".

In fact, in August 1791, during the debate on the final revision of this article, an earlier version submitted to the Assembly attributed to sovereignty only the quality of indivisibility. Robespierre demanded that inalienability be added.

On September 7, 1791, Siéyès declared: "France must not be an assembly of small nations, governed separately in democracy; it is by no means a collection of states; it is a unique entity, edified by integrating parties." Subsequently, on September 25, 1792, France declared itself to be "one and indivisible." Intermediate bodies and basic popular collectivities were considered to be illegitimate. A year later, this position was reiterated by the Jacobins in their denunciation of the "federalist danger." Accordingly, the revolutionaries would attempt to rid themselves of all linguistic dialects, and would demand suppression of the ancient provinces and their substitution with geometrically equal departments.

"THE PEOPLE" BECOME AN ABSTRACTION

Once the concept of "the nation" was legitimated, the concept of "the people" became an abstraction. This was the price "the people" had to pay for declaring themselves to be "sovereign." As Boroumand observes: "If 'the people,' as an objective reality, cannot be admitted to the sphere of national sovereignty, which is a metaphysical entity *par excellence*, then their metamorphosis into an ideal entity allow them to participate in the logic of national sovereignty without endangering the transcendent existence of 'the nation' incarnated in representation." In other words, "the people" are perceived to be a manifestation of the principle of unity and indivisibility, but without any presupposition of them being composed of particular communities and distinct entities. The idea of a nation as a unitary and transcendent entity, whose unity and indivisibility are necessarily independent of any external principle, ended by re-establishing the notion of a people *jusqu'à s'y substituer*, which has remained a tradition in French common law until today.

Finally, the revolutionary concept of sovereignty made nationality and citizenship synonymous: no longer was there any national who was not a citizen or any citizen who was not a national. Being so "indivisible" and unitary, "the people" had become an abstraction. That is why, even today, France is not a federal state and cannot recognize the existence of a Breton or a Corsican people. Thus, the same concept of sovereignty, understood as the "absolute and eternal power" of a republic and the source of all the rights and duties of the citizenry, obtained both during the *ancien régime* and the Revolution. Jacobinist sovereignty is no more restricted than Bodin's sovereignty. The revolutionaries denounced "federalism" on the same grounds as the absolute monarchy, when, for instance, the monarchy reproached the Protestants for seeking to "cantonize" France after the Swiss model.

They demonized and fought against the local particularities in the same manner in which royal power tried to limit the autonomy of the feudal lords by any means possible. In order to legitimate revolutionary justice, they employed the same arguments that Richelieu used to defend the discretionary power of the prince. The Revolution opposed national sovereignty to royal absolutism, not by challenging absolutism, but by transferring the absolute prerogatives of the king to the nation. As Mona Ozouf writes: "Certainly, the people of the Revolution appear to have separated themselves from the Old World by inventing a society of free and equal individuals. But, in reality, they inherited from absolutism an idea much more ancient and more constraining: the idea of national sovereignty, *i.e.*, a mythic, transcendent order of individuals. And this idea quickly discovered its efficacy when national sovereignty took the vacant place of the absolute sovereignty of the king.... The Terror, far from being the expedient of the created despair of a republic in distress, is inscribed in the logic of this element of the *ancien régime*." In fact, even if evidence suggests that the Terror violated the natural rights of individuals, it by no means violated the rights of the nation, which it claimed to guarantee and to preserve.

As Boroumand also writes: "The similarities between absolutism and Jacobinism are explicable. If the political reflexes and methods were the same before and after 1789, this means that they were moved by the same principle: the sovereignty of the nation. Thus, as Henri Mendras has observed, "what was vindication in the 16th century became in France an absolute doctrine, an intangible principle for the monarchy for two centuries, and then for the constitutions after 1791. This principle was a juridical fiction, an abstraction incarnated in the king, an absolute principle; the king disappeared, the Republic resumed. Liberal political thought also came back at that point in history, when it recognized the contradictory association in the revolutionary constitutional canon between the affirmation of the universality of human rights and the principle of the sovereignty of the nation. But, it proceeded in the inverse direction of the one prevailing at that time.

It sought to discover in the theory of human rights the foundations of a limitation of national sovereignty or, more precisely, the foundations of a transfer of sovereignty from the political to the legal sphere. Actually, with the exception of the followers of Hans Kelsen's legal positivism, the liberals do not refuse to discuss the concept of sovereignty, but they tend to raise it to the level of politics, in order to attribute it to law and, often through law, to the level of "morality." In this, they could learn from Bodin, who attributed great significance to law, despite the fact that he reached completely opposite conclusions.

AUSTINIAN (MONISTIC)THEORY OF SOVEREIGNTY

Different from the development in either France or Germany, was the course taken by the doctrine of sovereignty in England. Here the issue of popular sovereignty had long before been fought out, the theory of Locke had been accepted, and the question was never again seriously considered. The monarch had yielded up his pretensions to exclusive sovereignty, and was at best but "King in Parliament," and the efforts made by the monarchs in France and in the German States found no parallel in the English constitutional experience of the nineteenth century. Practically the Parliament was sovereign; the reigning house had its position by virtue of a Parliamentary act; the veto power had not been exercised since 1707; the political vitality and consciousness of the State were best represented in its two legislative bodies. There was no individual or body of individuals which could contend with the power of the King in Parliament. To Parliament there was, legally speaking, nothing inadmissible or impossible; from this point of view it was all-powerful and irresistible. There was no legal or constitutional limitation which could be invoked against it; there was no body which could pass upon the acts of the Legislature; it was the highest organ, the final interpreter in the sphere of politics and law. England was a centralized national state with a definite body possessing the supreme power, and exercising its power untrammeled by the restraints of constitution.

The political conditions were therefore favourable to the development of a sharply defined theory of sovereignty, stating its nature and character in the most precise terms; and, moreover, of a theory framed away from and uninfluenced by the conflict between king and people. The new doctrine was not a defence of the crown, as that of Bodin, or of the people as with Rousseau, or yet an attempt to compromise between the two. The point of view from which the theory of sovereignty had generally been treated was changed and the problems with it. The leaders in the new movement were inspired by a desire to bring greater clearness and precision into that confused mass of English law upon which Bentham made such vigorous assaults.

To effect the desired ends there was necessary a principle of legislation and a theory of law, and they were found in Utilitarianism in ethics and Positivism in jurisprudence. From this side the theory of sovereignty was now approached. The leader in the new movement was Jeremy Bentham, whose ideas on this subject are best expressed in the *Fragment on Government*, 1776. Bentham, in a violent and destructive criticism of Blackstone, rejects the contract theory of the nature of political society, and bases the whole structure on the foundation of Utilitarianism. Men submit to authority, it is argued, not because they have tacitly or expressly agreed to do so, but because they find such a course of conduct more favourable to their interest than the contrary would be. It is not the fulfillment of a promise as such, but the tendency to follow the line leading to the greatest happiness, that produces the submission to society. The distinguishing mark of a political society Bentham finds in the fact that there exists in the given community a ruling body and a body which is ruled. In his own words: "When a number of persons (whom we may style subjects) are supposed to be in the habit of paying obedience to a person or assemblage of persons of a known and certain description (whom we may call governor or governors), such persons altogether (subjects and governors) are said to be in a state of political society." The degree of obedience may and does in reality differ; perfect obedience is by no means necessary, is in fact impossible; but the existence of habitual command and obedience in some form constitutes the essence of the State. What then, we may ask, is the extent of the power which rests in the hands of the rulers. Has it limits of any kind; if so, of what nature? Legally speaking, declares Bentham, there is and can be no restraint on the power of the sovereign. "The field of the supreme governor's authority, though not ire, must unavoidably, I think, unless where limited by express convention, be allowed to be indefinite. Nor can I see any narrower or other bounds to it under this constitution or any other yet freer constitution, if there be one, than the most despotic."

Applying the principles of his favourite system, Bentham maintained that even if the power of the sovereign were theoretically limited, there could be no fixed and certain bounds established apart from those dictated by considerations of utility. True political liberty depends not on any theoretical limitation, but on a variety of circumstances, such as the mamler in which the force of the Government is distributed, the frequency and ease of change from governor to governed, the freedom of the press, the liberty of public association. Bentham's position was, then, that the power of the governing body, though practically capable of limitation, through the operation of the causes which determine the degree of obedience, was theoretically outside of any and all limitation or restriction whatever. It is conceded, however, that there may be a certain limitation on the power of the sovereign "by convention," by express agreement made by the governing body. The cases which Bentham has in mind are, it would seem, those arising between various States, and not within the limits of one State. In these instances there may be restrictions placed on the power of a State in other respects supreme; in other words, there may be a limited external sovereignty. Otherwise, reasons Bentham, we must hold that there is no such thing as Government in the German Empire, in the Dutch Provinces, in the Swiss Cantons.

Bentham regards the sovereignty as internally unlimited from the formal side, practically held in check by utilitarian considerations; externally it may be further restrained by the positive agreements made with other nations. The successor of Bentham was John Austin, the keenest of English jurists since the time of Hobbes. On the continent Austin exerted no influence, and is practically unknown down to the present time. Even in England, his work was at first but little noticed, and it was only after many years that his theories became influential in determining the direction of English jurisprudence. The work in which the doctrine of Austin was embodied was the *Lectures on Jurisprudence*, first published in 1832. His method was throughout logical and formal, his effort was constantly directed towards obtaining precision in the definition of terms, and then rigid and unyielding deduction of conclusions therefrom — a method recalling in many ways that of the author of the *Leviathan*, whom Austin had occasion more than once to defend.

The abstruseness and laboriousness of his style did much to prevent a general acquaintance with or acceptance of Austin's propositions. As with Bentham, the philosophy of Austin is through and through utilitarian, and the defence of Utilitarianism permeates his work. His theory of ethics is defended with as much, or even with more, enthusiasm than his theory of politics. Like Bentham, he rejects the social contract, the basis of the theories of Hobbes and Locke, and also the contract in the later forms given by the German philosophers: this he describes as "the German contract which never was made anywhere, but which is the necessary basis of political society and government." An original covenant, even as an hypothesis, would suppose, says Austin, "that the society about to be formed is composed entirely of adult members; that all these adult members are persons of the same mind and even of much sagacity and much judgement, and that being very sagacious and very judicious, they are also perfectly familiar, or are at least passably acquainted with political and ethical science." Granted these facts, one might construct a "coherent fiction." Austin inclines to the belief that the constitution of most societies has not been made by a contractual process, but is the result of a process of growth — the work of a long series of authors, composing the original members and many generations of their followers.

Austin's general point of view is indicated in the statement made, that the "philosophy of positive law" is concerned with "law as it necessarily is, rather than with law as it ought to be; with law as it must be, rather than with law as it must be if it be good;" that is to say, with really possible law rather than with ideal law. The starting point in the theory of Austin is his conception of law; this is the foundation upon which was erected the whole superstructure. It is his way of looking at law which determines his attitude towards questions of political science, and particularly towards that of sovereignty. What then was the Austinian notion of law? He defines a law as 'A command which obliges a person or persons and obliges generally to acts or forbearances of a class."

Law is essentially a command given by a superior to an inferior: God gives laws to man as his superior; men give laws to men as superiors, understanding here by the term superiority, "might." In any ease the essence of the law is the command given from the superior to the inferior, and binding by reason of the sanction which the superior is able to attach to it. There are two great classes of law, the divine, set by God for men, and the human law. Human law is again divided into two classes, namely, positive law, properly so-called, and positive morality. Both these classes are positive, that is to say, "placed" or "set" by a superior, as already indicated; but in the one case the superior is political, in which event the command given is a positive law proper, and in the other the superior is not a definite and determinate body, and the command given is a precept of morality, not in the true sense a positive law. It is called positive morality in distinction from the true or divine morality; *i.e.*, the law of God.

Of positive law there may be, according to Austin, three kinds, namely the laws given by monarchs or sovereign bodies, as supreme political superiors; those given by men in a state of subjection, as subordinate political superiors, that is to say by those persons who are high in the official series, but still lower than the highest; and thirdly by subjects not acting in any official capacity but merely as private persons in pursuance of legal rights, as the "laws" given by a guardian to his ward.

In accordance with this classification, Austin rules out altogether the greater part of the "constitutional" law of England, holding that it is not law at all, but, strictly speaking, must be regarded as "positive morality." In particular is this true of the so-called "laws" governing the relations between ruler and ruled. "All constitutional law," says Austin, "is as against the sovereign in that predicament," namely of being in reality not law at all, not positive law in the strictly defined Austinian sense, but merely positive morality. It is admitted, however, that much of this ethical material must be inserted in the "corpus juris" for "reasons of convenience." A knowledge of it is necessary to a proper understanding of the positive law itself.

But logically considered, in the strict analysis in which Austin delighted, the territory of constitutional law should be given over to the realm of ethics. Constitutional law is not given by a superior to an inferior (for reasons that will later appear); it is not stated in the form of a command; it is accompanied by no adequate and effective sanction. It fails therefore to meet the canons of requirement for positive law, and must accordingly be eliminated from the legal category. Law in the Austinian sense, is essentially the effective command of a superior. It is not at all a vague and general impression that something ought to be done, but a definite, precise order necessitating certain "acts or forbearances." Hence customary law or custom is also excluded from the field proper of positive law, for the reason that it lacks those qualities which constitute the Austinian law. Custom is not law in itself, and does not and cannot become law of itself, alone and unassisted. "Considered as moral rules formed into positive laws," says Austin, "customary laws are established by the state."

Mere custom cannot constitute a law proper; for, again applying the tests, it is not given by a definite superior, it is not stated in the form of a command, and finally it is not accompanied by an effective sanction. Custom becomes law, in the proper sense of the word, only when declared to be such by the state itself. It is *command*, not *custom* which is the essential element in the existence of law. With these observations on Austin's general theory of law, we enter on the consideration of the doctrine of sovereignty intimately connected therewith. Closely following Bentham, he says, "If a determinate human superior not in a habit of obedience to a like superior receive habitual obedience from the bulk of a given society, that determinate superior is sovereign in that society, and the society (including the superior) is a society political and independent." This is Austin's political society and sovereign.

It is to be observed that in his theory, as in that of Hobbes, the sovereign is the State, although the political society, the community, includes both sovereign or state, and subject. The community as a whole is not to be taken for the sovereign. "It is," asserts Austin, "only through an ellipsis or an abridged form of expression that the society is styled independent." "The part truly independent is not the society, but the sovereign portion of the society." Again, and more explicitly; "The State is usually synonymous with the sovereign. This is the meaning which I annex to the term, unless I employ it expressly with a different import."

He understood then, by the sovereign, a part of the society, not the whole community itself. This was not unlike the theory of Hobbes and his school, and the doctrine held by certain German writers, already considered, that the king, the government, the ruling body, is the State. These philosophers had used (and were still using) the theory in defence of the royal power against that of the people, and the argument that the king is the State served them well. Austin's exclusion of a part of the community was, however, no part of an argument against the people, but was a step in his effort to secure a definite and determinate sovereign power as the sole source of law. It is now necessary to enter yet more closely into the consideration of the sovereignty which was the centre of Austin's system. Particular emphasis is laid upon the following elements in its nature; first the habit of obedience on the part of the subject to the superior, with this addition to Bentham's proposition, that the superior must not be in a like habit of obedience to some still higher authority.

Again, the obedience must be rendered by the "bulk" or "generality" of the given society; and finally the obedience must be given to a "determinate" body. By a "habit" of obedience is understood general and regular submission to a recognized authority. The possibility of exceptions to the rule is by no means excluded, is even expressly recognized. Thus the presence of the allied armies in France for a time in 1814–15, or of the German army in 1871, even though the foreign military power received temporarily the obedience of the "bulk" of the community, did not suffice to make the invading powers sovereign in the political society. The obedience then given was not at all habitual and usual, but on the contrary it was exceptional and extraordinary.

It had not the regularity and continuity necessary to constitute a habit of obedience and a sovereignty in the Austinian sense. This "obedience" has, moreover, an external and an internal, a positive and a negative side: positively, the given superior must, to be sovereign, receive obedience from others: negatively, obedience must not be rendered to any other. Austin himself admits, however, that both of these criteria, the negative and the positive, are inadequate. It is, after all, uncertain just what constitutes the "bulk" of any given society; or how long the obedience must be continued in order to be fairly regarded as habitual; or whether we are to estimate obedience by the number of commands executed, or by the importance of those acceded to. Qualitatively and quantitatively the test is imperfect. There may even be, argues Austin, peoples in a state of natural society, not in the habit of obedience to any one, as is the case with certain tribes in North America.

It is necessary to conclude, therefore, that the positive test, that of the reception of obedience, is a fallible test. "It would not enable us to determine of every political society whether it were political or natural," that is to say whether a sovereign were really in existence. On the other hand, the negative test is also insufficient, and would not enable us to tell whether a political society were independent or subordinate. There is no nation wholly independent, no nation which does not at times render obedience to others; no power is wholly and absolutely independent. It seems from Austin's own statement, then, that habitual obedience can be determined at best with the greatest difficulty, and that it does not give an absolutely safe and sure basis upon which to build. It is always incomplete and uncertain.

The political society, the sovereign, must always rest upon a human habit. Farther back than this Austin found it impossible to penetrate. Given the necessary basis of habitual obedience, the most striking characteristic of the sovereignty, as conceived by Austin, was its definiteness and determinateness. As already stated, the sovereign must be a "determinate human superior." What is meant by a "determinate" body? Austin says: "If a body of persons be determinate, all the persons who compose it are determined and may be indicated."

A determinate body in the sense here used may be composed, first of persons indicated by characters or descriptions respectively appropriate to themselves, as for example the various members composing the firm A. B. and C., each one of whom is indicated or determined by characteristics peculiar to himself; or secondly the determinate body may be composed of all the members of a given class or classes, as the King, the members of Parliament. Such a determinate body, formed in either of these two ways, is capable of corporate conduct, "is capable as a body of positive or negative deportment;" whereas an indeterminate or indefinite body, is by its nature incapable of corporate conduct and of either positive or negative deportment. The most essential characteristic of the sovereignty, in the Austinian theory, is its definiteness — that it be clear-cut and concise, readily ascertainable. It must be located in a definite or determinate person or body of persons, who are marked out either by personal or by class characteristics. The Parliament of England is for example such a definite body (though Austin added the electorate), a Roman Triumvirate would satisfy the requirements, a king would of course be unexceptionable. At all events the distinction between ruler and ruled must stand out clearly and distinctly; there must be no doubt as to where the sovereign power really is; it must possess a "local habitation and a name."

By easy inference from the statements made, there is no sovereignty in existence, if there is no definite body to whom it can be attributed. The only sovereign recognized is a definite, determinate person or body of persons to whom the rest of the community renders habitual obedience. An association lacking this central body or organ is not yet an independent political society in the Austinian sense. Austin speaks of societies political but subordinate; but by strict deduction from his premises no society is political which is subordinate or dependent — which lacks the definite and determinate sovereign. The sovereign in the English nation is held by Austin to be the "king, peers and the electoral body of the commons," which he would regard as a determinate body.

This body is in the habit of receiving obedience from the bulk of the society and not in the habit of receiving commands from any other like determinate body, and is therefore sovereign in the community. In the United States the sovereignty rests with the state governments "as forming one aggregate body," understanding however by the government, "the body of citizens which appoints the ordinary legislature." Such bodies as these he regards as determinate, as capable of corporate conduct, and therefore as fitting repositories of the supreme power. The nature of the sovereignty as discussed by Austin was wholly absolute. The supreme power, whether vested in an individual or a body of individuals considered in their corporate capacity, was regarded as "incapable of legal limitation." To say that such an individual or body could be bound by a legal duty, would be equivalent to declaring it subject to some higher sovereign; "that is to say, a monarch or sovereign member bound by a legal duty were sovereign and not sovereign.

Supreme power limited by law is a flat contradiction in words." The sovereign is with Austin the source of law, hence above the binding force of its own decrees. The supreme power can be bound by no legal duties or obligations, since there is no power by whom such obligations can be interpreted or enforced. The law giver cannot be legally bound by his own law, however great the moral obligation incurred. Austin very tersely states that, "every supreme government is free from legal restraints, or (what is the same proposition dressed in a different phrase) every supreme government is legally despotic." The frequent objection made to this proposition is, he explains, due to a confusion of ideas, arising from the failure to distinguish between monarch and sovereign. But it does not follow that because the sovereign is despotic, legally speaking, that the monarch, the king, is also despotic in the unpopular sense of the term.

In a limited monarchy, the head of the government is loosely called a monarch or a sovereign. The power of this ruler or sovereign is not, however, true sovereignty; for it has been and may be subjected to indefinite limitations by, the provisions of the positive law, framed by the real ruler. The king in a limited monarchy, the king as found in the modern constitutional state, is not at all a genuine sovereign, possessing legally illimitable, despotic power. The true sovereign is back of the nominal ruler, *i.e.*, in England, the king, peers and the electoral body of the House of Commons. It is this body, and not the modern king, in whose hands rests the despotic power, the legally illimitable authority. Austin is not only ready to say that the sovereign has no legal duties, he approaches the question from the opposite side as well, and maintains that the sovereign can have no legal rights against its subjects. A legal right, it is urged, involves the existence of three parties; the two claimants and the umpire. But in case of a right of the sovereign against a subject, the sovereign would necessarily constitute two parties; it must be one of the claimants and at the same time the judge between itself and the other claimant — which would be impossible. The sovereign, the real sovereign, not the king, could have no rights against a subject, because to make this possible we must suppose another sovereign over and above the real ruler, which would be contrary to the hypothesis of an independent supreme power.

The sovereign can have no legal rights, since there is no law under which such rights can be given, save the will of the sovereign itself. The supreme power has neither legal rights nor legal duties; for all law, all that is legal, emanates from this very power whose rights or duties are in question. Kant said that the sovereign has rights but no duties as against the subject; Austin carried the proposition out to its logical end, and declared against both rights and duties. Austin's theory thus destroys the basis of public law in so far as it is regarded as the legal relation between governor and governed. There can be no system of law where there is no possibility of either a legal right or a legal duty. The relations are all *de facto* and in no way *de jure*.

As Locke had said long before, basing his proposition on the contract theory, the government and the people are always in a state of nature in regard to each other; for there is between them no common judge. Here the theory of Locke and that of the positive law agree. Neither is willing to recognize an ultimate system of legal rights and duties; they agree that the relations between ruler and ruled are necessarily, matters of fact and not of law. As already seen, Austin refused to constitutional law the character of true law, and consigned it to the domain of ethics; or it might be a "compound of positive morality and positive law," whatever that may mean. The act of the sovereign which violates the constitution "may be styled with propriety unconstitutional; it is not an infringement of law, simply and strictly so-called, and cannot be styled with propriety, illegal." As Austin reasons, the constitution cannot be law, because the sovereign cannot give to the sovereign a binding command; for, by hypothesis, the sovereign itself is the source of all legal obligation. The ruler cannot be bound by rules, though he may accept counsel and advice. Again, following out his premises, Austin refuses to admit any difference between a *de facto* and a *de jure* government. A sovereign Government, he argues, cannot be looked upon as either lawful or unlawful. "If it were lawful or unlawful in respect of the positive law of its own independent community, it were lawful or unlawful by virtue of its own appointment, which is absurd." On the other hand, if lawful or unlawful by virtue of the law of another community, "it were not an actual supreme but an actual subordinate Government, which is also absurd." It is useless, in Austin's opinion, to term a Government sovereign *de jure*, without specifying by what law it is or is not supreme. Now the only law by which it can be supreme is its own utterance, its own command, its own will.

Hence the Government is really being judged in last analysis by itself, and the expression Government *de jure* only amounts to saying that the Government is legal because it declares itself to be. A sovereign Government, so far as positive law is concerned, is neither legal nor illegal, just nor unjust. Austin does not even agree that "whatever is, is right;" it merely is. In the same spirit Austin declares that political or civil liberty is, "the liberty from legal obligation which is left or granted by a Government to any of its own subjects." Civil liberty is generally accompanied by a legal right, as its guarantee. Austin concludes that civil liberty is fostered by the very political restraint often considered as destructive of it, "that restraint from which the devotees of the idol liberty are so fearfully and blindly averse." Political liberty is a creature of law, the grant of the sovereign, a result of the legal system of which the supreme power is the source and centre. There is, as Austin reasons, no conflict between sovereignty and liberty, as the latter is dependent upon the existence and activity of the former.

The difficulty is not in seeing how liberty can exist with sovereignty, but how it could exist without sovereignty. Such was the Austinian theory of the supreme power, in method and result recalling, though not slavishly following, the work of the great English philosopher of the 17th century, Hobbes. The key to Austin's argument is the concept of law as the command of the sovereign; and in this connection "borrowing the language of Hobbes," he states that "the legislator is he, not by whose authority the law was first made, but by whose authority it continues to be a law." In other words, it is the sanction and not the source which is to hold first place in the definition of law. Austin's contemporaries, Savigny and the historical school in Germany, emphasized the sources of law. They examined custom, tradition, usage, observance; and the fabric created out of this material they regarded as law. Declaring that law is a growth rather than a product of conscious human activity, they opposed the codification of the German law, and, therefore, antagonized legislative interference with the development of the legal system. This tendency was, as we have seen, in perfect accord with the reaction against the spirit of the Revolution. Austin, on the other hand, was not a defender of the reaction, but supported Bentham's great movement for the codification and clarification of law by the political authorities. He was perfectly willing, anxious even, to foster the development of law by the aid of political interference. So far as legislation was concerned, Austin was a radical, Savigny a conservative. Austin attempted to draw a sharp line between law proper and custom.

Custom and usage are not law, he held, until the sovereign speaks. All rules and regulations which lack this sanction are simply excluded from the domain of positive law. Austin distinguishes between the social and the legal or political relations, barring the former from the field of law. As already shown, the important point is not how the rule was made, but by what authority it is enforced. On the one side are the rules accompanied by economic, religious, social sanctions; on the other those rules, alone positive laws, which are sealed by the sanction of the supreme political power in the community. It is to be noted, however, that although Austin denies that custom is law, in the proper sense of the term, and refuses to recognize it in his jurisprudence, it lies, nevertheless, at the basis of his entire system. Custom is not law, it is true, until it is endorsed by the sovereign; but, on the other hand, the sovereign is not sovereign until recognized by custom. Habitual obedience, the custom of obeying, constitutes the fundamental and essential basis of the political society and of the supreme power.

"If a determinate human superior, not in a habit of obedience to a like superior, receive habitual obedience," etc.; in other words, a habit or custom is at the foundation of the Austinian jurisprudence. Custom does not make law, but it makes the law-maker. The rule of custom ends, however, where the sovereignty begins, and, whenever the habit of obedience is so far developed that a state of political society is reached, containing a definite and determinate sovereign, the reign of custom ceases, except in so far as it must always continue to be the basis upon which the society rests. All else is regulated by the sovereign, whose will is law. Austin did not despise custom utterly. He recognized it once and for all as the source of the sovereign power, and from there on custom has no place as a law-maker.

One must have a starting point, and Austin's is a highly developed modern state, with a well-established habit of obedience. It might reasonably be asked, however, why the custom which serves as the basis of the sovereignty, as Austin recognizes in his doctrine of "habitual obedience" should not serve equally well as a basis for private law, or why it is inefficient in the creation of constitutional law? The Austinian answer is that a definite doctrine of sovereignty requires the assumption of the existence of a habit of command and obedience in the given community. The absoluteness of Austin's sovereign recalls that of Hobbes and Kant; the supreme power is by all regarded as "legally despotic" — as by definition incapable of limitation. Austin strenuously insisted upon the impossibility of restricting the sovereign, formally or legally; but "material" limitations are found at the basis of his system. The obedience to the ruler is always habitual, and never perfect; it has its source in the Austinian principle, in the benefits which result in utility. Hence it would follow that when the utility ceased to exist, the obedience would also come to an end, and the sovereignty find its limit.

The limitations found by other philosophers in the " purpose of the state," in respect for the "rights of man," in the moral or divine law, are all summed up, or find an equivalent, in the utilitarian principle laid down by Bentham and Austin. Legally the supreme government is absolutely despotic, practically its power depends upon considerations of a utilitarian nature; but back of the legal and into the realm of the practical the Austinian doctrine does not lead us The theory of Austin, though widely influential, did not escape severe and searching criticism at the hands of English writers. Coming from the study of early forms of society, Maine vigorously attacked the validity of the newly stated doctrine on the ground that it exclusively emphasized a single element in the concept of sovereignty and law, namely that of force. The theory neglects, urges Maine, the great body of historical facts, determining in the first place who the sovereign shall be, and in the second place, how and under what conditions his power shall be exercised; the doctrine is the result of abstraction. "The whole enormous aggregate of opinions, sentiments, beliefs, superstitions and prejudices; of ideas of all kinds, hereditary and acquired, some produced by institutions and some by the constitution of human nature — is rejected by the analytical jurists," and the eye fixed exclusively on one fact, common to political societies, namely the possession of force.

This is, to be sure, a notable characteristic of the state, but by no means the only one, and its insufficiency to explain all is at once evident when we examine a society of the more primitive type. Here it is found that order is maintained and political functions performed. not so much by the command of a determinate sovereign like the English Parliament, as in obedience to "an instinct almost as blind and unconscious as that which produces some of the movements of our bodies." Here the Austinian doctrine can scarcely be applied with any degree of success; its truth would here become nothing more than verbal, since the sovereign has, as a matter of fact, no such power as that attributed to him by Austin.

The analytical doctrine, Maine argues, has grown up in sight of the modern territorial state, with its centralized and relatively determinate political organization, and also in view of the intense legislative activity of the supreme political authority, as for example, indeed as the example, in the English state, with the English Parliament as its supreme legislature. In highly developed states such as this, it may be said that the Austinian theory is formally true, though only only formally even here; but where these advanced political conditions do not obtain, in forms of political society less perfectly organized, the doctrine is true only in the most purely verbal sense. The doctrine is applicable to a certain stage of political development only, and to but one side of that development — hence the accusation of excessive abstraction. Maine's idea was carried. still farther by Sidgwick, who agreed in general with the author of *Early Institutions*, but found it unnecessary to go back as far as the primitive types of society where Maine had found material for his argument.

Even in politically developed societies, it is not true that any and every command the sovereign chooses to lay down, will meet with obedience. Hence it follows, reasons Sidgwick, "that the proposition that the power of the sovereign is not legally limited becomes insignificant, since it does not mean that it is not subject to limitations which even lawyers will recognize, but merely that it is not limited by the sovereign's own commands — which no one can ever have supposed it to be." In many modern states, it may be said, moreover, that limits are set to the sovereign through the constitution. If, as in Belgium, there is a constitutional organ back of the ordinary government, then there is to be considered the "actual organ of government whose commands are habitually obeyed" and also the "possible organ whose power is legally unlimited."

The active sovereign is legally limited, while the organ legally unlimited is so seldom seen and so seldom acts that obedience to it can hardly be regarded as habitual. Even in a State like England, where the Parliament is checked by no constitutional limitations, there may be found a certain restraint in the control which the electors exercise over the members of the sovereign body. In emphasizing those general forces which tend to deter the existing governmental authority from some courses of action, Sidgwick asserts that there is really, "a certain sense in which the mass of the people, in any country, may be said to be the ultimate depository of political power." This statement is not to be too literally taken, however, as the purpose is merely to show that the power of the political sovereign is never wholly despotic in its nature, that it is always limited by the general opinion of the community; as Duden said, that the government can never act in opposition to its own basis. This, however, is an idea which Austin himself had never opposed.

That all government rests on habitual obedience, and that obedience is determined by motives of utility, was a fundamental proposition in the Austinian theory. It appears, then, that the effort of the critics has been to show that undue attention has been given by the analytical school to the purely legal side of the sovereignty, and that the great forces working back of the formal law have been comparatively neglected. In line with the German school, best typified by Savigny, they have demanded that not only the sanction of law be studied, but also its source; that not only the actually existing political authority be examined, but also the social and political forces upon which it rests, and upon whose balance its equilibrium depends. An attempt has recently been made to reconcile the doctrine which emphasizes the sovereignty found in the Government with that emphasizing the sovereignty found outside the Government.

The aim is to preserve all that is valuable in Austin's analysis without falling into mere formalism, and on the other hand to recognize the forces which produce sovereignty, without forgetting what the sovereignty really is in studying how it came to be. The leaders in the new movement are A. V. Dicey, and David G. Ritchie, and their advance is made by means of a distinction which is drawn between legal sovereignty and political sovereignty. The legal sovereign is understood to be the body whose commands are enforceable in the ordinary courts. It is the lawyer's sovereign, the ultimate legal authority, the last source to which law as law can be traced.

As Ritchie says, the command of this body is "good law" in the lawyer's sense, although not necessarily "a good law" in the layman's sense. Such a legal sovereign as for example the King in Parliament, is necessarily absolute and irresponsible, so far as the law goes; it is legally irresistible, legally despotic. Whatever its susceptibility to moral influences, or its liability to physical violence, it is nevertheless in the strictly and purely legal sense, despotic. Back of the legal sovereign, however, stands another power; "behind the sovereign which the lawyer recognizes there is another sovereign to whom the legal sovereign must bow."

This is the political sovereign, which Dicey says is that body in the state, "the will of which is ultimately obeyed by the citizens of the State." This sovereignty might be located in England in the "body of electors," or it might be found in the body of public sentiment or opinion to which the legal sovereign itself must ultimately render obedience. No matter what the opinion of the electorate may be, or what the public will may be, legally it possesses no power, it cannot be enforced in the courts of law.

Politically, however, it is supreme, it is the source of the legal sovereign, it must ultimately be obeyed. Legally this power has no effective organization, but it stands outside the domain of positive law, ultimately though not immediately determining what that domain shall be. Its "habit of obedience" makes and unmakes sovereigns. In this theory, then, the Austinian notion is recognized in the legal sovereign, the authority behind which the lawyer as lawyer need not go, and the notion of the historical school in the political sovereign — the true source of the ultimate political authority.

Strangely enough, a similar form of compromise was made by Locke in the attempt to reconcile the natural-right philosophy with the English monarchy. Now, however, the problem is not to harmonize popular custom and royal command, but rather custom and command in the abstract; or, if it is preferred, as fundamental facts in the world of political phenomena. The question is no longer how to find a modus vivendi for king and people, but how to show most clearly the existence of both the rigid and the flexible elements in the supreme political power. The answer given by Dicey and his school is reached not by dividing sovereignty, statically, as we might say, but rather in a dynamic sense. At any given moment there is a sovereign clothed in the forms of law, supreme within the bounds of law; but this sovereign, even the sphere of law itself, is fixed by the ultimate political sovereign, against whose will the spells of formal law are powerless. The validity of the doctrine depends upon the possibility of a clear distinction between "law " and "politics," between legal and political facts or phenomena.

4

Indian Political System

POLITICS OF INDIA

Politics of India take place in a framework of a federal parliamentary multi-party representative democratic republic. India is the world's largest democracy. In India, the Prime Minister of India is identified as the head of government of the nation, while the President of India is said to be the formal head of state and holds substantial reserve powers, placing him or her in approximately the same position as the British monarch. Executive power is enforced by the government. It can be noted that federal legislative power is vested in both the government of India and the two characteristic chambers of the Parliament of India. Also, it can be said that the judiciary is independent of both the executive and the legislature.

Looking at the constitution, India is a nation that is characterized to be "sovereign socialist secular democratic republic." India is the largest state by population with a democratically-elected government. Like the United States, India has a federal form of government, however, the central government in India has greater power in relation to its states, and its central government is patterned after the British parliamentary system. Regarding the former, "the Centre", the national government, can and has dismissed state governments if no majority party or coalition is able to form a government or under specific Constitutional clauses, and can impose direct federal rule known as President's rule. Locally, the Panchayati Raj system has several administrative functions. For most of the years since independence, the federal government has been guided by the Indian National Congress, In India the two largest political parties have been the Indian National Congress and the Bharatiya Janata Party. Presently the two parties have dominated the Indian politics, however regional parities too exist. From 1950 to 1990, barring two brief periods, the INC enjoyed a parliamentary majority.

The INC was out of power between 1977 and 1980, when the Janata Party won the election owing to public discontent with the corruption of the then Prime Minister Indira Gandhi. In 1989, a Janata Dal-led National Front coalition in alliance with the Left Front coalition won the elections but managed to stay in power for only two years. As the 1991 elections gave no political party a majority, the INC formed a minority government under Prime Minister P.V. Narasimha Rao and was able to complete its five-year term. The years 1996–1998 were a period of turmoil in the federal government with several short-lived alliances holding sway. The BJP formed a government briefly in 1996, followed by the United Front coalition that excluded both the BJP and the INC.

In 1998, the BJP formed the National Democratic Alliance with several other parties and became the first non-Congress government to complete a full five-year term. In the 2004 Indian elections, the INC won the largest number of Lok Sabha seats and formed a government with a coalition called the United Progressive Alliance, supported by various parties. In the 2009 Lok Sabha Elections, it won again with a surprising majority, the INC itself winning more than 200 seats. At the federal level, India is the most populous democracy in the world. While many neighbouring countries witness frequent coups, Indian democracy has been suspended only once. Nevertheless, Indian politics is often described as chaotic. More than a fifth of parliament members face criminal charges.

CENTRAL AND STATE GOVERNMENTS

The central government exercises its broad administrative powers in the name of the President, whose duties are largely ceremonial. The president and vice president are elected indirectly for 5-year terms by a special electoral college. The vice president assumes the office of president in case of the death or resignation of the incumbent president. The constitution designates the governance of India under two branches namely the executive branch and Real national executive power is centered in the Council of Ministers, led by the Prime Minister of India. The President appoints the Prime Minister, who is designated by legislators of the political party or coalition commanding a parliamentary majority. The President then appoints subordinate ministers on the advice of the Prime Minister. In reality, the President has no discretion on the question of whom to appoint as Prime Minister except when no political party or coalition of parties gains a majority in the Lok Sabha. Once the Prime Minister has been appointed, the President has no discretion on any other matter whatsoever, including the appointment of ministers. But all Central Government decisions are nominally taken in his/her name.

Legislative Branch

The constitution designates the Parliament of India as the legislative branch to oversee the operation of the government. India's bicameral parliament consists of the Rajya Sabha (Council of States) and the Lok Sabha (House of the People). The Council of Ministers is held responsible to the Lok Sabha.

State Government

States in India have their own elected governments, whereas Union Territories are governed by an administrator appointed by the president. Some of the state legislatures are bicameral, patterned after the two houses of the national parliament. The states' chief ministers are responsible to the legislatures in the same way the prime minister is responsible to parliament. Each state also has a presidentially appointed governor who may assume certain broad powers when directed by the central government. The central government exerts greater control over the union territories than over the States, although some territories have gained more power to administer their own affairs. Local state governments in India have less autonomy compared to their counterparts in the United States, Africa and Australia.

Judicial Branch

India's independent judicial system began under the British, and its concepts and procedures resemble those of Anglo-Saxon countries. The constitution designates the Supreme Court, the High Courts and the lower courts as the authority to resolve disputes among the people as well as the disputes related to the people and the government. The constitution through its articles relating to the judicial system provides a way to question the laws of the government, if the common man finds the laws as unsuitable for any community in India..

Local Governance

On April 24, 1993, the Constitutional (73rd Amendment) Act, 1992 came into force to provide constitutional status to the Panchayati Raj institutions. This Act was extended to Panchayats in the tribal areas of eight States, namely Andhra Pradesh, Bihar, Gujarat, Himachal Pradesh, Maharashtra, Madhya Pradesh, Orissa and Rajasthan from 24 December 1996. The Act aims to provide 3-tier system of Panchayati Raj for all States having population of over 2 million, to hold Panchayat elections regularly every 5 years, to provide reservation of seats for Scheduled Castes, Scheduled Tribes and Women, to appoint State Finance Commission to make recommendations as regards the financial powers of the Panchayats and to constitute District Planning Committee to prepare draft development plan for the district.

ROLE OF POLITICAL PARTIES

As like any other democracy, political parties represent different sections among the Indian society and regions, and their core values play a major role in the politics of India. Both the executive branch and the legislative branch of the government are run by the representatives of the political parties who have been elected through the elections. Through the electoral process, the people of India choose which majority in the lower house, a government can be formed by that party or the coalition. India has a multi-party system, where there are a number of national as well as regional parties. A regional party may gain a majority and rule a particular state.

If a party represents more than 4 states then such parties are considered as national parties. In the 61 years since India's independence, India has been ruled by the Indian National Congress for 48 of those years. The party enjoyed a parliamentary majority barring two brief periods during the 1970s and late 1980s. This rule was interrupted between 1977 to 1980, when the Janata Party coalition won the election owing to public discontent with the controversial state of emergency declared by the then Prime Minister Indira Gandhi. The Janata Dal won elections in 1989, but its government managed to hold on to power for only two years. Between 1996 and 1998, there was a period of political flux with the government being formed first by the right-wing nationalist Bharatiya Janata Party followed by a left-leaning United Front coalition.

In 1998, the BJP formed the National Democratic Alliance with smaller regional parties, and became the first non-INC and coalition government to complete a full five-year term. The 2004 Indian elections saw the INC winning the largest number of seats to form a government leading the United Progressive Alliance, and supported by left-parties and those opposed to the BJP. On 22 May 2004, Manmohan Singh was appointed the Prime Minister of India following the victory of the INC and the left front in the 2004 Lok Sabha election.

The UPA now rules India without the support of the left front. Previously, Atal Bihari Vajpayee had taken office in October 1999 after a general election in which a BJP-led coalition of 13 parties called the National Democratic Alliance emerged with a majority. Formation of coalition governments reflects the transition in Indian politics away from the national parties towards smaller, more narrowly-based regional parties. Some regional parties, especially in South India, are deeply aligned to the ideologies of the region unlike the national parties and thus the relationship between the central government and the state government in various states has not always been free of rancor. Disparity between the ideologies of the political parties ruling the centre and the state leads to severely skewed allocation of resources between the states.

EVOLUTION OF PARTY SYSTEM IN INDIA

The evolution of Indian party system can be traced to the formation of the Congress, as a political platform in 1885. Other parties and groups originated later. The Indian National Congress was formed as a response to the colonial rule and to achieve independence from the British rule.

After independence and with the adoption of a democratic Constitution, a new party system emerged in the wake of the first general elections based on universal adult franchise in 1952. During the post-independence period, the party system passed through various phases.

The first phase is known as the phase of one-party dominance because with the exception of Kerala during 1956–59, the ruling party both at the Centre and in the states was the Congress. The second phase (1967–1975) saw the emergence of a multi-party system in India. In the Assembly elections in 1967, Congress was defeated in eight States.

For the first time non-Congress parties formed governments in these states. These parties formed coalition governments. Then came the split in Congress into Congress (O) and Congress (N). However, the Congress again became a dominant force at the Centre after winning 1971 mid-term poll. Then came the emergency period (1975–77) which is known as the authoritarian period of Indian democracy.

With the lifting of emergency, the dominance of Congress ended. In the general elections of 1977 Congress was defeated by the Janata Party. Janata Party came into existence as a result of the merger of many opposition parties. But again in 1980 general elections Congress came back to power and remained in power till 1989. Janata Party emerged out of the merger of Congress (O) led by Morarji Desai, Bharatiya Lok Dal led by Ch. Charan Singh, Congress for Democracy (CFD) led by Jagjivan Ram and H. N. Bahuguna, the socialists led by George Fernandes and Jana Sangh led by L.K. Advani.

In 1989 elections, the National Front joined government with the support of BJP and the Left Front. But this formation could not last its tenure and elections for the tenth Lok Sabha were held in May-June, 1991. Congress again formed government at the Centre. In 1996 general elections BJP emerged as the single largest party and was asked to form government at the Centre. Since it could not prove its majority within the given time it had to resign.

The United Front which was a combination of thirteen parties, formed the government at the Centre with the external support of the Congress and the CPI(M). But this government also could not last its full term. Although the coalition government formed under the leadership of BJP after 1998 elections was defeated in Lok Sabha, the 1999 elections again provided them the opportunity to form government which lasted its full term under a multi-party coalition, known as National Democratic Alliance (NDA).

In the 14th general elections held in 2004, Congress emerged as the single largest party. It formed alliance with like minded parties and formed government at the Centre. The phase of Indian party system which began in 1989 and is still continuing has been aptly called a phase of coalition politics. No single party has been able to form government on its own at the Centre.

NATIONAL PARTIES AND REGIONAL PARTIES

India has two types of political parties–national parties and regional parties.

National parties are those which generally have influence all over the country. It is not necessary that a national party will have equal strength in all the states; it varies from State to State.

A party is recognised as a national party by the Election Commission on the basis of a formula. The political party which has secured not less than four per cent of the total valid votes in the previous general elections at least in four states, is given the status of a national party.

The number of national parties has been changing. In the year 2006:

- Indian National Congress,
- Bharatiya Janata Party,
- Communist Party of India (Marxist) [CPI(M)],
- Communist Party of India (CPI),
- Bahujan Samaj Party, and
- The Nationalist Congress Party were national parties.

However, there are other parties in India, which do not enjoy national influence. Their activities and influence are restricted to particular states or regions. Sometimes these parties are formed to voice demands of a specific region. These parties are neither weak nor short-lived.

Sometimes they prove to be very powerful in their respective regions. These are known as regional parties. Major regional parties are AIADMK and DMK in Tamil Nadu, Telugu Desam in Andhra Pradesh, Akali Dal in Punjab, National Conference in Jammu and Kashmir, Jharkhand Mukti Morcha in Jharkhand, Asom Gana Parishad in Assam and Nationalist Congress Party and Shiv Sena in Maharashtra.

MAJOR NATIONAL PARTIES IN INDIA

INDIAN NATIONAL CONGRESS

As you have already read, Indian National Congress was formed in the year 1885 in Bombay. W. C. Bonnarjee was the first President of the Indian National Congress. To begin with, Congress was an organisation of middle class intellectuals who were primarily concerned with political reforms in the British colonial rule. In the twenties under the leadership of Mahatma Gandhi, the Congress became a mass based organisation. The party started enjoying the support of the common people and played a very significant role in the freedom struggle.

After independence Jawahar Lal Nehru became the Prime Minsiter and led the Congress till his death in 1964. This was known as the 'Nehru era'. The Congress party won first five general elections in 1952, 1957, 1962, 1967 and 1971. In 1975 national emergency was declared which went on till 1977. In the elections of 1977, the Congress was defeated. However, in 1980 general elections, the Congress Party led by Indira Gandhi came back to power. Indira

Gandhi was assassinated in 1984 and during 1985 general elections, Rajiv Gandhi was the leader of the party.

Congress won the 1985 general elections with a larger majority. In 1989 though Congress could not get absolute majority, it was the single largest party. In the tenth general elections in 1991, Congress again emerged as the single largest party and formed the government at the Centre. In the 1996, general elections Congress could not form government at the Centre. In the 12th general elections in 1998, Congress could get only 140 Lok Sabha seats.

In the 1999 general elections Congress's strength was further reduced to 112. But in the 14th general elections Congress entered into alliance with other secular parties and secured the number of seats that provided it an opportunity to form a coalition government.

THE BHARATIYA JANATA PARTY (BJP)

The Bharatiya Janata Party (BJP) was formed in 1980. Since then it has extended its influence in the Hindi belt, Gujarat and Maharashtra. Since 1989, it has been trying to extend its base in South India also.

Since its formation in 1980, the BJP has been increasing its number of seats in the Lok Sabha gradually. In 1984, general elections it secured only two seats. In 1989 the number of seats increased to 88. In 1991 general elections BJP's strength in the Lok Sabha increased to 122 which rose to 161 in the 1996 elections. In 1998 it won 180 seats and in 1999 its number in Lok Sabha increased to 182.

In the 1999 general elections, BJP contested as an alliance partner in the National Democratic Alliance (NDA). In the recent 2004 general elections BJP as an alliance of NDA could not get the required majority. It is playing the role of the opposition party. The BJP has emerged as a significant national party but its support base as yet is limited to certain areas, rather than spread all over India.

THE COMMUNIST PARTIES

The two communist parties are the Communist Party of India (CPI) and the Communist Party of India (Marxist) [CPI(M)]. Next to the Congress, the Communist Party is the oldest in India. The communist movement began in the early twenties and the Communist Party was founded in 1925.

The communists participated in the national movement, though often they had serious differences with the Congress. The communists assert that the people should be economically equal and the society should not be divided into classes of rich and poor. The workers and peasants and other toiling people who do most of the productive work for the society, should be given due recognition and power. The communists were the main opposition in the Lok Sabha throughout the Nehru Era. In the first Lok Sabha they had 26 members, in the second and the third Lok Sabha, they had 27 and 29 members respectively. In 1957, the CPI won absolute majority in the Kerala Assembly and formed the first Communist government in India. In the early sixties specially after the Chinese aggression of 1962 there were serious differences among the members of the Communist Party. As a result, the party split into two. Those who broke away from CPI, formed CPI(M) in 1964.

The CPI(M)'s main support base has been concentrated in West Bengal, Kerala and Tripura, though it has registered its presence in Andhra Pradesh, Assam, Bihar, Maharashtra, Orissa and Punjab. The CPI has its pockets of influence in states like Andhra Pradesh, Assam, Bihar, Manipur, Orissa, Pondicherry, Punjab, etc.

Moreover CPI has been a part of the left front coalition in Kerala and West Bengal. In the Lok Sabha elections of 2004, both the CPI and the CPI (M) were alliance partners of the Congress. They are supporting the United Progressive Alliance (UPA) government at the Centre from outside.

BAHUJAN SAMAJ PARTY (BSP)

The BSP acquired the status of a national party in 1996. The BSP champions the cause of those sections which belong to low castes, deprived groups and minorities. In fact, these sections of Indian society (the Bahujan Samaj) form the majority of the Indian population. The BSP believes that this 'samaj' should be freed from the exploitation of the upper castes and by forming their own government. BSP's influence lies in states like Madhya Pradesh, Uttar Pradesh and Punjab. In 1995 and 1997 BSP was a partner in the coalition governments in Uttar Pradesh.

POLITICAL ISSUES

SOCIAL ISSUES

The lack of homogeneity in the Indian population causes division between different sections of the people based on religion, region, language, caste and race. This has led to the rise of political parties with agendas catering to one or a mix of these groups. Some parties openly profess their focus on a particular group, for example, the Dravida Munnetra Kazhagam's focus on the dravid population, and the Shiv Sena's pro-Marathi agenda. Some other parties claim to be universal in nature, but tend to draw support from particular sections of the population, for example, the Rashtriya Janata Dal (translated as National People's Party) has a vote bank among the Yadav and Muslim population of Bihar and the All India Trinamool Congress does not have any significant support outside West Bengal. The Bharatiya Janata Party, the party with the second largest number of MPs in the 15th Lok Sabha, has an image of being pro-Hindu, and anti-Muslim and anti-Christian. Such support from particular sections of the population affects the agenda and policies of such parties, and refute their claims of being universal representatives.

The Congress may be viewed as the most secular party with a national agenda, however it also practices vote bank politics to gain the support of minorities, especially Muslims, through appeasement and pseudo-secularist strategies. The narrow focus and vote bank politics of most parties, even in the central government and central legislature, sidelines national issues such as economic welfare and national security. Moreover, internal security is also threatened as incidences of political parties instigating and leading violence between two opposing groups of people is a frequent occurrence.

Economic Issues

Economic issues like poverty, unemployment, development are main issues that influence politics. *Garibi hatao* (eradicate poverty) has been a slogan of the Indian National Congress for long. The well known Bharatiya Janata Party is looked upon with grace as a political party that is indeed encouraging to free market economy, businesses and others. The Communist Party of India vehemently supports left-wing politics and has strongly opposed to socio-economic policies such as globalization, capitalism, foreign investments and privatization. The economic policies of most other parties do not go much further than providing populist subsidies and reservations. As a noteworthy case, the manifesto of the Samajwadi Party, the third largest party in the 15th Lok Sabha, for the 2009 general elections promised to reduce the use of computers upon being elected.

Law and Order

Just to name a few, terrorism, Naxalism, Religious violence and caste-related violence are important issues that affect the political environment of the Indian nation. Stringent anti-terror legislations like TADA, POTA and MCOCA have received much political attention, both in favour as well as criticism. Law and order issues such as action against organized crime are not issues that affect the outcomes of elections. On the other hand, there is a criminal-politician nexus. Many elected legislators have criminal cases against them. In July 2008 Washington Times reported that nearly a fourth of the 540 Indian Parliament members faced criminal charges, "including human trafficking, immigration rackets, embezzlement, rape and even murder".

GOVERNORS OF STATES OF INDIA

The Governors and Lieutenant-Governors of the states and territories of India have similar powers and functions at the state level as that of the President of India at Union level. Governors exist in the states while Lieutenant-Governors exist in union territories and in the National Capital Territory of

Delhi. The Governor acts as the nominal head whereas the real power lies in the hand of the Chief Ministers of the states and the Chief Minister's Council of Ministers. In India, a Lieutenant governor is in charge of a Union Territory. However the rank is present only in the union territories of Andaman and Nicobar Islands, Delhi and Pondicherry (the other territories have an administrator appointed, who is an IAS officer). Lieutenant-Governors hold the same rank as a Governor of a state in the list of precedence. The Governors and Lieutenant-Governors are appointed by the President for a term of 5 years.

Powers and Functions

The Governor enjoys many different types of powers:

- Executive powers related to administration, appointments and removals,
- Legislative powers related to lawmaking and the state legislature, that is Vidhan Sabha or Vidhan Parishad,
- Discretionary powers to be carried out according to the discretion of the Governor.

Executive Powers

The Constitution vests in the Governor all the executive powers of the State Government. The Governor appoints the Chief Minister who enjoys the support of the majority in the Vidhan Sabha. The Governor also appoints the other members of the Council of Ministers and distributes portfolios to them on the advice of the Chief Minister. The Council of Ministers remain in power during the 'pleasure' of the Governor, but in the real sense it means the pleasure of the Vidhan Sabha. As long as the majority in the Vidhan Sabha supports the government, the Council of Ministers cannot be dismissed. The Governor appoints the Chief Minister of a state. He also appoints the Advocate General and the chairman and members of the State Public Service Commission. The President consults the Governor in the appointment of judges of the High Courts and the Governor appoints the judges of the District Courts.

Legislative Powers

The Governor summons the sessions of both houses of the state legislature and prorogues them. The Governor can even dissolve the Vidhan Sabha. These powers are formal and the Governor while using these powers must act according to the advice of the Council of Ministers headed by the Chief Minister. The Governor inaugurates the state legislature by addressing it after the assembly elections and also at the beginning of the first session every year. The Governor's address on these occasions generally outlines new policies of the state government. A bill that the state legislature has passed, can become a law only after the Governor gives assent. The Governor can return a bill to the state legislature, if it is not a money bill, for reconsideration. However, if the state legislature sends it back to the Governor for the second time, the Governor must assent to it. The Governor has the power to reserve certain bills for the President. When the state legislature is not in session and the Governor considers it necessary to have a law, then the Governor can promulgate ordinances. These ordinances are submitted to the state legislature at its next session. They remain valid for no more than six weeks from the date the state legislature is reconvened unless approved by it earlier.

Financial Powers

Money bills can be introduced in the State Legislative Assembly only on the prior recommendation of the Governor. He also causes to be laid before the State Legislature the annual financial statement which is the State Budget. Further no demand for grant shall be made except on his recommendation. He can also make advances out of the Contingency Fund of the State to meet any unforeseen expenditure. Moreover, he constitutes the State Finance Commission.

Discretionary Powers

Normally, the Governor has to act on the aid and advice of the Council of ministers headed by the Chief Minister. However, there are situations when the Governor has to act as per his own judgement and take decisions on his own. These are called the discretionary powers of the Governor. The Governor exercises them in the following cases:

In the Appointment of the Chief Minister of a State

When no party gets a majority in the Vidhan Sabha, the Governor can either ask the leader of the single largest party or the consensus leader of two or more parties (that is, a coalition party) to form the government. The Governor then appoints the leader of the largest party to Chief Minister.

In informing the President of the Failure of Constitutional Machinery in a State

The Governor can send a report to the President informing him or her that the State's constitutional functioning has been compromised and recommending the President impose "President's rule" upon the state.

Removal

The term of Governor's office is normally 5 years but it can be terminated earlier by:

- Dismissal by the President on the advice of the Prime Minister of the country, at whose pleasure the Governor holds office.
- Resignation by the governor

VIDHAN SABHA

The Vidhan Sabhas also known as Legislative Assemblies are the lower houses of state legislature in of the different states of India. Members of a Vidhan Sabha are direct representatives of the people of the particular state as they are directly elected by an electorate consisting of all adult citizens of that state. Its maximum size as outlined in the Constitution of India is not more than 500 members and not less than 60. However, the size of the Vidhan Sabha can be less than 60 members through an Act of Parliament, such is the case in the states of Goa, Sikkim and Mizoram. The Governor can appoint 1 member to represent the Anglo-Indian community if he or she finds that community to not be adequately represented in the House. Each Vidhan Sabha is formed for a five year term after which all seats are up for election. During a State of Emergency, its term may be extended past five years or it may be dissolved. It can also be dissolved if a motion of no confidence is passed within it against the majority party or coalition.

Qualifications Required to Become a Member

To become a member of a Vidhan Sabha, a person must be a citizen of India, not less than 25 years of age. He should be mentally sound and should not be bankrupt. He should also state an affidavit that there are no criminal procedures against him. The members of a Vidhan Sabha elect a Speaker of Vidhan Sabha who is responsible for the conduct of business of the body, and also a Deputy Speaker to preside during the Speaker's absence. The Speaker acts as a neutral judge and manages all debates and discussions in the house. Usually he is a member of the stronger political party A Vidhan Sabha holds equal legislative power with the upper house of state legislature, the Vidhan Parishad ('Legislative Council'), except in the area of money bills in which case the Vidhan Sabha has the ultimate authority. If conflicting legislation is enacted by the two Houses, a joint sitting is held to resolve the differences. In such a session, the members of the Vidhan Sabha would generally prevail, since the Vidhan Sabha includes more than twice as many members as the Vidhan Parishad.

Special Powers of the Vidhan Sabha

A motion of no confidence against the government in the state can only be introduced in the Vidhan Sabha. If it is passed by a majority vote, then the Chief Minister and his Council of Ministers must collectively resign. A money bill can only be introduced in Vidhan Sabha. After it is passed in the Vidhan Sabha, it is sent to the Vidhan Parishad, where it can be kept for a maximum time of 14 days. Unless the Vidhan Parishad rejects it or 14 days lapse or the suggestions made by the Vidhan Parishad are not acceptable to the Vidhan Sabha, the bill is considered passed. The budget of state is also presented in the Vidhan Sabha by the Finance Minister of the state in the name of the Governor of that state. In matters related to ordinary bills, after it is passed by the originating house (that is either Vidhan Sabha or Vidhan Parishad) it is sent to the other house, where it can be kept for a maximum period of 6 months time. If the other house rejects the bill or 6 months pass or the suggestions made by the other house is not acceptable to the originating house, it results in a situation of deadlock. This is resolved by the Governor by calling a joint session of both houses which is presided over by the speaker of the Vidhan Sabha and decided by a simple majority. Since the Vidhan Sabha has greater numerical strength, it is in a position of advantage unless fractured by many different parties.

VIDHAN PARISHAD

The Vidhan Parishad (Legislative Council) forms a part of the state legislatures of India. In six of India's 28 states (Uttar Pradesh, Bihar, Karnataka, Maharashtra, Jammu and Kashmir and Andhra Pradesh), the Legislative Council serves as the indirectly-elected upper house of a bicameral legislature. It is also a permanent house because it cannot be dissolved.

Every Member of Legislative Council serves for a six-year term, with terms staggered so that the terms of one-third of members expire every two years. MLCs must be citizens of India not under 30 years of age, mentally sound and not bankrupt, and on the voter's list of the state from which he or she is contesting the election. The size of the Vidhan Parishad cannot be more than one-third the membership of the Vidhan Sabha, the Legislative Assembly of that state. But its size cannot be less than 40, except in Jammu and Kashmir where there are 36 by an act of Parliament. MLCs are chosen in the following manner:

- One-third are elected by members of local bodies such as corporations, municipalities, and zilla parishads.
- One-third are elected by members of Legislative Assembly from among the persons who are not members of the Assembly.
- One-twelfth are elected persons who are graduates of three years' standing residing in that state.
- One-twelfth are elected by persons engaged for at least three years in teaching in educational institutions within the state not lower than secondary schools, including colleges and universities.
- One-sixth are nominated by the governor from persons having knowledge or practical experience in fields such as literature, science, arts, the co-operative movement and social service.

In April 2007, the State of Andhra Pradesh re-established its Legislative Council. The State's main opposition party, the Telugu Desam Party, has stated that it would abolish the council again if it comes to power in the state. But

Telugu Desam Party could not come to the power for the past 7 years. After the victory of the Akali Dal-BJP in Punjab, newly elected Chief Minister Prakash Singh Badal stated that he would re-constitute the state's Vidhan Parishad.

PANCHAYATI RAJ

The panchayat raj is a South Asian political system mainly in India, Pakistan, and Nepal. "Panchayat" literally means assembly of five wise and respected elders chosen and accepted by the village community. Traditionally, these assemblies settled disputes between individuals and villages. Modern Indian government has decentralized several administrative functions to the village level, empowering elected gram panchayats. Gram panchayats are not to be confused with the unelected khap panchayats (or caste panchayats) found in some parts of India.Panchayati Or Panchaayati Raj is a system of governance in which gram panchayats are the basic units of administration.

It has 3 levels: village, block and district. The term 'panchayat raj' is relatively new, having originated during the British administration. 'Raj' literally means governance or government. Mahatma Gandhi advocated *Panchayati Raj*, a decentralized form of Government where each village is responsible for its own affairs, as the foundation of India's political system. His term for such a vision was "Gram Swaraj" (Village Self-governance). It was adopted by state governments during the 1950s and 60s as laws were passed to establish Panchayats in various states.

It also found backing in the Indian Constitution, with the 73rd amendment in 1993 to accommodate the idea. The Amendment Act of 1993 contains provision for devolution of powers and responsibilities to the panchayats to both for preparation of plans for economic development and social justice and for implementation in relation to twenty-nine subjects listed in the eleventh schedule of the constitution. The panchayats receive funds from three sources – (i) local body grants, as recommended by the Central Finance Commission, (ii) funds for implementation of centrally-sponsored schemes, and funds released by the state governments on the recommendations of the State Finance Commissions. In the history of Panchayati Raj in India, on 24 April 1993, the Constitutional (73rd Amendment) Act, 1992 came into force to provide constitutional status to the Panchayati Raj institutions. This Act was extended to Panchayats in the tribal areas of eight States, namely Andhra Pradesh, Bihar, Gujarat, Himachal Pradesh, Maharashtra, Madhya Pradesh, Orissa and Rajasthan from 24 December 1996. Now panchayati raj system exists in all the states except Nagaland, Meghalaya and Mizoram. Also all the UTs except Delhi. The Act aims to provide 3-tier system of Panchayati Raj for all States having population of over 2 million, to hold Panchayat elections regularly every 5 years, to provide reservation of seats for Scheduled Castes, Scheduled Tribes and Women, to appoint State Finance Commission to make recommendations as regards the financial powers of the Panchayats and to constitute District Planning Committee to prepare draft development plan for the district. The 3-tier system of Panchayati Raj consists of a) village level panchayat b) block level panchayat c) district level panchayat. Powers and responsibilities are delegated to Panchayats at the appropriate level:-

- Preparation of plan for economic development and social justice.
- Implementation of schemes for economic development and social justice in relation to 29 subjects given in Eleventh Schedule of the Constitution.
- To levy, collect and appropriate taxes, duties, tolls and fees.

Village level Panchayat

It is called a Panchayat at the village level. It is a local body working for the good of the village. The number of members usually ranges from 7 to 31; occasionally, groups are larger, but they never have fewer than 7 members. The block-level institution is called the Panchayat Samiti. The district-level institution is called the Zilla Parishad.

Departments

The common departments in the Samiti are as follows:

- General administration
- Finance
- Public works
- Agriculture
- Health
- Education
- Social welfare
- Information Technology and others.

Functions

- Implement schemes for the development of agriculture.
- Establishment of primary health centres and primary schools.
- Supply of drinking water, drainage, construction/repair of roads.
- Development of cottage and small-scale industries and opening of cooperative societies.
- Establishment of youth organisations.

District Level Panchayat

In the district level of the panchayati raj system you have the "zilla parishad". It looks after the administration of the rural area of the district and its office is located at the district headquarters. The Hindi word Parishad means Council and Zilla Parishad translates to District Council. It is headed by the "District Collector" or the "Distric Magistrate" or the "Deputy Comminissioner". it is the link between the state government and the panchayat samiti (local seld government at the block level)

GRAM PANCHAYAT

Gram panchayats are local governments at the village or small town level in India. As per 2002 there were about 265,000 gram panchayats in India. The gram panchayat is the foundation of the Panchayat System. A gram panchayat can be set up in villages with minimum population of 300. Sometimes two or more villages are clubbed together to form group-gram panchayat when the population of the individual villages is less than 300.

Sarpanch/ Chairperson

The Sarpanch or Chairperson is the head of the Gram Panchayat. The elected members of the Gram Panchayat elect from among themselves a Sarpanch and a Deputy Sarpanch for a term of five years. In some places the panchayat president is directly elected by village people. The Sarpanch presides over the meetings of the Gram Panchayat and supervises it's working.

He implements the development schemes of the village. The Deputy Sarpanch, who has the power to make his own decisions, assists the Sarpanch in his work. The Sarpanch has the responsibilities of

- Looking after street lights, construction and repair work of the roads in the villages and also the village markets, fairs, festivals and celebrations.
- Keeping a record of births, deaths and marriages in the village.
- Looking after public health and hygiene by providing facilities for sanitation and drinking water.
- Providing for education.
- Implementing development schemes for agriculture and animal husbandry.

Sources of Income

The main source of income of the Gram Panchayat is the property tax levied on the buildings and the open spaces within the village. Other sources of income include professional tax, taxes on pilgrimage, animal trade, grant received from the State Government in proportion of land revenue and the grants received from the Zilla Parishad.

Gram Sabha

All men and women in the village who are above 18 years of age form the Gram Sabha. The Gram Sabha meets quarterly a year. The probable dates for Gram Sabha have been suggested on four Public Holidays in order to facilitate maximum participation of the general public, *viz.* 26 January, 1 May, 15 August (Independence Day), 14 November (Children's Day).

Meetings of the Gram Sabha are convened to ensure the development of the people through their participation and mutual co-operation. The annual budget and the development schemes for the village are placed before the Gram Sabha for consideration and approval. The Sarpanch and his assistants answer the questions put by the people. The different problems and difficulties of the people are also discussed in the Gram Sabha. All decisions of community development should take in Special Gramsabha only.

Principles of Decentralization

Dr S B Sen committee, a committee appointed by the Government of Kerala in 1996, had suggested the following principles, which was later adopted by the Second Administrative Reforms Commission, for local governance:-

- Subsidiarity
- Democratic decentralisation
- Delineation of functions
- Devolution of functions in real terms
- Convergence
- Citizen centricity

Gram sabha is conducted two times in a year...December and June

PANCHAYAT SAMITI

Panchayat samiti is a local government body at the tehsil or Taluka level in India. It works for the villages of the Tehsil or Taluka that together are called a Development Block. The Panchayat Samiti is the link between the Gram Panchayat and the district administration.

There are a number of variations of this institution in various states. It is known as *Mandal Praja Parishad* in Andhra Pradesh, *Taluka panchayat* in Gujarat, *Mandal Panchayat* in Karnataka, etc. Every taluka in maharashtra has a panchayat samiti all the villages of a taluka make a development block."the panchayat samiti co-ordinates the develo-pmentactivities of all the villages in a development block.

Constitution

It is composed of ex-officio members (all sarpanchas of the panchayat samiti area, the MPs and MLAs of the area and the SDO of the subdivision), coopted members (representatives of SC/ST and women), associate members (a farmer of the area, a representative of the cooperative societies and one of the marketing services) and some elected members. A man or woman contesting the panchayat samiti elections must have completed 21 years of age;he/must be a citizen of india. The samiti is elected for 5 years and is headed by the chairman and the deputy chairman. Membere can propose a motion of no confidence against them. The administrative head of the panchayat samiti is the block development officer. He is appointed by the state governmet. His dutis include preparing samiti's budget,preparing a report of the activites of the panchayat samiti.

Departments

The common departments in the Samiti are:

- General administration
- Finance
- Public works
- Agriculture
- Health
- Education
- Social welfare
- Information Technology

There is an officer for every department. A government appointed block development officer is the executive officer to the samiti and the chief of its administration.

Functions

- Implement schemes for the development of agriculture.
- Establishment of Primary Health Centres and primary schools.
- Supply of drinking water, drainage, construction/repair of roads.
- Development of cottage and small-scale industries and opening of cooperative societies.
- Establishment of youth organisations.

Sources of Income

The main source of income of the panchayat samiti are grants-in-aid and loans from the State Government. THE ZILLA PARISHAD ALSO GIVES IT SOME GRANTS ON THE BASIS OF LAND REVENUE COLLECTED.

ZILLA PARISHAD

Zilla Parishad is a local government body at the district level in India. It looks after the administration of the rural area of the district and its office is located at the district headquarters. The Hindi word *Parishad* means Council and *Zilla Parishad* translates to *District Council*

Constitution

Members of the Zilla Parishad are elected from the district on the basis of adult franchise for a term of five years. Zilla Parishad has minimum of 50 and maximum of 75 members. There are seats reserved for Scheduled Castes, Scheduled Tribes, backward classes and women. The Chairmen of all the Panchayat Samitis form the members of Zilla Parishad. The Parishad is headed by a President and a Vice-President.

Administrative Structure

The Chief Executive Officer, who is an IAS officer, heads the administrative machinery of the Zilla Parishad. The CEO supervises the divisions of the Parishad and executes its development schemes.

Functions

- Provide essential services and facilities to the rural population and the planning and execution of the development programmes for the district.
- Supply improved seeds to farmers. Inform them of new techniques of training. Undertake construction of small-scale irrigation projects and percolation tanks. Maintain pastures and grazing lands.
- Set up and run schools in villages. Execute programmes for adult literacy. Run libraries.
- Start Primary Health Centers and hospitals in villages. Start mobile hospitals for hamlets, vaccination drives against epidemics and family welfare campaigns.
- Construct bridges and roads.
- Execute plans for the development of the scheduled castes and tribes. Run ashramshalas for adivasi children. Set up free hostels for scheduled caste students.
- Encourage entrepreneurs to start small-scale industries like cottage industries, handicraft, agriculture produce processing mills, dairy farms, etc. Implement rural employment schemes.
- They construct roads, schools, and public properties.And they take care of the public properties.
- They even supply work for the poor people. (tribes, scheduled caste, lower caste)

Sources of Income

- Taxes on water, pilgrimage, markets, etc.
- Fixed grant from the State Government in proportion with the land revenue and money for works and schemes assigned to the Parishad.

ELECTION COMMISSION OF INDIA

Elections enable every adult citizen of the country to participate in the process of government formation. You must have observed that elections are held in our country frequently. These include elections to elect members of the Lok Sabha, Rajya Sabha, State Legislative Assemblies (Vidhan Sabhas) Legislative Councils (Vidhan Parishad) and of, President and Vice-President of India. Elections are also held for local bodies such as municipalities, municipal corporations and Panchayati Raj justifications.

If you have attained the age of 18, you must have voted in some of these elections. If not, you will have the opportunity to vote in the next round of elections. These elections are held on the basis of universal adult franchise, which means all Indians of 18 years of age and above have the right to vote, irrespective of their caste, colour, religion, sex or place of birth.

Election is a complex exercise. It involves schedules rules and machinery. This chapter will give you a clear depiction of the voting procedure, as also about filing of nominations, their scrutiny and the campaigns carried out by the parties and the candidates before actual polling. In this chapter you will read about the Election Commission, electoral system in India and also some suggestions for electoral reforms.

The architects of the Indian Constitution attached special significance to an independent electoral machinery for the conduct of elections. The Constitution of India provides for an Election Commission of India which is responsible for superintendence direction and control of all elections.

It is responsible for conducting elections to both the Houses of Parliament and State Legislatures and for the offices of President and Vice-President. Besides, it is also responsible for the preparation revision, updation and maintenance of lists of voters. It delimits constituencies for election to the Parliament and the State Legislatures, fixes the election programme and settles election disputes. It performs many other functions related to elections.

Composition

The Election Commission consists of the Chief Election Commissioner and such other Election Commissioners as may be decided by the President from time to time. Ever since the first Chief Election Commissioner was appointed in 1950, there was no other Election Commissioner till 1989.

The Chief Election Commissioner was assisted by a larger number of officials. The Election Commission became a multi-member body on 16 October 1989 when the President appointed two more Election Commissioners. The senior of the two Election Commissioners is appointed as the Chief Election Commissioner.

Tenure and Removal

Chief Election Commissioner and other Election Commissioners are appointed for a term of six years, or till the age of 65 whichever is earlier. It is important that Chief Election Commissioner and other Election

Commissioners should be free from all political interferences. Therefore, even if they are appointed by the President, they cannot be removed by him. And no changes can be brought in the conditions of service and the tenure of office after their appointment.

The Chief Election Commissioner cannot be removed from office, except on the grounds and in the manner on which the Supreme Court judges can be removed. However, since the other Election Commissioners and the Regional Election Commissioners work under the Chief Commissioner, they may be removed by the President on his recommendations.

POWERS AND FUNCTIONS OF THE ELECTION COMMISSION

The primary function of the Election Commission is to conduct free and fair elections in India. For this purpose, the Election Commission has the following functions:

Delimitation of Constituencies

To facilitate the process of elections, a country has to be divided into several constituencies.

- *Constituency*: It is territorial area from where a candidate contests elections

The task of delimiting constituencies is generally performed by the Delimitation Commission consisting of five serving or retired judges of the Supreme Court and the Chief Election Commissioner who is its ex-officio member. All secretarial assistance (at all levels, national, state, district) is provided to the Delimitation Commission by the Election Commission. The Delimitation Commission is constituted by the Government from time to time.

Preparation of Electoral Rolls

Each constituency has a comprehensive list of voters. It is known as the Electoral Roll, or the Voters' List. The Commission prepares the Electoral Roll for Parliament as well as Legislative Assembly elections. The Electoral Roll of every constituency contains the names of all the persons who have right to vote in that constituency. The electoral roll is also revised from time to time generally before every general election, by-election and mid-term election in the constituency.

General Election	Election to constitute a new Lok Sabha or Assembly is called General Election.
By-Election	If at any time there is a mid-term vacancy due to the death or resignation of a member either in Lok Sabha or Legislative Assembly only one seat falls vacant. The election for that seat is known as by-election.
Mid-term Election	If the Lok Sabha or State Assembly is dissolved before completion of five years and the election is held to constitute new Lok Sabha or new State Assembly, etc. is called midterm election.

The revision is carried out from house to house by the enumerators appointed by Election Commission and all eligible voters are registered.

A person can be registered as a voter if he/she fulfils the following conditions:

- He/she is a citizen of India.
- He/she is 18 years of age.
- He/she is resident of the constituency.

Recognition of Political Parties

One of the important functions of the Election Commission is to recognise political parties as all India (National) or State (Regional) Political Parties. If in a general election, a particular party gets four per cent of the total valid votes polled in any four states it is recognised as an all India (National) Party. If a party gets four per cent of the total valid votes in a state, it is recognized as a State or regional party. The Indian National Congress, the Bharatiya Janata Party (BJP), the Communist Party of India (CPI), The Communist Party of India (Marxist) the Bahujan Samaj Party (BSP) and the Nationalist Congress Party are at present major recognised national parties.

Allotment of Symbol

Political Parties have symbols which are allotted by the Election Commission. For example, Hand is the symbol of the Indian National Congress, Lotus is the symbol of the Bharatiya Janata Party (BJP) and Elephant is the symbol of Bahujan Samaj Party.

These symbols are significant for the following reasons:

- They are a help for the illiterate voters who cannot read the names of the candidates.
- They help in differentiating between two candidates having the same name.

OFFICERS ON ELECTION DUTY STRUCTURE OF GOVERNMENT

To ensure that elections are held in free and fair manner, the Election Commission appoints thousands of polling personnel to assist in the election work. These personnel are drawn among magistrates, police officers, civil servants, clerks, typists, school teachers, drivers, peons etc. Out of these there are three main officials who play very important role in the conduct of free and fair election. They are Returning Officer, Presiding Officer and Polling Officers.

Returning Officer

In every constituency, one Officer is designated as Returning Officer by the Commission in consultation with the concerned State government. However, an Officer can be nominated as Returning Officer for more than one constituency. All the nomination papers are submitted to the Returning Officer.

Papers are scrutinised by him/her and if they are in order, accepted by him/her. Election symbols are allotted by him/her in accordance with the directions issued by the Election Commission. He/she also accepts withdrawal of the candidates and announces the final list. He/she supervises all the polling booths, votes are counted under his/her supervision and finally result is announced by him/her. In fact, the Returning Officer is the overall incharge of the efficient and fair conduct of elections in the concerned constituency.

Presiding Officers

Every constituency has a large number of polling booths. Each polling booth on an average caters to about a thousands votes. Every such booth is under the charge of an officer who is called the Presiding Officer. He/she supervises the entire process polling in the polling booth and ensures that every voter gets an opportunity to cast vote freely. After the polling is over he/she seals all the ballot boxes and deliver them to the Returning Officer.

Polling Officers

Every Presiding Officer is assisted by three to four polling officers. They check the names of the voters in the electoral roll, put indelible ink on the finger of the voter, issue ballot papers and ensure that votes are secretly cast by each voter.

[*Indelible Ink:* This ink cannot be removed easily. It is put on the first finger of the right hand of the voter so that a person does not come again to cast vote for the second time. This is done to avoid impersonation.]

ELECTORAL PROCESS

Elections in India are conducted according to the procedure laid down by law. The following process is observed.

Notification for Election

The process of election officially begins when on the recommendation of Election Commission, the President in case of Lok Sabha and the Governor in case of State Assembly issue a notification for the election. Seven days are given to candidates to file nomination. The seventh day is the last date after the issue of notification excluding Sunday.

Scrutiny of nomination papers is done on the day normally after the last date of filing nominations. The candidate can withdraw his/her nomination on the second day after the scrutiny of papers. Election is held not earlier than twentieth day after the withdrawal.

Filing of Nomination

A person who intends to contest an election is required to file the nomination paper in a prescribed form indicating his name, age, postal address and serial number in the electoral rolls. The candidate is required to be duly proposed and seconded by at least two voters registered in the concerned constituency. Every candidate has to take an oath or make affirmation. These papers are then submitted to the Returning Officer designated by the Election Commission.

Security Deposit

Every candidate has to make a security deposit at the time of filing nomination. For Lok Sabha every candidate has to make a security deposit of ₹10,000/- and for State Assembly ₹5,000. But candidates belonging to Scheduled Castes and Scheduled Tribes are required to deposit ₹5,000/– for if contesting the Lok Sabha elections and ₹2,500/– for contesting Vidhan Sabha elections. The security deposit is forfeited if the candidate fails to get at least 1/6 of the total valid votes polled.

Scrutiny and Withdrawal

All nomination papers received by the Returning Officer are scrutinised on the day fixed by the Election Commission. This is done to ensure that all papers are filled according to the procedure laid down and accompanied by required security deposit.

The Returning Officer is empowered to reject a nomination paper on any one of the following ground:

- If the candidate is less than 25 years of age.
- If he/she has not made security deposit.
- If he/she is holding any office of profit.
- If he/she is not listed as a voter anywhere in the country

The second day after the scrutiny of nomination papers is the last date for the withdrawal of the candidates. In case that day happens to be a holiday or Sunday, the day immediately after that is fixed as the last day for the withdrawal.

Election Campaign

Campaigning is the process by which a candidate tries to persuade the voters to vote for him rather than others. During this period, the candidates try to travel through their constituency to influence as many voters as possible to vote in their favour. In the recent times, the Election Commission has granted all the recognised National and Regional Parties, free access to the State-owned electronic media, the All India Radio (AIR) and the Doordarshan to do their campaigning. The total free time is fixed by the Election Commission which is allotted to all the political parties. Campaigning stops 48 hours before the day of polling. A number of campaign techniques are involved in the election process.

Some of these are:

- Holding of public meetings

- Distribution of handbills, highlighting the main issues of their election manifesto (election manifesto is a document issued by political party. It is declaration of policies and programmes of the party concerned.
- Door to door appeal by influential people in the party.
- Broadcasting and telecasting of speeches by various political leaders.

Model Code of Conduct

During the campaign period the political parties and the contesting candidates are expected to abide by a model code of conduct evolved by the Election Commission of India on the basis of the consensus among political parties. It comes into force the moment schedule of election is announced by the Election Commission.

The code of conduct is as follows:

- Political Parties and contesting candidates should not use religious places for election campaign.
- Such speeches should not be delivered in a way to create hatred among different communities belonging to different religions, castes and languages, etc.
- Official machinery should not be used for election work.
- No new grants can be sanctioned, no new schemes or projects can be started once the election dates are announced.
- One cannot misuse mass media for partisan coverage.

Scrutinisation of Expenses

Though the Election Commission provides free access for a limited time to all the recognised National and State parties for their campaign, this does not mean that political parties do not spend anything on their elections campaign. The political parties and the candidates contesting election spend large sum of amount on their election campaign. However, the Election Commission has the power to scrutinise the election expenses to be incurred by the candidates.

There is a ceiling on expenses to be incurred in Parlia-mentary as well as State Assembly elections. Every candidate is required to file an account of his election expenses within 45 days of declaration of results. In case of default or if the candidate has incurred (expenses) more than the prescribed limit, the Election Commission can take appropriate action and the candidate elected may be disqualified and his election may be countermanded.

Polling, Counting and Declaration of Result

In order to conduct polling, large number of polling booths are set up in each constituency. Each booth is placed under the charge of a Presiding Officer with the Polling Officers to help the process. A voter casts his/her vote secretly in an enclosure, so that no other person comes to know of the choice he/she has made. It is known as secret ballot. After the polling is over, ballot boxes are sealed in the presence of agents of the candidates. Agents ensure that no voter is denied right to vote, provided the voter turns up comes within the prescribed time limit.

Electronic Voting Machines (EVMs)

The Election Commission has started using tamper proof electronic voting machines to ensure free and fair elections. Each machine has the names and symbols of the candidates Structure of Government in a constituency. One Electronic Voting Machine (EVM) can accommodate maximum of 16 candidates. But if the number exceeds 16, then more than one EVM may be used. If the number of candidates is very large, ballot papers may be used.

The voter has to press the appropriate button to vote for the candidate of his/her choice. As soon as the button is pressed, the machine is automatically switched off. Then comes the turn of the next voter. The machine is easy to operate, and with this the use of ballot paper and ballot boxes is done away with.

When the machine is used, the counting of votes becomes more convenient and faster. The EVMs were used in all the seven Lok Sabha constituencies in Delhi in 1999, and later in all the State Assembly constituencies. In 2004 General Elections EVMs were used all over the country for Lok Sabha elections.

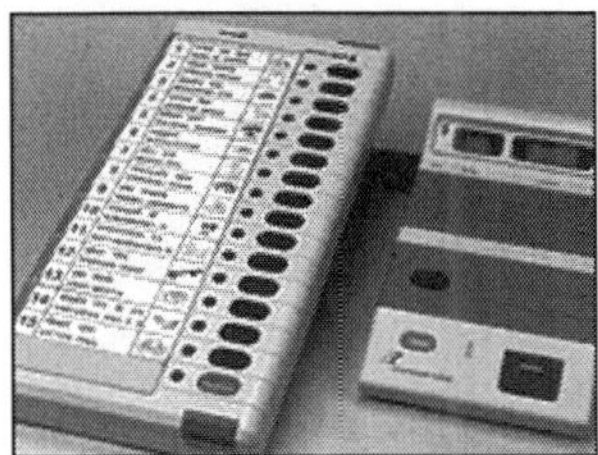

Fig. Electronic Voting Machine (EVM)

The sealed ballot boxes or EVMs are shifted in tight security to the counting centre. Counting takes place under the supervision of the Returning Officer and in the presence of candidates and their agents. If there is any doubt about the validity or otherwise of a vote, decision of the Returning Officer is final. As soon as counting is over, the candidate securing the maximum number of votes is declared elected (or returned) by the Returning Officer.

Re-poll

If at the time of polling, a booth is captured by some anti-social elements, the Election Commission may order holding of re-poll in either the entire constituency or particular booths.

Countermanding of Election

If a duly nominated candidate belonging to a recognised party dies at any time after the last date of nomination and before the commencement of polling, the Election Commission orders countermanding the elections. This is not just postponement of polling. The entire election process, beginning from nominations is initiated afresh in the concerned constituency.

SHORTCOMINGS OF INDIAN ELECTORAL SYSTEM

There has been universal appreciation of the Indian electoral system. People have hailed the manner in which elections have been conducted in India. But there are its weaknesses. It has been seen that in spite of the efforts of Election Commission to ensure free and fair election, there are certain shortcomings of our Electoral system.

Money Power

The role of unaccounted money in elections has become a serious problem. The political parties collect funds from companies and business houses, and then use this money to influence the voter to vote in their favour. The business contributions are mostly in cash and are not unaccounted. Many other corrupt practices are also adopted during election such as bribing, rigging or voters intimidation, impersonation and providing transport and conveyance of voters to and fro the polling stations. The reports of liquor being distributed in poor areas are frequent during election.

Muscle Power

Earlier the criminals used to support the candidates by intimidating the voter at a gunpoint to vote according to their direction. Now they themselves have come out openly by contesting the elections leading to criminalisation of politics. As a result violence during elections has also increased.

Caste and Religion

Generally the candidates are given tickets by the political parties on the consideration whether the candidate can muster the support of numerically larger castes and communities and possesses enough resources. Even the electorates vote on the caste and communal lines. Communal loyalties of the voters are used at the time of propaganda campaign.

Misuse of Government Machinery

All the political parties do not have equal opportunity in respect of access to resources. The party in power is always in advantageous position then the opposition parties. There is widespread allegation that the party in power accomplishes misuse of government machinery. All these features lead to violence, booth capturing, rigging bogus voting, forcible removal of ballot papers, ballot boxes burning of vehicles, etc. which result into loss of public faith in elections.

ELECTORAL REFORMS

In order to restore the confidence of the public in the democratic electoral system, many electoral reforms have been recommended from time to time by Tarkunde Committee and Goswami Committee which were particularly appointed to study and report on the scheme for Electoral Reforms in the year 1974 and 1990 respectively. Out of these recommendations some have been implemented. In fact, it was under the chairmanship of the then Chief Election Commissioner, T.N. Seshan, that Election Commission initiated many more measures to ensure free and fair elections.

Some of the reforms which have been implemented so far are as follows:

- The voting age has been lowered from 21 years to 18 years. This has helped increase the number of voters and response confidence in the youth of the country.
- Another landmark change has been the increase in the amount of security deposit by the candidate to prevent many non-serious condidates from contesting elections with a ulterior motive.
- The photo identity cards have been introduced to eradicate bogus voting or impersonation.
- With the introduction of Electronic Voting Machine (EVM) the voting capturing, rigging, and bogus voting may not be possible. The use of EVM will in the long run result in reducing the cost of holding elections and also the incidence of tampering during counting of votes.
- If a discrepancy is found between the member of votes polled and number of total votes counted, the Returning officer away report the matter forthwith to Election Commission. Election Commission on such report may either declare the poll at the particular polling station as void and give a date for fresh poll or countermand election in that constituency.

There is no doubt that India needs drastic poll reforms but still the fact remains that Indian elections have been largely free and fair and successfully conducted. It gives the country the proud distinction of being the largest democracy in the world.

5

Political Power

INTRODUCTION

Political power (*imperium* in Latin) is a type of power held by a group in a society which allows administration of some or all of public resources, including labour and wealth. There are many ways to obtain possession of such power. At the nation-state level political legitimacy for political power is held by the representatives of national sovereignty.

Political powers are not limited to heads of states, however the extent to which a person (such as Joseph Kony, Subcomandante Marcos, or Russell Means) or group such as an insurgency, terrorist group, or multinational corporation possesses such power is related to the amount of societal influence they can wield, formally or informally. In many cases this is not contained within a single state and it refers to international power. Political scientists have frequently defined power as *"the ability to influence the behaviour of others"* with or without resistance.

For analytical reasons, I.C. MacMillan separates the concepts power:

- Power is the capacity to restructure actual situations. —I.C. Macmillan

One of the most famous references to power comes from the Chinese communist leader Mao Zedong

- Political power grows from the barrel of a gun.— Mao Zedong

This quote has been widely misinterpreted, however. Mao explained further that, "Our principle is that the Party commands the gun, and the gun must never be allowed to command the Party." In contrast to Mao Zedong, Hannah Arendt claims that power and violence are opposites and that power is:

- "The human ability...to act in concert."

COMPLIANCE

Power is a complex social interaction between those who command and those who obey. For power to be effective there must be consent, cooperation, and obedience. Broad-based defiance of the authority of those who hold power may significantly erode it or overthrow it.

POLITICAL POWER AND THE QUESTION OF GOOD AUTHORITY

Some opinions representative of Enlightenment, 19th century, modern, and post-modern views on the relationship between political power and concepts of justice, good and evil:

- Judicial power, that sure criterion of the goodness of a Government...is, in a word, a necessary evil.— Jean-Louis de Lolme
- The power to rule is a necessary evil, and by this same token, alas, it can be called a good.— Émile Chartier
- Constituted power is concentrated power.— Giorgio Agamben
- [Constituted power] is the product of a grey, incessant alchemy in which good and evil and, along with them, all the metals of traditional ethics reach their point of fusion. It thus becomes a question of irresponsibility and "impotentia judicandi" [the inability to judge]...though one that is situated not beyond good and evil, but rather before.— Giorgio Agamben

SEPARATION OF POWERS

The separation of powers, often imprecisely used interchangeably with the *trias politica* principle, is a model for the governance of a state. The model was first developed in ancient Greece and came into widespread use by the Roman Republic as part of the unmodified Constitution of the Roman Republic. Under this model, the state is divided into branches, each with separate and independent powers and areas of responsibility so that no one branch has more power than the other branches. The normal division of branches is into an executive, a legislature, and a judiciary. For similar reasons, the concept of separation of church and state has been adopted in a number of countries, to varying degrees depending on the applicable legal structures and prevalent views towards the proper role of religion in society.

Montesquieu's Tripartite System

The term is ascribed to French Enlightenment political philosopher Baron de Montesquieu. Montesquieu described division of political power among an executive, a legislature, and a judiciary. He based this model on the British constitutional system, in which he perceived a separation of powers among the monarch, Parliament, and the courts of law. Subsequent writers have noted that this was misleading, because the United Kingdom had a very closely connected legislature and executive, with further links to the judiciary (though combined with judicial independence). Montesquieu did specify that "the independence of the judiciary has to be real, and not apparent merely". "The judiciary was generally seen as the most important of powers, independent and unchecked", and also considered it dangerous.

Comparison with Other Systems

In democratic systems of governance based on the trias politica, a fundamental parallel and a fundamental difference exists between *presidential systems* and constitutional monarchic *parliamentary system* of government.

The parallel is that the 3 branches of government (legislative, executive, judicial) exist largely independent of each other. Each with its competences, prerogatives and its domain of activity, and exercising control over each other.

- The legislative body has control of the executive finances, and has judiciary powers, it also has control of the way the judiciary works.
- The judiciary often has control of laws not being contradictory to the constitution or other laws and it has the power to correct and control the way the executive body exercises it powers (to execute the law)

The difference is:

- In presidential systems the incumbent of the Head-of-state is elected to office, and after transfer of power the president appoints his administration (ministers etc.) or a government headed by a prime minister is formed within the parliament (based on the majority in the parliament) (like in France). The latter might lead to a "cohabitation" where a president and his government belong to different parties or to different coalition. Also further down the ladder of political power regional or local legislative bodies and the chief executive is elected (State governor and State Senate in the US, the Conseil Communal and Bourgemestre in France).
- In constitutional monarchic parliamentary systems only the legislative body is elected and a government formed on the basis of majority or coalitions of parties. Elected members of parliament have to resign from their mandate in order to accept an Executive office. This is true in regional and local councils are elected and the executive nominated.

In a parliamentary system, when the term of the legislature ends, so too may the tenure of the executive selected by that legislature. Although in a presidential system the executive's term may or may not coincide with the legislature's, their selection is technically independent of the legislature.

The 2 branch power systems may have systems in which certain branches have more than one power. Often a legislative body is elected, while the executive is nominated. The nominated executive branch also has power of presenting legislation, while the legislative body is only has a controlling function. In those system the judiciary is subservient to the executive and has no power to control either the executive or the legality of new legislative texts.

The separation of powers is a doctrine which provides a separate authority, which makes it possible for the authorities to check each others checks and balances (Executive Authority Act 1936).

Various Models

Constitutions with a high degree of separation of powers are found worldwide. The UK system is distinguished by a particular entwining of powers. In Italy the powers are completely separated, even if Council of Ministers need the vote of confidence from both chambers of Parliament, that's however formed by a wide number of members (almost 1,000). A number of Latin American countries have electoral branches of government.

Countries with little separation of power include New Zealand and Canada. Canada makes limited use of separation of powers in practice, although in theory it distinguishes between branches of government. New Zealand also subscribes to the principle of 'Separation of Powers' through a series of constitutional safeguards. The Executive requires regular approval from the Legislature to carry out decisions. The Mixed Members Proportionate framework also caters for a coalition of parties to form government where a majority from a single party does not exist. The Judiciary is also free of government interference. If a series of judicial decisions result in an interpretation of the law which the Executive considers does not reflect the intention of the policy, the Executive can change the legislation. However, they can not direct or request a judicial officer to revise or reconsider a decision. These decisions are final. Should there be a dispute between the Executive and Judiciary, the Executive has no authority to direct the Judiciary, or its individual members.

Complete separation-of-powers systems are almost always presidential, although theoretically this need not be the case. There are a few historical exceptions, such as the Directoire system of revolutionary France. Switzerland offers an example of non-Presidential separation of powers today: It is run by a seven-member executive branch, the Federal Council. However, some might argue that Switzerland does not have a strong separation of powers system, as the Federal Council is appointed by parliament (but not dependent on parliament), and the judiciary has no power of review.

Executive Branch

This is the branch of government charged with execution and enforcement of laws and policies and the administration of public affairs. The executive branch includes governors and their staffs. At the federal level, the executive includes the president, the vice president, staffs of appointed advisers and a variety of departments and agencies. The executive branch also proposes a great deal of legislation to congress and also appoints federal judges, including justices of the Supreme Court.

Legislative Branch

This is the branch of government which has the power to make laws; the legislative branch consists of congress and the fifty state legislatures. At which both state and federal levels, legislature is made up of popularly elected representatives that propose laws that are sensitive to the needs and interests of their local constituents.

Judicial Branch

This is the branch of government in charge of the interpretation of laws and the administration of justice. The court systems of the judicial branch are local, state, and federal governments, in which each of them are responsible for interpreting the laws passed by the legislative branch and are enforced always by the executive branch. Each one of these courts has either criminal cases or civil cases. Each one of these courts attempts to resolve each conflict in order to protect the individual rights by the constitution and also with the bounds of justice, of the U.S law.

Three Branches

Australia: Three Branches

Australia does not maintain a strict separation between the legislative and executive branches of government—indeed, government ministers are required to be a member of parliament—but the federal judiciary strictly guards its independence from the other two branches. However, under influence from the American constitution, the Australian constitution does define the three branches of government separately, and this has been interpreted by the judiciary to induce an implicit separation of powers. State governments have a similar level of separation of power, but this is generally on the basis of convention, rather than constitution.

France

The government of France is divided up into 3 branches:

1. *Executive*: This includes the popularly elected president as well as the prime minister and cabinet.
2. *Legislature*: A bicameral legislature that includes the Senate (upper house) and the National Assembly (lower house).
3. *Judiciary*: This includes the judicial and administrative orders. It also includes a constitutional court.

Hong Kong (Chinese Special Administrative Region): Three Branches

Hong Kong is a largely self-governing Chinese territory pursuant to the Sino-British Joint Declaration, an international treaty registered with the United Nations. Currently, Hong Kong has three branches of government as codified in the Basic Law, which preserves the political setup of the British colonial era under the doctrine of one country, two systems:

- *Government*: Executive

- *Legislative Council*: Legislature
- *Judiciary (Court of Final Appeal and other courts and tribunals)*: Judiciary

The Chief Executive, elected by a 800-member Election Committee, is both head of the region and head of government, and chairs the Executive Council which composes of unofficial members and government secretaries. The law courts exercise the power of judicial review of constitutionality of legislations and administrative actions, and emphasis the separation of powers in their rulings. The Chief Justice also stated this position in the ceremonial opening of the legal year. However, politically separation of powers is usually argued against, with the leaders of the People's Republic of China, the sovereign of Hong Kong, requesting publicly for the three branches to cooperate, and pro-Beijing politicians emphasising an "executive-led" system.

India: Three Branches

- Parliament = Legislative
- Prime Minister, Cabinet, Government Departments and Civil Service = Executive
- Supreme Court = Judicial

The democratic system in India also offers a clear separation of powers. India follows a parliamentary system of government. The Judiciary branch is fairly independent of the other two branches. Executive powers are vested with the President who is assisted by the Cabinet Secretary and other Secretaries. All three branches have "checks and balances" over each other to maintain the balance of power. Executive branch is under the President of India, Vice-President of India and Cabinet Secretary (India).

United Kingdom: Three Branches

- *Parliament*: Legislature
- *Prime Minister, Cabinet, Government Departments and Civil Service*: Executive
- *Courts*: Judiciary

Although the doctrine of separation of power plays a role in the United Kingdom's constitutional doctrine, the UK constitution is often described as having "a weak separation of powers" A. V. Dicey, despite its constitution being the one to which Montesquieu originally referred. For example, in the United Kingdom, the executive forms a subset of the legislature, as did—to a lesser extent—the judiciary until the establishment of the Supreme Court of the United Kingdom. The Prime Minister, the Chief Executive, sits as a member of the Parliament of the United Kingdom, either as a peer in the House of Lords or as an elected member of the House of Commons (by convention, and as a result of the supremacy of the Lower House, the Prime Minister now sits in the House of Commons) and can effectively be removed from office by a simple majority vote. Furthermore, while the courts in the United Kingdom are undoubtedly amongst the most independent in the world, the Law Lords, who were the final arbiters of judicial disputes in the UK, until recently sat simultaneously in the House of Lords, the upper house of the legislature, although this arrangement ceased in 2009 when the Supreme Court of the United Kingdom came into existence. Furthermore, because of the existence of Parliamentary sovereignty, while the theory of separation of powers may be studied there, a system such as that of the UK is more accurately described as a "fusion of powers".

The development of the British constitution, which is not a codified document, is based on this fusion in the person of the Monarch, who has a formal role to play in the legislature (Parliament, which is where legal and political sovereignty lies, is the Crown-in-Parliament, and is summoned and dissolved by the Sovereign who must give his or her Royal Assent to all Bills so that they become Acts), the executive (the Sovereign appoints all ministers of His/Her Majesty's Government, who govern in the name of the Crown) and the judiciary (the Sovereign, as the fount of justice, appoints all senior judges, and all public prosecutions are brought in his or her name).

The British legal systems are based on common law traditions which require:

- Police or regulators cannot initiate complaints under criminal law but can only investigate (prosecution is mostly reserved for the Crown Prosecution Service), which prevents selective enforcement, *e.g.* the 'fishing expedition' which is often specifically forbidden.
- Prosecutors cannot withhold evidence from attorneys for the defendant; to do so results in mistrial or dismissal. Accordingly, their relation to police is no advantage.
- Defendants convicted can appeal, but only fresh and compelling evidence not available at trial can be introduced, restricting the power of the court of appeal to the process of law applied.

United States: Three Branches

In the United States Constitution, Article 1 Section I gives Congress only those "legislative powers herein granted" and proceeds to list those permissible actions in Article I Section 8, while Section 9 lists actions that are prohibited for Congress. The vesting clause in Article II places no limits on the Executive branch, simply stating that, "The Executive Power shall be vested in a President of the United States of America." The Supreme Court holds "The judicial Power" according to Article III, and it established the implication of Judicial review in Marbury vs Madison. The federal government refers to the branches as "branches of government", while some systems use "government" to describe the executive. The Executive branch has attempted to claim power arguing for separation of powers to include being the Commander in Chief of a standing army since the Civil war, executive orders, emergency powers and security classifications since WWII, national security, signing statements, and the scope of the unitary executive.

DIVISION OF POWER

A similar concept, termed "division of power", also consists of differentiated legislative, executive, and judicial powers. However, while separation of powers prohibits one branch from interfering with another, division of power permits such interference. For example, in Indonesia, the President (who wields executive power) can introduce a new bill, but the People's Consultative Assembly (holding legislative power) chooses to either legalize or reject the bill. The model here is the Checks and balances system introduced in the United States Constitution.

POWER PROJECTION

Power projection (or force projection) is a term used in military and political science to refer to the capacity of a state to conduct expeditionary warfare, *i.e.* to intimidate other nations and implement policy by means of force, or the threat thereof, in an area distant from its own territory. This ability is a crucial element of a state's power in international relations. Any state able to direct its military forces outside the limited bounds of its territory might be said to have *some* level of power projection capability, but the term itself is used most frequently in reference to militaries with a worldwide reach (or at least significantly broader than a state's immediate area). Even states with sizable hard power assets (such as a large standing army) may only be able to exert limited regional influence so long as they lack the means of effectively projecting their power on a global scale. Generally, only a select few states are able to overcome the logistical difficulties inherent in the deployment and direction of a modern, mechanized military force.

While traditional measures of power projection typically focus on hard power assets (tanks, soldiers, aircraft, naval vessels, etc.), the developing theory of soft power notes that power projection does not necessarily have to involve the active use of military forces in combat. Assets for power projection can often serve dual uses, as the deployment of various countries' militaries during the humanitarian response to the 2004 Indian Ocean earthquake illustrates. The ability of a state to project its forces into an area may serve as an effective diplomatic lever, influencing the decision-making process and acting as a potential deterrent on other states' behaviour.

Elements of Power Projection

As distance between a fighting force and its headquarters increases, command and control inevitably becomes more difficult. Modern-day power projection often makes use of high-tech communications and information technology to overcome these difficulties, a process sometimes described as the "Revolution in Military Affairs."

While a few long-range weapons—such as the intercontinental ballistic missiles (ICBMs) and certain types of cruise missiles—are capable of projecting deadly force in their own right, most discussion of power projection revolve around issues of military logistics. The ability to integrate naval and air forces with land armies as part of joint warfare is generally viewed as a key aspect of effective power projection; airlift and sealift capabilities allow a country to deploy units of soldiers or weapons to distant destinations not easily accessible by land forces.

The aircraft carrier battle group, strategic bomber, ballistic missile submarine, and strategic airlifter are all examples of power projection platforms. Military units designed to be light and mobile, such as airborne forces (paratroopers and air assault forces) and amphibious assault forces, are utilized in power projection. Forward basing is another method of power projection, which by pre-positioning military units or stockpiles of arms at strategically located military bases outside a country's territory, reduces the time and distance needed to mobilize them for combat in a distant theater of war.

Types of Power Projection Missions

Scholars have disaggregated military power projection into nine different aspects based on the political goals being sought and the level of force employed: Four of these relate to the employment of "soft" military power (securing sea lanes of communication, non-combatant evacuation operations, humanitarian response, and peacekeeping) and five are primarily concerned with "hard" military power (showing the flag, compellence/deterrence, punishment, armed intervention and conquest.)

Soft power projection:

- Securing sea lanes of communication: the protection of shipping lanes from attack by hostile states or irregular threats.
- Non-combatant evacuation operations: the evacuation of citizens or friendly third country civilians from a foreign country when they are endangered by war or civil unrest.
- Humanitarian response: the use of military forces abroad to assist in the aftermath of a natural disaster.
- Peace-keeping: military operations designed to support diplomatic efforts to reach a long-term political settlement to an on-going dispute.

Hard power projection:

- *Showing the flag*: The symbolic deployment of military forces to a region for the purposes of demonstrating political interest, resolve, or willingness to take more forceful military action.

- *Compulsion/deterrence*: The use of the threat of military force against another state to either induce it into or dissuade it from pursuing a given policy. In this form, power projection acts as a diplomatic tool, attempting to influence the decision-making process of foreign actors.
- *Punishment*: The punitive use of force against another state in response to their pursuit of a given policy.
- *Armed intervention*: The movement of military forces into another nation's territory for the purposes of influencing the internal affairs of the target country short of outright conquest.
- *Conquest*: The offensive use of military assets to forcibly occupy territory controlled or claimed by another state.

Examples

In the Russo-Japanese War of 1904–1905, the Japanese destruction of the Imperial Russian Navy's Pacific Fleet demonstrated Imperial Russia's inability to project force in the East. This immediately diminished Russia's diplomatic sway in that region. At the same time, Russia's western armies became less credible, as mobilization exposed organizational flaws and threw the western armies into chaos. This led analysts in Europe, such as German chief of staff Count Alfred von Schlieffen, to conclude that Russia would prove inept at projecting force in Europe, thus demoting Russia in European diplomatic relations.

Many other actions can be considered projections of force. The 19th century is full of these incidents, such as the 1864 Bombardment of Kagoshima and the Boxer Rebellion. More recently, the Falklands War provided an example of the United Kingdom's ability to project force far from home. The ability of the U.S. Navy, the British Royal Navy, and the French Navy to deploy large numbers of ships for long periods of time away from home are unique projection abilities.

POLITICAL SCIENCE PERSPECTIVES

Within normative political analysis, there are also various levels of power as described by academics that add depth into the understanding of the notion of power and its political implications. Robert Dahl, a prominent American political scientist, first ascribed to political power the trait of decision-making as the source and main indicator of power. Later, two other political scientists, Peter Bachrach and Morton Baratz, decided that simply ascribing decision-making as the basis of power was too simplistic and they added what they termed a second dimension of power, agenda-setting by elites who worked in the backrooms and away from public scrutiny in order to exert their power upon society.

Lastly, British academic Steven Lukes added a third dimension of power, preference-shaping, which he claimed was another important aspect of normative power in politics which entails theoretical views similar to notions of cultural hegemony. These three dimensions of power are today often considered defining aspects of political power by political researchers.

A radical alternative view of the source of political power follows the formula: information plus authority permits the exercise of power. Political power is intimately related to information. Sir Francis Bacon's statement: "Nam et ipsa scientia potentia est" for knowledge itself is power, assumed authority as given.

Hannah Arendt begins by commenting that political theorists from right to left all seem to agree that violence is "the most flagrant manifestation of power." Arendt says that violence and power are opposites and defines power as the ability of citizens to act in concert. "Power is never the property of an individual; it belongs to the group and remains in existence only so long as the group keeps together.

When we say of somebody that he "is in power" we actually refer to his being empowered by a certain number of people to act in their name." From her perspective that power and violence are opposites, Arendt correctly judged that the invasion of Czechoslovakia in 1968 was a sign of the diminishing power of the Soviet Union and not a sign of power.

THEORY OF SEPARATION OF POWERS

The functions of the government are vast and varied. It is necessary to entrust these functions to specific organs, so that the responsibility for performing these functions may be effectively fixed.

The division of governmental power under any constitutions may be of two kinds; the functional division such as legislative, executive and judicial and the territorial division of federalism. Thus structurally considered government consists of three branches having for their functions:

- Legislation or law meaning
- Their execution or administration and
- Interpretation of these laws.

The three branches to which these functions belong are known as the Legislature, the Executive and the Judiciary respectively.Political liberty in a state is possible when restraints are imposed on the exercise of these powers. The functions of the government should be differentiated and assigned to separate organs to limit each section to its own sphere of action. So that these organs independently interact between themselves. This is what is known as the theory of separation of powers.

Montesquieu, the celebrated French scholar asserted that concentrated power is dangerous and leads to despotism of government. As a check against this danger he suggested to separate the functions of executive, legislature and the judiciary so that one may operate as a balance against the other.

However Montesquieu was not the first scholar to develop the theory of separations of powers. Its origin can be traced back to Aristotle, the father of Political Science. Of course he did not discuss the issue in great details. He only analysed the functions of the three branches of government, the deliberative, executive and the judiciary without suggesting their separation. Besides many other philosophers at a later stage from thirteenth century onwards gave some attention to the theory of separation of powers. Jean Bodiri one of the earliest thinkers of the modern period sees the importance of separating the executive and judicial powers.

But actually it acquired greater significance in eighteenth century. John Locke was one of the eighteenth century philosophers to pay greater attention to the problems of concentration of governmental power. He argued that the executive and legislative powers should be separate for the sake of liberty. Liberty suffers when the same human being makes the law and executed them.

THE THEORY

Montesquieu, the noted political philosopher of France is regarded as the chief architect of the principles of Separation of powers. He in his book *'The Spirit of Laws'* published in 1748 gave the classic exposition of the idea of separation of powers. During his days the Bouborne monarchy in France had established despotism and the people enjoyed no freedom. The monarch was the chief law giver, executor and the adjudicator. The statement by Louis XIV that "I am the state" outlined the character and nature of monarchial authority. Montesquieu, a great advocate of human dignity, developed the theory of separation of powers as a weapon to uphold the liberty of the people. He believed that the application of this theory would prevent the overgrowth of a particular organ which spells danger for political liberty. According to him every man entrusted with some power is bound to misuse it. When the executive and the legislative powers are given to the same person there can be no liberty.

Because it is apprehended that the same person may enact oppressive laws to execute them whimsically. Again there is no liberty, if the judicial power is not separated from the legislature and executive. If the judicial and legislative powers are exercised jointly the life and liberty of the subjects could be exposed to arbitrary control; for the judge could then be the legislator. If it joined to the executive power the judges might behave with violence and oppression. If the same person or body of persons exercise these three powers that of enacting laws, executing them and of trying the cases of individuals, he maintained, that could spell the doom of the whole system of governance. In simple words Montesquieu's view is that concentration of legislative, executive and judicial functions either in one single person or a body of persons results in abuse of authority and such an organisation becomes tyrannical. He argued that the three organs of government should be so organized that each should be entrusted to different persons and each should perform distinct functions within the sphere of power assigned to it.

DISADVANTAGES

Government is an organic unity. The various parts are closely interwoven. Therefore absolute separation of powers is both impossible and undesirable. In every modern government the executive has some kind of law making power to fill the gaps in the structure. Finer observes that rule making is no more or less than secondary legislation. The legislature in almost every country has to perform some judicial function by way of trying of impeachments.

Maciver feels that this theory of separation of powers leads to isolation and disharmony. The various branches of the government tend to exhibit a sense of understanding and cooperation to achieve its end when they work together. But when they are separated to carry on exclusive work of their branch they become arrogant and refuse to work with other branches of government. This gives rise to lot of administrative complications. Every branch suffers from the vice of exclusiveness leading to loss of cooperation and harmony producing inefficiency of the government.

The theory of separation of powers which upholds the system of checks and balances for the sake of equality of powers is based an wrong assumptions. It is not possible to accept the view that all organs of government mutually check each other. The theory also makes the mistakes in assuming that all the three branches of government are equally powerful. But precisely this is not the case. With the growth of positive states the legislature has been reduced to a subordinate position paving way for the executive supremacy which largely restricts and regulates the former.

Finally, the relationship between public liberty and separation of powers is not very significant. Liberty of the individuals largely depends on the psyche of the people, their outlook, the existing institutions, traditions, customs and political consciousness. The people of Great Britain are not less free than that of USA because there is less separation of powers in the former.

Yet however the theory of separation of powers is not altogether without any significance. The complexity of modern society and the accepted concepts of a welfare a state demand more and more action and service on the part of the government. The crux of the problem of modern government is to find a synthesis combining the answer to two needs, the need for the welfare of the state and the need for freedom for the people. The welfare state assumes concentration of power on the executive level and consequently supremacy of the executive over the legislative branch. Of course it becomes alarming unless controlling and balancing devices are properly developed to keep pace with the ever changing face of the executive power. The doctrine of separation of powers from that point of view because more important today that perhaps any other time.

POINTS TO REMEMBER

Montesquieu developed the theory of separation of powers. He pointed out that the legislative, executive and judicial powers of government should be vested in three separate organs. They should not be concentrated in the hands of one man or a group of men.

ADVANTAGES

- Separation of powers according to Montesquieu is the best guarantee of the liberty of people.
- Separation of power promotes efficiency in the administration.

CRITICISM

- Complete separation of powers is neither possible nor desirable.
- Separation of powers is likely to lead to inefficiency in administration.
- The theory is based on the supposition that all the three organs of the government are equality important, but in reality it is not so.
- Liberty of the people largely depends more on factors like their psyche, political culture, consciousness, and institutions than separation of powers

However, separation of power is useful if used judiciously to bring about a balance between the vigorous action of the welfare state and the enjoyment of the liberty of the people.

POWER AND POLITICS IN ORGANIZATIONAL LIFE

There are few business activities more prone to a credibility gap than the way in which executives approach organizational life. A sense of disbelief occurs when managers purport to make decisions in rationalistic terms while most observers and participants know that personalities and politics play a significant if not an overriding role.

Where does the error lie? In the theory which insists that decisions should be rationalistic and non-personal? Or in the practice which treats business organizations as political structures? Whatever else organizations may be (problem-solving instruments, sociotechnical systems, reward systems, and so on), they are political structures. This means that organizations operate by distributing authority and setting a stage for the exercise of power. It is no wonder, therefore, that individuals who are highly motivated to secure and use power find a familiar and hospitable environment in business.

At the same time, executives are reluctant to acknowledge the place of power both in individual motivation and in organizational relationships. Somehow, power and politics are dirty words. And in linking these words to the play of personalities in organizations, some managers withdraw into the safety of organizational logics.

The importance of personality factors and a sensitive use of the strengths and limitations of people in decisions on power distributions can improve the quality of organizational life.

POLITICAL PYRAMID

Organizations provide a power base for individuals. From a purely economic standpoint, organizations exist to create a surplus of income over costs by meeting needs in the marketplace. But organizations also are political structures which provide opportunities for people to develop careers and therefore provide platforms for the expression of individual interests and motives. The development of careers, particularly at high managerial and professional levels, depends on accumulation of power as the vehicle for transforming individual interests into activities which influence other people.

Scarcity and Competition

A political pyramid exists when people compete for power in an economy of scarcity. In other words, people cannot get the power they want just for the asking. Instead, they have to enter into the decisions on how to distribute authority in a particular formal organization structure. Scarcity of power arises under two sets of conditions:

- Where individuals gain power in absolute terms at someone else's expense.
- Where there is a gain comparatively—not literally at someone else's expense—resulting in a relative shift in the distribution of power.

6

The Concept of Authority

AUTHORITY

The word "authority" is derived from the Latin word auctoritas, meaning invention, advice, opinion, influence, or command. In English, the word 'authority' can be used to mean power given by the state (in the form of Members of Parliament, Judges, Police Officers, etc.) or by academic knowledge of an area (someone can be an authority on a subject). The word "Authority" with capital "A", refers to the governing body upon which such authority (with lower case "a") is vested; for example, the Puerto Rico Electric Power Authority or the Massachusetts Bay Transportation Authority.

AUTHORITY IN PHILOSOPHY

In government, *authority* is often used interchangeably with "power". However, their meanings differ: while "power" is defined as "the ability to influence somebody to do something that he/she would not have done", "authority" refers to a claim of legitimacy, the justification and right to exercise that power. For example, while a mob has the power to punish a criminal, for example by lynching, people who believe in the rule of law consider that only a court of law has the authority to punish a criminal.

Since the emergence of social sciences, authority has been a subject of research in a variety of empirical settings: the family (parental authority), small groups (informal authority of leadership), intermediate organizations, such as schools, churches, armies, industries and bureaucracies (organizational and bureaucratic authorities) and society-wide or inclusive organizations, ranging from the most primitive tribal society to the modern nation-state and intermediate organization (political authority). The definition of authority in contemporary social science is a matter of debate. According to Michaels, in the Encyclopaedia of Social Sciences, authority is the capacity, innate or acquired for exercising ascendancy over a group. Other scientists, however, argue that authority is not a capacity but a relationship. It is sanctioned power, institutionalized power.

In political philosophy, the jurisdiction of political authority, the location of sovereignty, the balancing of freedom and authority, and the requirements of political obligations have been core questions from Plato and Aristotle to the present. In many democratic societies, there is an ongoing discussion regarding the legitimate extent of governmental authority in general. In the United States, for instance, there is a widespread belief that the political system as it was instituted by the Founding Fathers should accord the populace as much freedom as reasonable, and that government should limit its authority accordingly.

In religion, there is a tendency to act in the belief that what will result will be different than what would have happened had a subservient act (*e.g.* prayer, meditation, service to others, etc.) not been performed- this is the essence of exercised authority.

What one does in expectation of meeting with the approval of the divine is derived from some means of obtained faith. The faith comes by being affected by the authoritative direction of the divine. Authoritative sources in religion communicate their direction through commandments and/or expressed approval of behaviour deemed to be acceptable or beneficial, with the expectation that the subject of this didactic process will use wisdom and understanding in their actions of service.

WEBER ON AUTHORITY

Max Weber, in his sociological and philosophical work, identified and distinguished three types of legitimate domination, that have sometimes been rendered in English translation as types of authority, because domination isn't seen as a political concept in the first place. Weber defined domination (authority) as the chance of commands being obeyed by a specifiable group of people.

Legitimate authority is that which is recognized as legitimate and justified by both the ruler and the ruled.

Weber divided legitimate authority into three types:

- The first type discussed by Weber is *Rational-legal authority*. It is that form of authority which depends for its legitimacy on formal rules and established laws of the state, which are usually written down and are often very complex. The power of the rational legal authority is mentioned in the constitution. Modern societies depend on legal-rational authority. Government officials are the best example of this form of authority, which is prevalent all over the world.
- The second type of authority is *Traditional authority*, which derives from long-established customs, habits and social structures. When power passes from one generation to another, then it is known as traditional authority. The right of hereditary monarchs to rule

furnishes an obvious example. The Tudor dynasty in England and the ruling families of Mewar, in Rajasthan (India) are some examples of traditional authority.

- The third form of authority is *Charismatic authority*. Here, the charisma of the individual or the leader plays an important role. Charismatic authority is that authority which is derived from "the gift of grace" or when the leader claims that his authority is derived from a "higher power" (*e.g.* God or natural law or rights) or "inspiration", that is superior to both the validity of traditional and rational-legal authority and followers accept this and are willing to follow this higher or inspired authority, in the place of the authority that they have hitherto been following. Examples in this regard can be NT Rama Rao, a matinee idol, who went on to become one of the most powerful Chief Ministers of Andhra Pradesh.

History has witnessed several social movements or revolutions, against a system of traditional or legal-rational authority, which are usually started by Charismatic authorities. Weber states that what distinguishes authority, from coercion, force and power on the one hand and leadership, persuasion and influence on the other hand, is legitimacy.

Superiors, he states, feel that they have a right to issue commands; subordinates perceive an obligation to obey. Social scientists agree that authority is but one of several resources available to incumbents in formal positions.

For example, a Head of State is dependent upon a similar nesting of authority. His legitimacy must be acknowledged, not just by citizens, but by those who control other valued resources: his immediate staff, his cabinet, military leaders and in the long run, the administration and political apparatus of the entire society.

- Authority can be created either expressly or by implication;
- Public entities act publicly, using the same means to communicate the grant of authority to their agents that they use to communicate this to third parties;
- Apparent authority describes the situation when a principal has placed restrictions on an agent that are not known to a third party;
- Restrictions on government agents are accomplished in the open, through laws and regulations;
- Everyone, including contractors, are supposed to know the laws and regulations of our government; and thus
- The concept of "apparent authority" is often inapt when dealing with the government, insofar as the only cognizable restrictions on the agent's authority are deemed known to third parties, shattering any appearance of authority.

AUTHORITY IN A LIBERAL DEMOCRATIC STATE

Every state has a number of institutions which exercise authority based on longstanding practices. Apart from this, every state sets up agencies which are competent in dealing with one particular matter. All this is set up within its charter. One example would be a port authority like the Port of London. They are usually created by special legislation and are run by a board of directors. Several agencies and institutions are created along the same lines and they exercise authority in certain matters. They are usually required to support themselves through property taxes or other forms of collection or fees for services.

7

The Concept of Rights

WHAT ARE RIGHTS

There are two types of right: Negative rights and Positive rights.

NEGATIVE RIGHTS

Put simply a negative right is the right to be left alone. Specifically it is the right to think and act free from the coercive force of others. Free from muggers, fraudsters and restrictive laws and taxes. A negative right is an absolute. Even the slightest violation breaks this right. Imagine that a man stops you in the street once a week and forces you to stand still for one minute - hardly a life changing violation - yet your right to be free of the coercion of others is being broken. The degree to which this right is violated changes from place to place but I know of no country where it is not routinely violated by the state.

Remember that a person cannot claim this right while violating the same in others. A mugger cannot claim a right to be left alone whilst mugging people.

The kind of society where this right is prevalent is a society whose government exists only to protect the individual from the force of others. The American Constitution and Bill of Rights are the closest examples - which, sadly, modern day America is abandoning daily.

POSITIVE RIGHTS

These are rights to something. A right to food, to health care, to education - whatever. The reality of a positive right is that whatever the object of the right is, it needs to be created before the 'right' can be fulfilled. This creates an obligation upon others to create it and it is the basis for slave societies and statist dictatorhips.

In the UK positive rights exist and each person who is taxed and restricted via legislation into providing the object of the right is working a proportion of his/her life as a slave. This may seem a bit extreme, but it isnt. Unless you agree entirely with your payment of every tax and everything the government then spends your money on, you are being forced to work for ends you have *not* given your consent to - just like a slave. Slavery was outlawed, but it crept back under the guise of the 'public good'.

The reason most people tolerate, or even give apathetic support to it, is because they are not thinking about which principles are being abandoned and which of their own rights they are giving up by doing so. Many people find the costs of obeying restricitive laws and paying 50 per cent in tax irritating but, amazingly, no more than that. "Its not all that bad!" They might say - I would suggest turning back the tide of controls and restrictions now before it is terribly bad - it has happened in other countries, however naively you might imagine "it cant happen here". The answer is to ask, whenever some new scheme is proposed by the government, "at whose expense?" and you will find that the expense is your freedom.

WHERE DO RIGHTS COME FROM?

A common question asked of political rights is where do they come from and how are they granted. There are several different justifications for the inclusion of rights in a constitutional system. These vary slightly depending on how the political philosophy views the individual. Since the enlightenment focused social endeavour on individual autonomy as the primary source, the notion of universal political rights have risen. This is present in republicanism, liberalism, libertarianism and progressivism. All these political philosophies focus on the individual as the dominant political entity.

Republicanism views the purpose of government as ensuring the liberty of the individual. Tyranny or despotism has no place in a republican system. The rights or just demands of an individual's agreeance to follow the will of the majority in a government system come with the assurance of freedom from tyranny or arbitrary government.

A bill of rights becomes a political technology that ensures the liberty of the individual and describes tyranny. It creates a sphere of exclusion for government that it cannot legislate over.

Dan Deniehy took a natural rights view of republicanism. This describes moral perfection as the end result of human achievement, maturation and growth. Deniehy writes that tyranny and despotism are the dominant affliction against this purpose.

Consequently the tyranny becomes a crime against mankind's destiny - a crime against nature. This is a non-religious argument for natural rights. The religious argument for natural rights is quite simply that rights are granted by God. This is less sophisticated than Deniehy's argument and reliant on faith.

Progressives view rights as an intrinsic function of being human. For this reason they are often called Human Rights by the progressive movement. The progressives view rights as being greater than the simply eradication of tyranny and protection of liberty as republicans do and often include more ambiguous rights of a social nature such as the right to dignity or the right to education.

These are fine principles to maintain, however, they do not have a place in a constitutional document as they are nearly impossible to quantify. For instance writing brutally explicit language on the right to dignity is impossible.

Libertarians view rights in terms of the intrinsic value of the individual. This philosophy often terms them individual rights. Libertarianism does not have the same focus on tyranny as republicanism does and is merely interested in the primacy and dominance of the individual as a political being.

Of these justifications for rights I believe the republican definition to be superior. It is constitutionally achievable through explicit constitutional language and separation of powers.

The focus on the eradication of tyranny and political equity are important principles in democratic and representative systems.

Under republicanism rights are a very essential political technology which better serves the protection of liberty from arbitrary government.

FUNDAMENTAL RIGHTS AND DUTIES

FUNDAMENTAL RIGHTS

Fundamental Rights are provided to the citizens by the Constitution of India. The Fundamental Rights and Duties are among the vital sections of the Constitution and prescribe the fundamental obligations of the state to its citizens and the duties of the citizens to the state. These are the essential elements of the Constitution and they were developed by the Constituent Assembly of India between 1947 and 1949. Part III of the Constitution of India describes the Fundamental Rights offered to the country`s citizens. Fundamental Rights are essential human rights that can are offered to every citizen irrespective of caste, race, creed, place of birth, religion or gender. Fundamental Rights are subjected to specific restrictions and enforceable by courts. These are equal to freedoms and these rights are essential for personal good and the society at large.

Fundamental Rights are preserved as they guarantee civil liberties to all the citizens of the country for a calm and pleasant life. These are individual rights and comprise freedom of speech and expression, freedom to practice religion, equality before law, freedom of association and peaceful assembly and the right to constitutional remedies for the safeguard of civil rights by means of writs such as habeas corpus. The concept of providing the fundamental rights to the citizens has been taken from the England`s Bill of Rights; United States Bill of Rights and also France`s Declaration of the Rights of Man. Anyone who is violating the fundamental rights will face punishments in the court of law.

The Constitution of India guarantees six Fundamental Rights to the citizens. Right to Equality is the foremost right guaranteed to the citizens of India. It is provided in Articles 14, 15, 16, 17 and 18 of the Constitution. This right is regarded as the principal foundation of all other rights and liberties. The Right to Equality guarantees equality before law as per which citizens shall be equally protected by the laws of the country. Article 15 of the constitution states that there will be social equality and equal accessibility to public areas and no person shall be discriminated on the basis of caste, religion and language. Equality in matters of public employment is provided in Article 16 of the Constitution of India that defines that all citizens can apply for government. Article 17 puts forth abolition of untouchability. The practice of untouchability is an offence and anyone found doing so is punishable by law. Abolition of titles is another right to equality described by the Article 18 of the constitution. It forbids the state from conferring any titles to the citizens of India. Among the Fundamental Rights, right to freedom is included in the Articles 19, 20, 21 and 22. Right to freedom includes Freedom of speech and expression, Freedom to assemble peacefully without arms, Freedom to form associations or unions and freedom to move freely throughout the territory of India. Furthermore, Right to freedom also states that citizens have the Freedom to reside and settle in any part of the territory of India and also have the Freedom to practice any profession or to carry on any occupation, trade or business. However, subject to reasonable restrictions by the State in the interest of the general public certain safeguards are envisaged to protect the citizens from exploitation and coercion.

Right against exploitation is another essential among the Fundamental Rights. This right is given in the Articles 23 and 24. It provides for two provisions such as abolition of trafficking in human beings and forced labour. The right also lays down abolition of employment of children below the age of 14 years in dangerous jobs like factories and mines. Right to freedom of religion is included under articles 25, 26, 27 and 28. It provides religious freedom to all citizens of India and sustains the principle of secularism in India. The Constitution provides that all religions are equal before the state and no religion shall be given preference over the other. Citizens are free to preach, practice and propagate any religion of their choice.

Fundamental Rights also provided Cultural and educational rights to its citizens and it is covered in Articles 29 and 30. According to this right any community which has a language and a script of its own has the right to conserve and develop them. No citizen can be discriminated against for admission in state aided institutions. All minorities, religious or linguistic, can set up their own educational institutions in order to preserve and develop their own culture. Right to constitutional remedies is also provided in the Constitution. This right authorises the citizens to move a court of law in case of any denial of the fundamental rights. The courts can issue various kinds of writs and these writs are such as habeas corpus, mandamus, prohibition, quo warranto and certiorari. These writs help preserving and safeguarding the fundamental rights of the citizens of India. Another prominent among the Fundamental Rights was the Right to property.

Right to property in order to guarantee to all citizens the right to acquire hold and dispose off property. However, the 44th Amendment Act of 1978 removed the right to property from the list of Fundamental Rights. Article 300-A, was added to the Constitution which provided that 'no person shall be deprived of his property save by authority of law.' Fundamental rights are the freedoms that are given to the country`s citizens. They help in protecting as well as preventing gross violations of human rights. They give emphasis to fundamental unity of the country by guaranteeing the access and use of the same facilities, irrespective of caste, colour, creed and religion to all citizens. The fundamental rights were provided primarily to protect individuals from any arbitrary state actions, but some rights are enforceable against individuals. Only through a constitutional amendment, the Fundamental Rights can be altered. In addition to that during national and state emergency, the Fundamental Rights remain suspended.

FUNDAMENTAL DUTIES

Fundamental Duties of India are guaranteed by the Constitution of India in Part IV. These fundamental duties are identified as the moral obligations that actually help in upholding the spirit of nationalism as well as to support the harmony of the nation. These duties are designed concerning the individuals and the nation. However, these fundamental duties are not legally enforceable. Furthermore, the citizens are morally obligated by the Constitution to perform these duties.

These Fundamental Duties were added by the 42nd Amendment Act in 1976. Article 51-A of the Constitution provides ten Fundamental Duties of the citizen. These duties can be classified accordingly as relating to the environment, duties towards the state and the nation and also towards self. However, the fundamental duties are non-justiciable, and the main purpose of incorporating is to encourage the sense of patriotism among the country`s citizens. The international instruments such as the Universal Declaration of Human Rights and International Covenant on Civil and Political Rights include reference of such fundamental duties. These Fundamental Duties are such commitments that expand to the citizens as well as the state at large. According to the Fundamental Duties all the citizens should respect the national symbols as well as the Constitution of the country. The fundamental duties of the land also intend to uphold the right of equality of all individuals, defend the environment and the public property, to build up scientific temper, to disown violence, to struggle towards excellence and to offer compulsory education. In addition, the 11th Fundamental Duty of the country was added in the year 2002 by the 86th Constitutional Amendment. It states that 'every citizen who is a parent or guardian, to offer opportunities for education to his child or, as the case may be, ward between the age of six and 14 years.'

Fundamental Duties of India are as follows:

- To abide by the Constitution and respect its ideals and institutions, the National Flag and the National Anthem;
- To cherish and follow the noble ideals which inspired our national struggle for freedom;
- To uphold and protect the sovereignty, unity and integrity of India;
- To defend the country and render national service when called upon to do so;
- To promote harmony and the spirit of common brotherhood amongst all the people of India transcending religious, linguistic and regional or sectional diversities; to renounce practices derogatory to the dignity of women;
- To value and preserve the rich heritage of our composite culture;
- To protect and improve the natural environment including forests, lakes, rivers and wild life, and to have compassion for living creatures;
- To develop the scientific temper, humanism and the spirit of enquiry and reform;
- To safeguard public property and to abjure violence;
- To strive towards excellence in all spheres of individual and collective activity so that the nation constantly rises to higher levels of endeavour and achievement.

LEGAL RIGHTS AND THE STATE

While claims for human rights appeal to our moral self, the degree of success of such appeals depends on a number of factors, most important of which is the support of governments and the law. This is why so much importance is placed on the legal recognition of rights.

A Bill of Rights is enshrined in the constitutions of many countries. Constitutions represent the highest law of the land and so constitutional recognition of certain rights gives them a primary importance. In our country we call them Fundamental Rights. Other laws and policies are supposed to respect the rights granted in the Constitution. The rights mentioned in the Constitution would be those which are considered to be of basic importance. In some cases these may be supplemented by claims which gain importance because of the particular history and customs of a country. In India, for instance, we have a provision to ban untouchability which draws attention to a traditional social practice in the country.

So important is the legal and constitutional recognition of our claims that several theorists define rights as claims that are recognised by the state. The legal endorsement certainly gives our rights a special status in society but it is not the basis on which rights are claimed. As we discussed earlier, rights have steadily been expanded and reinterpreted to include previously excluded groups and to reflect our contemporary understanding of what it means to lead a life of dignity and respect.

However, in most cases the claimed rights are directed towards the state. That is, through these rights people make demands upon the state. When I assert my right to education, I call upon the state to make provisions for my basic education. Society may also accept the importance of education and contribute to it on its own. Different groups may open schools and fund scholarships so that children of all classes can get the benefit of education. But the primarily responsibility rests upon the state. It is the state that must initiate necessary steps to ensure that my right to education is fulfilled.

Thus, rights place an obligation upon the state to act in certain kinds of ways. Each right indicates what the state must do as well as what it must not do. For instance, my right to life obliges the state to make laws that protect me from injury by others. It calls upon the state to punish those who hurt me or harm me. If a society feels that the right to life means a right to a good quality of life, it expects the state to pursue policies that provide for clean environment along with other conditions that may be necessary for a healthy life. In other words, my right here places certain obligations upon the state to act in a certain way.

Rights not only indicate what the state must do, they also suggest what the state must refrain from doing. My right to liberty as a person, for instance, suggests that the state can not simply arrest me at its own will. If it wishes to put me behind bars it must defend that action; it must give reasons for curtailing my liberty before a judicial court. This is why the police are required to produce an arrest warrant before taking me away. My rights thus place certain constraints upon state actions.

To put it another way, our rights ensure that the authority of the state is exercised without violating the sanctity of individual life and liberty. The state may be the sovereign authority; the laws it makes may be enforced with force, but the sovereign state exists not for its own sake but for the sake of the individual. It is people who matter more and it is their well-being that must be pursued by the government in power. The rulers are accountable for their actions and must not forget that law exists to ensure the good of the people.

KINDS OF RIGHTS

Most democracies today begin by drawing up a charter of political rights. Political rights give to the citizens the right to equality before law and the right to participate in the political process. They include such rights as the right to vote and elect representatives, the right to contest elections, the right to form political parties or join them.

Political rights are supplemented by civil liberties. The latter refers to the right to a free and fair trial, the right to express one's views freely, the right to protest and express dissent. Collectively, civil liberties and political rights form the basis of a democratic system of government. But, rights aim to protect the well-being of the individual. Political rights contribute to it by making the government accountable to the people, by giving greater importance to the concerns of the individual over that of the rulers and by ensuring that all persons have an opportunity to influence the decisions of the government.

However, our rights of political participation can only be exercised fully when our basic needs, of food, shelter, clothing, health, are met. For a person living on the pavements and struggling to meet these basic needs, political rights by themselves have little value. They require certain facilities like an adequate wage to meet their basic needs and reasonable conditions of work. Hence democratic societies are beginning to recognise these obligations and providing economic rights.

In some countries, citizens, particularly those with low incomes, receive housing and medical facilities from the state; in others, unemployed persons receive a certain minimum wage so that they can meet their basic needs. In India the government has recently introduced a rural employment guarantee scheme, among other measures to help the poor. Today, in addition to political and economic rights more and more democracies are recognising the cultural claims of their citizens. The right to have primary education in one's mother tongue, the right to establish institutions for teaching one's language and culture, are today recognised as being necessary for leading a good life. The list of rights has thus steadily increased in democracies. While some rights, primarily the right to life, liberty, equal treatment, and the right to political participation are seen as basic rights that must receive priority, other conditions that are necessary for leading a decent life, are being recognised as justified claims or rights.

Rights not only place obligations upon the state to act in a certain way — for instance, to ensure sustainable development — but they also place obligations upon each of us. Firstly, they compel us to think not just of our own personal needs and interests but to defend some things as being good for all of us. Protecting the ozone layer, minimising air and water pollution, maintaining the green cover by planting new trees and preventing cutting down of forests, maintaining the ecological balance, are things that are essential for all of us. They represent the 'common-good' that we must act to protect for ourselves as well as for the future generations who are entitled to inherit a safe and clean world without which they cannot lead a reasonably good life.

Secondly, they require that I respect the rights of others. If I say that I must be given the right to express my views I must also grant the same right to others. If I do not want others to interfere in the choices I make — the dress

I wear or the music I listen to — I must refrain from interfering in the choices that others make. I must leave them free to choose their music and clothes. I cannot use the right to free speech to incite a crowd to kill my neighbour. In exercising my rights, I cannot deprive others of their rights. My rights are, in other words, limited by the principle of equal and same rights for all.

Thirdly, we must balance our rights when they come into conflict. For instance, my right to freedom of expression allows me to take pictures; however, if I take pictures of a person bathing in his house without his consent and post them on the internet, that would be a violation of his right to privacy.

Fourthly, citizens must be vigilant about limitations which may be placed on their rights. A currently debated topic concerns the increased restrictions which many government are imposing on the civil liberties of citizens on the grounds of national security. Protecting national security may be defended as necessary for safeguarding the rights and well being of citizens.

But at what point could the restrictions imposed as necessary for security themselves become a threat to the rights of people? Should a country facing the threat of terrorist bombings be allowed to curtail the liberty of citizens? Should it be allowed to arrest people on mere suspicion? Should it be allowed to intercept their mail or tap their phones? Should it be allowed to use torture to extract confession?

In such situations the question to ask is whether the person concerned poses an imminent threat to society. Even arrested persons should be allowed legal counsel and the opportunity to present their case before a magistrate or a court of law. We need to be extremely cautious about giving governments powers which could be used to curtail the civil liberties of individuals for such powers can be misused.

Governments can become authoritarian and undermine the very reasons for which governments exist — namely, the well being of the members of the state. Hence, even though rights can never be absolute, we need to be vigilant in protecting our rights and those of others for they form the basis of a democratic society.

8

The Concept of Justice

Justice is a concept of moral rightness based on ethics, rationality, law, natural law, religion, or equity, along with the punishment of the breach of said ethics; justice is the act of being just and/or fair.

Most contemporary theories of justice, it is overwhelmingly important: John Rawls claims that "Justice is the first virtue of social institutions, as truth is of systems of thought." Justice can be thought of as distinct from and more fundamental than benevolence, charity, mercy, generosity or compassion. Justice has traditionally been associated with concepts of fate, reincarnation or Divine Providence, *i.e.* with a life in accordance with the cosmic plan. The association of justice with fairness has thus been historically and culturally rare and is perhaps chiefly a modern innovation.

Studies at UCLA in 2008 have indicated that reactions to fairness are "wired" into the brain and that, "Fairness is activating the same part of the brain that responds to food in rats... This is consistent with the notion that being treated fairly satisfies a basic need". Research conducted in 2003 at Emory University, Georgia, USA, involving Capuchin Monkeys demonstrated that other cooperative animals also possess such a sense and that "inequity aversion may not be uniquely human." indicating that ideas of fairness and justice may be instinctual in nature.

VARIATIONS OF JUSTICE

- *Utilitarianism* is a form of consequentialism, where punishment is forward-looking. Justified by the ability to achieve future social benefits resulting in crime reduction, the moral worth of an action is determined by its outcome.
- *Retributive justice* regulates proportionate response to crime proven by lawful evidence, so that punishment is justly imposed and considered as morally correct and fully deserved. The law of *retaliation* is a military theory of retributive justice, which says that reciprocity should be equal to the wrong suffered; "life for life, wound for wound, stripe for stripe."

- *Restorative justice* is concerned not so much with retribution and punishment as with making the victim whole and reintegrating the offender into society. This approach frequently brings an offender and a victim together, so that the offender can better understand the effect his/her offence had on the victim.
- *Distributive justice* is directed at the proper allocation of things — wealth, power, reward, respect — among different people.

UNDERSTANDINGS OF JUSTICE

Understandings of justice differ in every culture, as cultures are usually dependent upon a shared history, mythology and/or religion. Each culture's ethics create values which influence the notion of justice. Although there can be found some justice principles that are one and the same in all or most of the cultures, these are insufficient to create a unitary justice apprehension.

JUSTICE AS HARMONY

In his dialogue *Republic*, Plato uses Socrates to argue for justice that covers both the just person and the just City State. Justice is a proper, harmonious relationship between the warring parts of the person or city. Hence Plato's definition of justice is that justice is the having and doing of what is one's own. A just man is a man in just the right place, doing his best and giving the precise equivalent of what he has received. This applies both at the individual level and at the universal level.

A person's soul has three parts–reason, spirit and desire. Similarly, a city has three parts–Socrates uses the parable of the chariot to illustrate his point: a chariot works as a whole because the two horses' power is directed by the charioteer. Lovers of wisdom–philosophers, in one sense of the term–should rule because only they understand what is good. If one is ill, one goes to a doctor rather than a psychologist, because the doctor is expert in the subject of health.

Similarly, one should trust one's city to an expert in the subject of the good, not to a mere politician who tries to gain power by giving people what they want, rather than what's good for them. Socrates uses the parable of the ship to illustrate this point: the unjust city is like a ship in open ocean, crewed by a powerful but drunken captain, a group of untrustworthy advisors who try to manipulate the captain into giving them power over the ship's course and a navigator who is the only one who knows how to get the ship to port. For Socrates, the only way the ship will reach its destination–the good–is if the navigator takes charge.

Justice as Divine Command

Justice as a divine law is commanding, and indeed the whole of morality, is the authoritative command. Killing is wrong and therefore must be punished and if not punished what should be done? A famous paradox called the Euthyphro dilemma essentially asks: is something right because God commands it, or does God command it because it's right? If the former, then justice is arbitrary; if the latter, then morality exists on a higher order than God, who becomes little more than a passer-on of moral knowledge. Some Divine command advocates respond by saying that the dilemma is false: goodness is the very nature of God and is necessarily expressed in His commands. Another response is that the laws and moral principles are objective and self evident in nature. God embodies these laws and is therefore neither higher nor lower than the law. He sets an example for the good people among men to follow His way and also become an embodiment of the highest principles and morals.

Justice as Natural Law

For advocates of the theory that justice is part of natural law, it involves the system of consequences that naturally derives from any action or choice. In this, it is similar to the laws of physics: in the same way as the Third of Newton's laws of Motion requires that for every action there must be an equal and opposite reaction, justice requires just as individuals or groups what they actually deserve, merit, or are entitled to. Justice, on this account, is a universal and absolute concept: laws, principles, religions, etc., are merely attempts to codify that concept, sometimes with results that entirely contradict the true nature of justice.

Justice as Human Creation

In contrast to the understandings canvassed so far, justice may be understood as a human *creation*, rather than a *discovery* of harmony, divine command, or natural law. This claim can be understood in a number of ways, with the fundamental division being between those who argue that justice is the creation of *some* humans, and those who argue that it is the creation of *all* humans.

Justice as Trickery

In *Republic* by Plato, the character Thrasymachus argues that justice is the interest of the strong—merely a name for what the powerful or cunning ruler has imposed on the people.

Justice as Mutual Agreement

Thinkers in the social contract tradition, justice is derived from the mutual agreement of everyone concerned; or, in many versions, from what they would agree to under *hypothetical* conditions including equality and absence of bias.

Justice as a Subordinate Value

The utilitarian thinkers including John Stuart Mill, justice is not as fundamental as we often think. Rather, it is derived from the more basic standard of rightness, consequentialism: what is right is what has the best consequences. So, the proper principles of justice are those that tend to have the best consequences. These rules may turn out to be familiar ones such as keeping contracts; but equally, they may not, depending on the facts about real consequences. Either way, what is important is those consequences, and justice is important, if at all, only as derived from that fundamental standard.

Mill tries to explain our mistaken belief that justice is overwhelmingly important by arguing that it derives from two natural human tendencies: our desire to retaliate against those who hurt us, and our ability to put ourselves imaginatively in another's place. So, when we see someone harmed, we project ourselves into her situation and feel a desire to retaliate on her behalf. If this process is the source of our feelings about justice, that ought to undermine our confidence in them.

THEORIES OF DISTRIBUTIVE JUSTICE

Theories of distributive justice need to answer three questions:

1. *What goods* are to be distributed? Is it to be wealth, power, respect, some combination of these things?
2. *Between what entities* are they to be distributed? Humans, sentient beings, the members of a single society, nations?
3. What is the *proper* distribution? Equal, meritocratic, just as to social status, just as to need, based on property rights and non-aggression?

Distributive justice theorists generally do not answer questions of *who has the right* to enforce a particular favoured distribution. On the other hand, property rights theorists argue that there is no "favoured distribution." Rather, distribution should be based simply on whatever distribution results from non-coerced interactions or transactions. This section describes some widely held theories of distributive justice, and their attempts to answer these questions.

EGALITARIANISM

The egalitarian, justice can only exist within the coordinates of equality. This basic view can be elaborated in many different ways, just as to what goods are to be distributed—wealth, respect, opportunity—and what they are to be distributed equally between—individuals, families, nations, races, species. Commonly held egalitarian positions include demands for equality of opportunity and for equality of outcome. It affirms that freedom and justice without equality are hollow and that equality itself is the highest justice.

At a cultural level, egalitarian theories have developed in sophistication and acceptance during the past two hundred years. Among the notable broadly egalitarian philosophies are socialism, communism, anarchism, left-libertarianism, and progressivism, all of which propound economic, political, and legal egalitarianism, respectively. Several egalitarian ideas enjoy wide support among intellectuals and in the general populations of many countries. Whether any of these ideas have been significantly implemented in practice, however, remains a controversial question. One argument is that liberalism provides democracy with the experience of civic reformism. Without it, democracy loses any tie per centargumentative or practical per centto a coherent design of public policy endeavoring to provide the resources for the realization of democratic citizenship.

Giving People What They Deserve

In one sense, all theories of distributive justice claim that everyone should get what they deserve. Theories disagree on the basis for deserving. The main distinction is between theories that argue the basis of just deserts is held equally by everyone, and therefore derive egalitarian accounts of distributive justice—and theories that argue the basis of just deserts is unequally distributed on the basis of, for instance, hard work, and therefore derive accounts of distributive justice by which some should have more than others. This section deals with some popular theories of the second type.

M*eritocratic* theories, goods, especially wealth and social status, should be distributed to match individual *merit*, which is usually understood as some combination of talent and hard work. *Needs*-based theories, goods, especially such basic goods as food, shelter and medical care, should be distributed to meet individuals' basic needs for them. Marxism can be regarded as a needs-based theory on some readings of Marx's slogan "from each just as to his ability, to each just as to his need". *Contribution*-based theories, goods should be distributed to match an individual's contribution to the overall social good.

Fairness

In his *A Theory of Justice*, John Rawls used a social contract argument to show that justice, and especially distributive justice, is a form of fairness: an *impartial* distribution of goods. Rawls asks us to imagine ourselves behind a *veil of ignorance* that denies us all knowledge of our personalities, social statuses, moral characters, wealth, talents and life plans, and then asks what theory of justice we would choose to govern our society when the veil is lifted, if we wanted to do the best that we could for ourselves. We don't know who in particular we are, and therefore can't bias the decision in our own favour.

So, the decision-in-ignorance models fairness, because it excludes selfish bias. Rawls argues that each of us would reject the utilitarian theory of justice that we should maximize welfare because of the risk that we might turn out to be someone whose own good is sacrificed for greater benefits for others.

Instead, we would endorse Rawls's two principles of justice:

1. Each person is to have an equal right to the most extensive total

system of equal basic liberties compatible with a similar system of liberty for all.

2. Social and economic inequalities are to be arranged so that they are both
   - To the greatest benefit of the least advantaged, consistent with the just savings principle, and
   - Attached to offices and positions open to all under conditions of fair equality of opportunity.

This imagined choice justifies these principles as the principles of justice for us, because we would agree to them in a fair decision procedure. Rawls's theory distinguishes two kinds of goods –liberties and social and economic goods, *i.e.* wealth, income and power–and applies different distributions to them–equality between citizens for, equality unless inequality improves the position of the worst off for.

Property Rights (Non-Coercion)/Having the Right History

Robert Nozick's influential critique of Rawls argues that distributive justice is not a matter of the whole distribution matching an ideal *pattern*, but of each individual entitlement having the right kind of *history*.

It is just that a person has some good if and only if they came to have it by a history made up entirely of events of two kinds:

1. Just *acquisition*, especially by working on unowned things; and
2. Just *transfer*, that is free gift, sale or other agreement, but not theft.

If the chain of events leading up to the person having something meets this criterion, they are entitled to it: that they possess it is just, and what anyone else does or doesn't have or need is irrelevant.

On the basis of this theory of distributive justice, Nozick argues that all attempts to redistribute goods according to an ideal pattern, without the consent of their owners, are theft. In particular, redistributive taxation is theft.

Some property rights theorists also take a consequentialist view of distributive justice and argue that property rights based justice also has the effect of maximizing the overall wealth of an economic system. They explain that voluntary transactions always have a property called pareto efficiency. A pareto efficient transaction is one where at least one party ends up better off and neither party ends up worse off. The result is that the world is better off in an absolute sense and no one is worse off. Such consequentialist property rights theorists argue that respecting property rights maximizes the number of pareto efficient transactions in the world and minimized the number of non-pareto efficient transactions in the world. The result is that the world will have generated the greatest total benefit from the limited, scarce resources available in the world. Further, this will have been accomplished without taking anything away from anyone by coercion.

Welfare-Maximization

The utilitarian, justice requires the maximization of the total or average welfare across all relevant individuals. This may require sacrifice of some for the good of others, so long as everyone's good is taken impartially into account. Utilitarianism, in general, argues that the standard of justification for actions, institutions, or the whole world, is *impartial welfare consequentialism*, and only indirectly, if at all, to do with rights, property, need, or any other non-utilitarian criterion.

These other criteria might be indirectly important, to the extent that human welfare involves them. But even then, such demands as human rights would only be elements in the calculation of overall welfare, not uncrossable barriers to action.

THEORIES OF RETRIBUTIVE JUSTICE

Theories of retributive justice are concerned with punishment for wrongdoing, and need to answer three questions:

1. *Why* punish?
2. *Who* should be punished?
3. *What punishment* should they receive?

This section considers the two major accounts of retributive justice, and their answers to these questions. *Utilitarian* theories look forward to the future consequences of punishment, while *retributive* theories look back to particular acts of wrongdoing, and attempt to balance them with deserved punishment.

UTILITARIANISM

The utilitarian, as already noted, justice requires the maximization of the total or average welfare across all relevant individuals. Punishment is bad treatment of someone, and therefore can't be good *in itself*, for the utilitarian.

But punishment might be a necessary sacrifice that maximizes the overall good in the long term, in one or more of three ways:

1. *Deterrence*. The credible threat of punishment might lead people to make different choices; well-designed threats might lead people to make choices that maximize welfare.
2. *Rehabilitation*. Punishment might make bad people into better ones. For the utilitarian, all that 'bad person' can mean is 'person who's likely to cause bad things'. So, utilitarianism could recommend punishment that changes someone such that they are less likely to cause bad things.
3. *Security/Incapacitation*. Perhaps there are people who are irredeemable causers of bad things. If so, imprisoning them might maximize welfare by limiting their opportunities to cause harm and therefore the benefit lies within protecting society.

So, the reason for punishment is the maximization of welfare, and punishment should be of whomever, and of whatever form and severity, are needed to meet that goal. Worryingly, this may sometimes justify punishing the innocent, or inflicting disproportionately severe punishments, when that will have the best consequences overall. It also suggests that punishment might turn out *never* to be right, depending on the facts about what actual consequences it has.

Retributivism

The retributivist will think the utilitarian's argument disastrously mistaken. If someone does something wrong, we must respond to it, and to him or her, as an individual, not as a part of a calculation of overall welfare. To do otherwise is to disrespect him or her as an individual human being. If the crime had victims, it is to disrespect them, too. Wrongdoing must be balanced or made good in some way, and so the criminal *deserves* to be punished.

Retributivism emphasizes retribution–payback–rather than maximization of welfare. Like the theory of distributive justice as giving everyone what they deserve, it links justice with desert. It says that all guilty people, and only guilty people, deserve appropriate punishment. This matches some strong intuitions about just punishment: that it should be *proportional* to the crime, and that it should be of *only* and *all of* the guilty.

However, it is sometimes argued that retributivism is merely revenge in disguise. Despite this criticism, there are numerous differences between retribution and revenge: the former is impartial, has a scale of appropriateness and corrects a moral wrong, whereas the latter is personal, unlimited in scale, and often corrects a slight.

Restorative Justice

Restorative justice is an approach to justice that focuses on the needs of victims and offenders, instead of satisfying abstract legal principles or punishing the offender. Victims take an active role in the process, while offenders are encouraged to take responsibility for their actions, "to repair the harm they've done—by apologizing, returning stolen money, or community service". It is based on a theory of justice that considers crime and wrongdoing to be an offence against an individual or community rather than the state. Restorative justice that fosters dialogue between victim and offender shows the highest rates of victim satisfaction and offender accountability.

Mixed Theories

Some modern philosophers have argued that Utilitarian and Retributive theories are not mutually exclusive. For example, Andrew Von Hirsch, in his 1976 book Doing Justice, suggested that we have a moral obligation to punish greater crimes more than lesser ones. However, so long as we adhere to that constraint then utilitarian ideals would play a significant secondary role.

INSTITUTIONS

In a world where people are interconnected but they disagree, institutions are required to instantiate ideals of justice. These institutions may be justified by their approximate instantiation of justice, or they may be deeply unjust when compared with ideal standards — consider the institution of slavery. Justice is an ideal the world fails to live up to, sometimes despite good intentions, sometimes disastrously. The question of institutive justice raises issues of legitimacy, procedure, codification and interpretation, which are considered by legal theorists and by philosophers of law.

Another definition of justice is an independent investigation of truth. In a court room, lawyers, the judge and the jury are supposed to be independently investigating the truth of an alleged crime. In physics, a group of physicists examine data and theoretical concepts to consult on what might be the truth or reality of a phenomenon.

JUST DISTRIBUTION

How goods are justly to be distributed among members of a society is among the primary concerns of any government. Redistribution via taxation is generally seen as necessary; but to what extent wealth should be redistributed is controversial.

A further problem is that once wealth has been redistributed justly it will not remain in that just distribution. People will buy and sell goods, earn and squander wealth. Does this mean that in order to maintain a just distribution of wealth we must continuously redistribute it?

One theory is that any distribution of goods that derives from an initial just distribution via just transfers must itself be just. A particular distribution may be unequal, but if wealth was once distributed fairly, and if all transactions were freely entered into, then that inequality will be warranted; there will be no need to correct it.

JOHN RAWLS' THEORY OF JUSTICE

Social and political theories are philosophically justified through human nature because it provides the moral component to the concept of justice. Justice is a concept that is balanced between law and morality. Laws can be used for the good or bad of a nation's citizens. Those that support citizens and create and promote social harmony are considered just. The good of a citizen and social harmony, however, can be accounted for in different ways, most of which depend on the account of human nature that a theory uses. Rawls defends his account of justice as fairness by utilizing the family. Rawls's hypothetical model of human nature generates the principles of justice that are supposed to represent the moral basis of political government. His original defence of this position is in *A Theory of Justice.* These principles, humans need liberty and freedom to pursue their interests as long as they do not harm others. People accomplish happiness by freely pursuing interests within a supportive society. Rawls is considered to be a liberal political philosopher because of his argument that every citizen deserves the same opportunities to succeed as every other citizen. I will discuss Rawls's argument for justice as "fairness" in society and the family. I will begin with the two principles of justice that Rawls generated from his model. I will then briefly explain Rawls's defence of democratic equality, which he thinks is chosen by the principles.

Then, I will present a criticism that Susan Moller Okin makes against Rawls's model. I will present the main reasons why she argues against Rawls's hypothetical approach to justice. In conclusion, I will present Leonard Choptiany's criticism of Rawls's view and how it supports Okin's position.

Rawls argues that his principles of justice should be used to assess the justice of actual social institutions, such as political governments, that govern human beings. Rawls bases these principles on his argument that a certain form of justice is essential to human flourishing. Rawls, human beings have specific, clearly defined, characteristics that must be accounted for in any theory of justice.

He argues that his theory best captures these characteristics and generates a resource for evaluating real social institutions. Rawls belongs to a philosophical tradition called social contract theory. In general, this tradition uses a model of human nature to argue for a position on the concept of justice, how it should be met and how it should be enforced. The model is created by first clarifying the human features that must be met by the theory.

The model arrives at conclusions about justice by showing that humans with the features would agree to obey and enforce the rules of governance that emerge from the model. Rawls's theory, however, differs from traditional theories like John Locke's or Thomas Hobbes's. This is because Rawls makes it very clear that his model is a hypothetical model used for the purposes of generating conclusions specific to the concept of justice and nothing else. Rawls calls this "justice as fairness."

Fairness occurs when a society insures that each citizen is treated equally in the eyes of the law and is given equal opportunity to succeed in a socially balanced life of his or her own choosing. To contrast a model that captures "justice as fairness," Rawls imagines a hypothetical situation in which no one has any arbitrary advantage over anyone else. He calls this situation "the original position." The decision makers in this position are behind a "veil of ignorance," which means that they know nothing about who or what they are in real life. Rawls's original position creates a hypothetical state of equality that stops decision-makers from choosing principles that may arbitrarily favour a person in the decision-maker's station in life. Rawls explains that,

- No one knows his or her place in society; no one knows her or his class position or social status; no one knows what abilities or handicaps he or she will have; and no one knows her or his conception of the good or his or her psychological tendencies.

These conditions create a "veil of ignorance." People cannot know their status in society. This ensures that whatever the rules are that people pick, they will apply equally to everyone and neither favour nor disadvantage anyone. Perfect equality would be an outcome of this veil of ignorance. Furthermore, principles of justice are the principles that rational and free persons concerned to further their own interests would accept in an initial position of equality as defining the fundamentals of the terms of their association.

The original position and the veil of ignorance are supposed to mirror a level of the playing field where everyone has an equal chance to win. The rules of association are like the rules of fair play, which each player must play and be judged by. Rawls argues that there are two distinctive principles that those behind the veil of ignorance would accept as governing principles in their decision-making.

The original position supports two principles which would regulate the distribution of social and economic advantages across society. The first principle states that, "Each person is to have an equal right to the most extensive basic liberty compatible with a similar liberty for others." The second principle states that, Social and economic qualities are to be arranged so that they are both reasonably expected to be to everyone's advantage and attached to positions and offices open to all..."

These principles apply to the basic structure of society. They regulate the rights and duties that citizens can fairly have through the distribution of social and economic advantages. Power relationships and economic classes would be based primarily on fairness, with a sensitivity to the fair use of talent and fair assessment of need. The first principle determines basic rights that we should naturally retain such as the political liberties, to vote or run for office, to own property and to have free speech. The ability for humans to flourish as productive autonomous creatures requires that these liberties be a protected part of their basic existence. The second principle describes the fair distribution of income and wealth and the fair design of organizations. Everyone would have the same chance to work, build wealth, and govern in public office without the prerequisite of wealth or power. The only prerequisite would be knowledge and skill. Rawls states that,

- While the distribution of wealth and income need not be equal, it must be to everyone's advantage, and at the same time, positions of authority must be accessible to all.

Rawls sees that economic barriers are some of the main sources of social injustice. These barriers prevent people from securing the education needed for competing in the job market. They can also stop people from entering public office, where they may make innovative contributions to the development of society. Protecting the basic rights of individuals as well as ensuring that they have a chance to compete fairly for jobs and public offices promotes advances in all the areas that contribute to human flourishing. Fair play in a state is important to its stability.

Fairness, in the form of the two principles, ensures that people have the chance to create a life for themselves if they are willing to work for it. Merit and ones contribution to society then becomes the basis of one's worth in society, both personal and social. No citizen, in turn, would have a legitimate reason to criticize or undermine the social institutions or rules that support such circumstances. Rawls, the rational person would be a supportive and law-abiding citizen.

A society filled with such persons would be stable. Once Rawls argues for the two principles of justice, he uses them to evaluate different types of political governments: natural liberty, natural aristocracy, liberal equality and democratic equality. He uses the principles of justice to show that three of the four fall short of promoting justice as fairness in one or more of the aspects outlined in the two principles. Only democratic equality fulfills the principle of justice.

Democratic equality guarantees citizens equal basic liberties through Rawls's first principle. His second principle consists of two principles that specify how the benefits of social cooperation are "open to all" and work "to everyone's advantage." Its guarantee of fair equality of opportunity requires that we not only judge people for jobs and offices by reference to their relevant talents and skills, but that we also establish institutional measures to correct for the ways in which class, race and gender might interfere with the normal development of marketable talents and skills.

Democratic equality fulfills the principles of justice because when there is true democracy, all of the people under the government will have equal opportunity in life. When everyone has the same opportunity in life, the principles' purpose will be achieved. Democratic equality is then the foundation for the principles of justice because equality allows mankind to accomplish anything. Rawls assumes that the two principles can be applied to any social institutions that occur in a democratic government as well.

Rawls claims that his model is based on reason and impartiality. Thus, the conclusions that one may reach using it are based on reason alone and apply to everyone. Rawls argues that although people should start at the same level in life, they don't. So, equity cannot be captured by the overly simplistic approach of making everyone have the same material goods, education and job. Natural talent creates difference; work ethic creates difference; temperament creates difference. All of these distinguish one person from another in their commerce with the rest of society and these things cannot be controlled without interfering with their contribution to the person and society. Rawls's basic liberties principle and difference principle provide ways to secure fairness without sacrificing the differing contributions.

The family is a social institution that, along with types of governments, can be evaluated using the principles of justice. The family, according to Rawls, is the ultimate source of members in the greater institutions of society. Hence, it is important to examine the psychological factors in the family that motivate people to obey or disobey rules and respect or disrespect other members of society. Rawls calls this development of a "sense of justice" in the family. It causes people to seek principles of justice that would come and play when they interact with people outside the family.

The three psychological factors of moral development are:

1. The morality of authority;
2. The morality of association; and
3. The morality of principles.

The morality of authority is the most primitive of stages and is in the form of a child. The love of parents for their children, which comes to be reciprocated, is important in his account of the development of a sense of self worth. By loving the child, they arouse in him a sense of his own value and the desire to become the sort of person they are. Healthy moral development in early life depends upon love, trust, affection, example, and guidance.

In the next stage, which is the morality of association, Rawls perceives the family as the first of many associations in which, by moving through a sequence of roles and positions, our moral understanding increases. The crucial aspect is the capacity in this stage of moral development. Our morality is shaped from how we perceive people for what they say and do, and what other peoples' ends, plans, and motives are in life. If this stage of development does not take place, "We cannot put ourselves into another's place and find out what we would do in his position," which we need to be able to do in order "to regulate our own conduct in the appropriate way by reference to it".

Rawls, however, uses only examples of the father associating with the stranger and demonstrating "judiciousness." What will later be shown in Okin is there is never a discussion of association and respect towards others with regard to fairness within the family. In the third stage, the morality of principles, the building on attachments formed in the family and participation in different roles in the various associations of society leads to the development of a person's "capacity for fellow feeling" and "to ties of friendship and mutual trust".

However this does not happen inside the family. In its normal form of right and justice, the morality of principles includes the virtues of the moralities of authority and association. It defines the last stage at which all the subordinate ideals are finally understood and organized into a coherent system by suitably general principles. By developing through the three stages of Rawls's psychological phases, people can evolve into good citizens and decision-makers for society. When a person is developing they are impacted on what their parents' relationship is to society. Children learn from their parents because they rely on them for everything. Parents are influential role models that help shape the future generations. By evolving through the three phases a person can enter the world with a capacity to know right from wrong, to make influential decisions and to become a citizen that other people respect.

For Rawls, justice starts with the family. That is where you discover role models and learn that others' needs are just as important as one's own. Rawls's original position is an abstract account that depicts people as indifferent and uninfluenced by their relationships with those they care about. In real life, humans are members of families. The original position does not address people who have a family or the special concerns and duties of women in the family either.

Susan Moller Okin argues that these psychological factors do not address people who have a family in the present time. Okin is concerned that these arguments foster a 1970s male dominant society where females do not have a voice within the family or the outside world. Rawls may respond that he talked about the family in his three psychological factors, but according to Okin, gender bias remains in the theory. He removes the "caring" from his original position causing proclamations to be indifferent claims rather than objective claims.

Okin criticizes Rawls for the ambiguous "he" that riddles his theory of justice. Of course, his overuse of the pronoun "he" is not Okin's most serious concern. Rather, it indicates a male perspective bias in the account that Rawls may not have recognized. Rawls briefly rules out formal legal discrimination on the grounds of sex. He fails to entirely address the justice of the gender system, which, with its roots in the sex roles of the family and its branches extending into virtually every corner of our lives, is one of the most fundamental and influential structures of society.

The woman's perspective is not fully addressed in the Rawls model. Rawls himself neglects gender and despite his initial statement about the place of the family in the basic structure, he does not consider whether or in what form the family is a just institution. He does not apply the principles of justice to the realm of human nurturance, a realm that is essential to the achievement and maintenance of justice in the society at large.

The family is not addressed as an institution that requires evaluation on the basis of justice. His three psychological factors are the only place where a reference is made about the family but not as a candidate for evaluation. It is just the factual foundation for a person's interest in justice. The sexism of the decision-makers could not be utilized to choose principles behind the veil or ignorance, but that is not enough. The original position only employs a disinterested, disaffected, self-interested perspective of one who does not have to be concerned with intimate emotionally based relationships. Okin points out that this perspective is one of the strangers working with other strangers, not one of someone who is a mother, sister, daughter, father, brother or son. According to Okin, at least two problems arise from such neglect. First, any relationship that is emotionally motivated is not addressed by the principles of justice.

This flaw can be seen in Rawls's own evaluation of the family where he neglects to apply the principles to the relationships between family members. Second, Rawls's original position removes the motivation to care about others, which removes the motivation to work at resolving problems on a more personal friendly basis, before they become major issues of violating a principle of justice. Okin's point is that the representative members of the original position are not just impartial but indifferent, which ignores a whole part of human life: the one that involves caring.

Okin observes that this neglect is most obvious in Rawls's discussion of the three psychological factors that help a person morally evolve in context of the family. Rawls's three stages of development emphasize learning how to fairly interact with strangers, not friends and family.

Okin argues that this exposes the fact that Rawls assumes that children do not need to learn that women, who are considered the primary care-givers of the family, deserve to be treated fairly in relationships. Of course, this is not necessarily exclusive to women. It is about the caregiver position in society. Rawls assumes that this position, which is traditionally taken by the wife/mother of the family, does not need to be treated fairly in the interactions of family members inside or outside of the family.

Okin supports this criticism by examining Rawls's morality of association. As a reminder, the morality of association is the second stage of Rawls's three psychological phases. This stage is where people learn through a sequence of roles and positions that our moral understanding increases. Okin observes that children's first examples of human interaction should be based on equality and reciprocality rather than on dependence and denomination.

Rawls's theory of moral development requires us to "put ourselves into another's place and find out what we would do in his position." Both parents must share in nurturing activities so the child can maintain an adult life in the capacity for empathy that under lies a sense of justice. Rawls neglects the family completely. Family justice must be of central importance for social justice, but Rawls leaves this out in his proposal.

Leonard Choptiany criticizes Rawls on his principles of justice and how all of society could not adopt these principles. Rawls's principles are not realistic to society–they are too hypothetical. Choptiany stresses they are neither necessary nor sufficient as principles of justice. Choptiany believes that Rawls's principles of justice are too far off for society to reach.

Rawls believed that his principles would be accepted freely by rational egoists in a "contractual state of nature" or "contract situation." Choptiany states that these principles give no specification of size of the inequality allowed in comparison with the amount of advantage provided. Any equality, no matter how great, would be justified by any advantage, no matter how slight. Rawls does not call this perfectly just, but he considers it "just" all the same.

Choptiany believes not everyone is represented or addressed in the principles of justice. He does not fully address that women are not represented in the principles of justice, but he clarifies on how not all men are recognized. Only the top tier men are being represented in Rawls's principles. Okins's criticism is an example specifically of how this happens to women. There are many loopholes in Rawls's principles of justice that Okin and Choptiany both recognize to be inconsistent to all of mankind.

They both raise different arguments from a male and female perspective. Even a male, Leonard Choptiany, is opposed to Rawls's principles of justice. Throughout Rawls argument the "he" is addressed which causes his credibility of a liberal political philosopher to be lost. The approach Rawls took even left out different races and ethnicities. This is specifically where Choptiany realises how not even all men are represented in this society. Rawls's argument is not strong enough because he left too many factors out. His principles of justice are too out of touch with the society of today. The principles are put on this elevated ladder that only reaches upper class men. In today's society the middle class makes up an overwhelming majority of the population. When a monumental amount of people are left out of the principles of justice how is it supposed to function? Rawls did want equality for mankind, but he chose not to address certain aspects of society. His principles would have no chance in the society of today.

With a solution to both these philosophers' arguments, Rawls needs to subtract the "he" and needs to come up with a more realistic way to achieve liberty. That is what comes down to both these philosophers argument: liberty. If not all men, women and children are addressed, how does Rawls suppose equality will happen? How is liberty going to be achieved if the objective is unrealistic? Choptiany believes his principles can not work overall, while Okin is displeased with how Rawls did not address women or the family. Rawls's general outlook was positive, but he needed to pose a more realistic way in achieving liberty.

SOCIAL JUSTICE

If in a society deep and persistent divisions exist between those who enjoy greater wealth and property, and the power which goes with such ownership, and those who are excluded and deprived, we would say that social justice is lacking there. We are not talking here merely about the different standards of living which may be enjoyed by different individuals in a society.

Justice does not require absolute equality and sameness in the way in which people live. But a society would be considered unjust if the differences between rich and poor are so great that they seem to be living in different worlds altogether, and if the relatively deprived have no chance at all to improve their condition however hard they may work. In other words, a just society should provide people with the basic minimum conditions to enable them to live healthy and secure lives and develop their talents as well as equal opportunities to pursue their chosen goals in society.

How can we decide what are the basic minimum conditions of life needed by people? Various methods of calculating the basic needs of people have been devised by different governments and by international organisations like the World Health Organisation. But in general it is agreed that the basic amount of nourishment needed to remain healthy, housing, supply of clean drinking water, education and a minimum wage would constitute an important part of these basic conditions.

Providing people with their basic needs is considered to be one of the responsibilities of a democratic government. However, providing such basic conditions of life to all citizens may pose a heavy burden on governments, particularly in countries like India which have a large number of poor people.

Even if we all agree that states should try and help the most disadvantaged members of the society to enjoy some degree of equality with others, disagreements could still arise regarding the best methods of achieving this goal. A debate is currently going on in our society, as well as in other parts of the world, about whether promoting open competition through free markets would be the best way of helping the disadvantaged without harming the betteroff members of a society, or whether the government should take on the responsibility of providing a basic minimum to the poor, if necessary even through a redistribution of resources.

In our country these different approaches are being supported by different political groups who debate the relative merits of different schemes for helping marginalised sections of the population such as the rural or urban poor.

FREE MARKETS VERSUS STATE INTERVENTION

Supporters of free markets maintain that as far as possible, individuals should be free to own property and enter into contracts and agreements with others regarding prices and wages and profits. They should be free to compete with each other to gain the greatest amount of benefit. This is a simple description of a free market. Supporters of the free market believe that if markets are left free of state interference the sum of market transactions would ensure overall a just distribution of benefits and duties in society. Those with merit and talent would be rewarded accordingly while the incompetent would get a lesser reward. They would maintain that whatever be the outcome of market distribution it would be just.

However, not all free market supporters today would support absolutely unregulated markets. Many would now be willing to accept certain restrictions, for instance, states could step in to ensure a basic minimum standard of living to all people so that they are able to compete on equal terms. But they might argue that even here the most efficient way of providing people with basic services might be to allow markets in health care, education, and such services, to develop. In other words, private agencies should be encouraged to provide such services while state policies should try to empower people to buy those services.

It might also be necessary for the state to give special help to the old and the sick who cannot compete. But apart from this the role of the state should only be to maintain a framework of laws and regulations to ensure that competition between individuals remains free of coercion and other obstacles. They maintain that a free market is the basis of a fair and just society. The market, it is said, does not care about the caste or religion of the person; it does not see whether you are a man or a woman. It is neutral and concerned with the talents and skills that you have. If you have the merit then nothing else matters.

One of the arguments put forward in favour of market distribution is that it gives us more choices. There is no doubt that the market system gives us more choices as consumers. We can choose the rice we eat and the school we go to, provided that we have the means to pay for them. But regarding basic goods and services what is important is the availability of good quality goods and services at a cost people can afford.

If private agencies do not find this profitable for them they may prefer not to enter that particular market, or to provide cheap and substandard services. That is why there may be few private schools in remote rural areas and the few which have been set up may be of low quality. The same would be true of health care or housing. In such situations the government might have to step in.

Another argument often heard in defence of free markets and private enterprise is that the quality of services they provide is often superior to that provided in government institutions. But the cost of such services may put them out of the reach of the poor. Private business tends to go where business would be most profitable and hence free markets eventually tend to work in the interest of the strong, the wealthy and the powerful. The result may be to deny, rather than extend, opportunities for those who are relatively weak and disadvantaged.

Arguments can be put forward on both sides of the debate but free markets often exhibit a tendency to work in favour of the already privileged. This is why many argue that to ensure social justice the state should step in to see that basic facilities are made available to all the members of a society.

In a democratic society disagreements about issues of distribution and justice are inevitable and even healthy because they force us to examine different points of view and rationally defend our own views. Politics is about the negotiation of such disagreements through debate. In our own country many kinds of social and economic inequalities exist and much remains to be done if they are to be reduced. Studying the different principles of justice should help us to discuss the issues involved and come to an agreement regarding the best way of pursuing justice.

9

The Concept of Liberty

Liberty is a moral and political principle, or Right, that identifies the condition in which human beings are able to govern themselves, to behave according to their own free will, and take responsibility for their actions. There are different conceptions of liberty, which articulate the relationship of individuals to society in different ways, including some which relate to life under a "social contract" or to existence in a "state of nature", and some which see the active exercise of freedom and rights as essential to liberty.

Individualist and classical liberal conceptions of liberty typically consist of the freedom of individuals from outside compulsion or coercion, also known as negative liberty, while Social liberal conceptions of liberty emphasize social structure and agency, or positive liberty. In feudal societies, a "liberty" was an area of allodial land in which the rights of the ruler, or monarch, had been waived.

LIBERTY PHILOSOPHY

Opinions on what constitute liberty can vary widely, but can be generally classified as positive liberty and negative liberty. Positive liberty asserts that freedom is found in a person's ability to exercise agency, particularly in the sense of having the power and resources to carry out their own will, without being inhibited by the structural inhibitions from society such as racism, classism or sexism. In the negative sense, one is considered free to the extent to which no person interferes with his or her activity. Thomas Hobbes, for example, *"a free man is he that... is not hindered to do what he hath the will to do."*

John Stuart Mill, in his work, *On Liberty*, was the first to recognize the difference between liberty as the freedom to act and liberty as the absence of coercion. In his book, *Two Concepts of Liberty*, Isaiah Berlin formally framed the differences between these two perspectives as the distinction between two opposite concepts of liberty: positive liberty and negative liberty. The latter designates a negative condition in which an individual is protected from tyranny and the arbitrary exercise of authority, while the former refers to having the means or opportunity, rather than the lack of restraint, to do things.

Mill offered insight into the notions of *soft tyranny* and *mutual liberty* with his *harm principle*. It can be seen as important to understand these concepts when discussing liberty since they all represent little pieces of the greater puzzle known as freedom. In a philosophical sense, it can be said that morality must supersede tyranny in any legitimate form of government. Otherwise, people are left with a societal system rooted in backwardness, disorder, and regression.

The concept of negative liberty has several noteworthy aspects. First, negative liberty defines a realm or "zone" of freedom. In Berlin's words, "liberty in the negative sense involves an answer to the question 'What is the area within which the subject — a person or group of persons — is or should be left to do or be what he is able to do or be, without interference by other persons." Some philosophers have disagreed on the extent of this realm while accepting the main point that liberty defines that realm in which one may act unobstructed by others. Second, the restriction implicit in negative liberty is imposed by a person or persons and not due to causes such as nature, lack, or incapacity. Helvetius expresses this point clearly: "The free man is the man who is not in irons, nor imprisoned in a jail, nor terrorized like a slave by the fear of punishment... it is not lack of freedom not to fly like an eagle or swim like a whale."

The dichotomy of positive and negative liberty is considered specious by political philosophers in traditions such as socialism, social democracy, libertarian socialism, and Marxism. Some of them argue that positive and negative liberty are indistinguishable in practice, while others claim that one kind of liberty cannot exist independently of the other. A common argument is that the preservation of negative liberty requires positive action on the part of the government or society to prevent some individuals from taking away the liberty of others.

A socialist, liberal and progressive defines liberty as being connected to the reasonably equitable distribution of wealth, arguing that the unrestrained concentration of wealth into only a few hands negates liberty. In other words, without relatively equal ownership, the subsequent concentration of power and influence into a small portion of the population inevitably results in the domination of the wealthy and the subjugation of the poor. Thus, freedom and material equality are seen as intrinsically connected. On the other hand, the classical liberal argues that wealth cannot be evenly distributed without force being used against individuals which reduces individual liberty.

FREEDOM AS A TRIADIC RELATION

In 1980, Gerald MacCallum argued that proponents of positive and negative liberty converge on a single definition of liberty, but simply have different approaches in establishing it. MacCallum, freedom is a triadic relationship: "x is/is not free from y to do/not to do or become/not become z". In this way, rather than defining liberty in terms of two separate paradigms, positive and negative liberty, he defined liberty as a single, complete formula.

The question is whether this formula fully captures what positive liberty means. Positive liberty, understood as "internal forces which determine how a person shall act" is saying more than 'x is free to do z.' One is free when one *becomes* the ideal of oneself, which includes MacCallum's triadic relation; but the latter alone is insufficient to fully capture what positive liberty means.

LIBERTY AND POLITICAL THOUGHT

Concepts of Liberty in History

The first known use of the word *freedom* in a political context dates back to the 24th century BC, in a text describing the restoration of social and economic liberty in Lagash, a Sumerian city-state. Urukagina, the king of Lagash, established the first known legal code to protect citizens from the rich and powerful. Known as a great reformer, Urukagina established laws that forbade compelling the sale of property and required the charges against the accused to be stated before any man accused of a crime could be punished. This is the first known example of any form of due process in the history of humanity.

Like Urukagina, most ancient freedoms focused on *negative liberty*, protecting the less fortunate from harassment or imposition. Other ancient legal codes, such as the Code of Hammurabi, similarly forbade compulsion in economic matters, like the sale of land, and made it clear that when a rich man murders a poor one, it is still murder. Still, these codes depended on a certain virtuousness of kings and ministers, which was far from reliable.

The modern concept of liberty has its origins in the Greek concepts of freedom and slavery. To be free, to the Greeks, was to not have a master, to be independent from a master. That was the original Greek concept of freedom. It is closely linked with the concept of democracy, as Aristotle put it:

"This, then, is one note of liberty which all democrats affirm to be the principle of their state. Another is that a man should live as he likes. This, they say, is the privilege of a freeman, since, on the other hand, not to live as a man likes is the mark of a slave. This is the second characteristic of democracy, whence has arisen the claim of men to be ruled by none, if possible, or, if this is impossible, to rule and be ruled in turns; and so it contributes to the freedom based upon equality."

So to the Greeks democracy was the system of government of a free society.

The populations of the Persian Empire enjoyed some degree of freedom. Citizens of all religions and ethnic groups were given the same rights and had the same freedom of religion, women had the same rights as men, and slavery was abolished. All the palaces of the kings of Persia were built by paid workers in an era where slaves typically did such work. In the Buddhist Maurya Empire of ancient India, citizens of all religions and ethnic groups had some rights to freedom, tolerance, and equality. The need for tolerance on an egalitarian basis can be found in the Edicts of Ashoka the Great, which emphasize the importance of tolerance in public policy by the government. The slaughter or capture of prisoners of war was also condemned by Ashoka. Slavery was also non-existent in the Maurya Empire. However, just as to Hermann Kulke and Dietmar Rothermund, "Ashoka's orders seem to have been resisted right from the beginning."

Roman law also embraced certain limited forms of liberty, even under the rule of the Roman Emperors. However, these liberties were accorded only to Roman citizens. Still, the Roman citizen enjoyed a combination of positive liberty and negative liberty. Many of the liberties enjoyed under Roman law endured through the Middle Ages, but were enjoyed solely by the nobility, never by the common man. The idea of unalienable and universal liberties had to wait until the Age of Enlightenment.

In Chinese, freedom is written is the character for self, and you is the character to follow, with an additional connotation of reason. Liberty thus implies a necessary connection between individualism and a rational duty.

SOCIAL CONTRACT

The social contract theory, invented by Hobbes, John Locke and Rousseau, were among the first to provide a political classification of rights, in particular through the notion of sovereignty and of natural rights. The thinkers of the Enlightenment reasoned the assertion that law governed both heavenly and human affairs, and that law gave the king his power, rather than the king's power giving force to law. The divine right of kings was thus opposed to the sovereign's unchecked *auctoritas*.

This conception of law would find its culmination in Montesquieu's thought. The conception of law as a relationship between individuals, rather than families, came to the fore, and with it the increasing focus on individual liberty as a fundamental reality, given by "Nature and Nature's God," which, in the ideal state, would be as expansive as possible. The Enlightenment created then, among other ideas, *liberty*: that is, of a free individual being most free within the context of a state which provides stability of the laws. Later, more radical philosophies such as socialism articulated themselves in the course of the French Revolution and in the 19th century.

Modern Perspectives

The modern conceptions of democracy, whether representative democracies or other types of democracies, are all found on the Rousseauist idea of popular sovereignty. Liberalism is a political current embracing several historical and present-day ideologies that claim defence of individual liberty as the purpose of government. Two main strands are apparent, although both are founded on an individualist ideology. Economic liberalism is the right of the individual to contract, trade and operate in a market free of constraint. Social liberalism is the right to dissent from orthodox tenets or established authorities in political or religious matters. Both are core political issues, and highly contentious. Article 3 of the Universal Declaration of Human Rights states that "*Everyone has the right to life, liberty, and security of person.*"

MILL'S CONCEPT OF LIBERTY

Born in London in 1806, son of James Mill, philosopher, economist and senior official in the East India Company, Mill gave a vivid and moving account of his life, and especially of his extraordinary education, in the Autobiography (1873) that he wrote towards the end of his life. Mill led an active career as an administrator in the East India Company from which he retired only when the Company's administrative functions in India were takenover by the British government following the Mutiny of 1857. In addition, he was a Liberal MP for Westminster 1865-8, and as a young man in the 1830s edited the *London* and *Westminster Review*, a radical quarterly journal. He died at Aix-En-Provence in 1873.

Mill was educated by his father, with the advice and assistance of Jeremy Bentham and Francis Place. He learned Greek at three, Latin a little later; by the age of 12, he was a competent logician and by 16 a well-trained economist. At 20 he suffered a nervous breakdown that persuaded him that more was needed in life than devotion to the public good and an analytically sharp intellect. Having grown up a utilitarian, he now turned to Coleridge, Wordsworth and Goethe to cultivate his aesthetic sensibilities. From 1830 to his death, he tried to persuade the British public of the necessity of a scientific approach to understanding social, political and economic change while not neglecting the insights of poets and other imaginative writers.

His *System of Logic* (1843) was an ambitious attempt to give an account not only of logic, as the title suggests, but of the methods of science and their applicability to social as well as purely natural phenomena. Mill's conception of logic was not entirely that of modern logicians; besides formal logic, what he,' he thought that there was a logic of proof, that is, a logic that would show how evidence proved or tended to prove the conclusions we draw from the evidence. That led him to the analysis of causation, and to an account of inductive reasoning that remains the starting point of most modern discussions. Mill's account of explanation in science was broadly that explanation seeks the causes of events where it is events in which we are interested; or seeks more general laws where we are concerned to explain less general laws as special cases of those laws.

Mill's discussion of the possibility of finding a scientific explanation of social events has worn equally well; Mill was as unwilling to suppose that the social sciences would become omniscient about human behaviour as to suppose that there was no prospect of explaining social affairs at any deeper level than that of common sense. Throughout the System of Logic Mill attacked the 'intuitionist' philosophy of William Whewell and Sir William Hamilton.

This was the view that explanations rested on intuitively compelling principles rather than on general, causal laws, and that ultimately the search for such intuitively compelling principles rested on understanding the universe as a divine creation governed by principles that a rational deity must choose. Mill thought that intuitionism was bad philosophy, and a comfort to political conservatism into the bargain. His Examination of Sir William Hamilton's *Philosophy* (1865) carried the war into the enemy camp with a vengeance; it provoked vigorous controversy for some twenty years or so, but is now the least readable of Mill's works. To the public at large, Mill was better known as the author of *Principles of Political Economy* (1848), a work that tried to show that economics was not the 'dismal science' that its radical and literary critics had supposed. Its philosophical interest lay in Mill's reflections on the difference between what economics measured and what human beings really valued: leading Mill to argue that we should sacrifice economic growth for the sake of the environment, and should limit population as much to give ourselves breathing space as in order to fend off the risk of starvation for the overburdened poor. Mill also allowed that conventional economic analysis could not show that socialism was unworkable, and suggested as his own ideal an economy of worker-owned cooperatives. Commentators have argued inconclusively over whether this is a form of socialism or merely 'workers' capitalism.

Mill remains most nearly our contemporary in the area of moral and political philosophy. However, His *Utilitarianism* (1861) remains the classic defence of the view that we ought to aim at maximizing the welfare of all sentient creatures, and that welfare consists of their happiness. Mill's defence of the view that we ought to pursue happiness because we do pursue happiness, has been the object of savage attack by, among others, F. H. Bradley in his *Ethical Studies* (1874) and G. E. Moore in *Principia Ethica* (1903). But others have argued that on this particular point, Mill was misinterpreted by his critics. His insistence that happiness was to be assessed not merely by quantity but by quality—the doctrine that a dissatisfied Socrates is not only better than a satisfied fool, but somehow happier, too—has puzzled generations of commentators.

And his attempt to show that justice can be accounted for in utilitarian terms is still important as a riposte to such writers as John Rawls. During his lifetime, it was his essay "On Liberty" (1859) that aroused the greatest controversy, and the most violent expressions of approval and disapproval. The essay was sparked by the feeling that Mill and his wife, Harriet Taylor, constantly expressed in their letters to one another: that they lived in a society where bold and adventurous individuals were becoming all too rare. Critics have sometimes thought that Mill was frightened by the prospect of a mass democracy in which working-class opinion would be oppressive and perhaps violent. The truth is that Mill was frightened by middle-class conformism much more than by anything to be looked for from an enfranchised working class. It was a fear he had picked up from reading Alexis de Tocqueville's *Democracy in America* (1836, 1840); America was a prosperous middle-class society, and Mill feared that it was also a society that cared nothing for individual liberty.

Mill lays down "one very simple principle" to govern the use of coercion in society - and by coercion he means both legal penalties and the operation of public opinion; it is that we may only coerce others in self-defence - either to defend ourselves, or to defend others from harm. Crucially, this rules out paternalistic interventions to save people from themselves, and ideal interventions to make people behave "better". It has long exercised critics to explain how a utilitarian can subscribe to such a principle of self-restraint. In essence, Mill argues that only by adopting the self-restraint principle can we seek out the truth, experience the truth as 'our own,' and fully develop individual selves.

Of Mill's shorter works, two others deserve mention. The *Subjection of Women* (1869) was thought to be excessively radical in Mill's time but is now seen as a classic statement of liberal feminism. Its essential case is that if freedom is a good for men, it is for women, and that every argument against this view drawn from the supposedly different 'nature' of men and women has been superstitious special pleading. If women have different natures, the only way to discover what they are is by experiment, and that requires that women should have access to everything to which men have access. Only after as many centuries of freedom as there have been centuries of oppression will we really know what our natures are.

Mill published *The Subjection of Women* late in life to avoid controversies that would lessen the impact of his other work. He chose not to have his *Three Essays on Religion* (1874) published until after his death. They argued, among other things, that it is impossible that the universe is governed by an omnipotent and loving God, but not unlikely that a less omnipotent benign force is at work in the world. They thus tended to disappoint those of Mill's admirers who looked for a tougher and more abrasive agnosticism, while doing nothing to appease critics who deplored the fact that he was any kind of agnostic. But they remain models of the calm discussion of contentious topics, and highly readable to this day.

MILL'S VIEW ON LIBERTY: INTRODUCTORY

The subject of this essay is not the so-called Liberty of the will, so unfortunately opposed to the misnamed doctrine of philosophical necessity; but civil, or social liberty: the nature and limits of the power which can be legitimately exercised by society over the individual. A question seldom stated, and hardly ever discussed, in general terms, but which profoundly influences the practical controversies of the age by its latent presence, and is likely soon to make itself recognized as the vital question of the future. It is so far from being new, that, in a certain sense, it has divided mankind, almost from the remotest ages, but in the stage of progress into which the more civilised portions of the species have now entered, it presents itself under new conditions, and requires a different and more fundamental treatment.

The struggle between Liberty and Authority is the most conspicuous feature in the portions of history with which we are earliest familiar, particularly in that of Greece, Rome, and England. But in old times this contest was between subjects, or some classes of subjects, and the government. By liberty, was meant protection against the tyranny of the political rulers. The rulers were conceived as in a necessarily antagonistic position to the people whom they ruled.

They consisted of a governing One, or a governing tribe or caste, who derived their authority from inheritance or conquest; who, at all events, did not hold it at the pleasure of the governed, and whose supremacy men did not venture, perhaps did not desire, to contest, whatever precautions might be taken against its oppressive exercise. Their power was regarded as necessary, but also as highly dangerous; as a weapon which they would attempt to use against their subjects, no less than against external enemies. To prevent the weaker members of the community from being preyed upon by innumerable vultures, it was needful that there should be an animal of prey stronger than the rest, commissioned to keep them down. But as the king of the vultures would be no less bent upon preying upon the flock than any of the minor harpies, it was indispensable to be in a perpetual attitude of defence against his beak and claws.

The aim, therefore, of patriots, was to set limits to the power which the ruler should be suffered to exercise over the community; and this limitation was what they meant by liberty. It was attempted in two ways. First, by obtaining a recognition of certain immunities, called political liberties or rights, which it was to be regarded as a breach of duty in the ruler to infringe, and which, if he did infringe, specific resistance, or general rebellion, was held to be justifiable. A second, and generally a later expedient, was the establishment of constitutional checks; by which the consent of the community, or of a body of some sort supposed to represent its interests, was made a necessary condition to some of the more important acts of the governing power.

To the first of these modes of limitation, the ruling power, in most European countries, was compelled, more or less, to submit. It was not so with the second; and to attain this, or when already in some degree possessed, to attain it more completely, became everywhere the principal object of the lovers of liberty.

And so long as mankind were content to combat one enemy by another, and to be ruled by a master, on condition of being guaranteed more or less efficaciously against his tyranny, they did not carry their aspirations beyond this point.

A time, however, came in the progress of human affairs, when men ceased to think it a necessity of nature that their governors should be an independent power, opposed in interest to themselves. It appeared to them much better that the various magistrates of the State should be their tenants or delegates, revocable at their pleasure. In that way alone, it seemed, could they have complete security that the powers of government would never be abused to their disadvantage. By degrees, this new demand for elective and temporary rulers became the prominent object of the exertions of the popular party, wherever any such party existed; and superseded, to a considerable extent, the previous efforts to limit the power of rulers. As the struggle proceeded for making the ruling power emanate from the periodical choice of the ruled, some persons began to think that too much importance had been attached to the limitation of the power itself. That was a resource against rulers whose interests were habitually opposed to those of the people. What was now wanted was, that the rulers should be identified with the people; that their interest and will should be the interest and will of the nation. The nation did not need to be protected against its own will.

There was no fear of its tyrannizing over itself. Let the rulers be effectually responsible to it, promptly removable by it, and it could afford to trust them with power of which it could itself dictate the use to be made. Their power was but the nation's own power, concentrated, and in a form convenient for exercise. This mode of thought, or rather perhaps of feeling, was common among the last generation of European liberalism, in the continental section of which, it still apparently predominates. Those who admit any limit to what a government may do, except in the case of such governments as they think ought not to exist, stand out as brilliant exceptions among the political thinkers of the continent. A similar tone of sentiment might by this time have been prevalent in our own country, if the circumstances which for a time encouraged it had continued unaltered.

But, in political and philosophical theories, as well as in persons, success discloses faults and infirmities which failure might have concealed from observation. The notion, that the people have no need to limit their power over themselves, might seem axiomatic, when popular government was a thing only dreamed about, or read of as having existed at some distant period of the past. Neither was that notion necessarily disturbed by such temporary aberrations as those of the French Revolution, the worst of which were the work of an usurping few, and which, in any case, belonged, not to the permanent working of popular institutions, but to a sudden and convulsive outbreak against monarchical and aristocratic despotism. In time, however, a democratic republic came to occupy a large portion of the earth's surface, and made itself felt as one of the most powerful members of the community of nations; and elective and responsible government became subject to the observations and criticisms which wait upon a great existing fact. It was now perceived that such phrases as 'self-government', and 'the power of the people over themselves', do not express the true state of the case. The 'people' who exercise the power, are not always the same people with those over whom it is exercised, and the 'self-government' spoken of, is not the government of each by himself, but of each by all the rest.

The will of the people, moreover, practically means, the will of the most numerous or the most active part of the people; the majority, or those who succeed in making themselves accepted as the majority; the people, consequently, may desire to oppress a part of their number; and precautions are as much needed against this, as against any other abuse of power. The limitation, therefore, of the power of government over individuals, loses none of its importance when the holders of power are regularly accountable to the community, that is, to the strongest party therein. This view of things, recommending itself equally to the intelligence of thinkers and to the inclination of those important classes in European society to whose real or supposed interests democracy is adverse, has had no difficulty in establishing itself; and in political speculations 'the tyranny of the majority' is now generally included among the evils against which society requires to be on its guard.

Like other tyrannies, the tyranny of the majority was at first, and is still vulgarly, held in dread, chiefly as operating through the acts of the public authorities. But reflecting persons perceived that when society is itself the tyran—society collectively, over the separate individuals who compose it—its means of tyrannizing are not restricted to the acts which it may do by the hands of its political functionaries. Society can and does execute its own mandates: and if it issues wrong mandates instead of right, or any mandates at all in things with which it ought not to meddle, it practises a social tyranny more formidable than many kinds of political oppression, since, though not usually upheld by such extreme penalties, it leaves fewer means of escape, penetrating much more deeply into the details of life, and enslaving the soul itself.

Protection, therefore, against the tyranny of the magistrate is not enough; they need protection also against the tyranny of the prevailing opinion and feeling; against the tendency of society to impose, by other means than civil penalties, its own ideas and practices as rules of conduct on those who dissent from them; to fetter the development, and, if possible, prevent the formation, of any individuality not in harmony with its ways, and compel all characters to fashion themselves upon the model of its own. There is a limit to the legitimate interference of collective opinion with individual independence; and to find that limit, and maintain it against encroachment, is as indispensable to a good condition of human affairs, as protection against political despotism. But though this proposition is not likely to be contested in general terms, the practical question, where to place the limit--how to make the fitting adjustment between individual independence and social control--is a subject on which nearly everything remains to be done. All that makes existence valuable to any one, depends on the enforcement of restraints upon the actions of other people. Some rules of conduct, therefore, must be imposed, by law in the first place, and by opinion on many things which are not fit subjects for the operation of law.

What these rules should be, is the principal question in human affairs; but if we except a few of the most obvious cases, it is one of those which least progress has been made in resolving. No two ages, and scarcely any two countries, have decided it alike; and the decision of one age or country is a wonder to another. Yet the people of any given age and country no more suspect any difficulty in it, than if it were a subject on which mankind had always been agreed.

The rules which obtain among themselves appear to them self-evident and self-justifying. This all but universal illusion is one of the examples of the magical influence of custom, which is not only, as the proverb says a second nature, but is continually mistaken for the first. The effect of custom, in preventing any misgiving respecting the rules of conduct which mankind impose on one another, is all the more complete because the subject is one on which it is not generally considered necessary that reasons should be given, either by one person to others, or by each to himself. People are accustomed to believe and have been encouraged in the belief by some who aspire to the character of philosophers, that their feelings, on subjects of this nature, are better than reasons, and render reasons unnecessary. The practical principle which guides them to their opinions on the regulation of human conduct, is the feeling in each person's mind that everybody should be required to act as he, and those with whom he sympathises, would like them to act. No one, indeed, acknowledges to himself that his standard of judgement is his own liking; but an opinion on a point of conduct, not supported by reasons, can only count as one person's preference; and if the reasons, when given, are a mere appeal to a similar preference felt by other people, it is still only many people's liking instead of one. To an ordinary man, however, his own preference, thus supported, is not only a perfectly satisfactory reason, but the only one he generally has for any of his notions of morality, taste, or propriety, which are not expressly written in his religious creed; and his chief guide in the interpretation even of that. Men's opinions, accordingly, on what is laudable or blamable, are affected by all the multifarious causes which influence their wishes in regard to the conduct of others, and which are as numerous as those which determine their wishes on any other subject.

Sometimes their reason--at other times their prejudices or superstitions: often their social affections, not seldom their anti-social ones, their envy or jealousy, their arrogance or contemptuousness: but most commonly, their desires or fears for themselves--their legitimate or illegitimate self-interest. Wherever there is an ascendant class, a large portion of the morality of the country emanates from its class interests, and its feelings of class superiority. The morality between Spartans and Helots, between planters and Negroes, between princes and subjects, between nobles and roturiers, between men and women, has been for the most part the creation of these class interests and feelings: and the sentiments thus generated, react in turn upon the moral feelings of the members of the ascendant class, in their relations among themselves.

Where, on the other hand, a class, formerly ascendant, has lost its ascendency, or where its ascendency is unpopular, the prevailing moral sentiments frequently bear the impress of an impatient dislike of superiority. Another grand determining principle of the rules of conduct, both in act and forbearance which have been enforced by law or opinion, has been the servility of mankind towards the supposed preferences or aversions of their temporal masters, or of their gods.

This servility though essentially selfish, is not hypocrisy; it gives rise to perfectly genuine sentiments of abhorrence; it made men burn magicians and heretics. Among so many baser influences, the general and obvious interests of society have of course had a share, and a large one, in the direction of the moral sentiments: less, however, as a matter of reason, and on their own account, than as a consequence of the sympathies and antipathies which grew out of them: and sympathies and antipathies which had little or nothing to do with the interests of society, have made themselves felt in the establishment of moralities with quite as great force.

The likings and dislikings of society, or of some powerful portion of it, are thus the main thing which has practically determined the rules laid down for general observance, under the penalties of law or opinion. And in general, those who have been in advance of society in thought and feeling, have left this condition of things unassailed in principle, however they may have come into conflict with it in some of its details.

They have occupied themselves rather in enquiring what things society ought to like or dislike, than in questioning whether its likings or dislikings should be a law to individuals. They preferred endeavouring to alter the feelings of mankind on the particular points on which they were themselves heretical, rather than make common cause in defence of freedom, with heretics generally. The only case in which the higher ground has been taken on principle and maintained with consistency, by any but an individual here and there, is that of religious belief: a case instructive in many ways, and not least so as forming a most striking instance of the fallibility of what is called the moral sense: for the odium theologicum, in a sincere bigot, is one of the most unequivocal cases of moral feeling.

Those who first broke the yoke of what called itself the Universal Church, were in general as little willing to permit difference of religious opinion as that church itself. But when the heat of the conflict was over, without giving a complete victory to any party, and each church or sect was reduced to limit its hopes to retaining possession of the ground it already occupied; minorities, seeing that they had no chance of becoming majorities, were under the necessity of pleading to those whom they could not convert, for permission to differ. It is accordingly on this battle-field, almost solely, that the rights of the individual against society have been asserted on broad grounds of principle, and the claim of society to exercise authority over dissentients openly controverted.

The great writers to whom the world owes what religious liberty it possesses, have mostly asserted freedom of conscience as an indefeasible right, and denied absolutely that a human being is accountable to others for his religious belief. Yet so natural to mankind is intolerance in whatever they really care about, that religious freedom has hardly anywhere been practically realised, except where religious indifference, which dislikes to have its peace disturbed by theological quarrels, has added its weight to the scale. In the minds of almost all religious persons, even in the most tolerant countries, the duty of toleration is admitted with tacit reserves. One person will bear with dissent in matters of church government, but not of dogma; another can tolerate everybody, short of a Papist or an Unitarian; another, every one who believes in revealed religion; a few extend their charity a little further, but stop at the belief in a God and in a future state. Wherever the sentiment of the majority is still genuine and intense, it is found to have abated little of its claim to be obeyed.

In England, from the peculiar circumstances of our political history, though the yoke of opinion is perhaps heavier, that of law is lighter, than in most other countries of Europe; and there is considerable jealousy of direct interference, by the legislative or the executive power with private conduct; not so much from any just regard for the independence of the individual, as from the still subsisting habit of looking on the government as representing an opposite interest to the public. The majority have not yet learnt to feel the power of the government, their power, or its opinions their opinions. When they do so, individual liberty will probably be as much exposed to invasion from the government, as it already is from public opinion. But, as yet, there is a considerable amount of feeling ready to be called forth against any attempt of the law to control individuals in things in which they have not hitherto been accustomed to be controlled by it; and this with very little discrimination as to whether the matter is, or is not, within the legitimate sphere of legal control; insomuch that the feeling, highly salutary on the whole, is perhaps quite as often misplaced as well grounded in the particular instances of its application. There is, in fact, no recognized principle by which the propriety or impropriety of government interference is customarily tested. People decide according to their personal preferences.

Some, whenever they see any good to be done, or evil to be remedied, would willingly instigate the government to undertake the business; while others prefer to bear almost any amount of social evil, rather than add one to the departments of human interests amenable to governmental control. And men range themselves on one or the other side in any particular case, according to this general direction of their sentiments; or according to the degree of interest which they feel in the particular thing which it is proposed that the government should do; or according to the belief they entertain that the government would, or would not, do it in the manner they prefer; but very rarely on account of any opinion to which they consistently adhere, as to what things are fit to be done by a government. And it seems to me that, in consequence of this absence of rule or principle, one side is at present as often wrong as the other; the interference of government is, with about equal frequency, improperly invoked and improperly condemned.

The object of this essay is to assert one very simple principle, as entitled to govern absolutely the dealings of society with the individual in the way of compulsion and control, whether the means used be physical force in the form of legal penalties, or the moral coercion of public opinion. That principle is, that the sole end for which mankind are warranted, individually or collectively in interfering with the liberty of action of any of their number, is self-protection. That the only purpose for which power can be rightfully exercised over any member of a civilized community, against his will, is to prevent harm to others. His own good, either physical or moral, is not a sufficient warrant. He cannot rightfully be compelled to do or forbear because it will be better for him to do so, because it will make him happier, because, in the opinions of others, to do so would be wise, or even right. These are good reasons for remonstrating with him, or reasoning with him, or persuading him, or entreating him, but not for compelling him, or visiting him with any evil, in case he do otherwise. To justify that, the conduct from which it is desired to deter him must be calculated to produce evil to someone else. The only part of the conduct of any one, for which he is amenable to society, is that which concerns others. In the part which merely concerns himself, his independence is, of right, absolute. Over himself, over his own body and mind, the individual is sovereign.

It is, perhaps, hardly necessary to say that this doctrine is meant to apply only to human beings in the maturity of their faculties. We are not speaking of children, or of young persons below the age which the law may fix as that of manhood or womanhood. Those who are still in a state to require being taken care of by others, must be protected against their own actions as well as against external injury. For the same reason, we may leave out of consideration those backward states of society in which the race itself may be considered as in its non-age. The early difficulties in the way of spontaneous progress are so great, that there is seldom any choice of means for overcoming them; and a ruler full of the spirit of improvement is warranted in the use of any expedients that will attain an end, perhaps otherwise unattainable. Despotism is a legitimate mode of government in dealing with barbarians, provided the end be their improvement, and the means justified by actually effecting that end.

Liberty, as a principle, has no application to any state of things anterior to the time when mankind have become capable of being improved by free and equal discussion. Until then, there is nothing for them but implicit obedience to an Akbar or a Charlemagne, if they are so fortunate as to find one. But as soon as mankind have attained the capacity of being guided to their own improvement by conviction or persuasion, compulsion, either in the direct form or in that of pains and penalties for non-compliance, is no longer admissible as a means to their own good, and justifiable only for the security of others. It is proper to state that I forego any advantage which could be derived to my argument from the idea of abstract right as a thing independent of utility. I regard utility as the ultimate appeal on all ethical questions; but it must be utility in the largest sense, grounded on the permanent interests of man as a progressive being. Those interests, I contend, authorise the subjection of individual spontaneity to external control, only in respect to those actions of each, which concern the interest of other people. If anyone does an act hurtful to others, there is a prima facie case for punishing him, by law, or, where legal penalties are not safely applicable, by general disapprobation. There are also many positive acts for the benefit of others, which he may rightfully be compelled to perform; such as, to give evidence in a court of justice; to bear his fair share in the common defence, or in any other joint work necessary to the interest of the society of which he enjoys the protection; and to perform certain acts of individual beneficence, such as saving a fellow-creature's life, or interposing to protect the defenceless against ill-usage, things which whenever it is obviously a man's duty to do, he may rightfully be made responsible to society for not doing.

A person may cause evil to others not only by his actions but by his inaction, and in either case he is justly accountable to them for the injury. The latter case, it is true, requires a much more cautious exercise of compulsion than the former. To make any one answerable for doing evil to others, is the rule; to make him answerable for not preventing evil, is, comparatively speaking, the exception. Yet there are many cases clear enough and grave enough to justify that exception. In all things which regard the external relations of the individual, he is de jure amenable to those whose interests are concerned, and if need be, to society as their protector. There are often good reasons for not holding him to the responsibility; but these reasons must arise from the special expediencies of the case: either because it is a kind of case in which he is on the whole likely to act better, when left to his own discretion, than when controlled in any way in which society have it in their power to control him; or because the attempt to exercise control would produce other evils, greater than those which it would prevent.

When such reasons as these preclude the enforcement of responsibility, the conscience of the agent himself should step into the vacant judgement-seat, and protect those interests of others which have no external protection; judging himself all the more rigidly, because the case does not admit of his being made accountable to the judgement of his fellow-creatures.

But there is a sphere of action in which society, as distinguished from the individual, has, if any, only an indirect interest; comprehending all that portion of a person's life and conduct which affects only himself, or, if it also affects others, only with their free, voluntary, and undeceived consent and participation. When we say only himself, we mean directly, and in the first instance: for whatever affects himself, may affect others through himself; and the objection which may be grounded on this contingency, will receive consideration in the sequel. This, then, is the appropriate region of human liberty.

It comprises, first, the inward domain of consciousness; demanding liberty of conscience, in the most comprehensive sense; liberty of thought and feeling; absolute freedom of opinion and sentiment on all subjects, practical or speculative, scientific, moral, or theological. The liberty of expressing and publishing opinions may seem to fall under a different principle, since it belongs to that part of the conduct of an individual which concerns other people; but, being almost of as much importance as the liberty of thought itself, and resting in great part on the same reasons, is practically inseparable from it.

Secondly, the principle requires liberty of tastes and pursuits; of framing the plan of our life to suit our own character; of doing as we like, subject to such consequences as may follow; without impediment from our fellow-creatures, so long as what we do does not harm them even though they should think our conduct foolish, perverse, or wrong. Thirdly, from this liberty of each individual, follows the liberty, within the same limits, of combination among individuals; freedom to unite, for any purpose not involving harm to others: the persons combining being supposed to be of full age, and not forced or deceived.

No society in which these liberties are not, on the whole, respected, is free, whatever may be its form of government; and none is completely free in which they do not exist absolute and unqualified. The only freedom which deserves the name, is that of pursuing our own good in our own way, so long as we do not attempt to deprive others of theirs, or impede their efforts to obtain it. Each is the proper guardian of his own health, whether bodily, or mental or spiritual. Mankind are greater gainers by suffering each other to live as seems good to themselves, than by compelling each to live as seems good to the rest. Though this doctrine is anything but new, and, to some persons, may have the air of a truism, there is no doctrine which stands more directly opposed to the general tendency of existing opinion and practice. Society has expended fully as much effort in the attempt to compel people to conform to its notions of personal, as of social excellence.

The ancient commonwealths thought themselves entitled to practise, and the ancient philosophers countenanced, the regulation of every part of private conduct by public authority, on the ground that the state had a deep interest in the whole bodily and mental discipline of every one of its citizens, a mode of thinking which may have been admissible in small republics surrounded by powerful enemies, in constant peril of being subverted by foreign attack or internal commotion, and to which even a short interval of relaxed energy and self-command might so easily be fatal, that they could not afford to wait for the salutary permanent effects of freedom.

In the modern world, the greater size of political communities the separation between the spiritual and temporal authority, prevented so great an interference by law in the details of private life; but the engines of moral repression have been wielded more strenuously against divergence from the reigning opinion in self-regarding, than even in social matters; religion, the most powerful of the elements which have entered into the formation of moral feeling, having almost always been governed either by the ambition of a hierarchy, seeking control over every department of human conduct, or by the spirit of Puritanism. And some of those modern reformers who have placed themselves in strongest opposition to the religions of the past, have been nowhere behind either churches or sects in their assertion of the right of spiritual domination: M. Compte, in particular, whose social system, as unfolded in his *Trait de Politique Positive*, aims at establishing a despotism of society over the individual, surpassing anything contemplated in the political ideal of the most rigid disciplinarian among the ancient philosophers.

Apart from the peculiar tenets of individual thinkers, there is also in the world at large an increasing inclination to stretch unduly the powers of society over the individual, both by the force of opinion and even by that of legislation: and as the tendency of all the changes taking place in the world is to strengthen society, and diminish the power of the individual, this encroachment is not one of the evils which tend spontaneously to disappear, but, on the contrary, to grow more and more formidable. The disposition of mankind, whether as rulers or as fellow-citizens, to impose their own opinions and inclinations as a rule of conduct on others, is so energetically supported by some of the best and by some of the worst feelings incident to human nature, that it is hardly ever kept under restraint by anything but want of power; and as the power is not declining, but growing, unless a strong barrier of moral conviction can be raised against the mischief, we must expect, in the present circumstances of the world, to see it increase. It will be convenient for the argument, if, instead of at once entering upon the general thesis, we confine ourselves in the first instance to a single branch of it, on which the principle here stated is, if not fully, yet to a certain point, recognized by the current opinions.

This one branch is the Liberty of Thought: from which it is impossible to separate the cognate liberty of speaking and of writing.

Although these liberties, to some considerable amount, form part of the political morality of all countries which profess religious toleration and free institutions, the grounds, both philosophical and practical, on which they rest, are perhaps not so familiar to the general mind, nor so thoroughly appreciated by many even of the leaders of opinion, as might have been expected. Those grounds, when rightly understood, are of much wider application than to only one division of the subject, and a thorough consideration of this part of the question will be found the best introduction to the remainder. Those to whom nothing which we are about to say will be new, may therefore, we hope, excuse us, if on a subject which for now three centuries has been so often discussed, we venture on one discussion more.

THE LIBERTY OF THOUGHT AND DISCUSSION

The time, it is to be hoped, is gone by when any defence would be necessary of the 'liberty of the press' as one of the securities against corrupt or tyrannical government. No argument, we may suppose, can now be needed, against permitting a legislature or an executive, not identified in interest with the people, to prescribe opinions to them, and determine what doctrines or what arguments they shall be allowed to hear. This aspect of the question, besides, has been so often and so triumphantly enforced by preceding writers, that it needs not be specially insisted on in this place. Though the law of England, on the subject of the press, is as servile to this day as it was in the time of the Tudors, there is little danger of its being actually put in force against political discussion, except during some temporary panic, when fear of insurrection drives ministers and judges from their propriety; and, speaking generally, it is not, in constitutional countries, to be apprehended that the government, whether completely responsible to the people or not, will often attempt to control the expression of opinion, except when in doing so it makes itself the organ of the general intolerance of the public. Let us suppose, therefore, that the government is entirely at one with the people, and never thinks of exerting any power of coercion unless in agreement with what it conceives to be their voice.

But I deny the right of the people to exercise such coercion, either by themselves or by their government. The power itself is illegitimate. The best government has no more title to it than the worst. It is as noxious, or more noxious, when exerted in accordance with public opinion, than when in opposition to it. If all mankind minus one, were of one opinion, and only one person were of the contrary opinion, mankind would be no more justified in silencing that one person, than he, if he had the power, would be justified in silencing mankind. Were an opinion a personal possession of no value except to the owner; if to be obstructed in the enjoyment of it were simply a private injury, it would make some difference whether the injury was inflicted only on a few persons or on many.

But the peculiar evil of silencing the expression of an opinion is, that it is robbing the human race; posterity as well as the existing generation; those who dissent from the opinion, still more than those who hold it. If the opinion is right, they are deprived of the opportunity of exchanging error for truth: if wrong, they lose, what is almost as great a benefit, the clearer perception and livelier impression of truth, produced by its collision with error. It is necessary to consider separately these two hypotheses, each of which has a distinct branch of the argument corresponding to it. We can never be sure that the opinion we are endeavouring to stifle is a false opinion; and if we were sure, stifling it would be an evil still. First: the opinion which it is attempted to suppress by authority may possibly be true.

Those who desire to suppress it, of course deny its truth; but they are not infallible. They have no authority to decide the question for all mankind, and exclude every other person from the means of judging. To refuse a hearing to an opinion, because they are sure that it is false, is to assume that their certainty is the same thing as absolute certainty. All silencing of discussion is an assumption of infallibility. Its condemnation may be allowed to rest on this common argument, not the worse for being common. Unfortunately for the good sense of mankind, the fact of their fallibility is far from carrying the weight in their practical judgement, which is always allowed to it in theory; for while every one well knows himself to be fallible, few think it necessary to take any precautions against their own fallibility, or admit the supposition that any opinion of which they feel very certain, may be one of the examples of the error to which they acknowledge themselves to be liable.

Absolute princes, or others who are accustomed to unlimited deference, usually feel this complete confidence in their own opinions on nearly all subjects. People more happily situated, who sometimes hear their opinions disputed, and are not wholly unused to be set right when they are wrong, place the same unbounded reliance only on such of their opinions as are shared by all who surround them, or to whom they habitually defer: for in proportion to a man's want of confidence in his own solitary judgement, does he usually repose, with implicit trust, on the infallibility of 'the world' in general. And the world, to each individual, means the part of it with which he comes in contact; his party, his sect, his church, his class of society: the man may be called, by comparison, almost liberal and large-minded to whom it means anything so comprehensive as his own country or his own age.

Nor is his faith in this collective authority at all shaken by his being aware that other ages, countries, sects, churches, classes, and parties have thought, and even now think, the exact reverse. He devolves upon his own world the responsibility of being in the right against the dissentient worlds of other people; and it never troubles him that mere accident has decided which of these numerous worlds is the object of his reliance, and that the same causes which make him a Churchman in London, would have made him a Buddhist or a Confucian in Pekin. Yet it is as evident in itself as any amount of argument can make it, that ages are no more infallible than individuals; every age having held many opinions which subsequent ages have deemed not only false but absurd; and it is as certain that many opinions, now general, will be rejected by future ages, as it is that many, once general, are rejected by the present.

The objection likely to be made to this argument, would probably take some such form as the following. There is no greater assumption of infallibility in forbidding the propagation of error, than in any other thing which is done by public authority on its own judgement and responsibility. Judgement is given to men that they may use it. Because it may be used erroneously, are men to be told that they ought not to use it at all? To prohibit what they think pernicious, is not claiming exemption from error, but fulfilling the duty incumbent on them, although fallible, of acting on their conscientious conviction. If we were never to act on our opinions, because those opinions may be wrong, we should leave all our interests uncared for, and all our duties unperformed. An objection which applies to all conduct can be no valid objection to any conduct in particular.

It is the duty of governments, and of individuals, to form the truest opinions they can; to form them carefully, and never impose them upon others unless they are quite sure of being right. But when they are sure, it is not conscientiousness but cowardice to shrink from acting on their opinions, and allow doctrines which they honestly think dangerous to the welfare of mankind, either in this life or in another, to be scattered abroad without restraint, because other people, in less enlightened times, have persecuted opinions now believed to be true.

Let us take care, it may be said, not to make the same mistake: but governments and nations have made mistakes in other things, which are not denied to be fit subjects for the exercise of authority: they have laid on bad taxes, made unjust wars. Ought we therefore to lay on no taxes, and, under whatever provocation, make no wars? Men, and governments, must act to the best of their ability. There is no such thing as absolute certainty, but there is assurance sufficient for the purposes of human life. We may, and must, assume our opinion to be true for the guidance of our own conduct: and it is assuming no more when we forbid bad men to pervert society by the propagation of opinions which we regard as false and pernicious. I answer, that it is assuming very much more. There is the greatest difference between presuming an opinion to be true, because, with every opportunity for contesting it, it has not been refuted, and assuming its truth for the purpose of not permitting its refutation. Complete liberty of contradicting and disproving our opinion, is the very condition which justifies us in assuming its truth for purposes of action; and on no other terms can a being with human faculties have any rational assurance of being right.

When we consider either the history of opinion, or the ordinary conduct of human life, to what is it to be ascribed that the one and the other are no worse than they are? Not certainly to the inherent force of the human understanding; for, on any matter not self-evident, there are ninety-nine persons totally incapable of judging of it, for one who is capable; and the capacity of the hundredth person is only comparative; for the majority of the eminent men of every past generation held many opinions now known to be erroneous, and did or approved numerous things which no one will now justify. Why is it, then, that there is on the whole a preponderance among mankind of rational opinions and rational conduct?

If there really is this preponderance--which there must be, unless human affairs are, and have always been, in an almost desperate state--it is owing to a quality of the human mind, the source of everything respectable in man, either as an intellectual or as a moral being, namely, that his errors are corrigible. He is capable of rectifying his mistakes by discussion and experience. Not by experience alone. There must be discussion, to show how experience is to be interpreted. Wrong opinions and practices gradually yield to fact and argument: but facts and arguments, to produce any effect on the mind, must be brought before it. Very few facts are able to tell their own story, without comments to bring out their meaning. The whole strength and value, then, of human judgement, depending on the one property, that it can be set right when it is wrong, reliance can be placed on it only when the means of setting it right are kept constantly at hand. In the case of any person whose judgement is really deserving of confidence, how has it become so? Because he has kept his mind open to criticism of his opinions and conduct.

Because it has been his practice to listen to all that could be said against him; to profit by as much of it as was just, and expound to himself, and upon occasion to others, the fallacy of what was fallacious. Because he has felt, that the only way in which a human being can make some approach to knowing the whole of a subject, is by hearing what can be said about it by persons of every variety of opinion, and studying all modes in which it can be looked at by every character of mind. No wise man ever acquired his wisdom in any mode but this; nor is it in the nature of human intellect to become wise in any other manner.

The steady habit of correcting and completing his own opinion by collating it with those of others, so far from causing doubt and hesitation in carrying it into practice, is the only stable foundation for a just reliance on it: for, being cognizant of all that can, at least obviously, be said against him, and having taken up his position against all gainsayers knowing that he has sought for objections and difficulties, instead of avoiding them, and has shut out no light which can be thrown upon the subject from any quarter--he has a right to think his judgement better than that of any person, or any multitude, who have not gone through a similar process. It is not too much to require that what the wisest of mankind, those who are best entitled to trust their own judgement, find necessary to warrant their relying on it, should be submitted to by that miscellaneous collection of a few wise and many foolish individuals, called the public. The most intolerant of churches, the Roman Catholic Church, even at the canonization of a saint, admits, and listens patiently to, a 'devil's advocate'. The holiest of men, it appears, cannot be admitted to posthumous honours, until all that the devil could say against him is known and weighed.

If even the Newtonian philosophy were not permitted to be questioned, mankind could not feel as complete assurance of its truth as they now do. The beliefs which we have most warrant for, have no safeguard to rest on, but a standing invitation to the whole world to prove them unfounded. If the challenge is not accepted, or is accepted and the attempt fails, we are far enough from certainty still; but we have done the best that the existing state of human reason admits of; we have neglected nothing that could give the truth a chance of reaching us: if the lists are kept open, we may hope that if there be a better truth, it will be found when the human mind is capable of receiving it; and in the meantime we may rely on having attained such approach to truth, as is possible in our own day. This is the amount of certainty attainable by a fallible being, and this the sole way of attaining it.

Strange it is, that men should admit the validity of the arguments for free discussion, but object to their being "pushed to an extreme", not seeing that unless the reasons are good for an extreme case, they are not good for any case. Strange that they should imagine that they are not assuming infallibility when they acknowledge that there should be free discussion on all subjects which can possibly be doubtful, but think that some particular principle or doctrine should be forbidden to be questioned because it is so certain, that is, because they are certain that it is certain. To call any proposition certain, while there is anyone who would deny its certainty if permitted, but who is not permitted, is to assume that we ourselves, and those who agree with us, are the judges of certainty, and judges without hearing the other side.

In the present age--which has been described as "destitute of faith, but terrified at scepticism"--in which people feel sure, not so much that their opinions are true, as that they should not know what to do without them--the claims of an opinion to be protected from public attack are rested not so much on its truth, as on its importance to society. There are, it is alleged, certain beliefs, so useful, not to say indispensable to well-being, that it is as much the duty of governments to uphold those beliefs, as to protect any other of the interests of society. In a case of such necessity, and so directly in the line of their duty, something less than infallibility may, it is maintained, warrant, and even bind, governments, to act on their own opinion, confirmed by the general opinion of mankind. It is also often argued, and still oftener thought, that none but bad men would desire to weaken these salutary beliefs; and there can be nothing wrong, it is thought, in restraining bad men, and prohibiting what only such men would wish to practise. This mode of thinking makes the justification of restraints on discussion not a question of the truth of doctrines, but of their usefulness; and flatters itself by that means to escape the responsibility of claiming to be an infallible judge of opinions.

But those who thus satisfy themselves, do not perceive that the assumption of infallibility is merely shifted from one point to another. The usefulness of an opinion is itself matter of opinion: as disputable, as open to discussion and requiring discussion as much, as the opinion itself. There is the same need of an infallible judge of opinions to decide an opinion to be noxious, as to decide it to be false, unless the opinion condemned has full opportunity of defending itself. And it will not do to say that the heretic may be allowed to maintain the utility or harmlessness of his opinion, though forbidden to maintain its truth. The truth of an opinion is part of its utility.

If we would know whether or not it is desirable that a proposition should be believed, is it possible to exclude the consideration of whether or not it is true? In the opinion, not of bad men, but of the best men, no belief which is contrary to truth can be really useful: and can we prevent such men from urging that plea, when they are charged with culpability for denying some doctrine which they are told is useful, but which they believe to be false? Those who are on the side of received opinions, never fail to take all possible advantage of this plea; we do not find them handling the question of utility as if it could be completely abstracted from that of truth: on the contrary, it is because their doctrine is 'the truth', that the knowledge or the belief of it is held to be so indispensable. There can be no fair discussion of the question of usefulness, when an argument so vital may be employed on one side, but not on the other. And in point of fact, when law or public feeling do not permit the truth of an opinion to be disputed, they are just as little tolerant of a denial of its usefulness. The utmost they allow is an extenuation of its absolute necessity or of the positive guilt of rejecting it. In order more fully to illustrate the mischief of denying a hearing to opinions because we, in our own judgement, have condemned them, it will be desirable to fix down the discussion to a concrete case; and we choose, by preference, the cases which are least favourable to us–in which the argument against freedom of opinion, both on the score of truth and on that of utility, is considered the strongest. Let the opinions impugned be the belief in a God and in a future state, or any of the commonly received doctrines of morality. To fight the battle on such ground, gives a great advantage to an unfair antagonist; since he will be sure to say, Are these the doctrines which you do not deem sufficiently certain to be taken under the protection of law? Is the belief in a God one of the opinions, to feel sure of which, you hold to be assuming infallibility?

But I must be permitted to observe, that it is not the feeling sure of a doctrine which I call an assumption of infallibility. It is the undertaking to decide that question for others, without allowing them to hear what can be said on the contrary side. And I denounce and reprobate this pretension not the less, if put forth on the side of my most solemn convictions. However positive any one's persuasion may be, not only of the falsity, but of the pernicious consequences--not only of the pernicious consequences, but the immorality and impiety of an opinion; yet if, in pursuance of that private judgement, though backed by the public judgement of his country or his contemporaries, he prevents the opinion from being heard in its defence, he assumes infallibility. And so far from the assumption being less objectionable or less dangerous because the opinion is called immoral or impious, this is the case of all others in which it is most fatal.

These are exactly the occasions on which the men of one generation commit those dreadful mistakes which excite the astonishment and horror of posterity. It is among such that we find the instances memorable in history, when the arm of the law has been employed to root out the best men and the noblest doctrines; with deplorable success as to the men, though some of the doctrines have survived to be invoked, in defence of similar conduct towards those who dissent from them, or from their received interpretation.

Mankind can hardly be too often reminded, that there was once a man named Socrates, between whom and the legal authorities and public opinion of his time, there took place a memorable collision. Born in an age and country abounding in individual greatness, this man has been handed down to us by those who best knew both him and the age, as the most virtuous man in it; while we know him as the head and prototype of all subsequent teachers of virtue, the source equally of the lofty inspiration of Plato and the judicious utilitarianism of Aristotle, "i maestri di colour che sanno", the two headsprings of ethical as of all other philosophy.

This acknowledged master of all the eminent thinkers who have since lived--whose fame, still growing after more than two thousand years, all but outweighs the whole remainder of the names which make his native city illustrious--was put to death by his countrymen, after a judicial conviction, for impiety and immorality. Impiety, in denying the gods recognised by the state; indeed his accuser asserted that he believed in no gods at all. Immorality, in being, by his doctrines and instructions, a "corrupter of youth." Of these charges the tribunal, there is every ground for believing, honestly found him guilty, and condemned the man who probably of all then born had deserved best of mankind, to be put to death as a criminal.

To pass from this to the only other instance of judicial iniquity, the mention of which, after the condemnation of Socrates, would not be an anti-climax: the event which took place on Calvary rather more than eighteen hundred years ago. The man who left on the memory of those who witnessed his life and conversation, such an impression of his moral grandeur, that eighteen subsequent centuries have done homage to him as the Almighty in person, was ignominiously put to death, as what? As a blasphemer. Men did not merely mistake their benefactor; they mistook him for the exact contrary of what he was, and treated him as that prodigy of impiety, which they themselves are now held to be, for their treatment of him. The feelings with which mankind now regard these lamentable transactions, especially the latter of the two, render them extremely unjust in their judgement of the unhappy actors.

These were, to all appearance, not bad men--not worse than men most commonly are, but rather the contrary; men who possessed in a full, or somewhat more than a full measure, the religious, moral, and patriotic feelings of their time and people: the very kind of men who, in all times, our own included, have every chance of passing through life blameless and respected. The high-priest who rent his garments when the words were pronounced, which, according to all the ideas of his country, constituted the blackest guilt, was in all probability quite as sincere in his horror and indignation, as the generality of respectable and pious men now are in the religious and moral sentiments they profess; and most of those who now shudder at his conduct, if they had lived in his time and been born Jews, would have acted precisely as he did. Orthodox Christians who are tempted to think that those who stoned to death the first martyrs must have been worse men than they themselves are, ought to remember that one of those persecutors was Saint Paul.

Let us add one more example, the most striking of all, if the impressiveness of an error is measured by the wisdom and virtue of him who falls into it. If ever anyone, possessed of power, had grounds for thinking himself the best and most enlightened among his contemporaries, it was the Emperor Marcus Aurelius. Absolute monarch of the whole civilized world, he preserved through life not only the most unblemished justice, but what was less to be expected from his Stoical breeding, the tenderest heart. The few failings which are attributed to him, were all on the side of indulgence: while his writings, the highest ethical product of the ancient mind, differ scarcely perceptibly, if they differ at all, from the most characteristic teachings of Christ.

This man, a better Christian in all but the dogmatic sense of the word, than almost any of the ostensibly Christian sovereigns who have since reigned, persecuted Christianity. Placed at the summit of all the previous attainments of humanity, with an open, unfettered intellect, and a character which led him of himself to embody in his moral writings the Christian ideal, he yet failed to see that Christianity was to be a good and not an evil to the world, with his duties to which he was so deeply penetrated. Existing society he knew to be in a deplorable state. But such as it was, he saw or thought he saw, that it was held together and prevented from being worse, by belief and reverence of the received divinities. As a ruler of mankind, he deemed it his duty not to suffer society to fall in pieces; and saw not how, if its existing ties were removed, any others could be formed which could again knit it together.

The new religion openly aimed at dissolving these ties: unless, therefore, it was his duty to adopt that religion, it seemed to be his duty to put it down, inasmuch then as the theology of Christianity did not appear to him true or of divine origin; inasmuch as this strange history of a crucified God was not credible to him, and a system which purported to rest entirely upon a foundation to him so wholly unbelievable, could not be foreseen by him to be that renovating agency which, after all abatements, it has in fact proved to be; the gentlest and most amiable of philosophers and rulers, under a solemn sense of duty, authorized the persecution of Christianity. To my mind this is one of the most tragical facts in all history. It is a bitter thought, how different a thing the Christianity of the world might have been, if the Christian faith had been adopted as the religion of the empire under the auspices of Marcus Aurelius instead of those of Constantine.

But it would be equally unjust to him and false to truth, to deny, that no one plea which can be urged for punishing anti-Christian teaching, was wanting to Marcus Aurelius for punishing, as he did, the propagation of Christianity. No Christian more firmly believes that Atheism is false, and tends to the dissolution of society, than Marcus Aurelius believed the same things of Christianity; he who, of all men then living, might have been thought the most capable of appreciating it. Unless any one who approves of punishment for the promulgation of opinions, flatters himself that he is a wiser and better man than Marcus Aurelius--more deeply versed in the wisdom of his time, more elevated in his intellect it—more earnest in his search for truth, or more single-minded in his devotion to it when found;--let him abstain from that assumption of the joint infallibility of himself and the multitude, which the great Antoninus made with so unfortunate a result. Aware of the impossibility of defending the use of punishment for restraining irreligious opinions, by any argument which will not justify Marcus Antoninus, the enemies of religious freedom, when hard pressed, occasionally accept this consequence, and say, with Dr. Johnson, that the persecutors of Christianity were in the right; that persecution is an ordeal through which truth ought to pass, and always passes successfully, legal penalties being, in the end, powerless against truth, though sometimes beneficially effective against mischievous errors. This is a form of the argument for religious intolerance, sufficiently remarkable not to be passed without notice.

A theory which maintains that truth may justifiably be persecuted because persecution cannot possibly do it any harm, cannot be charged with being intentionally hostile to the reception of new truths; but we cannot commend the generosity of its dealing with the persons to whom mankind are indebted for them. To discover to the world something which deeply concerns it, and of which it was previously ignorant; to prove to it that it had been mistaken on some vital point of temporal or spiritual interest, is as important a service as a human being can render to his fellow-creatures, and in certain cases, as in those of the early Christians and of the Reformers, those who think with Dr. Johnson believe it to have been the most precious gift which could be bestowed on mankind.

That the authors of such splendid benefits should be requited by martyrdom; that their reward should be to be dealt with as the vilest of criminals, is not, upon this theory, a deplorable error and misfortune, for which humanity should mourn in sackcloth and ashes, but the normal and justifiable state of things. The propounder of a new truth, according to this doctrine, should stand, as stood, in the legislation of the Locrians, the proposer of a new law, with a halter round his neck, to be instantly tightened if the public assembly did not, on hearing his reasons, then and there adopt his proposition. People who defend this mode of treating benefactors, cannot be supposed to set much value on the benefit; and I believe this view of the subject is mostly confined to the sort of persons who think that new truths may have been desirable once, but that we have had enough of them now.

But, indeed, the dictum that truth always triumphs over persecution, is one of those pleasant falsehoods which men repeat after one another till they pass into commonplaces, but which all experience refutes. History teems with instances of truth put down by persecution. If not suppressed forever, it may be thrown back for centuries. To speak only of religious opinions: the Reformation broke out at least twenty times before Luther, and was put down. Arnold of Brescia was put down. Fra Dolcino was put down. Savonarola was put down. The Albigeois were put down.

The Vaudois were put down. The Lollards were put down. The Hussites were put down. Even after the era of Luther, wherever persecution was persisted in, it was successful. In Spain, Italy, Flanders, the Austrian empire, Protestantism was rooted out; and, most likely, would have been so in England, had Queen Mary lived, or Queen Elizabeth died. Persecution has always succeeded, save where the heretics were too strong a party to be effectually persecuted. No reasonable person can doubt that Christianity might have been extirpated in the Roman empire. It spread, and became predominant, because the persecutions were only occasional, lasting but a short time, and separated by long intervals of almost undisturbed propagandism. It is a piece of idle sentimentality that truth, merely as truth, has any inherent power denied to error, of prevailing against the dungeon and the stake. Men are not more zealous for truth than they often are for error, and a sufficient application of legal or even of social penalties will generally succeed in stopping the propagation of either. The real advantage which truth has, consists in this, that when an opinion is true, it may be extinguished once, twice, or many times, but in the course of ages there will generally be found persons to rediscover it, until some one of its reappearances falls on a time when from favourable circumstances it escapes persecution until it has made such head as to withstand all subsequent attempts to suppress it.

It will be said, that we do not now put to death the introducers of new opinions: we are not like our fathers who slew the prophets, we even build sepulchres to them. It is true we no longer put heretics to death; and the amount of penal infliction which modern feeling would probably tolerate, even against the most obnoxious opinions, is not sufficient to extirpate them. But let us not flatter ourselves that we are yet free from the stain even of legal persecution. Penalties for opinion, or at least for its expression, still exist by law; and their enforcement is not, even in these times, so unexampled as to make it at all incredible that they may some day be revived in full force. In the year 1857, at the summer assizes of the county of Cornwall, an unfortunate man, said to be of unexceptionable conduct in all relations of life, was sentenced to twenty-one months imprisonment, for uttering, and writing on a gate, some offensive words concerning Christianity.

Within a month of the same time, at the Old Bailey, two persons, on two separate occasions, were rejected as jurymen, and one of them grossly insulted by the judge and one of the counsel, because they honestly declared that they had no theological belief; and a third, a foreigner, for the same reason, was denied justice against a thief. This refusal of redress took place in virtue of the legal doctrine, that no person can be allowed to give evidence in a court of justice, who does not profess belief in a God and in a future state; which is equivalent to declaring such persons to be outlaws, excluded from the protection of the tribunals; who may not only be robbed or assaulted with impunity, if no one but themselves, or persons of similar opinions, be present, but anyone else may be robbed or assaulted with impunity, if the proof of the fact depends on their evidence.

The assumption on which this is grounded, is that the oath is worthless, of a person who does not believe in a future state; a proposition which betokens much ignorance of history in those who assent to it and would be maintained by no one who had the smallest conception how many of the persons in greatest repute with the world, both for virtues and for attainments, are well known, at least to their intimates, to be unbelievers.

The rule, besides, is suicidal, and cuts away its own foundation. Under pretence that atheists must be liars, it admits the testimony of all atheists who are willing to lie, and rejects only those who brave the obloquy of publicly confessing a detested creed rather than affirm a falsehood. A rule thus self-convicted of absurdity so far as regards its professed purpose, can be kept in force only as a badge of hatred, a relic of persecution; a persecution, too, having the peculiarity that the qualification for undergoing it is the being clearly proved not to deserve it. The rule, and the theory it implies, are hardly less insulting to believers than to infidels. For if he who does not believe in a future state necessarily lies, it follows that they who do believe are only prevented from lying, if prevented they are, by the fear of hell. As suggested, not do the authors and abettors of the rule the injury of supposing, that the conception which they have formed of Christian virtue is drawn from their own consciousness. These, indeed, are but rags and remnants of persecution, and may be thought to be not so much an indication of the wish to persecute, as an example of that very frequent infirmity of English minds, which makes them take a preposterous pleasure in the assertion of a bad principle, when they are no longer bad enough to desire to carry it really into practice. But unhappily there is no security in the state of the public mind, that the suspension of worse forms of legal persecution, which has lasted for about the space of a generation, will continue. In this age the quiet surface of routine is as often ruffled by attempts to resuscitate past evils, as to introduce new benefits.

What is boasted of at the present time as the revival of religion, is always, in narrow and uncultivated minds, at least as much the revival of bigotry; and where there is the strongest permanent leaven of intolerance in the feelings of a people, which at all times abides in the middle classes of this country, it needs but little to provoke them into actively persecuting those whom they have never ceased to think proper objects of persecution. For it is this--it is the opinions men entertain, and the feelings they cherish, respecting those who disown the beliefs they deem important, which makes this country not a place of mental freedom. For a long time past, the chief mischief of the legal penalties is that they strengthen the social stigma. It is that stigma which is really effective, and so effective is it, that the profession of opinions which are under the ban of society is much less common in England, than is, in many other countries, the avowal of those which incur risk of judicial punishment. In respect to all persons but those whose pecuniary circumstances make them independent of the goodwill of other people, opinion, on this subject, is as efficacious as law; men might as well be imprisoned, as excluded from the means of earning their bread. Those whose bread is already secured, and who desire no favours from men in power, or from bodies of men, or from the public, have nothing to fear from the open avowal of any opinions, but to be ill-thought of and ill-spoken of, and this it ought not to require a very heroic mould to enable them to bear.

There is no room for any appeal and misericordiam on behalf of such persons. But though we do not now inflict so much evil on those who think differently from us, as it was formerly our custom to do, it may be that we do ourselves as much evil as ever by our treatment of them. Socrates was put to death, but the Socratic philosophy rose like the sun in heaven, and spread its illumination over the whole intellectual firmament. Christians were cast to the lions, but the Christian Church grew up a stately and spreading tree, overtopping the older and less vigorous growths, and stifling them by its shade. Our merely social intolerance, kills no one, roots out no opinions, but induces men to disguise them, or to abstain from any active effort for their diffusion.

With us, heretical opinions do not perceptibly gain or even lose, ground in each decade or generation; they never blaze out far and wide, but continue to smoulder in the narrow circles of thinking and studious persons among whom they originate, without ever lighting up the general affairs of mankind with either a true or a deceptive light. It thus is kept up a state of things very satisfactory to some minds, because, without the unpleasant process of fining or imprisoning anybody, it maintains all prevailing opinions outwardly undisturbed, while it does not absolutely interdict the exercise of reason by dissentients afflicted with the malady of thought. A convenient plan for having peace in the intellectual world, and keeping all things going on therein very much as they do already. But the price paid for this sort of intellectual pacification, is the sacrifice of the entire moral courage of the human mind.

A state of things in which a large portion of the most active and enquiring intellects find it advisable to keep the genuine principles and grounds of their convictions within their own breasts, and attempt, in what they address to the public, to fit as much as they can of their own conclusions to premises which they have internally renounced, cannot send forth the open, fearless characters, and logical, consistent intellects who once adorned the thinking world. The sort of men who can be looked for under it, are either mere conformers to commonplace, or time-servers for truth whose arguments on all great subjects are meant for their hearers, and are not those which have convinced themselves. Those who avoid this alternative, do so by narrowing their thoughts and interests to things which can be spoken of without venturing within the region of principles, that is, to small practical matters, which would come right of themselves, if but the minds of mankind were strengthened and enlarged, and which will never be made effectually right until then; while that which would strengthen and enlarge men's minds, free and daring speculation on the highest subjects, is abandoned.

Those in whose eyes this reticence on the part of heretics is no evil, should consider in the first place, that in consequence of it there is never any fair and thorough discussion of heretical opinions; and that such of them as could not stand such a discussion, though they may be prevented from spreading, do not disappear. But it is not the minds of heretics that are deteriorated most, by the ban placed on all enquiry which does not end in the orthodox conclusions. The greatest harm done is to those who are not heretics, and whose whole mental development is cramped, and their reason cowed, by the fear of heresy. Who can compute what the world loses in the multitude of promising intellects combined with timid characters, who dare not follow out any bold, vigorous, independent train of thought, lest it should land them in something which would admit of being considered irreligious or immoral? Among them we may occasionally see some man of deep conscientiousness, and subtile and refined understanding, who spends a life in sophisticating with an intellect which he cannot silence, and exhausts the resources of ingenuity in attempting to reconcile the promptings of his conscience and reason with orthodoxy, which yet he does not, perhaps, to the end succeed in doing.

No one can be a great thinker who does not recognize, that as a thinker it is his first duty to follow his intellect to whatever conclusions it may lead. Truth gains more even by the errors of one who, with due study and preparation, thinks for himself, than by the true opinions of those who only hold them because they do not suffer themselves to think. Not that it is solely, or chiefly, to form great thinkers, that freedom of thinking is required. On the contrary, it is as much, and even more indispensable, to enable average human beings to attain the mental stature which they are capable of. There have been, and may again be, great individual thinkers, in a general atmosphere of mental slavery.

But there never has been, nor ever will be, in that atmosphere, an intellectually active people. Where any people has made a temporary approach to such a character, it has been because the dread of heterodox speculation was for a time suspended. Where there is a tacit convention that principles are not to be disputed; where the discussion of the greatest questions which can occupy humanity is considered to be closed, we cannot hope to find that generally high scale of mental activity which has made some periods of history so remarkable. Never when controversy avoided the subjects which are large and important enough to kindle enthusiasm, was the mind of a people stirred up from its foundations, and the impulse given which raised even persons of the most ordinary intellect to something of the dignity of thinking beings.

Of such we have had an example in the condition of Europe during the times immediately following the Reformation; another, though limited to the Continent and to a more cultivated class, in the speculative movement of the latter half of the eighteenth century; and a third, of still briefer duration, in the intellectual fermentation of Germany during the Goethian and Fichtean period. These periods differed widely in the particular opinions which they developed; but were alike in this, that during all three the yoke of authority was broken. In each, an old mental despotism had been thrown off, and no new one had yet taken its place.

The impulse given at these three periods has made Europe what it now is. Every single improvement which has taken place either in the human mind or in institutions, may be traced distinctly to one or other of them. Appearances have for some time indicated that all three impulses are well-nigh spent; and we can expect no fresh start, until we again assert our mental freedom. Let us now pass to the second division of the argument, and dismissing the Supposition that any of the received opinions may be false, let us assume them to be true, and examine into the worth of the manner in which they are likely to be held, when their truth is not freely and openly canvassed. However unwillingly a person who has a strong opinion may admit the possibility that his opinion may be false, he ought to be moved by the consideration that however true it may be, if it is not fully, frequently, and fearlessly discussed, it will be held as a dead dogma, not a living truth.

There is a class of persons who think it enough if a person assents undoubtingly to what they think true, though he has no knowledge whatever of the grounds of the opinion, and could not make a tenable defence of it against the most superficial objections. Such persons, if they can once get their creed taught from authority, naturally think that no good, and some harm, comes of its being allowed to be questioned. Where their influence prevails, they make it nearly impossible for the received opinion to be rejected wisely and considerately, though it may still be rejected rashly and ignorantly; for to shut out discussion entirely is seldom possible, and when it once gets in, beliefs not grounded on conviction are apt to give way before the slightest semblance of an argument. Waiving, however, this possibility--assuming that the true opinion abides in the mind, but abides as a prejudice, a belief independent of, and proof against, argument--this is not the way in which truth ought to be held by a rational being. This is not knowing the truth. Truth, thus held, is but one superstition the more, accidentally clinging to the words which enunciate a truth.

If the intellect and judgement of mankind ought to be cultivated, a thing which Protestants at least do not deny, on what can these faculties be more appropriately exercised by any one, than on the things which concern him so much that it is considered necessary for him to hold opinions on them? If the cultivation of the understanding consists in one thing more than in another, it is surely in learning the grounds of one's own opinions. Whatever people believe, on subjects on which it is of the first importance to believe rightly, they ought to be able to defend against at least the common objections. But, some one may say, "Let them be taught the grounds of their opinions. It does not follow that opinions must be merely parroted because they are never heard controverted.

Persons who learn geometry do not simply commit the theorems to memory, but understand and learn likewise the demonstrations; and it would be absurd to say that they remain ignorant of the grounds of geometrical truths, because they never hear any one deny, and attempt to disprove them." Undoubtedly: and such teaching suffices on a subject like mathematics, where there is nothing at all to be said on the wrong side of the question. The peculiarity of the evidence of mathematical truths is, that all the argument is on one side. There are no objections, and no answers to objections.

But on every subject on which difference of opinion is possible, the truth depends on a balance to be struck between two sets of conflicting reasons. Even in natural philosophy, there is always some other explanation possible of the same facts; some geocentric theory instead of heliocentric, some phlogiston instead of oxygen; and it has to be shown why that other theory cannot be the true one: and until this is shown and until we know how it is shown, we do not understand the grounds of our opinion. But when we turn to subjects infinitely more complicated, to morals, religion, politics, social relations, and the business of life, three-fourths of the arguments for every disputed opinion consist in dispelling the appearances which favour some opinion different from it. The greatest orator, save one, of antiquity, has left it on record that he always studied his adversary's case with as great, if not with still greater, intensity than even his own. What Cicero practised as the means of forensic success, requires to be imitated by all who study any subject in order to arrive at the truth. He who knows only his own side of the case, knows little of that.

His reasons may be good, and no one may have been able to refute them. But if he is equally unable to refute the reasons on the opposite side; if he does not so much as know what they are, he has no ground for preferring either opinion. The rational position for him would be suspension of judgement, and unless he contents himself with that, he is either led by authority, or adopts, like the generality of the world, the side to which he feels most inclination. Nor is it enough that he should hear the arguments of adversaries from his own teachers, presented as they state them, and accompanied by what they offer as refutations. This is not the way to do justice to the arguments, or bring them into real contact with his own mind. He must be able to hear them from persons who actually believe them; who defend them in earnest, and do their very utmost for them.

He must know them in their most plausible and persuasive form; he must feel the whole force of the difficulty which the true view of the subject has to encounter and dispose of, else he will never really possess himself of the portion of truth which meets and removes that difficulty. Ninety-nine in a hundred of what are called educated men are in this condition, even of those who can argue fluently for their opinions.

Their conclusion may be true, but it might be false for anything they know: they have never thrown themselves into the mental position of those who think differently from them, and considered what such persons may have to say; and consequently they do not, in any proper sense of the word, know the doctrine which they themselves profess. They do not know those parts of it which explain and justify the remainder; the considerations which show that a fact which seemingly conflicts with another is reconcilable with it, or that, of two apparently strong reasons, one and not the other ought to be preferred. All that part of the truth which turns the scale, and decides the judgement of a completely informed mind, they are strangers to; nor is it ever really known, but to those who have attended equally and impartially to both sides, and endeavored to see the reasons of both in the strongest light. So essential is this discipline to a real understanding of moral and human subjects, that if opponents of all important truths do not exist, it is indispensable to imagine them and supply them with the strongest arguments which the most skilful devil's advocate can conjure up.

To abate the force of these considerations, an enemy of free discussion may be supposed to say, that there is no necessity for mankind in general to know and understand all that can be said against or for their opinions by philosophers and theologians. That it is not needful for common men to be able to expose all the misstatements or fallacies of an ingenious opponent. That it is enough if there is always somebody capable of answering them, so that nothing likely to mislead uninstructed persons remains unrefuted. That simple minds, having been taught the obvious grounds of the truths inculcated on them, may trust to authority for the rest, and being aware that they have neither knowledge nor talent to resolve every difficulty which can be raised, may repose in the assurance that all those which have been raised have been or can be answered, by those who are specially trained to the task. Conceding to this view of the subject the utmost that can be claimed for it by those most easily satisfied with the amount of understanding of truth which ought to accompany the belief of it; even so, the argument for free discussion is no way weakened. For even this doctrine acknowledges that mankind ought to have a rational assurance that all objections have been satisfactorily answered; and how are they to be answered if that which requires to be answered is not spoken? or how can the answer be known to be satisfactory, if the objectors have no opportunity of showing that it is unsatisfactory? If not the public, at least the philosophers and theologians who are to resolve the difficulties, must make themselves familiar with those difficulties in their most puzzling form; and this cannot be accomplished unless they are freely stated, and placed in the most advantageous light which they admit of. The Catholic Church has its own way of dealing with this embarrassing problem.

It makes a broad separation between those who can be permitted to receive its doctrines on conviction, and those who must accept them on trust. Neither, indeed, are allowed any choice as to what they will accept; but the clergy, such at least as can be fully confided in, may admissibly and meritoriously make themselves acquainted with the arguments of opponents, in order to answer them, and may, therefore, read heretical books; the laity, not unless by special permission, hard to be obtained. This discipline recognizes a knowledge of the enemy's case as beneficial to the teachers, but finds means, consistent with this, of denying it to the rest of the world: thus giving to the elite more mental culture, though not more mental freedom, than it allows to the mass.

By this device it succeeds in obtaining the kind of mental superiority which its purposes require; for though culture without freedom never made a large and liberal mind, it can make a clever *nisi prius* advocate of a cause. But in countries professing Protestantism, this resource is denied; since Protestants hold, at least in theory, that the responsibility for the choice of a religion must be borne by each for himself, and cannot be thrown off upon teachers. Besides, in the present state of the world, it is practically impossible that writings which are read by the instructed can be kept from the uninstructed. If the teachers of mankind are to be cognizant of all that they ought to know, everything must be free to be written and published without restraint.

If, however, the mischievous operation of the absence of free discussion, when the received opinions are true, were confined to leaving men ignorant of the grounds of those opinions, it might be thought that this, if an intellectual, is no moral evil, and does not affect the worth of the opinions, regarded in their influence on the character. The fact, however, is, that not only the grounds of the opinion are forgotten in the absence of discussion, but too often the meaning of the opinion itself. The words which convey it, cease to suggest ideas, or suggest only a small portion of those they were originally employed to communicate. Instead of a vivid conception and a living belief, there remain only a few phrases retained by rote; or, if any part, the shell and husk only of the meaning is retained, the finer essence being lost. The great stage in human history which this fact occupies and fills, cannot be too earnestly studied and meditated on.

It is illustrated in the experience of almost all ethical doctrines and religious creeds. They are all full of meaning and vitality to those who originate them, and to the direct disciples of the originators. Their meaning continues to be felt in undiminished strength, and is perhaps brought out into even fuller consciousness, so long as the struggle lasts to give the doctrine or creed an ascendency over other creeds. At last it either prevails, and becomes the general opinion, or its progress stops; it keeps possession of the ground it has gained, but ceases to spread further. When either of these results has become apparent, controversy on the subject flags, and gradually dies away.

The doctrine has taken its place, if not as a received opinion, as one of the admitted sects or divisions of opinion: those who hold it have generally inherited, not adopted it; and conversion from one of these doctrines to another, being now an exceptional fact, occupies little place in the thoughts of their professors.

Instead of being, as at first, constantly on the alert either to defend themselves against the world, or to bring the world over to them, they have subsided into acquiescence, and neither listen, when they can help it, to arguments against their creed, nor trouble dissentients with arguments in its favour. From this time may usually be dated the decline in the living power of the doctrine. We often hear the teachers of all creeds lamenting the difficulty of keeping up in the minds of believers a lively apprehension of the truth which they nominally recognize, so that it may penetrate the feelings, and acquire a real mastery over the conduct.

No such difficulty is complained of while the creed is still fighting for its existence: even the weaker combatants then know and feel what they are fighting for, and the difference between it and other doctrines; and in that period of every creed's existence, not a few persons may be found, who have realized its fundamental principles in all the forms of thought, have weighed and considered them in all their important bearings, and have experienced the full effect on the character, which belief in that creed ought to produce in a mind thoroughly imbued with it. But when it has come to be an hereditary creed, and to be received passively, not actively--when the mind is no longer compelled, in the same degree as at first, to exercise its vital powers on the questions which its belief presents to it, there is a progressive tendency to forget all of the belief except the formularies, or to give it a dull and torpid assent, as if accepting it on trust dispensed with the necessity of realizing it in consciousness, or testing it by personal experience; until it almost ceases to connect itself at all with the inner life of the human being. Then are seen the cases, so frequent in this age of the world as almost to form the majority, in which the creed remains as it were outside the mind, encrusting and petrifying it against all other influences addressed to the higher parts of our nature; manifesting its power by not suffering any fresh and living conviction to get in, but itself doing nothing for the mind or heart, except standing sentinel over them to keep them vacant.

To what an extent doctrines intrinsically fitted to make the deepest impression upon the mind may remain in it as dead beliefs, without being ever realized in the imagination, the feelings, or the understanding, is exemplified by the manner in which the majority of believers hold the doctrines of Christianity. By Christianity we here mean what is accounted such by all churches and sects--the maxims and precepts contained in the New Testament. These are considered sacred, and accepted as laws, by all professing Christians.

Yet it is scarcely too much to say that not one Christian in a thousand guides or tests his individual conduct by reference to those laws. The standard to which he does refer it, is the custom of his nation, his class, or his religious profession. He has thus, on the one hand, a collection of ethical maxims, which he believes to have been vouchsafed to him by infallible wisdom as rules for his government; and on the other, a set of every-day judgements and practices, which go a certain length with some of those maxims, not so great a length with others, stand in direct opposition to some, and are, on the whole, a compromise between the Christian creed and the interests and suggestions of worldly life. To the first of these standards he gives his homage; to the other his real allegiance.

All Christians believe that the blessed are the poor and humble, and those who are ill-used by the world; that it is easier for a camel to pass through the eye of a needle than for a rich man to enter the kingdom of heaven; that they should judge not, lest they be judged; that they should swear not at all; that they should love their neighbour as themselves; that if one take their cloak, they should give him their coat also; that they should take no thought for the morrow; that if they would be perfect, they should sell all that they have and give it to the poor. They are not insincere when they say that they believe these things. They do believe them, as people believe what they have always heard lauded and never discussed. But in the sense of that living belief which regulates conduct, they believe these doctrines just up to the point to which it is usual to act upon them.

The doctrines in their integrity are serviceable to pelt adversaries with; and it is understood that they are to be put forward as the reasons for whatever people do that they think laudable. But any one who reminded them that the maxims require an infinity of things which they never even think of doing would gain nothing but to be classed among those very unpopular characters who affect to be better than other people. The doctrines have no hold on ordinary believers--are not a power in their minds. They have an habitual respect for the sound of them, but no feeling which spreads from the words to the things signified, and forces the mind to take them in, and make them conform to the formula. Whenever conduct is concerned, they look round for Mr. A and B to direct them how far to go in obeying Christ.

Now we may be well assured that the case was not thus, but far otherwise, with the early Christians. Had it been thus, Christianity never would have expanded from an obscure sect of the despised Hebrews into the religion of the Roman empire. When their enemies said, "See how these Christians love one another" they assuredly had a much livelier feeling of the meaning of their creed than they have ever had since. And to this cause, probably, it is chiefly owing that Christianity now makes so little progress in extending its domain, and after eighteen centuries, is still nearly confined to Europeans and the descendants of Europeans.

Even with the strictly religious, who are much in earnest about their doctrines, and attach a greater amount of meaning to many of them than people in general, it commonly happens that the part which is thus comparatively active in their minds is that which was made by Calvin, or Knox, or some such person much nearer in character to themselves. The sayings of Christ coexist passively in their minds, producing hardly any effect beyond what is caused by mere listening to words so amiable and bland. There are many reasons, doubtless, why doctrines which are the badge of a sect retain more of their vitality than those common to all recognized sects, and why more pains are taken by teachers to keep their meaning alive; but one reason certainly is, that the peculiar doctrines are more questioned, and have to be oftener defended against open gainsayers. Both teachers and learners go to sleep at their post, as soon as there is no enemy in the field.

The same thing holds true, generally speaking, of all traditional doctrines--those of prudence and knowledge of life, as well as of morals or religion. All languages and literatures are full of general observations on life, both as to what it is, and how to conduct oneself in it; observations which everybody knows, which everybody repeats, or hears with acquiescence, which are received as truisms, yet of which most people first truly learn the meaning, when experience, generally of a painful kind, has made it a reality to them. How often, when smarting under some unforeseen misfortune or disappointment, does a person call to mind some proverb or common saying familiar to him all his life, the meaning of which, if he had ever before felt it as he does now, would have saved him from the calamity.

There are indeed reasons for this, other than the absence of discussion: there are many truths of which the full meaning cannot be realized, until personal experience has brought it home. But much more of the meaning even of these would have been understood, and what was understood would have been far more deeply impressed on the mind, if the man had been accustomed to hear it argued pro and con by people who did understand it. The fatal tendency of mankind to leave off thinking about a thing when it is no longer doubtful, is the cause of half their errors. A contemporary author has well spoken of "the deep slumber of a decided opinion".

But what! Is the absence of unanimity an indispensable condition of true knowledge? Is it necessary that some part of mankind should persist in error, to enable any to realize the truth? Does a belief cease to be real and vital as soon as it is generally received--and is a proposition never thoroughly understood and felt unless some doubt of it remains? As soon as mankind have unanimously accepted a truth, does the truth perish within them? The highest aim and best result of improved intelligence, it has hitherto been thought, is to unite mankind more and more in the acknowledgment of all important truths: and does the intelligence only last as long as it has not achieved its object? Do the fruits of conquest perish by the very completeness of the victory?

We affirm no such thing. As mankind improve, the number of doctrines which are no longer disputed or doubted will be constantly on the increase: and the well-being of mankind may almost be measured by the number and gravity of the truths which have reached the point of being uncontested. The cessation, on one question after another, of serious controversy, is one of the necessary incidents of the consolidation of opinion; a consolidation as salutary in the case of true opinions, as it is dangerous and noxious when the opinions are erroneous. But though this gradual narrowing of the bounds of diversity of opinion is necessary in both senses of the term, being at once inevitable and indispensable, we are not therefore obliged to conclude that all its consequences must be beneficial.

The loss of so important an aid to the intelligent and living apprehension of a truth, as is afforded by the necessity of explaining it to, or defending it against, opponents, though not sufficient to outweigh, is no trifling drawback from, the benefit of its universal recognition. Where this advantage can no longer be had, I confess I should like to see the teachers of mankind endeavoring to provide a substitute for it; some contrivance for making the difficulties of the question as present to the learner's consciousness, as if they were pressed upon him by a dissentient champion, eager for his conversion.

But instead of seeking contrivances for this purpose, they have lost those they formerly had. The Socratic dialectics, so magnificently exemplified in the dialogues of Plato, were a contrivance of this description. They were essentially a negative discussion of the great questions of philosophy and life, directed with consummate skill to the purpose of convincing any one who had merely adopted the commonplaces of received opinion, that he did not understand the subject--that he as yet attached no definite meaning to the doctrines he professed; in order that, becoming aware of his ignorance, he might be put in the way to attain a stable belief, resting on a clear apprehension both of the meaning of doctrines and of their evidence. The school disputations of the Middle Ages had a somewhat similar object.

They were intended to make sure that the pupil understood his own opinion, and the opinion opposed to it, and could enforce the grounds of the one and confute those of the other. These last-mentioned contests had indeed the incurable defect, that the premises appealed to were taken from authority, not from reason; and, as a discipline to the mind, they were in every respect inferior to the powerful dialectics which formed the intellects of the 'Socratici viri': but the modern mind owes far more to both than it is generally willing to admit, and the present modes of education contain nothing which in the smallest degree supplies the place either of the one or of the other.

A person who derives all his instruction from teachers or books, even if he escape the besetting temptation of contenting himself with cram, is under no compulsion to hear both sides; accordingly it is far from a frequent accomplishment, even among thinkers, to know both sides; and the weakest part of what everybody says in defence of his opinion, is what he intends as a reply to antagonists. It is the fashion of the present time to disparage negative logic --that which points out weaknesses in theory or errors in practice, without establishing positive truths. Such negative criticism would indeed be poor enough as an ultimate result; but as a means to attaining any positive knowledge or conviction worthy the name, it cannot be valued too highly; and until people are again systematically trained to it, there will be few great thinkers, and a low general average of intellect, in any but the mathematical and physical departments of speculation.

On any other subject no one's opinions deserve the name of knowledge, except so far as he has either had forced upon him by others, or gone through of himself, the same mental process which would have been required of him in carrying on an active controversy with opponents. That, therefore, which when absent, it is so indispensable, but so difficult, to create, how worse than absurd is it to forego, when spontaneously offering itself! If there are any persons who contest a received opinion, or who will do so if law or opinion will let them, let us thank them for it, open our minds to listen to them, and rejoice that there is someone to do for us what we otherwise ought, if we have any regard for either the certainty or the vitality of our convictions, to do with much greater labour for ourselves.

It still remains to speak of one of the principal causes which make diversity of opinion advantageous, and will continue to do so until mankind shall have entered a stage of intellectual advancement which at present seems at an incalculable distance. We have hitherto considered only two possibilities: that the received opinion may be false, and some other opinion, consequently, true; or that, the received opinion being true, a conflict with the opposite error is essential to a clear apprehension and deep feeling of its truth. But there is a commoner case than either of these; when the conflicting doctrines, instead of being one true and the other false, share the truth between them; and the non-conforming opinion is needed to supply the remainder of the truth, of which the received doctrine embodies only a part. Popular opinions, on subjects not palpable to sense, are often true, but seldom or never the whole truth.

They are a part of the truth; sometimes a greater, sometimes a smaller part, but exaggerated, distorted, and disjoined from the truths by which they ought to be accompanied and limited. Heretical opinions, on the other hand, are generally some of these suppressed and neglected truths, bursting the bonds which kept them down, and either seeking reconciliation with the truth contained in the common opinion, or fronting it as enemies, and setting themselves up, with similar exclusiveness, as the whole truth. The latter case is hitherto the most frequent, as, in the human mind, one-sidedness has always been the rule, and many-sidedness the exception. Hence, even in revolutions of opinion, one part of the truth usually sets while another rises.

Even progress, which ought to superadd, for the most part only substitutes one partial and incomplete truth for another; improvement consisting chiefly in this, that the new fragment of truth is more wanted, more adapted to the needs of the time, than that which it displaces. Such being the partial character of prevailing opinions, even when resting on a true foundation; every opinion which embodies somewhat of the portion of truth which the common opinion omits, ought to be considered precious, with whatever amount of error and confusion that truth may be blended. No sober judge of human affairs will feel bound to be indignant because those who force on our notice truths which we should otherwise have overlooked, overlook some of those which we see. Rather, he will think that so long as popular truth is one-sided, it is more desirable than otherwise that unpopular truth should have one-sided asserters too; such being usually the most energetic, and the most likely to compel reluctant attention to the fragment of wisdom which they proclaim as if it were the whole. Thus, in the eighteenth century, when nearly all the instructed, and all those of the uninstructed who were led by them, were lost in admiration of what is called civilization, and of the marvels of modern science, literature, and philosophy, and while greatly overrating the amount of unlikeness between the men of modern and those of ancient times, indulged the belief that the whole of the difference was in their own favour; with what a salutary shock did the paradoxes of Rousseau explode like bombshells in the midst, dislocating the compact mass of one-sided opinion, and forcing its elements to recombine in a better form and with additional ingredients.

Not that the current opinions were on the whole farther from the truth than Rousseau's were; on the contrary, they were nearer to it; they contained more of positive truth, and very much less of error. Nevertheless there lay in Rousseau's doctrine, and has floated down the stream of opinion along with it, a considerable amount of exactly those truths which the popular opinion wanted; and these are the deposit which was left behind when the flood subsided. The superior worth of simplicity of life, the enervating and demoralizing effect of the trammels and hypocrisies of artificial society, are ideas which have never been entirely absent from cultivated minds since Rousseau wrote; and they will in time produce their due effect, though at present needing to be asserted as much as ever, and to be asserted by deeds, for words, on this subject, have nearly exhausted their power.

In politics, again, it is almost a commonplace, that a party of order or stability, and a party of progress or reform, are both necessary elements of a healthy state of political life; until the one or the other shall have so enlarged its mental grasp as to be a party equally of order and of progress, knowing and distinguishing what is fit to be preserved from what ought to be swept away. Each of these modes of thinking derives its utility from the deficiencies of the other; but it is in a great measure the opposition of the other that keeps each within the limits of reason and sanity. Unless opinions favourable to democracy and to aristocracy, to property and to equality, to co-operation and to competition, to luxury and to abstinence, to sociality and individuality, to liberty and discipline, and all the other standing antagonisms of practical life, are expressed with equal freedom, and enforced and defended with equal talent and energy, there is no chance of both elements obtaining their due; one scale is sure to go up, and the other down.

Truth, in the great practical concerns of life, is so much a question of the reconciling and combining of opposites, that very few have minds sufficiently capacious and impartial to make the adjustment with an approach to correctness, and it has to be made by the rough process of a struggle between combatants fighting under hostile banners. On any of the great open questions just enumerated, if either of the two opinions has a better claim than the other, not merely to be tolerated, but to be encouraged and countenanced, it is the one which happens at the particular time and place to be in a minority.

That is the opinion which, for the time being, represents the neglected interests, the side of human well-being which is in danger of obtaining less than its share. We are aware that there is not, in England, any intolerance of differences of opinion on most of these topics. They are adduced to show, by admitted and multiplied examples, the universality of the fact, that only through diversity of opinion is there, in the existing state of human intellect, a chance of fair play to all sides of the truth. When there are persons to be found, who form an exception to the apparent unanimity of the world on any subject, even if the world is in the right, it is always probable that dissentients have something worth hearing to say for themselves, and that truth would lose something by their silence. It may be objected, "But some received principles, especially on the highest and most vital subjects, are more than half-truths. The Christian morality, for instance, is the whole truth on that subject and if anyone teaches a morality which varies from it, he is wholly in error."

As this is of all cases the most important in practice, none can be fitter to test the general maxim. But before pronouncing what Christian morality is or is not, it would be desirable to decide what is meant by Christian morality. If it means the morality of the *New Testament*, I wonder that any one who derives his knowledge of this from the book itself, can suppose that it was announced, or intended, as a complete doctrine of morals. The Gospel always refers to a pre-existing morality, and confines its precepts to the particulars in which that morality was to be corrected, or superseded by a wider and higher; expressing itself, moreover, in terms most general, often impossible to be interpreted literally, and possessing rather the impressiveness of poetry or eloquence than the precision of legislation.

To extract from it a body of ethical doctrine, has never been possible without eking it out from the *Old Testament*, that is, from a system elaborate indeed, but in many respects barbarous, and intended only for a barbarous people. St. Paul, a declared enemy to this Judaical mode of interpreting the doctrine and filling up the scheme of his Master, equally assumes a pre-existing morality, namely, that of the Greeks and Romans; and his advice to Christians is in a great measure a system of accommodation to that; even to the extent of giving an apparent sanction to slavery. What is called Christian, but should rather be termed theological, morality, was not the work of Christ or the Apostles, but is of much later origin, having been gradually built up by the Catholic Church of the first five centuries, and though not implicitly adopted by moderns and Protestants, has been much less modified by them than might have been expected. For the most part, indeed, they have contented themselves with cutting off the additions which had been made to it in the Middle Ages, each sect supplying the place by fresh additions, adapted to its own character and tendencies.

That mankind owe a great debt to this morality, and to its early teachers, I should be the last person to deny; but I do not scruple to say of it, that it is, in many important points, incomplete and one-sided, and that unless ideas and feelings, not sanctioned by it, had contributed to the formation of European life and character, human affairs would have been in a worse condition than they now are. Christian morality has all the characters of a reaction; it is, in great part, a protest against Paganism. Its ideal is negative rather than positive; passive rather than active; Innocence rather than Nobleness; Abstinence from Evil, rather than energetic Pursuit of Good: in its precepts 'thou shalt not' predominates unduly over 'thou shalt'. In its horror of sensuality, it made an idol of asceticism, which has been gradually compromised away into one of legality.

It holds out the hope of heaven and the threat of hell, as the appointed and appropriate motives to a virtuous life: in this falling far below the best of the ancients, and doing what lies in it to give to human morality an essentially selfish character, by disconnecting each man's feelings of duty from the interests of his fellow-creatures, except so far as a self-interested inducement is offered to him for consulting them. It is essentially a doctrine of passive obedience; it inculcates submission to all authorities found established; who indeed are not to be actively obeyed when they command what religion forbids, but who are not to be resisted, far less rebelled against, for any amount of wrong to ourselves. And while, in the morality of the best Pagan nations, duty to the state holds even a disproportionate place, infringing on the just liberty of the individual; in purely Christian ethics that grand department of duty is scarcely noticed or acknowledged.

It is in the Koran, not the *New Testament*, that we read the maxim--"A ruler who appoints any man to an office, when there is in his dominions another man better qualified for it, sins against God and against the state." What little recognition the idea of obligation to the public obtains in modern morality, is derived from Greek and Roman sources, not from Christian; as, even in the morality of private life, whatever exists of magnanimity, high-mindedness, personal dignity, even the sense of honour, is derived from the purely human, not the religious part of our education, and never could have grown out of a standard of ethics in which the only worth, professedly recognized, is that of obedience.

As far as any one from pretending that these defects are necessarily inherent in the Christian ethics, in every manner in which it can be conceived, or that the many requisites of a complete moral doctrine which it does not contain, do not admit of being reconciled with it. We believe that the sayings of Christ are all, that I can see any evidence of their having been intended to be; that they are irreconcilable with nothing which a comprehensive morality requires; that everything which is excellent in ethics may be brought within them, with no greater violence to their language than has been done to it by all who have attempted to deduce from them any practical system of conduct whatever. But it is quite consistent with this, to believe that they contain and were meant to contain, only a part of the truth; that many essential elements of the highest morality are among the things which are not provided for, nor intended to be provided for, in the recorded deliverances of the Founder of Christianity, and which have been entirely thrown aside in the system of ethics erected on the basis of those deliverances by the Christian Church.

And this being so, we think it a great error to persist in attempting to find in the Christian doctrine that complete rule for our guidance, which its author intended it to sanction and enforce, but only partially to provide. we believe, too, that this narrow theory is becoming a grave practical evil, detracting greatly from the value of the moral training and instruction, which so many well-meaning persons are now at length exerting themselves to promote. I much fear that by attempting to form the mind and feelings on an exclusively religious type, and discarding those secular standards which heretofore coexisted with and supplemented the Christian ethics, receiving some of its spirit, and infusing into it some of theirs, these will result, and is even now resulting, a low, abject, servile type of character, which, submit itself as it may to what it deems the Supreme Will, is incapable of rising to or sympathizing in the conception of Supreme Goodness.

We believe that other ethics than anyone which can be evolved from exclusively Christian sources, must exist side by side with Christian ethics to produce the moral regeneration of mankind; and that the Christian system is no exception to the rule that in an imperfect state of the human mind, the interests of truth require a diversity of opinions. It is not necessary that in ceasing to ignore the moral truths not contained in Christianity, men should ignore any of those which it does contain.

Such prejudice, or oversight, when it occurs, is altogether an evil; but it is one from which we cannot hope to be always exempt, and must be regarded as the price paid for an inestimable good. The exclusive pretension made by a part of the truth to be the whole, must and ought to be protested against, and if a reactionary impulse should make the protestors unjust in their turn, this one-sidedness, like the other, may be lamented, but must be tolerated. If Christians would teach infidels to be just to Christianity, they should themselves be just to infidelity. It can do truth no service to blink the fact, known to all who have the most ordinary acquaintance with literary history, that a large portion of the noblest and most valuable moral teaching has been the work, not only of men who did not know, but of men who knew and rejected, the Christian faith.

I do not pretend that the most unlimited use of the freedom of enunciating all possible opinions would put an end to the evils of religious or philosophical sectarianism. Every truth which men of narrow capacity are in earnest about, is sure to be asserted, inculcated, and in many ways even acted on, as if no other truth existed in the world, or at all events none that could limit or qualify the first. I acknowledge that the tendency of all opinions to become sectarian is not cured by the freest discussion, but is often heightened and exacerbated thereby; the truth which ought to have been, but was not, seen, being rejected all the more violently because proclaimed by persons regarded as opponents.

But it is not on the impassioned partisan, it is on the calmer and more disinterested bystander, that this collision of opinions works its salutary effect. Not the violent conflict between parts of the truth, but the quiet suppression of half of it, is the formidable evil: there is always hope when people are forced to listen to both sides; it is when they attend only to one that errors harden into prejudices, and truth itself ceases to have the effect of truth, by being exaggerated into falsehood. And since there are few mental attributes more rare than that judicial faculty which can sit in intelligent judgement between two sides of a question, of which only one is represented by an advocate before it, truth has no chance but in proportion as every side of it, every opinion which embodies any fraction of the truth, not only finds advocates, but is so advocated as to be listened to. We have now recognized the necessity to the mental well-being of mankind of freedom of opinion, and freedom of the expression of opinion, on four distinct grounds; which as suggested, now briefly recapitulate. First, if any opinion is compelled to silence, that opinion may, for aught we can certainly know, be true. To deny this is to assume our own infallibility. Secondly, though the silenced opinion be an error, it may, and very commonly does, contain a portion of truth; and since the general or prevailing opinion on any object is rarely or never the whole truth, it is only by the collision of adverse opinions that the remainder of the truth has any chance of being supplied.

Thirdly, even if the received opinion be not only true, but the whole truth; unless it is suffered to be, and actually is, vigorously and earnestly contested, it will, by most of those who receive it, be held in the manner of a prejudice, with little comprehension or feeling of its rational grounds. And not only this, but, fourthly, the meaning of the doctrine itself will be in danger of being lost, or enfeebled, and deprived of its vital effect on the character and conduct: the dogma becoming a mere formal profession, inefficacious for good, but cumbering the ground, and preventing the growth of any real and heartfelt conviction, from reason or personal experience.

Before quitting the subject of freedom of opinion, it is fit to take notice of those who say, that the free expression of all opinions should be permitted, on condition that the manner be temperate, and do not pass the bounds of fair discussion. Much might be said on the impossibility of fixing where these supposed bounds are to be placed; for if the test be offence to those whose opinion is attacked, I think experience testifies that this offence is given whenever the attack is telling and powerful, and that every opponent who pushes them hard, and whom they find it difficult to answer, appears to them, if he shows any strong feeling on the subject, an intemperate opponent. But this, though an important consideration in a practical point of view, merges in a more fundamental objection. Undoubtedly the manner of asserting an opinion, even though it be a true one, may be very objectionable, and may justly incur severe censure. But the principal offences of the kind are such as it is mostly impossible, unless by accidental self-betrayal, to bring home to conviction.

The gravest of them is, to argue sophistically, to suppress facts or arguments, to misstate the elements of the case, or misrepresent the opposite opinion. But all this, even to the most aggravated degree, is so continually done in perfect good faith, by persons who are not considered, and in many other respects may not deserve to be considered, ignorant or incompetent, that it is rarely possible on adequate grounds conscientiously to stamp the misrepresentation as morally culpable; and still less could law presume to interfere with this kind of controversial misconduct. With regard to what is commonly meant by intemperate discussion, namely, invective, sarcasm, personality, and the like, the denunciation of these weapons would deserve more sympathy if it were ever proposed to interdict them equally to both sides; but it is only desired to restrain the employment of them against the prevailing opinion: against the unprevailing they may not only be used without general disapproval, but will be likely to obtain for him who uses them the praise of honest zeal and righteous indignation. Yet whatever mischief arises from their use, is greatest when they are employed against the comparatively defenceless; and whatever unfair advantage can be derived by any opinion from this mode of asserting it, accrues almost exclusively to received opinions. The worst offence of this kind which can be committed by a polemic, is to stigmatize those who hold the contrary opinion as bad and immoral men.

To calumny of this sort, those who hold any unpopular opinion are peculiarly exposed, because they are in general few and uninfluential, and nobody but themselves feels much interest in seeing justice done to them; but this weapon is, from the nature of the case, denied to those who attack a prevailing opinion: they can neither use it with safety to themselves, nor if they could, would it do anything but recoil on their own cause.

In general, opinions contrary to those commonly received can only obtain a hearing by studied moderation of language, and the most cautious avoidance of unnecessary offence, from which they hardly ever deviate even in a slight degree without losing ground: while unmeasured vituperation employed on the side of the prevailing opinion, really does deter people from professing contrary opinions, and from listening to those who profess them. For the interest, therefore, of truth and justice, it is far more important to restrain this employment of vituperative language than the other; and, for example, if it were necessary to choose, there would be much more need to discourage offensive attacks on infidelity, than on religion.

It is, however, obvious that law and authority have no business with restraining either, while opinion ought, in every instance, to determine its verdict by the circumstances of the individual case; condemning every one, on whichever side of the argument he places himself, in whose mode of advocacy either want of candor, or malignity, bigotry or intolerance of feeling manifest themselves, but not inferring these vices from the side which a person takes, though it be the contrary side of the question to our own; and giving merited honour to every one, whatever opinion he may hold, who has calmness to see and honesty to state what his opponents and their opinions really are, exaggerating nothing to their discredit, keeping nothing back which tells, or can be supposed to tell, in their favour.

This is the real morality of public discussion; and if often violated, we are happy to think that there are many controversialists who to a great extent observe it, and a still greater number who conscientiously strive towards it. These words had scarcely been written, when, as if to give them an emphatic contradiction, occurred the Government Press Prosecutions of 1858. That ill-judged interference with the liberty of public discussion has not, however, induced us to alter a single word in the text, nor has it at all weakened our conviction that, moments of panic excepted, the era of pains and penalties for political discussion has, in our own country, passed away. For, in the first place, the prosecutions were not persisted in; and in the second, they were never, properly speaking, political prosecutions. The offence charged was not that of criticizing institutions, or the acts or persons of rulers, but of circulating what was deemed an immoral doctrine, the lawfulness of Tyrannicide.

If the arguments of the present stage are of any validity, there ought to exist the fullest liberty of professing and discussing, as a matter of ethical conviction, any doctrine, however immoral it may be considered. It would, therefore, be irrelevant and out of place to examine here, whether the doctrine of Tyrannicide deserves that title. We will content ourself with saying, that the subject has been at all times one of the open questions of morals, that the act of a private citizen in striking down a criminal, who, by raising himself above the law, has placed himself beyond the reach of legal punishment or control, has been accounted by whole nations, and by some of the best and wisest of men, not a crime, but an act of exalted virtue and that, right or wrong, it is not of the nature of assassination but of civil war. As such, we hold that the instigation to it, in a specific case, may be a proper subject of punishment, but only if an overt act has followed, and at least a probable connection can be established between the act and the instigation.

Even then it is not a foreign government, but the very government assailed, which alone, in the exercise of self-defence, can legitimately punish attacks directed against its own existence. Ample warning may be drawn from the large infusion of the passions of a persecutor, which mingled with the general display of the worst parts of our national character on the occasion of the Sepoy insurrection.

The ravings of fanatics or charlatans from the pulpit may be unworthy of notice; but the heads of the Evangelical party have announced as their principle, for the government of Hindus and Mahomedans, that no schools be supported by public money in which the Bible is not taught, and by necessary consequence that no public employment be given to any but real or pretended Christians.

An Under-Secretary of State, in a speech delivered to his constituents on the 12th of November, 1857, is reported to have said: "Toleration of their faith", "the superstition which they called religion, by the British Government, had had the effect of retarding the ascendency of the British name, and preventing the salutary growth of Christianity.... Toleration was the great corner-stone of the religious liberties of this country; but do not let them abuse that precious word toleration. As he understood it, it meant the complete liberty to all, freedom of worship, among Christians, who worshipped upon the same foundation. It meant toleration of all sects and denominations of Christians who believed in the one mediation." We desire to call attention to the fact, that a man who has been deemed fit to fil a high office in the government of this country, under a liberal ministry, maintains the doctrine that all who do not believe in the divinity of Christ are beyond the pale of toleration. Who, after this imbecile display, can indulge the illusion that religious persecution has passed away, never to return?

Individuality, as One of the Elements of Well-being

Such being the reasons which make it imperative that human beings should be free to form opinions, and to express their opinions without reserve; and such the baneful consequences to the intellectual, and through that to the moral nature of man, unless this liberty is either conceded, or asserted in spite of prohibition; let us next examine whether the same reasons do not require that men should be free to act upon their opinions--to carry these out in their lives, without hindrance, either physical or moral, from their fellow-men, so long as it is at their own risk and peril.

This last proviso is of course indispensable. No one pretends that actions should be as free as opinions. On the contrary, even opinions lose their immunity, when the circumstances in which they are expressed are such as to constitute their expression a positive instigation to some mischievous act. An opinion that corn-dealers are starvers of the poor, or that private property is robbery, ought to be unmolested when simply circulated through the press, but may justly incur punishment when delivered orally to an excited mob assembled before the house of a corn-dealer, or when handed about among the same mob in the form of a placard.

Acts of whatever kind, which, without justifiable cause, do harm to others, may be, and in the more important cases absolutely require to be, controlled by the unfavourable sentiments, and, when needful, by the active interference of mankind. The liberty of the individual must be thus far limited; he must not make himself a nuisance to other people. But if he refrains from molesting others in what concerns them, and merely acts according to his own inclination and judgement in things which concern himself, the same reasons which show that opinion should be free, prove also that he should be allowed, without molestation, to carry his opinions into practice at his own cost. That mankind are not infallible; that their truths, for the most part, are only half-truths; that unity of opinion, unless resulting from the fullest and freest comparison of opposite opinions, is not desirable, and diversity not an evil, but a good, until mankind are much more capable than at present of recognizing all sides of the truth, are principles applicable to men's modes of action, not less than to their opinions. As it is useful that while mankind are imperfect there should be different opinions, so is it that there should be different experiments of living; that free scope should be given to varieties of character, short of injury to others; and that the worth of different modes of life should be proved practically, when anyone thinks fit to try them. It is desirable, in short, that in things which do not primarily concern others, individuality should assert itself. Where, not the person's own character, but the traditions of customs of other people are the rule of conduct, there is wanting one of the principal ingredients of human happiness, and quite the chief ingredient of individual and social progress.

In maintaining this principle, the greatest difficulty to be encountered does not lie in the appreciation of means towards an acknowledged end, but in the indifference of persons in general to the end itself. If it were felt that the free development of individuality is one of the leading essentials of well-being; that it is not only a coordinate element with all that is designated by the terms civilization, instruction, education, culture, but is itself a necessary part and condition of all those things; there would be no danger that liberty should be undervalued, and the adjustment of the boundaries between it and social control would present no extraordinary difficulty. But the evil is, that individual spontaneity is hardly recognized by the common modes of thinking as having any intrinsic worth, or deserving any regard on its own account.

The majority, being satisfied with the ways of mankind as they now are cannot comprehend why those ways should not be good enough for everybody; and what is more, spontaneity forms no part of the ideal of the majority of moral and social reformers, but is rather looked on with jealousy, as a troublesome and perhaps rebellious obstruction to the general acceptance of what these reformers, in their own judgement, think would be best for mankind. Few persons, out of Germany, even comprehend the meaning of the doctrine which Wilhelm von Humboldt, so eminent both as a savant and as a politician, made the text of a treatise--that "the end of man, or that which is prescribed by the eternal or immutable dictates of reason, and not suggested by vague and transient desires, is the highest and most harmonious development of his powers to a complete and consistent whole"; that, therefore, the object "towards which every human being must ceaselessly direct his efforts, and on which especially those who design to influence their fellow-men must ever keep their eyes, is the individuality of power and development"; that for this there are two requisites, "freedom, and a variety of situations;" and that from the union of these arise "individual vigour and manifold diversity", which combine themselves in "originality".

Little, however, as people are accustomed to a doctrine like that of Von Humboldt, and surprising as it may be to them to find so high a value attached to individuality, the question, one must nevertheless think, can only be one of degree. No one's idea of excellence in conduct is that people should do absolutely nothing but copy one another. No one would assert that people ought not to put into their mode of life, and into the conduct of their concerns, any impress whatever of their own judgement, or of their own individual character. On the other hand, it would be absurd to pretend that people ought to live as if nothing whatever had been known in the world before they came into it; as if experience had as yet done nothing towards showing that one mode of existence, or of conduct, is preferable to another.

Nobody denies that people should be so taught and trained in youth, as to know and benefit by the ascertained results of human experience. But it is the privilege and proper condition of a human being, arrived at the maturity of his faculties, to use and interpret experience in his own way. It is for him to find out what part of recorded experience is properly applicable to his own circumstances and character.

The traditions and customs of other people are, to a certain extent, evidence of what their experience has taught them; presumptive evidence, and as such, have a claim to this deference: but, in the first place, their experience may be too narrow; or they may not have interpreted it rightly. Secondly, their interpretation of experience may be correct but unsuitable to him. Customs are made for customary circumstances, and customary characters: and his circumstances or his character may be uncustomary. Thirdly, though the customs be both good as customs, and suitable to him, yet to conform to custom, merely as custom, does not educate or develop in him any of the qualities which are the distinctive endowment of a human being.

The human faculties of perception, judgement, discriminative feeling, mental activity, and even moral preference, are exercised only in making a choice. He who does anything because it is the custom, makes no choice. He gains no practice either in discerning or in desiring what is best. The mental and moral, like the muscular powers, are improved only by being used. The faculties are called into no exercise by doing a thing merely because others do it, no more than by believing a thing only because others believe it. If the grounds of an opinion are not conclusive to the person's own reason, his reason cannot be strengthened, but is likely to be weakened by his adopting it: and if the inducements to an act are not such as are consentaneous to his own feelings and character, it is so much done towards rendering his feelings and character inert and torpid, instead of active and energetic.

He who lets the world, or his own portion of it, choose his plan of life for him, has no need of any other faculty than the ape-like one of imitation. He who chooses his plan for himself, employs all his faculties. He must use observation to see, reasoning and judgement to foresee, activity to gather materials for decision, discrimination to decide, and when he has decided, firmness and self-control to hold to his deliberate decision. And these qualities he requires and exercises exactly in proportion as the part of his conduct which he determines according to his own judgement and feelings is a large one.

It is possible that he might be guided in some good path, and kept out of harm's way, without any of these things. But what will be his comparative worth as a human being? It really is of importance, not only what men do, but also what manner of men they are that do it. Among the works of man, which human life is rightly employed in perfecting and beautifying, the first in importance surely is man himself. Supposing it were possible to get houses built, corn grown, battles fought, causes tried, and even churches erected and prayers said, by machinery--by automatons in human form--it would be a considerable loss to exchange for these automatons even the men and women who at present inhabit the more civilized parts of the world, and who assuredly are but starved specimens of what nature can and will produce. Human nature is not a machine to be built after a model, and set to do exactly the work prescribed for it, but a tree, which requires to grow and develop itself on all sides, according to the tendency of the inward forces which make it a living thing. It will probably be conceded that it is desirable people should exercise their understandings, and that an intelligent following of custom, or even occasionally an intelligent deviation from custom, is better than a blind and simply mechanical adhesion to it. To a certain extent it is admitted, that our understanding should be our own: but there is not the same willingness to admit that our desires and impulses should be our own likewise; or that to possess impulses of our own, and of any strength, is anything but a peril and a snare. Yet desires and impulses are as much a part of a perfect human being, as beliefs and restraints: and strong impulses are only perilous when not properly balanced; when one set of aims and inclinations is developed into strength, while others, which ought to coexist with them, remain weak and inactive. It is not because men's desires are strong that they act ill; it is because their consciences are weak.

There is no natural connection between strong impulses and a weak conscience. The natural connection is the other way. To say that one person's desires and feelings are stronger and more various than those of another, is merely to say that he has more of the raw material of human nature, and is therefore capable, perhaps of more evil, but certainly of more good. Strong impulses are but another name for energy. Energy may be turned to bad uses; but more good may always be made of an energetic nature, than of an indolent and impassive one. Those who have most natural feeling, are always those whose cultivated feelings may be made the strongest. The same strong susceptibilities which make the personal impulses vivid and powerful, are also the source from whence are generated the most passionate love of virtue, and the sternest self-control.

It is through the cultivation of these, that society both does its duty and protects its interests: not by rejecting the stuff of which heroes are made, because it knows not how to make them. A person whose desires and impulses are his own--are the expression of his own nature, as it has been developed and modified by his own culture--is said to have a character. One whose desires and impulses are not his own, has no character, no more than a steam-engine has a character. If, in addition to being his own, his impulses are strong, and are under the government of a strong will, he has an energetic character. Whoever thinks that individuality of desires and impulses should not be encouraged to unfold itself, must maintain that society has no need of strong natures--is not the better for containing many persons who have much character--and that a high general average of energy is not desirable.

In some early states of society, these forces might be, and were, too much ahead of the power which society then possessed of disciplining and controlling them. There has been a time when the element of spontaneity and individuality was in excess, and the social principle had a hard struggle with it. The difficulty then was, to induce men of strong bodies or minds to pay obedience to any rules which required them to control their impulses. To overcome this difficulty, law and discipline, like the Popes struggling against the Emperors, asserted a power over the whole man, claiming to control all his life in order to control his character—-which society had not found any other sufficient means of binding. But society has now fairly got the better of individuality; and the danger which threatens human nature is not the excess, but the deficiency, of personal impulses and preferences. Things are vastly changed, since the passions of those who were strong by station or by personal endowment were in a state of habitual rebellion against laws and ordinances, and required to be rigorously chained up to enable the persons within their reach to enjoy any particle of security.

In carlier times, from the highest class of society down to the lowest every one lives as under the eye of a hostile and dreaded censorship. Not only in what concerns others, but in what concerns only themselves, the individual, or the family, do not ask themselves--what do I prefer? or, what would suit my character and disposition? or, what would allow the best and highest in me to have fair play, and enable it to grow and thrive? They ask themselves, what is suitable to my position? what is usually done by persons of my station and pecuniary circumstances? or what is usually done by persons of a station and circumstances superior to mine? We do not mean that they choose what is customary, in preference to what suits their own inclination.

It does not occur to them to have any inclination, except for what is customary. Thus the mind itself is bowed to the yoke: even in what people do for pleasure, conformity is the first thing thought of; they like in crowds; they exercise choice only among things commonly done: peculiarity of taste, eccentricity of conduct, are shunned equally with crimes: until by dint of not following their own nature, they have no nature to follow: their human capacities are withered and starved: they become incapable of any strong wishes or native pleasures, and are generally without either opinions or feelings of home growth, or properly their own. Now is this, or is it not, the desirable condition of human nature?

It is so, on the Calvinistic theory. According to that, the one great offence of man is Self-will. All the good of which humanity is capable, is comprised in Obedience. You have no choice; thus you must do, and no otherwise; "whatever is not a duty is a sin". Human nature being radically corrupt, there is no redemption for anyone until human nature is killed within him. To one holding this theory of life, crushing out any of the human faculties, capacities, and susceptibilities, is no evil: man needs no capacity, but that of surrendering himself to the will of God: and if he uses any of his faculties for any other purpose but to do that supposed will more effectually, he is better without them. That is the theory of Calvinism; and it is held, in a mitigated form, by many who do not consider themselves Calvinists; the mitigation consisting in giving a less ascetic interpretation to the alleged will of God; asserting it to be his will that mankind should gratify some of their inclinations; of course not in the manner they themselves prefer, but in the way of obedience, that is, in a way prescribed to them by authority; and, therefore, by the necessary conditions of the case, the same for all. In some such insidious form there is at present a strong tendency to this narrow theory of life, and to the pinched and hidebound type of human character which it patronizes. Many persons, no doubt, sincerely think that human beings thus cramped and dwarfed, are as their Maker designed them to be; just as many have thought that trees are a much finer thing when clipped into pollards, or cut out into figures of animals, than as nature made them. But if it be any part of religion to believe that man was made by a good Being, it is more consistent with that faith to believe, that this Being gave all human faculties that they might be cultivated and unfolded, not rooted out and consumed, and that he takes delight in every nearer approach made by his creatures to the ideal conception embodied in them, every increase in any of their capabilities of comprehension, of action, or of enjoyment.

There is a different type of human excellence from the Calvinistic; a conception of humanity as having its nature bestowed on it for other purposes than merely to be abnegated. "Pagan self-assertion" is one of the elements of human worth, as well as "Christian self-denial". There is a Greek ideal of self-development, which the Platonic and Christian ideal of self-government blends with, but does not supersede. It may be better to be a John Knox than an Alcibiades, but it is better to be a Pericles than either; nor would a Pericles, if we had one in these days, be without anything good which belonged to John Knox.

It is not by wearing down into uniformity all that is individual in themselves, but by cultivating it and calling it forth, within the limits imposed by the rights and interests of others, that human beings become a noble and beautiful object of contemplation; and as the works partake the character of those who do them, by the same process human life also becomes rich, diversified, and animating, furnishing more abundant aliment to high thoughts and elevating feelings, and strengthening the tie which binds every individual to the race, by making the race infinitely better worth belonging to. In proportion to the development of his individuality, each person becomes more valuable to himself, and is therefore capable of being more valuable to others. There is a greater fulness of life about his own existence, and when there is more life in the units there is more in the mass which is composed of them. As much compression as is necessary to prevent the stronger specimens of human nature from encroaching on the rights of others, cannot be dispensed with; but for this there is ample compensation even in the point of view of human development.

The means of development which the individual loses by being prevented from gratifying his inclinations to the injury of others, are chiefly obtained at the expense of the development of other people. And even to himself there is a full equivalent in the better development of the social part of his nature, rendered possible by the restraint put upon the selfish part. To be held to rigid rules of justice for the sake of others, develops the feelings and capacities which have the good of others for their object. But to be restrained in things not affecting their good, by their mere displeasure, develops nothing valuable, except such force of character as may unfold itself in resisting the restraint. If acquiesced in, it dulls and blunts the whole nature. To give any fair play to the nature of each, it is essential that different persons should be allowed to lead different lives. In proportion as this latitude has been exercised in any age, has that age been noteworthy to posterity. Even despotism does not produce its worst effects, so long as Individuality exists under it; and whatever crushes individuality is despotism, by whatever name it may be called, and whether it professes to be enforcing the will of God or the injunctions of men.

Having said that Individuality is the same thing with development, and that it is only the cultivation of individuality which produces, or can produce, well-developed human beings, I might here close the argument: for what more or better can be said of any condition of human affairs, than that it brings human beings themselves nearer to the best thing they can be? or what worse can be said of any obstruction to good, than that it prevents this? Doubtless, however, these considerations will not suffice to convince those who most need convincing; and it is necessary further to show, that these developed human beings are of some use to the undeveloped--to point out to those who do not desire liberty, and would not avail themselves of it, that they may be in some intelligible manner rewarded for allowing other people to make use of it without hindrance.In the first place, then, we would suggest that they might possibly learn something from them. It will not be denied by anybody, that originality is a valuable element in human affairs. There is always need of persons not only to discover new truths, and point out when what were once truths are true no longer, but also to commence new practices, and set the example of more enlightened conduct, and better taste and sense in human life. This cannot well be gainsaid by anybody who does not believe that the world has already attained perfection in all its ways and practices. It is true that this benefit is not capable of being rendered by everybody alike: there are but few persons, in comparison with the whole of mankind, whose experiments, if adopted by others, would be likely to be any improvement on established practice.

But these few are the salt of the earth; without them, human life would become a stagnant pool. Not only is it they who introduce good things which did not before exist; it is they who keep the life in those which already existed. If there were nothing new to be done, would human intellect cease to be necessary? Would it be a reason why those who do the old things should forget why they are done, and do them like cattle, not like human beings? There is only too great a tendency in the best beliefs and practices to degenerate into the mechanical; and unless there were a succession of persons whose ever-recurring originality prevents the grounds of those beliefs and practices from becoming merely traditional, such dead matter would not resist the smallest shock from anything really alive, and there would be no reason why civilization should not die out, as in the Byzantine Empire. Persons of genius, it is true, are, and are always likely to be, a small minority; but in order to have them, it is necessary to preserve the soil in which they grow.

Genius can only breathe freely in an atmosphere of freedom. Persons of genius are, *ex vi termini*, more individual than any other people--less capable, consequently, of fitting themselves, without hurtful compression, into any of the small number of moulds which society provides in order to save its members the trouble of forming their own character. If from timidity they consent to be forced into one of these moulds, and to let all that part of themselves which cannot expand under the pressure remain unexpanded, society will be little the better for their genius. If they are of a strong character, and break their fetters they become a mark for the society which has not succeeded in reducing them to common-place, to point at with solemn warning as 'wild', 'erratic', and the like; much as if one should complain of the Niagara river for not flowing smoothly between its banks like a Dutch canal.

One must insist thus emphatically on the importance of genius, and the necessity of allowing it to unfold itself freely both in thought and in practice, being well aware that no one will deny the position in theory, but knowing also that almost every one, in reality, is totally indifferent to it. People think genius a fine thing if it enables a man to write an exciting poem, or paint a picture. But in its true sense, that of originality in thought and action, though no one says that it is not a thing to be admired, nearly all, at heart, think they can do very well without it. Unhappily this is too natural to be wondered at. Originality is the one thing which unoriginal minds cannot feel the use of.

They cannot see what it is to do for them: how should they? If they could see what it would do for them, it would not be originality. The first service which originality has to render them, is that of opening their eyes: which being once fully done, they would have a chance of being themselves original. Meanwhile, recollecting that nothing was ever yet done which some one was not the first to do, and that all good things which exist are the fruits of originality, let them be modest enough to believe that there is something still left for it to accomplish, and assure themselves that they are more in need of originality, the less they are conscious of the want.

In sobre truth, whatever homage may be professed, or even paid, to real or supposed mental superiority, the general tendency of things throughout the world is to render mediocrity the ascendant power among mankind. In ancient history, in the Middle Ages, and in a diminishing degree through the long transition from feudality to the present time, the individual was a power in himself; and if he had either great talents or a high social position, he was a considerable power. At present individuals are lost in the crowd. In politics it is almost a triviality to say that public opinion now rules the world. The only power deserving the name is that of masses, and of governments while they make themselves the organ of the tendencies and instincts of masses.

This is as true in the moral and social relations of private life as in public transactions. Those whose opinions go by the name of public opinion, are not always the same sort of public: in America, they are the whole white population; in England, chiefly the middle class. But they are always a mass, that is to say, collective mediocrity.

And what is still greater novelty, the mass do not now take their opinions from dignitaries in Church or State, from ostensible leaders, or from books. Their thinking is done for them by men much like themselves, addressing them or speaking in their name, on the spur of the moment, through the newspapers. We are not complaining of all this. We do not assert that anything better is compatible, as a general rule, with the present low state of the human mind. But that does not hinder the government of mediocrity from being mediocre government. No government by a democracy or a numerous aristocracy, either in its political acts or in the opinions, qualities, and tone of mind which it fosters, ever did or could rise above mediocrity, except in so far as the sovereign Many have let themselves be guided by the counsels and influence of a more highly gifted and instructed One or Few. The initiation of all wise or noble things, comes and must come from individuals; generally at first from some one individual. The honour and glory of the average man is that he is capable of following that initiative; that he can respond internally to wise and noble things, and be led to them with his eyes open. We are not countenancing the sort of "hero-worship" which applauds the strong man of genius for forcibly seizing on the government of the world and making it do his bidding in spite of itself.

All he can claim is, freedom to point out the way. The power of compelling others into it, is not only inconsistent with the freedom and development of all the rest, but corrupting to the strong man himself. It does seem, however, that when the opinions of masses of merely average men are everywhere become or becoming the dominant power, the counterpoise and corrective to that tendency would be, the more and more pronounced individuality of those who stand on the higher eminences of thought.

It is in these circumstances most especially, that exceptional individuals, instead of being deterred, should be encouraged in acting differently from the mass. In other times there was no advantage in their doing so, unless they acted not only differently, but better. In this age the mere example of non-conformity, the mere refusal to bend the knee to custom, is itself a service. Precisely because the tyranny of opinion is such as to make eccentricity a reproach, it is desirable, in order to break through that tyranny, that people should be eccentric. Eccentricity has always abounded when and where strength of character has abounded; and the amount of eccentricity in a society has generally been proportional to the amount of genius, mental vigour, and moral courage which it contained. That so few now dare to be eccentric, marks the chief danger of the time.

We have said that it is important to give the freest scope possible to uncustomary things, in order that it may in time appear which of these are fit to be converted into customs. But independence of action, and disregard of custom are not solely deserving of encouragement for the chance they afford that better modes of action, and customs more worthy of general adoption, may be struck out; nor is it only persons of decided mental superiority who have a just claim to carry on their lives in their own way. There is no reason that all human existences should be constructed on some one, or some small number of patterns. If a person possesses any tolerable amount of common sense and experience, his own mode of laying out his existence is the best, not because it is the best in itself, but because it is his own mode. Human beings are not like sheep; and even sheep are not undistinguishably alike. A man cannot get a coat or a pair of boots to fit him, unless they are either made to his measure, or he has a whole warehouseful to choose from: and is it easier to fit him with a life than with a coat, or are human beings more like one another in their whole physical and spiritual conformation than in the shape of their feet?

If it were only that people have diversities of taste that is reason enough for not attempting to shape them all after one model. But different persons also require different conditions for their spiritual development; and can no more exist healthily in the same moral, than all the variety of plants can in the same physical atmosphere and climate. The same things which are helps to one person towards the cultivation of his higher nature, are hindrances to another. The same mode of life is a healthy excitement to one, keeping all his faculties of action and enjoyment in their best order, while to another it is a distracting burden, which suspends or crushes all internal life. Such are the differences among human beings in their sources of pleasure, their susceptibilities of pain, and the operation on them of different physical and moral agencies, that unless there is a corresponding diversity in their modes of life, they neither obtain their fair share of happiness, nor grow up to the mental, moral, and aesthetic stature of which their nature is capable.

Why then should tolerance, as far as the public sentiment is concerned, extend only to tastes and modes of life which extort acquiescence by the multitude of their adherents? Nowhere is diversity of taste entirely unrecognized; a person may without blame, either like or dislike rowing, or smoking, or music, or athletic exercises, or chess, or cards, or study, because both those who like each of these things, and those who dislike them, are too numerous to be put down. But the man, and still more the woman, who can be accused either of doing 'what nobody does', or of not doing 'what everybody does', is the subject of as much depreciatory remark as if he or she had committed some grave moral delinquency. Persons require to possess a title, or some other badge of rank, or the consideration of people of rank, to be able to indulge somewhat in the luxury of doing as they like without detriment to their estimation. To indulge somewhat, we repeat: for whoever allow themselves much of that indulgence, incur the risk of something worse than disparaging speeches--they are in peril of a commission *de lunatico*, and of having their property taken from them and given to their relations.

There is one characteristic of the present direction of public opinion, peculiarly calculated to make it intolerant of any marked demonstration of individuality. The general average of mankind are not only moderate in intellect, but also moderate in inclinations: they have no tastes or wishes strong enough to incline them to do anything unusual, and they consequently do not understand those who have, and class all such with the wild and intemperate whom they are accustomed to look down upon.

Now, in addition to this fact which is general, we have only to suppose that a strong movement has set in towards the improvement of morals, and it is evident what we have to expect. In these days such a movement has set in; much has actually been effected in the way of increased regularity of conduct, and discouragement of excesses; and there is a philanthropic spirit abroad, for the exercise of which there is no more inviting field than the moral and prudential improvement of our fellow-creatures.

These tendencies of the times cause the public to be more disposed than at most former periods to prescribe general rules of conduct, and endeavour to make every one conform to the approved standard. And that standard, express or tacit, is to desire nothing strongly. Its ideal of character is to be without any marked character; to maim by compression, like a Chinese lady's foot, every part of human nature which stands out prominently, and tends to make the person markedly dissimilar in outline to common-place humanity.

As is usually the case with ideals which exclude one half of what is desirable, the present standard of approbation produces only an inferior imitation of the other half. Instead of great energies guided by vigorous reason, and strong feelings strongly controlled by a conscientious will, its result is weak feelings and weak energies, which therefore can be kept in outward conformity to rule without any strength either of will or of reason. Already energetic characters on any large-scale are becoming merely traditional. There is now scarcely any outlet for energy in this country except business. The energy expended in that may still be regarded as considerable. What little is left from that employment, is expended on some hobby; which may be a useful, even a philanthropic hobby, but is always some one thing, and generally a thing of small dimensions. The greatness of England is now all collective: individually small, we only appear capable of anything great by our habit of combining; and with this our moral and religious philanthropists are perfectly contented. But it was men of another stamp than this that made England what it has been; and men of another stamp will be needed to prevent its decline. The despotism of custom is everywhere the standing hindrance to human advancement, being in unceasing antagonism to that disposition to aim at something better than customary, which is called, according to circumstances, the spirit of liberty, or that of progress or improvement. The spirit of improvement is not always a spirit of liberty, for it may aim at forcing improvements on an unwilling people; and the spirit of liberty, in so far as it resists such attempts, may ally itself locally and temporarily with the opponents of improvement; but the only unfailing and permanent source of improvement is liberty, since by it there are as many possible independent centres of improvement as there are individuals.

The progressive principle, however, in either shape, whether as the love of liberty or of improvement, is antagonistic to the sway of Custom, involving at least emancipation from that yoke; and the contest between the two constitutes the chief interest of the history of mankind. The greater part of the world has, properly speaking, no history, because the despotism of Custom is complete.

This is the case over the whole East. Custom is there, in all things, the final appeal; Justice and right mean conformity to custom; the argument of custom no one, unless some tyrant intoxicated with power, thinks of resisting. And we see the result. Those nations must once have had originality; they did not start out of the ground populous, lettered, and versed in many of the arts of life; they made themselves all this, and were then the greatest and most powerful nations in the world. What are they now? The subjects or dependents of tribes whose forefathers wandered in the forests when theirs had magnificent palaces and gorgeous temples, but over whom custom exercised only a divided rule with liberty and progress.

A people, it appears, may be progressive for a certain length of time, and then stop: when does it stop? When it ceases to possess individuality. If a similar change should befall the nations of Europe, it will not be in exactly the same shape: the despotism of custom with which these nations are threatened is not precisely stationariness. It proscribes singularity, but it does not preclude change, provided all change together. We have discarded the fixed costumes of our forefathers; everyone must still dress like other people, but the fashion may change once or twice a year. We thus take care that when there is change, it shall be for change's sake, and not from any idea of beauty or convenience; for the same idea of beauty or convenience would not strike all the world at the same moment, and be simultaneously thrown aside by all at another moment. But we are progressive as well as changeable: we continually make new inventions in mechanical things, and keep them until they are again superseded by better; we are eager for improvement in politics, in education, even in morals, though in this last our idea of improvement chiefly consists in persuading or forcing other people to be as good as ourselves. It is not progress that we object to; on the contrary, we flatter ourselves that we are the most progressive people who ever lived.

It is individuality that we war against: we should think we had done wonders if we had made ourselves all alike; forgetting that the unlikeness of one person to another is generally the first thing which draws the attention of either to the imperfection of his own type, and the superiority of another, or the possibility, by combining the advantages of both, of producing something better than either. We have a warning example in China--a nation of much talent, and, in some respects, even wisdom, owing to the rare good fortune of having been provided at an early period with a particularly good set of customs, the work, in some measure, of men to whom even the most enlightened European must accord, under certain limitations, the title of sages and philosophers. They are remarkable, too, in the excellence of their apparatus for impressing, as far as possible, the best wisdom they possess upon every mind in the community, and securing that those who have appropriated most of it shall occupy the posts of honour and power.

Surely the people who did this have discovered the secret of human progressiveness, and must have kept themselves steadily at the head of the movement of the world. On the contrary, they have become stationary--have remained so for thousands of years; and if they are ever to be farther improved, it must be by foreigners. They have succeeded beyond all hope in what English philanthropists are so industriously working at--in making a people all alike, all governing their thoughts and conduct by the same maxims and rules; and these are the fruits. The modern regime of public opinion is, in an unorganized form, what the Chinese educational and political systems are in an organized; and unless individuality shall be able successfully to assert itself against this yoke, Europe, notwithstanding its noble antecedents and its professed Christianity, will tend to become another China.

What is it that has hitherto preserved Europe from this lot? What has made the European family of nations an improving, instead of a stationary portion of mankind? Not any superior excellence in them, which when it exists, exists as the effect, not as the cause; but their remarkable diversity of character and culture. Individuals, classes, nations, have been extremely unlike one another: they have struck out a great variety of paths, each leading to something valuable; and although at every period those who travelled in different paths have been intolerant of one another, and each would have thought it an excellent thing if all the rest could have been compelled to travel his road, their attempts to thwart each other's development have rarely had any permanent success, and each has in time endured to receive the good which the others have offered. Europe is, wholly indebted to this plurality of paths for its progressive and many-sided development. But it already begins to possess this benefit in a considerably less degree. It is decidedly advancing towards the Chinese ideal of making all people alike. M. de Tocqueville, in his last important work, remarks how much more the Frenchmen of the present day resemble one another, than did those even of the last generation.

The same remark might be made of Englishmen in a far greater degree. In a passage already quoted from Wilhelm von Humboldt, he points out two things as necessary conditions of human development, because necessary to render people unlike one another; namely, freedom, and variety of situations. The second of these two conditions is in this country every day diminishing. The circumstances which surround different classes and individuals, and shape their characters, are daily becoming more assimilated. Formerly, different ranks, different neighbourhoods, different trades and professions lived in what might be called different worlds; at present, to a great degree, in the same. Comparatively speaking, they now read the same things, listen to the same things, see the same things, go to the same places, have their hopes and fears directed to the same objects, have the same rights and liberties, and the same means of asserting them. Great as are the differences of position which remain, they are nothing to those which have ceased. And the assimilation is still proceeding.

All the political changes of the age promote it, since they all tend to raise the low and to lower the high. Every extension of education promotes it, because education brings people under common influences, and gives them access to the general stock of facts and sentiments. Improvements in the means of communication promote it, by bringing the inhabitants of distant places into personal contact, and keeping up a rapid flow of changes of residence between one place and another.

The increase of commerce and manufactures promotes it, by diffusing more widely the advantages of easy circumstances, and opening all objects of ambition, even the highest, to general competition, whereby the desire of rising becomes no longer the character of a particular class, but of all classes. A more powerful agency than even all these, in bringing about a general similarity among mankind, is the complete establishment, in this and other free countries, of the ascendancy of public opinion in the State.

As the various social eminences which enabled persons entrenched on them to disregard the opinion of the multitude, gradually became levelled; as the very idea of resisting the will of the public, when it is positively known that they have a will, disappears more and more from the minds of practical politicians; there ceases to be any social support for non-conformity--any substantive power in society, which, itself opposed to the ascendancy of numbers, is interested in taking under its protection opinions and tendencies at variance with those of the public.

The combination of all these causes forms so great a mass of influences hostile to Individuality, that it is not easy to see how it can stand its ground. It will do so with increasing difficulty, unless the intelligent part of the public can be made to feel its value--to see that it is good there should be differences, even though not for the better, even though, as it may appear to them, some should be for the worse. If the claims of Individuality are ever to be asserted, the time is now, while much is still wanting to complete the enforced assimilation. It is only in the earlier stages that any stand can be successfully made against the encroachment. The demand that all other people shall resemble ourselves, grows by what it feeds on.

If resistance waits till life is reduced nearly to one uniform type, all deviations from that type will come to be considered impious, immoral, even monstrous and contrary to nature. Mankind speedily become unable to conceive diversity, when they have been for some time unaccustomed to see it the Sphere and Duties of government, from the German of Baron Wilhelm von Humboldt, Sterling's Essays. There is something both contemptible and frightful in the sort of evidence on which, of late years, any person can be judicially declared unfit for the management of his affairs; and after his death, his disposal of his property can be set aside, if there is enough of it to pay the expenses of litigation--which are charged on the property itself.

All of the minute details of his daily life are pried into, and whatever is found which, seen through the medium of the perceiving and escribing faculties of the lowest of the low, bears an appearance unlike absolute commonplace, is laid before the jury as evidence of insanity, and often with success; the jurors being little, if at all, less vulgar and ignorant than the witnesses; while the judges, with that extraordinary want of knowledge of human nature and life which continually astonishes us in English lawyers, often help to mislead them. These trials speak volumes as to the state of feeling and opinion among the vulgar with regard to human liberty. So far from setting any value on individuality--so far from respecting the rights of each individual to act, in things indifferent, as seems good to his own judgement and inclinations, judges and juries cannot even conceive that a person in a state of sanity can desire such freedom. In former days, when it was proposed to burn atheists, charitable people used to suggest putting them in a madhouse instead: it would be nothing surprising now-a-days were we to see this done, and the doers applauding themselves, because, instead of persecuting for religion, they had adopted so humane and Christian a mode of treating these unfortunates, not without a silent satisfaction at their having thereby obtained their deserts.

The Limits to the Authority of Society over the Individual

What, then, is the rightful limit to the sovereignty of the individual over himself? Where does the authority of society begin? How much of human life should be assigned to individuality, and how much to society? Each will receive its proper share, if each has that which more particularly concerns it. To individuality should belong the part of life in which it is chiefly the individual that is interested; to society, the part which chiefly interests society.

Though society is not founded on a contract, and though no good purpose is answered by inventing a contract in order to deduce social obligations from it, everyone who receives the protection of society owes a return for the benefit, and the fact of living in society renders it indispensable that each should be bound to observe a certain line of conduct towards the rest. This conduct consists, first, in not injuring the interests of one another; or rather certain interests, which, either by express legal provision or by tacit understanding, ought to be considered as rights; and secondly, in each person's bearing his share of the labours and sacrifices incurred for defending the society or its members from injury and molestation.

These conditions, society is justified in enforcing, at all costs to those who endeavour to withhold fulfilment. Nor is this all that society may do. The acts of an individual may be hurtful to others, or wanting in due consideration for their welfare, without going the length of violating any of their constituted rights. The offender may then be justly punished by opinion, though not by law. As soon as any part of a person's conduct affects prejudicially the interests of others, society has jurisdiction over it, and the question whether the general welfare will or will not be promoted by interfering with it, becomes open to discussion. But there is no room for entertaining any such question when a person's conduct affects the interests of no persons besides himself, or needs not affect them unless they like. In all such cases there should be perfect freedom, legal and social, to do the action and stand the consequences. It would be a great misunderstanding of this doctrine, to suppose that it is one of selfish indifference, which pretends that human beings have no business with each other's conduct in life, and that they should not concern themselves about the well-doing or well-being of one another, unless their own interest is involved. Instead of any diminution, there is need of a great increase of disinterested exertion to promote the good of others. But disinterested benevolence can find other instruments to persuade people to their good, than whips and scourges, either of the literal or the metaphorical sort. I am the last person to undervalue the self-regarding virtues; they are only second in importance, if even second, to the social. It is equally the business of education to cultivate both. But even education works by conviction and persuasion as well as by compulsion, and it is by the former only that, when the period of education is past, the self-regarding virtues should be inculcated. Human beings owe to each other help to distinguish the better from the worse, and encouragement to choose the former and avoid the latter.

They should be forever stimulating each other to increased exercise of their higher faculties, and increased direction of their feelings and aims towards wise instead of foolish, elevating instead of degrading, objects and contemplations. But neither one person, nor any number of persons, is warranted in saying to another human creature of ripe years, that he shall not do with his life for his own benefit what he chooses to do with it. He is the person most interested in his own well-being, the interest which any other person, except in cases of strong personal attachment, can have in it, is trifling, compared with that which he himself has; the interest which society has in him individually is fractional, and altogether indirect: while, with respect to his own feelings and circumstances, the most ordinary man or woman has means of knowledge immeasurably surpassing those that can be possessed by any one else.

The interference of society to overrule his judgement and purposes in what only regards himself, must be grounded on general presumptions; which may be altogether wrong, and even if right, are as likely as not to be misapplied to individual cases, by persons no better acquainted with the circumstances of such cases than those are who look at them merely from without. In this department, therefore, of human affairs, Individuality has its proper field of action. In the conduct of human beings towards one another, it is necessary that general rules should for the most part be observed, in order that people may know what they have to expect; but in each person's own concerns, his individual spontaneity is entitled to free exercise. Considerations to aid his judgement, exhortations to strengthen his will, may be offered to him, even obtruded on him, by others; but he, himself, is the final judge. All errors which he is likely to commit against advice and warning, are far outweighed by the evil of allowing others to constrain him to what they deem his good.

I do not mean that the feelings with which a person is regarded by others, ought not to be in any way affected by his self-regarding qualities or deficiencies. This is neither possible nor desirable. If he is eminent in any of the qualities which conduce to his own good, he is, so far, a proper object of admiration. He is so much the nearer to the ideal perfection of human nature.

If he is grossly deficient in those qualities, a sentiment the opposite of admiration will follow. There is a degree of folly, and a degree of what may be called lowness or depravation of taste, which, though it cannot justify doing harm to the person who manifests it, renders him necessarily and properly a subject of distaste, or, in extreme cases, even of contempt: a person could not have the opposite qualities in due strength without entertaining these feelings. Though doing no wrong to any one, a person may so act as to compel us to judge him, and feel to him, as a fool, or as a being of an inferior order: and since this judgement and feeling are a fact which he would prefer to avoid, it is doing him a service to warn him of it beforehand, as of any other disagreeable consequence to which he exposes himself. It would be well, indeed, if this good office were much more freely rendered than the common notions of politeness at present permit, and if one person could honestly point out to another that he thinks him in fault, without being considered unmannerly or presuming. We have a right, also, in various ways, to act upon our unfavourable opinion of any one, not to the oppression of his individuality, but in the exercise of ours. We are not bound, for example, to seek his society; we have a right to avoid it, for we have a right to choose the society most acceptable to us. We have a right, and it may be our duty, to caution others against him, if we think his example or conversation likely to have a pernicious effect on those with whom he associates. We may give others a preference over him in optional good offices, except those which tend to his improvement.

In these various modes a person may suffer very severe penalties at the hands of others, for faults which directly concern only himself; but he suffers these penalties only in so far as they are the natural, and, as it were, the spontaneous consequences of the faults themselves, not because they are purposely inflicted on him for the sake of punishment. A person who shows rashness, obstinacy, self-conceit--who cannot live within moderate means--who cannot restrain himself from hurtful indulgences--who pursues animal pleasures at the expense of those of feeling and intellect--must expect to be lowered in the opinion of others, and to have a less share of their favourable sentiments, but of this he has no right to complain, unless he has merited their favour by special excellence in his social relations, and has thus established a title to their good offices, which is not affected by his demerits towards himself.

What I contend for is, that the inconveniences which are strictly inseparable from the unfavourable judgement of others, are the only ones to which a person should ever be subjected for that portion of his conduct and character which concerns his own good, but which does not affect the interests of others in their relations with him. Acts injurious to others require a totally different treatment. Encroachment on their rights; infliction on them of any loss or damage not justified by his own rights; falsehood or duplicity in dealing with them; unfair or ungenerous use of advantages over them; even selfish abstinence from defending them against injury--these are fit objects of moral reprobation, and, in grave cases, of moral retribution and punishment. And not only these acts, but the dispositions which lead to them, are properly immoral, and fit subjects of disapprobation which may rise to abhorrence.

Cruelty of disposition; malice and ill-nature; that most anti-social and odious of all passions, envy; dissimulation and insincerity, irascibility on insufficient cause, and resentment disproportioned to the provocation; the love of domineering over others; the desire to engross more than one's share of advantages; the pride which derives gratification from the abasement of others; the egotism which thinks self and its concerns more important than everything else, and decides all doubtful questions in his own favour;--these are moral vices, and constitute a bad and odious moral character: unlike the self-regarding faults previously mentioned, which are not properly immoralities, and to whatever pitch they may be carried, do not constitute wickedness. They may be proofs of any amount of folly, or want of personal dignity and self-respect; but they are only a subject of moral reprobation when they involve a breach of duty to others, for whose sake the individual is bound to have care for himself. What are called duties to ourselves are not socially obligatory, unless circumstances render them at the same time duties to others. The term duty to oneself, when it means anything more than prudence, means self-respect or self-development; and for none of these is anyone accountable to his fellow-creatures, because for none of them is it for the good of mankind that he be held accountable to them.

The distinction between the loss of consideration which a person may rightly incur by defect of prudence or of personal dignity, and the reprobation which is due to him for an offence against the rights of others, is not a merely nominal distinction. It makes a vast difference both in our feelings and in our conduct towards him, whether he displeases us in things in which we think we have a right to control him, or in things in which we know that we have not.

If he displeases us, we may express our distaste, and we may stand aloof from a person as well as from a thing that displeases us; but we shall not therefore feel called on to make his life uncomfortable. We shall reflect that he already bears, or will bear, the whole penalty of his error; if he spoils his life by mismanagement, we shall not, for that reason, desire to spoil it still further: instead of wishing to punish him, we shall rather endeavour to alleviate his punishment, by showing him how he may avoid or cure the evils his conduct tends to bring upon him. He may be to us an object of pity, perhaps of dislike, but not of anger or resentment; we shall not treat him like an enemy of society: the worst we shall think ourselves justified in doing is leaving him to himself, If we do not interfere benevolently by showing interest or concern for him. It is far otherwise if he has infringed the rules necessary for the protection of his fellow-creatures, individually or collectively. The evil consequences of his acts do not then fall on himself, but on others; and society, as the protector of all its members, must retaliate on him; must inflict pain on him for the express purpose of punishment, and must take care that it be sufficiently severe. In the one case, he is an offender at our bar, and we are called on not only to sit in judgement on him, but, in one shape or another, to execute our own sentence: in the other case, it is not our part to inflict any suffering on him, except what may incidentally follow from our using the same liberty in the regulation of our own affairs, which we allow to him in his.

The distinction here pointed out between the part of a person's life which concerns only himself, and that which concerns others, many persons will refuse to admit. How can any part of the conduct of a member of society be a matter of indifference to the other members? No person is an entirely isolated being;

it is impossible for a person to do anything seriously or permanently hurtful to himself, without mischief reaching at least to his near connections, and often far beyond them. If he injures his property, he does harm to those who directly or indirectly derived support from it, and usually diminishes, by a greater or less amount, the general resources of the community.

If he deteriorates his bodily or mental faculties, he not only brings evil upon all who depended on him for any portion of their happiness, but disqualifies himself for rendering the services which he owes to his fellow-creatures generally; perhaps becomes a burden on their affection or benevolence; and if such conduct were very frequent, hardly any offence that is committed would detract more from the general sum of good. Finally, if by his vices or follies a person does no direct harm to others, he is nevertheless injurious by his example; and ought to be compelled to control himself, for the sake of those whom the sight or knowledge of his conduct might corrupt or mislead. And even if the consequences of misconduct could be confined to the vicious or thoughtless individual, ought society to abandon to their own guidance those who are manifestly unfit for it? If protection against themselves is confessedly due to children and persons under age, is not society equally bound to afford it to persons of mature years who are equally incapable of self-government? If gambling, or drunkenness, or incontinence, or idleness, or uncleanliness, are as injurious to happiness, and as great a hindrance to improvement, as many or most of the acts prohibited by law, why should not law, so far as is consistent with practicability and social convenience, endeavour to repress these also?

And as a supplement to the unavoidable imperfections of law, ought not opinion at least to organize a powerful police against these vices, and visit rigidly with social penalties those who are known to practice them? There is no question here about restricting individuality, or impeding the trial of new and original experiments in living. The only things it is sought to prevent are things which have been tried and condemned from the beginning of the world until now; things which experience has shown not to be useful or suitable to any person's individuality. There must be some length of time and amount of experience, after which a moral or prudential truth may be regarded as established, and it is merely desired to prevent generation after generation from falling over the same precipice which has been fatal to their predecessors.

We fully admit that the mischief which a person does to himself, may seriously affect, both through their sympathies and their interests, those nearly connected with him, and in a minor degree, society at large. When, by conduct of this sort, a person is led to violate a distinct and assignable obligation to any other person or persons, the case is taken out of the self-regarding class, and becomes amenable to moral disapprobation in the proper sense of the term. If, for example, a man, through intemperance or extravagance, becomes unable to pay his debts, or, having undertaken the moral responsibility of a family, becomes from the same cause incapable of supporting or educating them, he is deservedly reprobated, and might be justly punished; but it is for the breach of duty to his family or creditors, not for the extravagance. If the resources which ought to have been devoted to them, had been diverted from them for the most prudent investment, the moral culpability would have been the same. If someone murdered his uncle to get money for his mistress, but if he had done it to set himself up in business, he would equally have been hanged. Again, in the frequent case of a man who causes grief to his family by addiction to bad habits, he deserves reproach for his unkindness or ingratitude; but so he may for cultivating habits not in themselves vicious, if they are painful to those with whom he passes his life, or who from personal ties are dependent on him for their comfort.

Whoever fails in the consideration generally due to the interests and feelings of others, not being compelled by some more imperative duty, or justified by allowable self-preference, is a subject of moral disapprobation for that failure, but not for the cause of it, nor for the errors, merely personal to himself, which may have remotely led to it. In like manner, when a person disables himself, by conduct purely self-regarding, from the performance of some definite duty incumbent on him to the public, he is guilty of a social offence. No person ought to be punished simply for being drunk; but a soldier or a policeman should be punished for being drunk on duty. Whenever, in short, there is a definite damage, or a definite risk of damage, either to an individual or to the public, the case is taken out of the province of liberty, and placed in that of morality or law.

But with regard to the merely contingent or, as it may be called, constructive injury which a person causes to society, by conduct which neither violates any specific duty to the public, nor occasions perceptible hurt to any assignable individual except himself; the inconvenience is one which society can afford to bear, for the sake of the greater good of human freedom. If grown persons are to be punished for not taking proper care of themselves, rather it were for their own sake, than under pretence of preventing them from impairing their capacity of rendering to society benefits which society does not pretend it has a right to exact. But we cannot consent to argue the point as if society had no means of bringing its weaker members up to its ordinary standard of rational conduct, except waiting till they do something irrational, and then punishing them, legally or morally, for it. Society has had absolute power over them during all the early portion of their existence: it has had the whole period of childhood and non-age in which to try whether it could make them capable of rational conduct in life. The existing generation is master both of the training and the entire circumstances of the generation to come; it cannot indeed make them perfectly wise and good, because it is itself so lamentably deficient in goodness and wisdom; and its best efforts are not always, in individual cases, its most successful ones; but it is perfectly well able to make the rising generation, as a whole, as good as, and a little better than, itself.

If society lets any considerable number of its members grow up mere children, incapable of being acted on by rational consideration of distant motives, society has itself to blame for the consequences. Armed not only with all the powers of education, but with the ascendency which the authority of a received opinion always exercises over the minds who are least fitted to judge for themselves; and aided by the natural penalties which cannot be prevented from falling on those who incur the distaste or the contempt of those who know them; let not society pretend that it needs, besides all this, the power to issue commands and enforce obedience in the personal concerns of individuals, in which, on all principles of justice and policy, the decision ought to rest with those who are to abide the consequences. Nor is there anything which tends more to discredit and frustrate the better means of influencing conduct, than a resort to the worse.

If there be among those whom it is attempted to coerce into prudence or temperance, any of the material of which vigorous and independent characters are made, they will infallibly rebel against the yoke. No such person will ever feel that others have a right to control him in his concerns, such as they have to prevent him from injuring them in theirs; and it easily comes to be considered a mark of spirit and courage to fly in the face of such usurped authority, and do with ostentation the exact opposite of what it enjoins; as in the fashion of grossness which succeeded, in the time of Charles II., to the fanatical moral intolerance of the Puritans. With respect to what is said of the necessity of protecting society from the bad example set to others by the vicious or the self-indulgent; it is true that bad example may have a pernicious effect, especially the example of doing wrong to others with impunity to the wrong-doer. But we are now speaking of conduct which, while it does no wrong to others, is supposed to do great harm to the agent himself: and we do not see how those who believe this, can think otherwise than that the example, on the whole, must be more salutary than hurtful, since, if it displays the misconduct, it displays also the painful or degrading consequences which, if the conduct is justly censured, must be supposed to be in all or most cases attendant on it.

But the strongest of all the arguments against the interference of the public with purely personal conduct, is that when it does interfere, the odds are that it interferes wrongly, and in the wrong place. On questions of social morality, of duty to others, the opinion of the public, that is, of an overruling majority, though often wrong, is likely to be still oftener right; because on such questions they are only required to judge of their own interests; of the manner in which some mode of conduct, if allowed to be practised, would affect themselves. But the opinion of a similar majority, imposed as a law on the minority, on questions of self-regarding conduct, is quite as likely to be wrong as right; for in these cases public opinion means, at the best, some people's opinion of what is good or bad for other people; while very often it does not even mean that; the public, with the most perfect indifference, passing over the pleasure or convenience of those whose conduct they censure, and considering only their own preference.

There are many who consider as an injury to themselves any conduct which they have a distaste for, and resent it as an outrage to their feelings; as a religious bigot, when charged with disregarding the religious feelings of others, has been known to retort that they disregard his feelings, by persisting in their abominable worship or creed. But there is no parity between the feeling of a person for his own opinion, and the feeling of another who is offended at his holding it; no more than between the desire of a thief to take a purse, and the desire of the right owner to keep it. And a person's taste is as much his own peculiar concern as his opinion or his purse. It is easy for anyone to imagine an ideal public, which leaves the freedom and choice of individuals in all uncertain matters undisturbed, and only requires them to abstain from modes of conduct which universal experience has condemned. But where has there been seen a public which set any such limit to its censorship? or when does the public trouble itself about universal experience. In its interferences with personal conduct it is seldom thinking of anything but the enormity of acting or feeling differently from itself; and this standard of judgement, thinly disguised, is held up to mankind as the dictate of religion and philosophy, by nine–tenths of all moralists and speculative writers. These teach that things are right because they are right; because we feel them to be so.

They tell us to search in our own minds and hearts for laws of conduct binding on ourselves and on all others. What can the poor public do but apply these instructions, and make their own personal feelings of good and evil, if they are tolerably unanimous in them, obligatory on all the world?

The evil here pointed out is not one which exists only in theory; and it may perhaps be expected that I should specify the instances in which the public of this age and country improperly invests its own preferences with the character of moral laws. That is too weighty a subject to be discussed parenthetically, and by way of illustration. Yet examples are necessary, to show that the principle is of serious and practical moment, and that we are not endeavouring to erect a barrier against imaginary evils. And it is not difficult to show, by abundant instances, that to extend the bounds of what may be called moral police, until it encroaches on the most unquestionably legitimate liberty of the individual, is one of the most universal of all human propensities.

As a first instance, consider the antipathies which men cherish on no better grounds than that persons whose religious opinions are different from theirs, do not practice their religious observances, especially their religious abstinences. To cite a rather trivial example, nothing in the creed or practice of Christians does more to envenom the hatred of Mahomedans against them, than the fact of their eating pork. There are few acts which Christians and Europeans regard with more unaffected disgust, than Mussulmans regard this particular mode of satisfying hunger. It is, in the first place, an offence against their religion; but this circumstance by no means explains either the degree or the kind of their repugnance; for wine also is forbidden by their religion, and to partake of it is by all Mussulmans accounted wrong, but not disgusting.

Their aversion to the flesh of the 'unclean beast' is, on the contrary, of that peculiar character, resembling an instinctive antipathy, which the idea of uncleanness, when once it thoroughly sinks into the feelings, seems always to excite even in those whose personal habits are anything but scrupulously cleanly and of which the sentiment of religious impurity, so intense in the Hindus, is a remarkable example.

Suppose now that in a people, of whom the majority were Mussulmans, that majority should insist upon not permitting pork to be eaten within the limits of the country. This would be nothing new in Mahomedan countries. Would it be a legitimate exercise of the moral authority of public opinion? and if not, why not? The practice is really revolting to such a public. They also sincerely think that it is forbidden and abhorred by the Deity. Neither could the prohibition be censured as religious persecution. It might be religious in its origin, but it would not be persecution for religion, since nobody's religion makes it a duty to eat pork. The only tenable ground of condemnation would be, that with the personal tastes and self-regarding concerns of individuals the public has no business to interfere.

To come somewhat nearer home: the majority of Spaniards consider it a gross impiety, offensive in the highest degree to the Supreme Being, to worship him in any other manner than the Roman Catholic; and no other public worship is lawful on Spanish soil. The people of all Southern Europe look upon a married clergy as not only irreligious, but unchaste, indecent, gross, disgusting. What do Protestants think of these perfectly sincere feelings, and of the attempt to enforce them against non-Catholics? Yet, if mankind are justified in interfering with each other's liberty in things which do not concern the interests of others, on what principle is it possible consistently to exclude these cases? or who can blame people for desiring to suppress what they regard as a scandal in the sight of God and man? No stronger case can be shown for prohibiting anything which is regarded as a personal immorality, than is made out for suppressing these practices in the eyes of those who regard them as impieties; and unless we are willing to adopt the logic of persecutors, and to say that we may persecute others because we are right, and that they must not persecute us because they are wrong, we must beware of admitting a principle of which we should resent as a gross injustice the application to ourselves.

The preceding instances may be objected to, although unreasonably, as drawn from contingencies impossible among us: opinion, in this country, not being likely to enforce abstinence from meats, or to interfere with people for worshipping, and for either marrying or not marrying, according to their creed or inclination. The next example, however, shall be taken from an interference with liberty which we have by no means passed all danger of. Wherever the Puritans have been sufficiently powerful, as in New England, and in Great Britain at the time of the Commonwealth, they have endeavoured, with considerable success, to put down all public, and nearly all private, amusements: especially music, dancing, public games, or other assemblages for purposes of diversion, and the theatre. There are still in this country large bodies of persons by whose notions of morality and religion these recreations are condemned; and those persons belonging chiefly to the middle class, who are the ascendant power in the present social and political condition of the kingdom, it is by no means impossible that persons of these sentiments may at some time or other command a majority in Parliament.

How will the remaining portion of the community like to have the amusements that shall be permitted to them regulated by the religious and moral sentiments of the stricter Calvinists and Methodists? Would they not, with considerable peremptoriness, desire these intrusively pious members of society to mind their own business? This is precisely what should be said to every government and every public, who have the pretension that no person shall enjoy any pleasure which they think wrong. But if the principle of the pretension be admitted, no one can reasonably object to its being acted on in the sense of the majority, or other preponderating power in the country; and all persons must be ready to conform to the idea of a Christian commonwealth, as understood by the early settlers in New England, if a religious profession similar to theirs should ever succeed in regaining its lost ground, as religions supposed to be declining have so often been known to do.

To imagine another contingency, perhaps more likely to be realized than the one last mentioned. There is confessedly a strong tendency in the modern world towards a democratic constitution of society, accompanied or not by popular political institutions. It is affirmed that in the country where this tendency is most completely realized--where both society and the government are most democratic--the United States--the feeling of the majority, to whom any appearance of a more showy or costly style of living than they can hope to rival is disagreeable, operates as a tolerably effectual sumptuary law, and that in many parts of the Union it is really difficult for a person possessing a very large income, to find any mode of spending it, which will not incur popular disapprobation. Though such statements as these are doubtless much exaggerated as a representation of existing facts, the state of things they describe is not only a conceivable and possible, but a probable result of democratic feeling, combined with the notion that the public has a right to a veto on the manner in which individuals shall spend their incomes.

We have only further to suppose a considerable diffusion of Socialist opinions, and it may become infamous in the eyes of the majority to possess more property than some very small amount, or any income not earned by manual labour. Opinions similar in principle to these, already prevail widely among the artisan class, and weigh oppressively on those who are amenable to the opinion chiefly of that class, namely, its own members. It is known that the bad workmen who form the majority of the operatives in many branches of industry, are decidedly of opinion that bad workmen ought to receive the same wages as good, and that no one ought to be allowed, through piecework or otherwise, to earn by superior skill or industry more than others can without it. And they employ a moral police, which occasionally becomes a physical one, to deter skilful workmen from receiving, and employers from giving, a larger remuneration for a more useful service. If the public have any jurisdiction over private concerns, I cannot see that these people are in fault, or that any individual's particular public can be blamed for asserting the same authority over his individual conduct, which the general public asserts over people in general.

But, without dwelling upon supposititious cases, there are, in our own day, gross usurpations upon the liberty of private life actually practised, and still greater ones threatened with some expectation of success, and opinions proposed which assert an unlimited right in the public not only to prohibit by law everything which it thinks wrong, but in order to get at what it thinks wrong, to prohibit any number of things which it admits to be innocent.

Under the name of preventing intemperance the people of one English colony, and of nearly half the United States, have been interdicted by law from making any use whatever of fermented drinks, except for medical purposes: for prohibition of their sale is in fact, as it is intended to be, prohibition of their use. And though the impracticability of executing the law has caused its repeal in several of the states which had adopted it, including the one from which it derives its name, an attempt has notwithstanding been commenced, and is prosecuted with considerable zeal by many of the professed philanthropists, to agitate for a similar law in this country. The association, or 'Alliance' as it terms itself, which has been formed for this purpose, has acquired some notoriety through the publicity given to a correspondence between its Secretary and one of the very few English public men who hold that a politician's opinions ought to be founded on principles.

Lord Stanley's share in this correspondence is calculated to strengthen the hopes already built on him, by those who know how rare such qualities as are manifested in some of his public appearances, unhappily are among those who figure in political life. The organ of the Alliance, who would "deeply deplore the recognition of any principle which could be wrested to justify bigotry and persecution," undertakes to point out the "broad and impassable barrier" which divides such principles from those of the association. "All matters relating to thought, opinion, conscience, appear to me," he says, "to be without the sphere of legislation; all pertaining to social act, habit, relation, subject only to a discretionary power vested in the State itself, and not in the individual, to be within it." No mention is made of a third class, different from either of these, *viz.*, acts and habits which are not social, but individual; although it is to this class, surely, that the act of drinking fermented liquors belongs. Selling fermented liquors, however, is trading, and trading is a social act. But the infringement complained of is not on the liberty of the seller, but on that of the buyer and consumer; since the State might just as well forbid him to drink wine, as purposely make it impossible for him to obtain it. The Secretary, however, says, "I claim, as a citizen, a right to legislate whenever my social rights are invaded by the social act of another". And now for the definition of these 'social rights'. "If anything invades my social rights, certainly the traffic in strong drink does. It destroys my primary right of security, by constantly creating and stimulating social disorder. It invades my right of equality, by deriving a profit from the creation of a misery, I am taxed to support. It impedes my right to free moral and intellectual development, by surrounding my path with dangers, and by weakening and demoralizing society, from which I have a right to claim mutual aid and intercourse."

A theory of 'social rights', the like of which probably never before found its way into distinct language--being nothing short of this--that it is the absolute social right of every individual, that every other individual shall act in every respect exactly as he ought; that whosoever fails thereof in the smallest particular, violates my social right, and entitles me to demand from the legislature the removal of the grievance.

So monstrous a principle is far more dangerous than any single interference with liberty; there is no violation of liberty which it would not justify; it acknowledges no right to any freedom whatever, except perhaps to that of holding opinions in secret, without ever disclosing them; for the moment an opinion which I consider noxious, passes any one's lips, it invades all the 'social rights' attributed to me by the Alliance. The doctrine ascribes to all mankind a vested interest in each other's moral, intellectual, and even physical perfection, to be defined by each claimant according to his own standard. Another important example of illegitimate interference with the rightful liberty of the individual, not simply threatened, but long since carried into triumphant effect, is Sabbatarian legislation. Without doubt, abstinence on one day in the week, so far as the exigencies of life permit, from the usual daily occupation, though in no respect religiously binding on any except Jews, is a highly beneficial custom. And inasmuch as this custom cannot be observed without a general consent to that effect among the industrious classes, therefore, in so far as some persons by working may impose the same necessity on others, it may be allowable and right that the law should guarantee to each, the observance by others of the custom, by suspending the greater operations of industry on a particular day.

But this justification, grounded on the direct interest which others have in each individual's observance of the practice, does not apply to the self-chosen occupations in which a person may think fit to employ his leisure; nor does it hold good, in the smallest degree, for legal restrictions on amusements. It is true that the amusement of some is the day's work of others; but the pleasure, not to say the useful recreation, of many, is worth the labour of a few, provided the occupation is freely chosen, and can be freely resigned. The operatives are perfectly right in thinking that if all worked on Sunday, seven days' work would have to be given for six days' wages: but so long as the great mass of employments are suspended, the small number who for the enjoyment of others must still work, obtain a proportional increase of earnings; and they are not obliged to follow those occupations, if they prefer leisure to emolument.

If a further remedy is sought, it might be found in the establishment by custom of a holiday on some other day of the week for those particular classes of persons. The only ground, therefore, on which restrictions on Sunday amusements can be defended, must be that they are religiously wrong; a motive of legislation which never can be too earnestly protested against. "*Deorum injuriae Diis curae*." It remains to be proved that society or any of its officers holds a commission from on high to avenge any supposed offence to Omnipotence, which is not also a wrong to our fellow-creatures. The notion that it is one man's duty that another should be religious, was the foundation of all the religious persecutions ever perpetrated, and if admitted, would fully justify them. Though the feeling which breaks out in the repeated attempts to stop railway travelling on Sunday, in the resistance to the opening of Museums, and the like, has not the cruelty of the old persecutors, the state of mind indicated by it is fundamentally the same. It is a determination not to tolerate others in doing what is permitted by their religion, because it is not permitted by the persecutor's religion. It is a belief that God not only abominates the act of the misbeliever, but will not hold us guiltless if we leave him unmolested.

I cannot refrain from adding to these examples of the little account commonly made of human liberty, the language of downright persecution which breaks out from the press whenever it feels called on to notice the remarkable phenomenon of Mormonism. Much might be said on the unexpected and instructive fact, that an alleged new revelation, and a religion, founded on it, the product of palpable imposture, not even supported by the prestige of extraordinary qualities in its founder, is believed by hundreds of thousands, and has been made the foundation of a society, in the age of newspapers, railways, and the electric telegraph. What here concerns us is, that this religion, like other and better religions, has its martyrs; that its prophet and founder was, for his teaching, put to death by a mob; that others of its adherents lost their lives by the same lawless violence; that they were forcibly expelled, in a body, from the country in which they first grew up; while, now that they have been chased into a solitary recess in the midst of a desert, many in this country openly declare that it would be right to send an expedition against them, and compel them by force to conform to the opinions of other people.

The article of the Mormonite doctrine which is the chief provocative to the antipathy which thus breaks through the ordinary restraints of religious tolerance, is its sanction of polygamy; which, though permitted to Mahomedans, and Hindus, and Chinese, seems to excite unquenchable animosity when practised by persons who speak English, and profess to be a kind of Christians. No one has a deeper disapprobation than I have of this Mormon institution; both for other reasons, and because, far from being in any way countenanced by the principle of liberty, it is a direct infraction of that principle, being a mere riveting of the chains of one half of the community, and an emancipation of the other from reciprocity of obligation towards them. Still, it must be remembered that this relation is as much voluntary on the part of the women concerned in it, and who may be deemed the sufferers by it, as is the case with any other form of the marriage institution; and however surprising this fact may appear, it has its explanation in the common ideas and customs of the world, which teaching women to think marriage the one thing needful, make it intelligible that many a woman should prefer being one of several wives, to not being a wife at all.

Other countries are not asked to recognize such unions, or release any portion of their inhabitants from their own laws on the score of Mormonite opinions. But when the dissentients have conceded to the hostile sentiments of others, far more than could justly be demanded; when they have left the countries to which their doctrines were unacceptable, and established themselves in a remote corner of the earth, which they have been the first to render habitable to human beings; it is difficult to see on what principles but those of tyranny they can be prevented from living thereunder what laws they please, provided they commit no aggression on other nations, and allow perfect freedom of departure to those who are dissatisfied with their ways.

A recent writer, in some respects of considerable merit, proposes not a crusade, but a civilizade, against this polygamous community, to put an end to what seems to him a retrograde step in civilization. It also appears so to me, but I am not aware that any community has a right to force another to be civilized. So long as the sufferers by the bad law do not invoke assistance from other communities, I cannot admit that persons entirely unconnected with them ought to step in and require that a condition of things with which all who are directly interested appear to be satisfied, should be put an end to because it is a scandal to persons some thousands of miles distant, who have no part orconcern in it.

Let them send missionaries, if they please, to preach against it; and let them, by any fair means, oppose the progress of similar doctrines among their own people. If civilization has got the better of barbarism when barbarism had the world to itself, it is too much to profess to be afraid lest barbarism, after having been fairly got under, should revive and conquer civilization. A civilization that can thus succumb to its vanquished enemy must first have become so degenerate, that neither its appointed priests and teachers, nor anybody else, has the capacity, or will take the trouble, to stand up for it. If this be so, the sooner such a civilization receives notice to quit, the better. It can only go on from bad to worse, until destroyed and regenerated by energetic barbarians.

The case of the Bombay Parsees is a curious instance in point. When this industrious and enterprising tribe, the descendants of the Persian fire-worshippers, flying from their native country before the Caliphs, arrived in Western India, they were admitted to toleration by the Hindu sovereigns, on condition of not eating beef. When those regions afterwards fell under the dominion of Mahomedan conquerors, the Parsees obtained from them a continuance of indulgence, on condition of refraining from pork. What was at first obedience to authority became a second nature, and the Parsees to this day abstain both from beef and pork. Though not required by their religion, the double abstinence has had time to grow into a custom of their tribe; and custom, in the East, is a religion.

NEGATIVE AND POSITIVE LIBERTY

While Isaiah Berlin is often credited with distinguishing positive from negative liberty, this view was in fact put forward in the nineteenth century by, among others, the English political philosopher, T. H. Green who contributed to understanding what positive liberty, or freedom, implies. Green put the matter this way:

We shall probably all agree that freedom, rightly understood, is the greatest of blessings; that its attainment is the true end of all our efforts as citizens. But when we thus speak of freedom, we should consider carefully what we mean by it. We do not mean merely freedom from restraint or compulsion. We do not mean merely freedom to do as we like irrespective of what it is that we like.

We do not mean a freedom that can be enjoyed by one man or one set of men at the cost of a loss of freedom to others. When we speak of freedom as something to be so highly prized, we mean a positive power or capacity of doing or enjoying something worth doing or enjoying, and that, too, something that we do or enjoy in common with others. We mean by it a power which each man exercises through the help or security given him by his fellow-men, and which he in turn helps to secure for them. When we measure the progress of a society by its growth in freedom, we measure it by the increasing development and exercise on the whole of those powers of contributing to social good with which we believe the members of the society to be endowed; in short, by the greater power on the part of the citizens as a body to make the most and best of themselves.

There are very formidable defenders of the idea of positive liberty among contemporary political philosophers–among them, Amartya Sen, Martha Nussbaum, Cass Sunstein, Ronald Dworkin, and Henry Shue. All of them conclude from their somewhat diverse approaches, that the freedom or liberty to make progress in one's life is even more important to respect, secure, and protect than negative liberty. Negative liberty, in the tradition of Locke's natural rights theory, is the condition of not being interfered with or intruded upon in one's person and estate. This liberty is dubbed "negative" because it requires that everyone abstain from acting aggressively, that they refrain from invasive or intrusive conduct. Positive liberty or rights involve securing, for those in need, the capabilities to achieve the ends they seek.

The underlying understanding of human nature in these two schools of political thought is markedly different. In the Lockean tradition of negative liberty–or the right to it–human beings are taken to have the capacity and responsibility to advance in their lives once a condition of negative freedom has been secured for them. In other words, free persons can and ought to strive to flourish in their lives and to this end they may only make use of provisions from others which are given or voluntarily exchanged. Social cooperation–in such areas as education, industry, science, philanthropy and the like–is deemed quite likely as a function of the self-responsible conduct everyone is expected to engage in.

With respect to the conception of human nature that underlies the notion of positive liberty, it is generally held that those who are indigent, poor, or are otherwise importantly lacking in provisions needed for their lives to flourish require support mandated from others so that they will become capable or enabled. Without such support, they will very likely languish in their deprived situations and will ultimately suffer the indignity of helplessness.

Implicit in the position of those who embrace the idea of positive liberty is an emphasis on the right of all citizens to take part in political decision-making. "Put in the simplest terms, one might say that a democratic society is a free society because it is a self-determined society, and that a member of that society is free to the extent that he or she participates in its democratic process." Furthermore, "there are also individualist applications of the concept of positive freedom. For example, it is sometimes said that a government should aim actively to create the conditions necessary for individuals to be self-sufficient or to achieve self-realization."

The basic idea here is that by enjoying this kind of positive political liberty–namely, the liberty to take part in the determination and configuration of laws and public policy–citizens are capable of securing for themselves the conditions that are needed for their flourishing. They are able to vote into law the appropriate and necessary distribution of society's resources.

Champions of negative liberty, who argue that laws and public policy ought to concentrate on extirpating society conduct that invades persons and properties of citizens–that is, that violate our negative rights–object to this idea on the grounds that voting for laws and public policies that involve distribution of society's resources amounts to unjust rights violations and discourage self-responsible behaviour. Supporters of a political theory predicated on positive liberty reject this on the grounds that without such mandated provisions, too many individuals will remain poor, ignorant, and helpless in innumerable ways.

The debate between the two schools hinges on numerous features of their respective positions. Are men and women who are forced to work for objectives to which they haven't give their consent being treated unjustly? And will these laws undermine the productivity of those being forced to work in this way? In a society where resources are conceived of as commonly owned, will this inevitably lead to what has been called the tragedy of the commons"? Or, alternatively, is the self-motivation that negative liberty appears to require simply a myth?

Are those who are deprived indeed capable of choosing to advance, thus moving from their deprived condition towards one where their goals can be fulfilled? Is the protection of negative liberty or rights going to favour those who are well endowed to start with so that they will necessarily be advantaged while their fellow citizens will be left deprived? Will this create a class of privileged citizens?

Both negative and positive liberty can be defended on either deontological or utilitarian grounds. The deontological approach–or something akin to this, such as a self-perfectionist or neo-Aristotelian position–implies that what is crucial in a human community is that the dignity of persons be respected and protected and thus are allowed to guide their lives by their own decisions, for better or for worse. Thus, it doesn't matter so much how well off members of the community are–what is crucial is whether justice, predicated on a conception of negative liberty, or rights, prevails. Some go on to argue that this is more likely than not to also secure widespread well being; but that is not their most crucial objective.

The utilitarian approach focuses on actual well being and how prevalent it is in a society that respects and protects either negative or positive liberty or rights. If, in fact, one of these approaches to community life–to the laws and public policies of the society–is most likely to produce widespread well being, over the long run, it will be deemed superior to the other. Among those who argue for positive liberty or rights, some hold that these are the only kind that in fact exist. For example, Henry Shue, in his book Basic Rights, maintains that since negative liberty or rights are ineffective without being protected, and their protection amounts to providing a service to others, negative liberty or rights actually amount to positive ones. Everyone is owed the protection of his or her negative liberty but this protection is something positive, something that needs to be provided so as to be practically useful, even meaningful.

A similar line of reasoning has been advanced by Cass Sunstein and Stephen Holmes, in their work The Cost of Right, Why Liberty Depends on Taxation. Without being dependent on taxes, which others owe as a reflection of one's positive right no one can enjoy negative liberty–it will go unsecured, unprotected. On the other hand, supporters of the notion of negative liberty or rights argue in response that unless the negative liberty or right exists, unless individuals have them, it is conceptually odd to speak of the need to secure or protect them.

We can be sure that this discussion will continue for some time since many deem it central to the issue of whether a robust welfare state or a society of limited government is the truly just political order, at least within the framework of the Western liberal political tradition. For example, the philosopher James P. Sterba has argued in several of his books, and is indeed planning several works, in support of welfare or positive liberty or rights, while the philosophers Jan Narveson, Eric Mack, Douglas B. Rasmussen, et al., have argued, instead, for negative liberty or rights.

It is, of course, possible to argue, also, that this entire discussion rests on the mistaken notion that individuals have rights. Communitarians, among them Auguste Comte, object to this view.

Comte argued, as far back as the early nineteenth century, as follows:

- "Everything we have belongs then to Humanity...Positivism never admits anything but duties, of all to all. For its social point of view cannot tolerate the notion of right, constantly based on individualism. We are born loaded with obligations of every kind, to our predecessors, to our successors, to our contemporaries. Later they only grow or accumulate before we can return any service. On what human foundation then could rest the idea of right, which in reason should imply some previous efficiency? Whatever may be our efforts, the longest life well employed will never enable us to pay back but an imperceptible part of what we have received. And yet it would only be after a complete return that we should be justly authorized to require reciprocity for the new services. All human rights then are as absurd as they are immoral. This, the definitive formula of human morality, gives a direct sanction exclusively to our instincts of benevolence, the common source of happiness and duty. Humanity, whose we are entirely."

Contemporary communitarians, such as Charles Taylor, also hold that human beings actually belong to some community or other and their conduct, their pursuit of various goals, are contingent upon gaining the sanction of the community–they have no right to act on their own initiative unless they gained the community's permission to do so. Any notion of individualism that takes it that people are independent agents is a false atomism.

Critics of communitarianism claim, however, that there are conceptual problems with denying some notion of individualism since in advancing their views communitarians are themselves conducting themselves individualistically. They are assuming that they have the right to voice their views, that they need no permission from the community to disagree with the community which is, at least in large portions of the West, individualistic.

Another source of support for the idea of positive liberty is a deterministic view of human behaviour, which is increasingly popular. Those who do not fare well may not be regarded as having failed but more as incapable of doing what needs to be done for them to get ahead in their lives. As John Rawls puts the matter, the assertion that we "deserve the superior character that enables us to make the effort to cultivate our talents is...problematic; for such character depends in good part upon fortunate family and social circumstances in early life for which we can claim no credit."

Thus, having more or less of what others have is of no moral significance but a matter of the various impersonal forces that shape a person's life. From this it may be inferred that all who are disadvantaged are victims of circumstances and do not deserve their lot. This is a view that counters the conception of negative liberty that libertarians embrace, namely that once adult men or women are free from interference from others, their flourishing or lack thereof in life must be largely their own achievement.

In any case, despite the attempt to dismiss the debate between advocates of negative and positive liberty, the issue appears to have staying power because political philosophers will continue to affirm certain kinds of liberties or rights for human beings. Which of those are the proper kind is something that will remain both theoretically and practically significant.

Libertarians are supporters only of negative liberty as a feature of a legal system, believing as they do that the goals of positive liberty advocates are attainable without involving government, without mandating what libertarians deem to amount to involuntary servitude from others so that people may flourish. Their position is supported from a variety of perspectives, of course, but it is central to all that individual human beings are sovereign and must not be used against their will by others, including the government.

10

Theory of Democracy

Democracy is a form of government in which all people have an equal say in the decisions that affect their lives. Ideally, this includes equal participation in the proposal, development and passage of legislation into law. It can also encompass social, economic and cultural conditions that enable the free and equal practice of political self-determination. The term comes from the Greek: 'rule of the people', which was coined from dêmos 'people' and Kratos 'power', in the middle of the 5th-4th century BC to denote the political systems then existing in some Greek city-states, notably Athens following a popular uprising in 508 BC.

According to some theories of democracy, popular sovereignty is the founding principle of such a system. However, the democratic principle has also been expressed as "the freedom to call something into being which did not exist before, which was not given… and which therefore, strictly speaking, could not be known." This type of freedom, which is connected to human 'natality', or the capacity to begin anew, sees democracy as "not only a political system… but an ideal, an aspiration, really, intimately connected to and dependent upon a picture of what it is to be human-of what it is a human should be to be fully human."

While there is no universally accepted definition of 'democracy', equality and freedom have both been identified as important characteristics of democracy since ancient times. These principles are reflected in all citizens being equal before the law and having equal access to legislative processes. For example, in a representative democracy, every vote has equal weight, no unreasonable restrictions can apply to anyone seeking to become a representative, and the freedom of its citizens is secured by legitimized rights and liberties which are generally protected by a constitution.

There are several varieties of democracy, some of which provide better representation and more freedom for their citizens than others. However, if any democracy is not structured so as to prohibit the government from excluding the people from the legislative process, or any branch of government from altering the separation of powers in its own favour, then a branch of the system can accumulate too much power and destroy the democracy. Representative Democracy, Consensus Democracy, and Deliberative Democracy are all major examples of attempts at a form of government that is both practical and responsive to the needs and desires of citizens. Many people use the term 'democracy' as shorthand for liberal democracy, which may include elements such as political pluralism; equality before the law; the right to petition elected officials for redress of grievances; due process; civil liberties; human rights; and elements of civil society outside the government.

In the United States, separation of powers is often cited as a central attribute, but in other countries, such as the United Kingdom, the dominant principle is that of parliamentary sovereignty. In other cases, 'democracy' is used to mean direct democracy. Though the term 'democracy' is typically used in the context of a political state, the principles are applicable to private organizations and other groups as well.

Majority rule is often listed as a characteristic of democracy. However, it is also possible for a minority to be oppressed by a 'tyranny of the majority' in the absence of governmental or constitutional protections of individual or group rights. An essential part of an 'ideal' representative democracy is competitive elections that are fair both substantively and procedurally. Furthermore, freedom of political expression, freedom of speech, and freedom of the press are considered to be essential, so that citizens are adequately informed and able to vote according to their own best interests as they see them. It has also been suggested that a basic feature of democracy is the capacity of individuals to participate freely and fully in the life of their society.

Democracy has its formal origins in Ancient Greece, but democratic practices are evident in earlier societies including Mesopotamia, Phoenicia and India. Other cultures since Greece have significantly contributed to the evolution of democracy such as Ancient Rome, Europe, and North and South America. The concept of representative democracy arose largely from ideas and institutions that developed during the European Middle Ages and the Age of Enlightenment and in the American and French Revolutions.

Democracy has been called the 'last form of government' and has spread considerably across the globe. The right to vote has been expanded in many jurisdictions over time from relatively narrow groups, with New Zealand the first nation to grant universal suffrage for all its citizens in 1893. Democracy is often confused with the republic form of government.

HISTORY OF DEMOCRACY

ANCIENT ORIGINS

The term Democracy first appeared in ancient Greek political and philosophical thought. The Greek city state of Athens, led by Cleisthenes, established what is generally held as the first democracy in 507 BCE.

Cleisthenes is referred to as "the father of Athenian democracy". The Athenian philosopher Plato contrasted democracy, the system of 'rule by the governed', with the alternative systems of monarchy, oligarchy and timocracy. Today Classical Athenian democracy is considered by many to have been a direct democracy. Originally it had two distinguishing features: first the allotment of ordinary citizens to the few government offices and the courts, and secondarily the assembly of all the citizens.

All citizens were eligible to speak and vote in the assembly, which set the laws of the city state. However, Athenian citizens were all-male, born from parents who were born in Athens, and excluded women, slaves, foreigners and males under 20 years old. Of the estimated 200,000 to 400,000 inhabitants there were between 60,000 to 30,000 citizens. The generals often held influence in the assembly. Pericles was, during his many years of de-facto political leadership, once elected general 15 years in a row. Even though the Roman Republic contributed significantly to certain aspects of democracy, only a minority of Romans were citizens with votes in elections for representatives. The votes of the powerful were given more weight through a system of Gerrymandering, so most high officials, including members of the Senate, came from a few wealthy and noble families. However, many notable exceptions did occur.

Middle Ages

During the Middle Ages, there were various systems involving elections or assemblies, although often only involving a small amount of the population, the election of Gopala in Bengal, the Polish-Lithuanian Commonwealth, the Althing in Iceland, the Løgting in the Faroe Islands, certain medieval Italian city-states such as Venice, the tuatha system in early medieval Ireland, the Veche in Novgorod and Pskov Republics of medieval Russia, Scandinavian Things, The states in Tirol and Switzerland and the autonomous merchant city of Sakai in the 16th century in Japan. However, participation was often restricted to a minority, and so may be better classified as oligarchy. Most regions in medieval Europe were ruled by clergy or feudal lords.

The Kouroukan Fouga or Kurukan Fuga is purported to be the constitution of the Mali Empire, created after the Battle of Krina by an assembly of notables to create a government for the newly established empire. It was first alluded to in print in Djibril Tamsir Niane's book, *Soundjata, ou la Epoupée Mandingue*. The Kouroukan Fouga divided the new empire into ruling clans that were represented at a great assembly called the Gbara. However, the charter made Mali more similar to a constitutional monarchy than a democratic republic.

A little closer to modern democracy were the Cossack republics of Ukraine in the 16th-17th centuries: Cossack Hetmanate and Zaporizhian Sich. The highest post - the Hetman - was elected by the representatives from the country's districts. Because these states were very militarised, the right to participate in Hetman's elections was largely restricted to those who served in the Cossack Army and over time was curtailed effectively limiting these rights to higher army ranks.

The Parliament of England had its roots in the restrictions on the power of kings written into Magna Carta, explicitly protected certain rights of the King's subjects, whether free or fettered - and implicitly supported what became English writ of habeas corpus, safeguarding individual freedom against unlawful imprisonment with right to appeal. The first elected parliament was De Montfort's Parliament in England in 1265. However only a small minority actually had a voice; Parliament was elected by only a few per cent of the population,, and the power to call parliament was at the pleasure of the monarch. The power of Parliament increased in stages over the succeeding centuries. After the Glorious Revolution of 1688, the English Bill of Rights of 1689 was enacted, which codified certain rights and increased the influence of Parliament. The franchise was slowly increased and Parliament gradually gained more power until the monarch became largely a figurehead. As the franchise was increased, it also was made more uniform, as many so-called rotten boroughs, with a handful of voters electing a Member of Parliament, were eliminated in the Reform Act of 1832.

Band societies, such as the Bushmen, which usually number 20-50 people in the band often do not have leaders and make decisions based on consensus among the majority. In Melanesia, farming village communities have traditionally been egalitarian and lacking in a rigid, authoritarian hierarchy. Although a 'Big man' or 'Big woman' could gain influence, that influence was conditional on a continued demonstration of leadership skills, and on the willingness of the community. Every person was expected to share in communal duties, and entitled to participate in communal decisions. However, strong social pressure encouraged conformity and discouraged individualism.

18th and 19th Centuries

The first nation in modern history to adopt a democratic constitution was the short-lived Corsican Republic in 1755. This Corsican Constitution was the first based on Enlightenment principles and even allowed for female suffrage, something that was granted in other democracies only by the twentieth century. Although not described as a democracy by the founding fathers, the United States founders also shared a determination to root the American experiment in the principle of natural freedom and equality. The United States Constitution, adopted in 1788, provided for an elected government and protected civil rights and liberties for some.

In the colonial period before 1776, and for some time after, often only adult white male property owners could vote; enslaved Africans, most free black people and most women were not extended the franchise. On the American frontier, democracy became a way of life, with widespread social, economic and political equality. However, slavery was a social and economic institution, particularly in eleven states in the American South, that a variety of organizations were established advocating the movement of black people from the United States to locations where they would enjoy greater freedom and equality.

During the 1820s and 1830s the American Colonization Society (ACS) was the primary vehicle for proposals to return black Americans to freedom in Africa, and in 1821 the ACS established the colony of Liberia, assisting thousands of former African-American slaves and free black people to move there from the United States. By the 1840s almost all property restrictions were ended and nearly all white adult male citizens could vote; and turnout averaged 60-80 per cent in frequent elections for local, state and national officials.

The system gradually evolved, from Jeffersonian Democracy to Jacksonian Democracy and beyond. In the 1860 United States Census the slave population in the United States had grown to four million, and in reconstruction after the Civil War the newly freed slaves became citizens with a nominal right to vote. Full enfranchisement of citizens was not secured until after the African-American Civil Rights Movement gained passage by the United States Congress of the Voting Rights Act of 1965.

In 1789, Revolutionary France adopted the Declaration of the Rights of Man and of the Citizen and, although short-lived, the National Convention was elected by all males in 1792. Universal male suffrage was definitely established in France in March 1848 in the wake of the French Revolution of 1848. In 1848, several revolutions broke out in Europe as rulers were confronted with popular demands for liberal constitutions and more democratic government.

The Australian colonies became democratic during the mid-19th century, with South Australia being the first government in the world to introduce women's suffrage in 1861. New Zealand granted suffrage to Mori men in 1867, white men in 1879, and women in 1893, thus becoming the first major nation to achieve universal suffrage. However, women were not eligible to stand for parliament until 1919. Liberal democracies were very few and often short-lived before the late 19th century, and various nations and territories have also claimed to be the first with universal suffrage.

20th and 21st Centuries

20th century transitions to liberal democracy have come in successive 'waves of democracy', variously resulting from wars, revolutions, decolonization, religious and economic circumstances. World War I and the dissolution of the Ottoman and Austro-Hungarian empires resulted in the creation of new nation-states from Europe, most of them at least nominally democratic.

In the 1920s democracy flourished, but the Great Depression brought disenchantment, and most of the countries of Europe, Latin America, and Asia turned to strong-man rule or dictatorships. Fascism and dictatorships flourished in Nazi Germany, Italy, Spain and Portugal, as well as non-democratic regimes in the Baltics, the Balkans, Brazil, Cuba, China, and Japan, among others.

World War II brought a definitive reversal of this trend in western Europe. The successful democratization of the American, British, and French sectors of occupied Germany, Austria, Italy, and the occupied Japan served as a model for the later theory of regime change. However, most of Eastern Europe, including the Soviet sector of Germany was forced into the non-democratic Soviet bloc. The war was followed by decolonization, and again most of the new independent states had nominally democratic constitutions. India emerged as the world's largest democracy and continues to be so.

By 1960, the vast majority of country-states were nominally democracies, although the majority of the world's populations lived in nations that experienced sham elections, and other forms of subterfuge A subsequent wave of democratization brought substantial gains towards true liberal democracy for many nations. Spain, Portugal and several of the military dictatorships in South America returned to civilian rule in the late 1970s and early 1980s. This was followed by nations in East and South Asia by the mid-to-late 1980s.

Economic malaise in the 1980s, along with resentment of communist oppression, contributed to the collapse of the Soviet Union, the associated end of the Cold War, and the democratization and liberalization of the former Eastern bloc countries. The most successful of the new democracies were those geographically and culturally closest to western Europe, and they are now members or candidate members of the European Union. Some researchers consider that contemporary Russia is not a true democracy and instead resembles a form of dictatorship. The liberal trend spread to some nations in Africa in the 1990s, most prominently in South Africa. Some recent examples of attempts of liberalization include the Indonesian Revolution of 1998, the Bulldozer Revolution in Yugoslavia, the Rose Revolution in Georgia, the Orange Revolution in Ukraine, the Cedar Revolution in Lebanon, the Tulip Revolution in Kyrgyzstan, and the Jasmine Revolution in Tunisia.

According to Freedom House, in 2007 there were 123 electoral democracies. According to World Forum on Democracy, electoral democracies now represent 120 of the 192 existing countries and constitute 58.2 per cent of the world's population. At the same time liberal democracies *i.e.* countries Freedom House regards as free and respectful of basic human rights and the rule of law are 85 in number and represent 38 per cent of the global population. As such, it has been speculated that this trend may continue in the future to the point where liberal democratic nation-states become the universal standard form of human society. This prediction forms the core of Francis Fukayama's

'End of History' controversial theory. These theories are criticized by those who fear an evolution of liberal democracies to post-democracy, and others who point out the high number of illiberal democracies.

FORMS OF DEMOCRACY

Democracy has taken a number of forms, both in theory and practice. The following kinds are not exclusive of one another: many specify details of aspects that are independent of one another and can co-exist in a single system.

REPRESENTATIVE

Representative democracy involves the selection of government officials by the people being represented. If the head of state is also democratically elected then it is called a democratic republic. The most common mechanisms involve election of the candidate with a majority or a plurality of the votes. Representatives may be elected or become diplomatic representatives by a particular district, or represent the entire electorate proportionally proportional systems, with some using a combination of the two. Some representative democracies also incorporate elements of direct democracy, such as referendums. A characteristic of representative democracy is that while the representatives are elected by the people to act in the people's interest, they retain the freedom to exercise their own judgement as how best to do so.

Parliamentary

Parliamentary democracy is a representative democracy where government is appointed by representatives as opposed to a 'presidential rule' wherein the president is both head of state and the head of government and is elected by the voters. Under a parliamentary democracy, government is exercised by delegation to an executive ministry and subject to ongoing review, checks and balances by the legislative parliament elected by the people. Parliamentary systems have the right to dismiss a prime minister at any point in time that they feel he or she is not doing their job to the expectations of the legislature.

This is done through a Vote of No Confidence where the legislature decides whether or not to remove the prime minister from office by a majority support for his or her dismissal. The prime minister can also call an election whenever he or she so chooses. Typically the prime minister will hold an election when he or she knows that they are in good favour with the public as to get re-elected.

Presidential

Presidential democracy is a system where the public elects the president through free and fair elections. The president serves as both the head of state and head of government controlling most of the executive powers. The president serves for a specific term and cannot exceed that amount of time. By being elected by the people, the president can say that he is the choice of the people and for the people. Elections typically have a fixed date and are not easily changed.

Combining head of state and head of government makes the president not only the face of the people but as the head of policy as well. The president has direct control over the cabinet, which are specifically appointed by the president himself.

The president cannot be easily removed from office by the legislature. While the president holds most of the executive powers, he cannot remove the legislative branch any easier than they could remove him form office. This increases separation of powers. This can also create unrest between the president and the legislature if they are of separate parties allowing one to block the other. This type of democracy is not common around the world today due to the conflicts it can lead to.

Semi-Presidential

A semi-presidential system is a system of democracy where the government contains both a Prime Minister and a President. This form of democracy is even less common than a presidential system. This system has both a Prime Minister with no fixed term and a President with a fixed term. Depending on the country, the separation of powers between the prime minister and president varies. In one instance, the president can hold more power than the prime minister making the prime minister accountable to both the legislature and president.

On the other hand, the Prime Minister can hold more power than the president. The president and Prime Minister share power while the president is holds separate power from the legislature. The President holds the role of commander in chief, controls foreign policy, and is the face of the people. The Prime Minister is expected to form the Presidents policies into legislature. This type of government can also create issues over who holds what responsibilities.

Liberal

A liberal democracy is a representative democracy in which the ability of the elected representatives to exercise decision-making power is subject to the rule of law, and usually moderated by a constitution that emphasizes the protection of the rights and freedoms of individuals, and which places constraints on the leaders and on the extent to which the will of the majority can be exercised against the rights of minorities. In a liberal democracy, it is possible for some large-scale decisions to emerge from the many individual decisions that citizens are free to make. In other words, citizens can 'vote with their feet' or 'vote with their dollars', resulting in significant informal government-by-the-masses that exercises many 'powers' associated with formal government elsewhere.

Direct

Direct democracy is a political system where the citizens participate in the decision-making personally, contrary to relying on intermediaries or representatives. The supporters of direct democracy argue that democracy is more than merely a procedural issue.

A direct democracy gives the voting population the power to:

1. Change constitutional laws,
2. Put forth initiatives, referendums and suggestions for laws,
3. Give binding orders to elective officials, such as revoking them before the end of their elected term, or initiating a lawsuit for breaking a campaign promise.

Of the three measures mentioned, most operate in developed democracies today. This is part of a gradual shift towards direct democracies. Examples of this include the extensive use of referendums in California with more than 20 million voters, and in Switzerland, where five million voters decide on national referendums and initiatives two to four times a year; direct democratic instruments are also well established at the cantonal and communal level. Vermont towns have been known for their yearly town meetings, held every March to decide on local issues. No direct democracy is in existence outside the framework of a different overarching form of government. Most direct democracies to date have been weak forms, relatively small communities, usually city-states. The world is yet to see a large, fundamental, working example of direct democracy as of yet, with most examples being small and weak forms.

Inclusive Democracy

Inclusive democracy is a political theory and political project that aims for direct democracy in all fields of social life: political democracy in the form of face-to-face assemblies which are confederated, economic democracy in a stateless, moneyless and marketless economy, democracy in the social realm, *i.e.* self-management in places of work and education, and ecological democracy which aims to reintegrate society and nature. The theoretical project of inclusive democracy emerged from the work of political philosopher Takis Fotopoulos in "*Towards An Inclusive Democracy*" and was further developed in *the journal Democracy and Nature*' and its successor *The International Journal of Inclusive Democracy*.

The basic unit of decision making in an inclusive democracy is the demotic assembly, *i.e.* the assembly of demos, the citizen body in a given geographical area which may encompass a town and the surrounding villages, or even neighbourhoods of large cities. An inclusive democracy today can only take the form of a confederal democracy that is based on a network of administrative councils whose members or delegates are elected from popular face-to-face democratic assemblies in the various demoi. Thus, their role is purely administrative and practical, not one of policy-making like that of representatives in representative democracy.The citizen body is advised by experts but it is the citizen body which functions as the ultimate decision-taker. Authority can be delegated to a segment of the citizen body to carry out specific duties, for example to serve as members of popular courts, or of regional and confederal councils. Such delegation is made, in principle, by lot, on a rotation basis, and is always recallable by the citizen body. Delegates to regional and confederal bodies should have specific mandates.

Participatory

A Parpolity or Participatory Polity is a theoretical form of democracy that is ruled by a Nested Council structure. The guiding philosophy is that people should have decision-making power in proportion to how much they are affected by the decision. Local councils of 25-50 people are completely autonomous on issues that affect only them, and these councils send delegates to higher level councils who are again autonomous regarding issues that affect only the population affected by that council. A council court of randomly chosen citizens serves as a check on the tyranny of the majority, and rules on which body gets to vote on which issue. Delegates can vote differently than their sending council might wish, but are mandated to communicate the wishes of their sending council. Delegates are recallable at any time. Referendums are possible at any time via votes of the majority of lower level councils, however, not everything is a referendum as this is most likely a waste of time. A parpolity is meant to work in tandem with a participatory economy.

Socialist

Socialist thought has several different views on democracy. Social democracy, democratic socialism, and the dictatorship of the proletariat are some examples. Many democratic socialists and social democrats believe in a form of participatory democracy and workplace democracy combined with a representative democracy. Within Marxist orthodoxy there is a hostility to what is commonly called 'liberal democracy,' which they simply refer to as parliamentary democracy because of its often centralized nature. Because of their desire to eliminate the political elitism they see in capitalism, Marxists, Leninists and Trotskyists believe in direct democracy implemented through a system of communes. This system ultimately manifests itself as council democracy and begins with workplace democracy.

Anarchist

Anarchists are split in this domain, depending on whether they believe that a majority-rule is tyrannic or not. The only form of democracy considered acceptable to many anarchists is direct democracy. Pierre-Joseph Proudhon argued that the only acceptable form of direct democracy is one in which it is recognized that majority decisions are not binding on the minority, even when unanimous. However, anarcho-communist Murray Bookchin criticized individualist anarchists for opposing democracy, and says 'majority rule' is consistent with anarchism.

Some anarcho-communists oppose the majoritarian nature of direct democracy, feeling that it can impede individual liberty and opt in favour of a non-majoritarian form of consensus democracy, similar to Proudhon's position on direct democracy. Henry David Thoreau, who did not self-identify as an anarchist but argued for 'a better government' and is cited as an inspiration by some anarchists, argued that people should not be in the position of ruling others or being ruled when there is no consent.

Iroquois

Iroquois society had a form of participatory democracy and representative democracy. Elizabeth Tooker, a Temple University professor of anthropology and an authority on the culture and history of the Northern Iroquois, has reviewed the claim that the Iroquois inspired the American Confederation and concluded they are myth rather than fact. The relationship between the Iroquois League and the Constitution is based on a portion of a letter written by Benjamin Franklin and a speech by the Iroquois chief Canasatego in 1744. Tooker concluded that the documents only indicate that some groups of Iroquois and white settlers realized the advantages of uniting against a common enemy, and that ultimately there is little evidence to support the idea that 18th century colonists were knowledgeable regarding the Iroquois system of governance.

What little evidence there is regarding this system indicates chiefs of different tribes were permitted representation in the Iroquois League council, and this ability to represent the tribe was hereditary. The council itself did not practice representative government, and there were no elections; deceased chiefs' successors were selected by the most senior woman within the hereditary lineage, in consultation with other women in the clan. Decision making occurred through lengthy discussion and decisions were unanimous, with topics discussed being introduced by a single tribe. Tooker concludes that "...there is virtually no evidence that the framers [of the Constitution] borrowed from the Iroquois" and that the myth that this was the case is the result of exaggerations and misunderstandings of a claim made by Iroquois linguist and ethnographer J.N.B. Hewitt after his death in 1937.

Sortition

Sometimes called 'democracy without elections,' sortition is the process of choosing decision makers via a random process. The intention is that those chosen will be representative of the opinions and interests of the people at large, and be more fair and impartial than an elected official. The technique was in widespread use in Athenian Democracy and is still used in modern jury selection.

Consensus

Consensus democracy requires varying degrees of consensus rather than just a mere democratic majority. It typically attempts to protect minority rights from domination by majority rule.

Supranational

Qualified majority voting is designed by the Treaty of Rome to be the principal method of reaching decisions in the European Council of Ministers. This system allocates votes to member states in part according to their population, but heavily weighted in favour of the smaller states. This might be seen as a form of representative democracy, but representatives to the Council might be appointed rather than directly elected. Some might consider the 'individuals' being democratically represented to be states rather than people, as with many other international organizations. European Parliament members are democratically directly elected on the basis of universal suffrage, may be seen as an example of a supranational democratic institution.

Cosmopolitan

Cosmopolitan democracy, also known as global democracy or World Federalism, is a political system in which democracy is implemented on a global scale, either directly or through representatives. An important justification for this kind of system is that the decisions made in national or regional democracies often affect people outside the constituency who, by definition, cannot vote. By contrast, in a cosmopolitan democracy, the people who are affected by decisions also have a say in them.

According to its supporters, any attempt to solve global problems is undemocratic without some form of cosmopolitan democracy. The general principle of cosmopolitan democracy is to expand some or all of the values and norms of democracy, including the rule of law; the non-violent resolution of conflicts; and equality among citizens, beyond the limits of the state. To be fully implemented, this would require reforming existing international organizations, *e.g.* the United Nations, as well as the creation of new institutions such as a World Parliament, which ideally would enhance public control over, and accountability in, international politics. Cosmopolitan Democracy has been promoted, among others, by physicist Albert Einstein, writer Kurt Vonnegut, columnist George Monbiot, and professors David Held and Daniele Archibugi.

The creation of the International Criminal Court in 2003 was seen as a major step forward by many supporters of this type of cosmopolitan democracy.

Non-Governmental

Aside from the public sphere, similar democratic principles and mechanisms of voting and representation have been used to govern other kinds of communities and organizations.

- Many non-governmental organizations decide policy and leadership by voting.
- Most trade unions choose their leadership through democratic elections.
- Cooperatives are enterprises owned and democratically controlled by their customers or workers.

MEANING OF DEMOCRACY

Seen from the above account of the development of the idea of democracy, it is next to impossible to give any universal definition of democracy. Cranston writes that democracy is nothing but different doctrines in different people‘s mind. C.D. Burns also complains: Tew words have been more loosely and variously defined than democracy. It has almost literally meant all things to all people‘. The UNESCO questionnaire had also pointed out the vagueness of the term: voices of complaints on the looseness and vagueness of current use of the word democracy have been heard at least since the days of the French Revolution‘.

One can agree with Laski that 'Democracy has a context in every sphere of life and in each of these spheres it raises its special problems which do not admit of satisfactory or universal generalization‘.

The difficulty with giving any precise definition of democracy lies also in the fact that the term has been understood not only as a form of government but also as an ideal or a way of life. The latter meaning takes a broader view of democracy which includes the ideals of democratic man, democratic society, democratic economic system and democratic morality.

A number of definitions have appeared from time to time associating democracy with the process of government, some of which are as follows:

- *Lincon:* Democracy is 'a government of the people, for the people and by the people‘.
- *Seelay:* Democracy is a form of government in which everyone has a share‘.
- *Sartori:* A democratic political system is one that makes the government responsive and accountable and its effectiveness depends first and foremost on the efficiency and skill of its leadership'.

- *Lipset:* Democracy...may be defined as a political systems which supplies regular constitutional opportunities for changing the governing officials and a social mechanism which permits the largest possible part of the population to influence major decisions by choosing among contenders for political office'.
- *Macpherson:* '...democracy is merely a mechanism for choosing and authorizing governments or in some other way getting laws and political decisions made'.
- *Schempeter:* 'The democratic method is that institutional arrangement for arriving at political decisions which realizes the common good by making the people itself decide issues through the election of individuals who are to assemble in order to carry out its will'.

From the various definition of this controversially interpreted political concept, the following ideas may be selected which are commonly associated with this democracy:

- A high level of political participation in the selection of public policies and public officials at regular intervals. It is the right and duty of all citizens to get involved in elections, public discussions and other aspects of political process.
- Meaningful and extensive competition among individuals and organizations for effective positions of government.
- Availability of civil and political liberties, sufficient to secure integrity of political competition and participation such as constitutional state, guarantee of basic rights such as right to vote, freedom to form organizations, free and fair elections, decentralization of political power, etc.

In short, democracy is associated with Participation, Competition and Civil and Political Liberties. Historically, it has been defended on grounds of fundamental values such as equality, liberty, moral self-development, social utility, satisfaction of wants, efficient decisions, etc.

GROWTH OF THE IDEA OF DEMOCRACY

For the greater part of human history, democracy was treated by intellectuals and political leaders with contempt. Democracy originally meant rule by the common people, the plebians.

It meant rule by the untrained, ignorant mob. Its egalitarian character was contrary to the naturally hierarchical character of society. Democracy considered what is right by the counting of heads rather than by any standard of truth or justice. Plato defined it as 'the worst form of government, less than tyranny'. In democracy, freedom degenerates into license and equality into insolence. Aristotle considered it as the rule of the poor, regardless of whether the poor were a majority or minority.

He emphasized three elements of democracy: i) intellectually, democracy meant equality, ii) constitutionally, it meant rule of the majority, and iii) socially it meant rule of the poor at the expense of the rich. On the other hand, Greek philosopher Cleon defined democracy as the rule 'of the people, by the people and for the people'. A classical theory of democracy was developed in Athens. It was justified on the grounds that citizens should enjoy political equality in order to be free to rule and be ruled in turn.

The key features of this democracy were: i) direct participation of citizens in the legislative and judicial functions, ii) assembly of the citizens being sovereign and had the power to legislate on all common affairs of the city, iii) public offices were filled through direct election, lot or rotation, and had short duration. However, this type of democracy was limited to small city-states, and had a slave economy which created 'free' time for citizens. And more importantly, citizenship was restricted a to relatively small number of people.

In the middle ages, one could not expect any theory of democracy or any demand for a democratic franchise. When feudalism prevailed, power depended on rank, whether inherited or acquired by force of arms. It was only in the seventeenth and eighteenth centuries that democracy became a respectable term. It were movements like Reformation and Renaissance that made the case for democratization of state, society, economy and politics. The initial theoretical thrust came from English puritans of the left such as Diggers and Levellers.

The classical democratic element was provided by John Locke who sought to free the individual from arbitrary government and establish him as an independent sovereign being guided by his conscience and right reason. Government, according to him, must derive its authority from the free consent of the governed. The equalitarian element of democracy was provided by Rousseau who sought to re-introduce elements of direct democracy through his theory of 'General Will'. However, while these philosophers provided the foundation of a plausible concept of democracy, they did not push their thought to logical conclusion. Their views were far away from the fact that people actually rule.

During eighteenth century, the American revolutionaries and constitutionalists such as Jefferson and Madison tried to lay down the institutional basis of democracy. In England, Bentham and James Mill advocated right to vote and representative government. J.S. Mill elaborated the aims, ideals and institutions of democracy which later on came to be known as classical-liberal democracy.

Implicit in his writings was the view that democracy was desirable not only because it produces public policies but also makes participation in a common undertaking rewarding. He saw democracy as participatory, developmental, educative and constructive. This type of democracy was endorsed by many subsequent liberal writers such as T.H. Green, Harold Laski,

R.M. MacIver, John Dewey, W. Wilson, etc. During the latter half of twentieth century, classical liberal theory of democracy was challenged not only by liberalism itself which produced a new theory known as Elite theory of Democracy, but also by two other non-liberal variants of democracy: the Marxist-communist or peoples‘ democracy, and a host of theories evolved by the underdeveloped countries.

The major thrust of the elite theory of democracy was that democracy as a government by the people was a myth and political power, far from being wielded by the people, was competed among the elitist/pluaralist groups. A new theory of democracy known as Participatory Democracy which has evolved in Europe and America during the last twenty-five years is trying to free democracy from the elitist elements. A powerful critique of liberal democracy and a radically different image of good society was provided by Marxism. Marxism rejected the whole idea of liberal democracy, terming it as 'class democracy‘ since capitalist society was a class-divided society. Instead, it proposed a new theory of democracy to be established by the working class after overthrowing the capitalist state.

This is known as the proletarian democracy or 'Dictatorship of the Proletariat‘. Again, after the second world war, a large number of Asian and African countries got independence from colonial rule either through revolutionary struggle or without any actual use of force. These revolutions were made by the leaders who were able to get support for their vision of building a future society. A part of this vision was democracy. However, these leaders arrived at their own theories of democracy by the conscious selection of those elements in both liberal and Marxist theories which they found applicable to the problems of their own people.

Thus we find that though democracy is a legitimate and universally appropriate form of government, different structural foundations or social pre-conditions produce quite different but possible democratic systems. However, in all kinds of democracies, the ultimate ethical principle at the most general level has been the same: to provide conditions for the free development of human capacities and to do this equally for all members of society. However, serious differences arise when we move from the general to the particular level in different societies. The different theories of democracy are nothing but different attempts to achieve this goal.

DEMOCRACY THEORY

Democracy means rule by the people. However, to define democracy as the rule of the people raises more questions rather than helping to clarify its meaning. There is a lot of disagreement on both what constitutes 'people‘ and what is meant by 'rule‘. If 'demos‘ means people, then the question is who constitute 'people‘, what is the scope and extent of their participation; what are the conditions which are conducive to participation. Similarly, if 'crats' means rule, then what is the scope of that rule; does rule mean control of the people over law and order, control over the economy and the public policies? What is the mechanism for those who do not want to participate? Just as there are innumerable questions, numerous answers have been given by different thinkers to these questions.

While some thinkers believe that all should directly participate in the decision-making, others believe that people can also participate through their representatives. Still others believe that rulers should be chosen by the people and should be accountable to them. The rulers should be accountable to the representatives of the people. Some believe that if the rulers act in the interest of the people, this will suffice. The different theories of democracy answer these questions in a systematic manner. For the purpose of our study, the following theories can be identified:

- Classical-liberal theory of democracy
- Elitist theory of democracy
- Pluralist theory of democracy
- Participatory democracy
- Marxist theory of democracy or peoples' democracy

While the classical-liberal and Elitist/Pluralist theories are representative democracy, the participatory theory and the peoples' democracy try to blend elements of direct democracy so as to make the participation of the common man in the decision-making process a reality.

CLASSICAL-LIBERAL THEORY OF DEMOCRACY

Liberalism supported the democratic ideas right from the beginning. In fact, it was only with the rise of liberalism in England and Europe that the path was cleared for democracy and it became a respectable concept. Democratic ideas were nothing but a logical requirement of the governance of a society which had freed itself from absolute power of the kings and religious traditions. The ideas of liberty, equality, rights, secularism and justice became the cornerstone of liberalism and democracy became a means of achieving them. The liberal democracies that we know were liberal first and democratic afterwards.

According to Macpherson, before democracy came in the western world, there came a society and politics of choice, a society and politics of competition, and a society and politics of market. It was the liberal state that was democratized and in the process, the democracy was liberalized. Early traces of classical-liberal democratic ideas are found in the writings of Thomas Moore's Utopia (1616), Winstanely's The Law of Freedom (1652) and English Puritanism as well as in the thinking of Levellers. However, it was the social contract theory which became crucial in establishing the foundation of democracy because the contract could be made only when all men were assumed to be equal. Thomas Hobbes in Leviathan (1651) elaborated the democratic principle that the government is created by the people through a social contract. It was John Locke who provided the formula that government must be by the people and aim solely at their good. The essence of his argument was that:

- ultimately all political power inheres in the people, the legitimate power of the government is a limited one; the government should not violate certain rights of the people, otherwise, the contract between the government and the people is dissolved, and individual rights are a part of man's nature. Ultimately, a government is dedicated to the needs of the individual and not vice versa.

Locke's ideas about politics were complemented by Adam Smith in the realm of economics. He opposed mercantalism promoted by the state and argued that the best economic decisions should be made by the people themselves. Freedom to produce, buy and sell, free and open competition, free economic exchange would give advantage to the best endeavours and most industrious proportionate opulence. The French philosopher Montesquieu elaborated the theory of separation of powers which had a great democratic appeal and influenced the making of American constitution. On the American continent, Jefferson. Madison and Hamilton tried to give institutional shape to the ideas of Locke, Adam Smith and Monesquieu.

VIEWS OF BENTHAM AND J.S. MILL

Jermy Bentham was the first modern liberal thinker who prepared the ground for the attitude towards democracy. He along with James Mill and J.S. Mill justified democracy on utilitarian grounds. He said that individuals require protection from the governors as well as from each other, and an assurance that those who govern pursue policies that are in consonance with the interests of the individual. Thus for him the problem was how to make sure that governments follow the wishes and interests of the community in matters of law and policy.

In other words, the problem was how to find a system of choosing and authorizing government which would make and enforce the laws needed by the society. The solution to this problem was representative democracy, constitutional government, regular elections, secret ballot, competition between parties and leaders, majority rule, etc. Thus Bentham came to see democratic franchise as essential to the goal of the greatest happiness of the greatest number. The only way to prevent the government despoiling the people was to make the governors frequently removable by the majority decision. However, his views on democratic franchise were not consistent.

Till 1802, he advocated limited franchise, in 1809 he called for a householder franchise limited to propertied class, in 1817 he talked about universal franchise for men. However, broadly speaking, liberal democracy with universal franchise and constitutional government was seen as the best protector of individual rights and laisses faire capitalist economy. It was J.S. Mill who set the course of democratic thought in the nineteenth century. Through his writings he sought to defend a concept of politics which increased individuality, representative government, efficient administration and non-interference in the economic affairs. While accepting the views of Bentham on democracy as a means of protecting the citizens from the oppression of the rulers, he supplemented it with another dimension—the moral worth of democracy for the improvement and development of mankind as a whole. His emphasis was more on what democracy could contribute to human development.

Macpherson has called Mill's views on democracy as 'Developmental democracy'. According to Mill, man is capable of developing his powers and capacities and a good society is one which permits and promotes these activities. Liberal democracy or representative government was important because it was an effective means for the free development of individuality.

Democracy drew people in the operations of government by giving them a right to vote which could bring a fall in government. Participation in political life such as voting, involvement in local administration and jury service was vital to create a direct interest in developing citizenry. Like Rousseau, Mill conceived democracy as a prime mechanism of moral self-development and highest and harmonious expansion of individual capacities.

However, while accepting participation in the elections as an essential means of human development, Mill did not favour universal franchise or the principle of one-man-one-vote. He was fearful that the working class being in majority, one-man-one-vote may lead to legislation in the interest of one particular class at the expense of other classes as well as of posterity. Instead, he recommended a system of plural voting for the members of the smaller classes so that neither of two classes should outweigh the other and impose class legislation.

While everyone should have vote, some should have several votes. In his later book, Representative Government (1861) he argued for plural vote for some along with the exclusion of others such as people receiving poor relief, bankrupts, illiterates, those not paying taxes, etc. While participation in the political process was necessary to improve people's quality, participation with equal weight was deemed to reinforce low quality. Hence those who had already attained superior quality, through education or property must not be made to yield their power to the rest. As he wrote 'It is not useful but hurtful that the constitution of the country should declare ignorance to be entitled to as much political power as knowledge'.

Thus, although from a purely arithmetical point of view, Mill could not be ranked as a full egalitarian yet his moral dimension was more democratic because it wanted to move towards a society of individuals more humanly developed. On the whole, he drew the conclusion that a representative democracy, the scope and powers of which are tightly restricted by the principle of liberty and laissez faire in economic relations is the best guarantee of free community and brilliant prosperity. The above ideas of classical-liberal democracy found further support in the writings of T.H. Green, Hobhouse, Lindsay, Barker, Laski, MacIver, John Dewey, W. Wilson, etc.

With the evolution of the party system in the twentieth century, the classical-liberal theory was further strengthened. The contradiction which Mill had seen between universal franchise and the class interest turned out to be unfounded. Franchise was extended to all adult population. In fact the early twentieth century liberal thinkers felt that the democratic party system had overcome the dangers of class government. For example, MacIver saw the party system as an effective way of reducing the multitudinous differences of opinion to relatively simple alternatives. Similarly, John Dewey felt that democracy was the best method to organize the scattered, mobile and manifold public.

PARTICIPATORY THEORY OF DEMOCRACY

The theories of democracy during the last 200 years have assumed that a proper system of government must provide opportunities for political participation by ordinary citizens in the affairs of the state. While the opportunity to vote in periodic elections is the minimum qualification for democracy, participatory democracy believes that comprehensive opportunities and forms of political participation are the essence of democracy. The participatory theory of democracy justifies participation both as an ideal, *i.e.*, why people should participate, and as a functional requirement, *i.e.*, how to and how much to participate in the affairs of the state. Though the term 'Participatory Democracy' is frequently used to cover a variety of models from classical Athens to Marxist tradition, the type of participatory democracy with which we are dealing here is a new model of democracy developed by certain Left Wing political writers from 1960s onwards. It was the result of the political upheavals, student movements, internal debates within the left wing ideology and dissatisfaction with liberal and Marxist ideas on democracy. Many writers have contributed to the development of this new model of democracy, but primarily it is associated with three names: Carole Pateman, C.B. Macpherson and N. Poulantzas. This theory was also developed as a counter model to Legal Democracy propounded by Hayek and Nozic. Although many writers have advocated participatory democracy as the appropriate response to twentieth century challenges, yet theory and practice of this model remains quite limited.

WHAT IS PARTICIPATORY DEMOCRACY

Participatory Democracy has developed as a reaction against the Elitist/

Pluralist theories of democracy. It is the common man's reaction against the 'expert'. In Elitist/Pluralist theories, power of decision-making is the monopoly of certain -elites or groups and the role of the masses is reduced only to the selection of elites once in few years. The participatory democracy seeks to distribute decision-making power more equitably.

The helplessness of the individual against the growth of the functions of the state and the concentration of decisionmaking power in a few hands led to a number of movements calling for the direct involvement of ordinary people in the decision-making. While adhering to equality and majority rule, participatory democracy wants to extend this political equality by some sort of grassroots decision-making of an authoritative nature. According to Cook and Morgan, participatory democracy has two broad features: i) decentralization of authoritative decision-making so as to bring it closer to the people affected by the decisions, ii) direct involvement of common man in making the decisions. Participatory democracy agrees with the classical liberal idea that democracy is not only a form of government but also a means of equal right to self-development.

Such a development can be achieved only in a participatory society—a society which cares for collective problems and helps in the formation of politically active citizens who take a continuous interest in the governing process. It believes in direct participation of citizens in the regulation of key institutions of society, making political parties more open and accountable, and maintaining an open institutional system to ensure the possibility of experimentation with new political forms of participation. Since Participatory Democracy wants to restore common man's participation, the natural questions are:

- Why is there a need for participation, and
- How to and how much participation?

NEED FOR PARTICIPATION

Participatory Democracy means involvement of common man in the authoritative decision-making. The early liberal thinkers like J.S. Mill had defended participation both on grounds of protecting the citizens from the oppression of the rulers and as a means of improvement and development of mankind as a whole. It were the elitist/pluralist theories which discouraged participation.

The theorists of Participatory Democracy want to restore participation once again. According to Carole Pateman, the free and equal individual is found rarely in the contemporary democracies. The formal existence of rights (though not unimportant) is of little value if they cannot be actually realized. Freedom can be assessed from the concrete liberties and opportunities available to the individual in the society to participate actively in the political and civic life.

Drawing upon the central notions of Rousseau and Mill, Pateman argues that participatory democracy fosters human development, enhances a sense of political efficacy, reduces the sense of estrangement from power centres, nurtures a concern for collective problems and contributes to the formation of an active citizenary capable of taking a more acute interest in government affairs. If people know that opportunities exist for effective participation in decision-making, and that participation is worthwhile, they would definitely like to participate actively.

Similarly, Macpherson writes that liberty of the individual can be fully realized only with the direct participation of the people in the regulation of the affairs of the state. Participation is a learning process. Participation changes the psychology of man since it socializes people into new beliefs, attitudes and values.

According to Cook and Morgan, it increases the political efficacy or a person's sense of effectively manipulating his environment. In an age when people find themselves helpless in the administrative complexity, a change in the decision-making through participation can overcome this sense of powerlessness and the resultant apathy.

Participation can lead to acquisition of more information on public affairs. Participants become aware of possible alternative solutions to problems. Participation can revive the feeling of community solidarity and increase the ability to cope up with the tensions of modern life. Participation also results in better decisions. Participatory democracy is everyman's revolt against the expert. Even ordinary people are experts in certain matters. They are better than elected representatives. Collective wisdom may be specially relevant to our times of rapidly expanding higher education in the industrial and technological societies. The more man knows collectively the better.

Also the best protection from tyranny is through the dispersal of power. Participatory democracy can rescue the individual from apathy, ignorance and alienation. Thus participation is the essence of democracy and without the involvement of common man in the decision-making, it is meaningless.

METHODS AND SCOPE OF PARTICIPATION

Now, if participation in the affairs of the government is a precondition for self-development, the question is what are the possible means available to the common man. Inspite of disagreement among various theorists regarding the means and extent of participation, one can pinpoint a number of means in the modern democratic state. Some of these are: voting in local or national elections; canvassing or otherwise campaigning in the elections, active membership of a political party; active membership of a pressure group; taking part in political demonstrations; industrial strikes with political objectives or other activities aimed at changing public policy; various forms of civil disobedience such as refusing to pay taxes; membership of consumer councils for publically owned industries, involvement in the implementation of social policies; various forms of community development programmes such as women development, family planning, environment issues etc; taking part in referendum, recall, etc.

The participatory democracy finds a number of shortcomings in the representative democracy and wants it to be supplemented by a number of measures by permitting the ordinary citizens to participate in the decisionmaking process. Opinions, however, differ as to how the people can directly and effectively participate and a number of alternatives have been and can be proposed. The classical-liberal democracy had evolved a number of participatory means such as elections, universal adult franchise, individual rights and civil liberties, freedom of thought and belief, participation in local government, public debates and jury service, etc. However, the recent supporters of participatory democracy consider these means inadequate.

According to them, modern mass democracies produce alienated, isolated citizens, and that the governments in reality lack legitimacy. The inequality in power and resources have limited the means of life, liberty and equality, thereby restricting the capacity of the individual to effectively participate in political life. The state being a part of the productive process, produces a number of inequalities in daily life through its laws. Elections are not always an adequate mechanism to ensure the accountability of the representatives. Hence peoples' control over the democratic process becomes an urgent matter.

According to Poulantzas, since the state has grown in size and power, institutions of direct democracy or self-management cannot simply replace the state because this will leave a vacuum which will be filled by bureaucracy. However, participation of people can be enhanced through two sets of changes: i) the state must be democratized by making parliament, the state bureaucracies and political parties more open and accountable, and ii) new forms of struggles at local level through factory-based politics, women's movements, ecological groups must ensure that society as well as the state are democratized. But how the two are to be interrelated is a big question mark. Macpherson also admits that the problem posed by size and number of modern states are formidable and it is very difficult to imagine a political system in which all citizens can be involved in a face-to-face discussion every time a public issue arises.

However, it does not mean that there is no scope for change. This can be achieved through a combination of competitive parties and organizations of direct democracy. There will always be issues and different interests around which political parties might form. Moreover, only competition between political parties guarantees a minimum response of government to the people.

However, this party system can be organized on less hierarchical principles making political administrators and managers more accountable to the people.

A substantial basis would be created for participatory democracy if i) parties are democratized according to the principle of 'direct democracy', ii) if these genuinely participatory parties operate within the parliamentary structure, iii) if they are supplemented by fully-managed organizations in the work-place and local community. Only such a political system can realize the democratic value of 'equal right to self-development'. According to Carole Pateman, participation can be increased by making democracy count in people's everyday life. This can be done by extending democratic control over those institutions which affect the daily life of the people. For this, democratic rights need to be extended to the economic enterprises and other institutions of society.

The political rights of the citizens must be supplemented by a similar set of rights in the sphere of work and community relations. There is no doubt that the institutions of direct democracy cannot be extended to all political, social and economic spheres because of a number of constraints. Also many of the liberal democratic institutions like competitive parties, political representatives, periodic elections are unavoidable elements of participatory society. But direct participation and control over immediate local issues, complemented by party and interest group competition in government spheres can most realistically advance the principle of participatory democracy. Also the opportunity of participation at work place can radically alter the nature of national politics.

Individuals would be able to learn more about the key issues in resource creation and hence would be better equipped to judge national questions, the performance of the representatives and participate in decisions of national importance when the opportunity arises. Through such methods, the representative democracy can be extended to change into participatory democracy.

CHARACTERISTICS OF PARTICIPATORY DEMOCRACY

The chief characteristics of Participatory Democracy can be enumerated as follows:

- It believes that democracy is not only a form of government but also a means of selfdevelopment. An equal right to self-development can be achieved through participatory society—a society which fosters a sense of political efficacy, nurtures a concern for collective problems and creates a kind of citizen who takes continues interest in the governing process.
- Apart from representative institutions, it calls for direct participation of citizens in the regulation of key institutions of society such as work place and local community.
- It wants to reorganize the party system so as to make the representatives directly accountable to the people.

- Only 'genuine' accountable political parties should operate the parliamentary system.
- It wants to maintain an open institutional system to ensure the possibility of new forms of democratic control.
- It wants to make a direct improvement in the poor resource base of individuals and social groups by extending economic rights and redistribution of material resources.
- It wants to minimize the hold of unaccountable bureaucratic power in both public and private life.

PROBLEMS OF PARTICIPATORY DEMOCRACY

According to David Held, while the participatory democracy recognizes many difficulties associated with the previous models of democracy (classical-liberal, earliest/pluralist, etc.) and represents an advance upon them, it leaves many questions unresolved. There is no doubt that we learn to participate by participating and that it does help foster an active and knowledgeable citizenship, still it does not mean that an increased participation *per se* will automatically bring a new revolution in human development.

There is no guarantee that people generally become more democratic, cooperative and dedicated to the common good. As Burnheim points out, it would probably be wiser to presuppose that people will not perform better either morally or intellectually than they do at present. There is every possibility that participation will lead to consistent strifes and clashes, leading to contradictions between individual liberty, distributive justice and democratic decisions.

Secondly, the participatory democracy is based on the belief that people in general want to extend the, sphere of control over their lives. However, it is one thing to recognize a right, and another to say that we must, irrespective of choice, must participate in public life. What if they do not want to do so? What if they do not really want to participate in the management of social and economic affairs.? What if they do not wish to become creatures of democratic reason? Or if they wield democratic power undemocratically, who is to check them? Thirdly, participatory democracy consider democracy not only a form of government but also a way of life and human self-improvement.

According to David Held, although participatory theorists are right in pursuing the implications of democratic principles for the organizational structure of society and state, yet they have not clearly resolved the highly complex relation between individual liberty, distributional matters and democratic process. By focusing on the desirability of collective decision-making, they leave these relations to be decided by democratic negotiations.

But the basic problem is: Should there be limits on the power of the people to change and alter political circumstances; should the relation between liberty and equality be left to the whims of democratic decisions. Participatory theorists are vague on these points. Fourthly, according to Cook and Morgan, as a system of government also, participatory democracy has not been able to build a systematic theory. Participation of ordinary citizen in the decision-making process both at local level and national raises a number of problems which have not been adequately dealt with at theoretical level.

Some of these problems are: i) What would be an appropriate unit for this kind of decision-making?, ii) What should be the proper size and function of the participatory unit, iii) The involvement of a large number of citizens may affect the efficiency and competence of the decisions, iv) How the decisions taken at the local levels may be coordinated with the political decisions at other levels and with the overall interest of the society at large.

Such innumerable problems have created a variety of difficulties for the implementation of participatory democracy but have also a lot of criticism from the New Right school of thinkers.

CRITICIMS OF BOURGEOIS CONCEPT OF DEMOCRACY

During 1840s, Marx and Engles associated themselves with democracy which they saw as an egalitarian movement leading to socialism. Marx wrote twelve essays during this period to express the principle tenets of his democratic convictions. 'Organ of Democracy was the subtitle of the journal which he edited.

Marx was fully convinced that only democracy could help in establishing the state on a rational basis. He criticized the aristocratic, hereditary domination of landed interests, and property qualification for franchise. He wanted the popular will to permeate the executive and legislative branches of the government. Similarly, he also attacked the non-democratic bureaucracy.

During this period, all his criticism of the despotic institutions was based upon his concept of humanism. His devotion to the goal of human freedom, respect for law as a human need, his concern for the separation of powers in a democratic state and his defence of the rights of the individual were all a part of the western liberal tradition. In the Paris Manuscripts of 1844, Marx put forward his concept of democracy which could accomplish general human emancipation.. Although he was critical of the rights granted by the bourgeois state, yet he realized the historical importance of these right in so far as they provided an opportunity to the working class to organize themselves against the oppression of the dominant class for general emancipation.

Similarly, he regarded the bourgeois freedom as only one step in the direction of man's total freedom. Marx was still to develop the class concept of democracy but his commitment to communism was quite clear, *i.e.*, it was to be classless and based upon the absence of exploitation of man by man. The first great democratic battles which Marx and Engles experienced were a series of uprisings that exploded across the major cities of Europe in 1848. However, the happenings of 1848 led them to reject the view that communism and democracy were synonymous. This was because while the democrats wished to overthrow feudalism and establish representative institutions within the capitalist society, they were not ready to allow power to descend to the working class. After the failure of revolutions in France and Germany, Marx saw the unreliability of the petty bourgeois democrats. Democracy was a progressive demand against autocracy but it was also the highest form of the capitalist state, and as such 'stands condemned if seen as an ultimate aim'.

However, the meaning of democracy was not different from that of the liberal notion, *i.e.*, constitutionalism, civil liberties, representative institutions and universal adult franchise. For liberals, this provided a satisfactory means of ascertaining and implementing the will of the people. However, for Marx, it made a mockery of its aim because the selfish and corrupt politicians misused democratic structure for their own personal ends.

'The formal values of liberal constitutionalism were wrong in a number of ways. Firstly, the basis of bourgeois democracy was the economic system in which the means of production were vested in the capitalist class. The state sanctioned the existence of private property, personal ownership of capital, profit motive in production, free competition, free contract and free market. In a classdivided society where bourgeoisie controlled and owned the means of production, it also controlled and dominated the state apparatus.

The state power, rights and privileges were exclusive to it and were defined in such a way that the working class did not possess them. Secondly, the state bureaucracy, courts and police, the army apparatus and maintenance of law and order were not neutral but served the interests of the dominant class. Here, we have the core of Marxist critique of bourgeois democracy. It is that 'the state parliament and the entire political sphere do not occupy neutral ground in which success is obtained purely on the basis of arguments and numerical appeal. On the other hand, for the working class, it was an enemy territory.

These are simply the devices to delude and deceive the masses into believing that the power of the state belonged to them while in reality this was controlled and exercised by the bourgeois minority'. Parliaments talked without being listened to. Parliamentary influence could not bring any fundamental change in the basic social and political power which is in the hands of the bourgeoisie.

Hence, democracy was nothing but a convenient form for the maintenance of class rule, to be used as and when and in so far as it serves the class interest. In short, the liberal bourgeois democracy hides its intentions, is a class state instead of a natural arbiter; it offers paper freedoms for real political freedoms; and it offers only political freedoms instead of general human emancipation'. However, while maintaining that bourgeois democracy was not real democracy for the working class and that working class cannot come to power through democratic means, Marx and Engles held the view that this kind of democracy could be used by the working class to organize itself, to raise the level of political consciousness and to achieve the level of proletarian revolution.

The main feature of the bourgeois democracy was universal suffrage which provided a 'school of development' for the working class and offered definite but limited possibilities for the revolutionary movements. The question of suffrage was also connected with the 'transition to socialism'. Marx was willing to allow that there might be some isolated cases where the transition would be achieved by non-violent means, though he was very sceptical about such a process and took it for granted that it would not be the common pattern.

Nevertheless the notion that a revolutionary party has no interest in the bourgeois parliament finds no confirmation in the writings of Marx and Engles. For them, the revolutionary and the parliamentary paths were not opposed but complementary to each other. They accepted parliamentary tactics as one part of class struggle. But theirs was a vigourous, radical and suspicious parliamentarianism, and involving no renunciation of other forms of struggle'.

PEOPLES' DEMOCRACY OR DICTATORSHIP OF THE PROLETARIAT

Marx and Engles accepted the Enlightenment ideal of democracy as a participatory activity. However, he saw this notion of democracy as incompatible with the parliamentary model of bourgeois democracy which viewed politics as a specialised activity restricted to a relatively harmless sphere. For Marx, genuine democracy, as distinct from the sham bourgeois democracy, comes into existence only after the proletarian revolution. The Paris Commune of 1871 provided an actual indication of 'the political form at last discovered under which to work out the economic emancipation of labour. For Marx, the significance of the Paris Commune was that it had begun to dismantle the state apparatus and given power to the people.

The whole initiative hitherto exercised by the state was laid into the hands of the Commune, whose municipal council was elected by universal suffrage and a majority of whose members were working men or acknowledged representatives of the working class. The Commune was to be a working, not a parliamentary body, executive and legislative at the same time'. It got rid of the police, suppressed the standing army and replaced it by armed people. Like the rest of the public servants, magistrates and judges were to be elected, responsible and revocable, and all public services had to be done at workmen's wages.

In short, in the Commune, Marx saw an attempt to give power to the working class and to bring into being a regime as close to direct democracy as possible. Marx and Engles pointed to the Paris Commune as illustrating what they meant by people's democracy as the Dictatorship of the Proletariat.

However, the term Dictatorship of the Proletariat as understood by Marx and Engles and as it was interpreted by Lenin in the context of Russian Revolution deserves careful consideration. According to Selucky, the term was used by Marx not more than five times while Hal Draper finds this phrase used by Marx and Engles not more than eleven times.

The study of the concept in the context of its appearance proves adequately the democratic credentials of Marx and Engles. In The Class Struggles in France, Marx referred to the class dictatorship of the proletariat as the inevitable transit point to the abolition of class differences generally. In The Critique of the Gotha Programme (1875), he wrote, 'Between the capitalist and the communist society lies the period of the revolutionary transformation of the one into the other.

There corresponds to this also a political transition period in which the state can be noting but the revolutionary dictatorship of the proletariat'. After the seizure of power by the workers in the Paris Commune, Marx further elaborated the idea of democracy. This view of democracy cannot be understood without reference to the Dictatorship of the Proletariat. Democracy and Dictatorship of the Proletariat were not mutually exclusive concepts but this dictatorship permitted a clear distinction between the bourgeois democracy and the proletarian democracy.

Marx and Engles conceived of every state as the dictatorship of the ruling class. They used the term dictatorship in the sense of rule of a particular social class and not as a government of a single party. For them the concept was not primarily a political concept but a social one. The opposite of this phrase was the 'dictatorship of the bourgeoisie' which signified the different forms of bourgeois governments such as absolute monarchy, constitutional monarchy, democratic republics. Similarly the Dictatorship of the Proletariat was used to signify the different forms of proletariat governments. Marx and Engles were more concerned with the content rather than the form of post-revolutionary state.

Democracy meant no more no less than rule by the majority. Since Marx and Engles were certain that at the time of socialist revolution, the proletariat would be in the majority, this very notion of democracy merely suggests that 'the dictatorship of the proletariat meant to be the rule of the majority by the majority and for the majority.' It was peoples' democracy in the real sense of the terms. According to Marx and Engles, revolution could be violent or peaceful depending upon the presence of democratic political possibilities. However, whether peaceful or not, the socialist revolution must be democratic.

Although, at the time of Communist Manifesto, there was no possibility of bringing any social change through peaceful, parliamentary means, yet the Manifesto declared that 'the first task after the revolution would be to raise the working class to the level of democracy'. Inspite of being deficient and incomplete, both Marx and Engles positively assessed the historical importance of political emancipation of man (political right), universal suffrage and right to representation and association granted by the bourgeois democracy.

Marx and Engles, as is well known, anticipated the possibility that socialism could be introduced peacefully by parliamentary means in countries like England and United States. Towards the end of his life, Engles explicitly declared that 'dictatorship of the proletariat' would express itself under the political form of bourgeois parliamentary republic. He wrote, 'If one thing is certain, it is that our Party and the working class can only come to power under the form of democratic republic. This is even the specific form of dictatorship of the proletariat as the great French revolution had already shown.'

CHIEF CHARACTERISTICS OF PEOPLES' DEMOCRACY

- Democracy is essentially a participatory activity by the working class in the affairs of the state through direct democratic means. It is a rule by the majority, of the majority and for the majority.
- Peoples' democracy can be established only after the proletarian revolution and raising the working class to the level of political decision-making. It requires the defeat of the bourgeoisie and their class privileges and the unity of the working class.
- At economic level, peoples' democracy means social ownership of the means of production, appropriation of all large-scale private capital, central control of production in the hands of the state, rapid increase of productive forces, state control of transportation and communication, equal liability of All citizens to work, and public direction of employment.
- At political level, democracy means integration of executive and legislative functions; all government personnel to be directly elected and subject to recall; election and recall of magistrates; replacement of army and police force by people's malitia; full local autonomy; public officials to be paid no more than workmen's wages.
- At social level, there will be no inheritance; free education for all children; heavy graduated taxation, reunion of town and country through more equitable distribution of population over the whole country; integration of work and non-work environments; sustained development of forces of production so that all basic needs are met and people have sufficient time to pursue non-work activities.
- People's democracy is a transition stage between capitalist democracy and communism. After the abolition of classes and the establishment of socialist society will start the higher stage of communism. It will be a society based upon abolition of scarcity and private property, elimination of markets, exchange and money, end of social division

of labour. Here government and politics will be replaced by self-regulation, all public affairs will be governed collectively, administrative tasks will be done by rotation or election; and all public questions will be decided on consensus. Thus communism will herald not only the end of politics but also of democracy as a form of government. It will become a part of habit and a way of life. It will turn into self-rule in the real sense of the term.

CHANGES MADE BY LENIN AND STALIN IN THE CONCEPT OF DICTATORSHIP OF THE PROLETARIAT

The Marxist concept of democracy as the Dictatorship of the Proletariat as developed by Lenin and Stalin, and the establishment of peoples' democracies in USSR and other communist countries introduced major variations in the original concept. Lenin called DP as the major idea of Marx regarding the state, the main content of socialist revolution and necessary for workers for their victory.

However, he gave different interpretations of this concept at different times. In 1918, he called revolutionary dictatorship of the proletariat as the 'rule won and maintained by the use of violence of the proletariat against the bourgeoisie, rule that is unrestricted by any laws'. In 1919, he shifted emphasis from the use of force to the organizational task of building socialism. In 1920. he made clear that the dictatorship of the proletariat can be exercised neither by the proletariat class as a. whole nor by a mass proletariat organization but only through its vanguard—the Party, on behalf of the proletariat. The question of democracy was examined by Lenin in relation to three phases: Capitalist Democracy, Socialist Democracy, and Communist Democracy.

Defining democracy, he wrote, 'Democracy is a form of state, one of its varieties'. In a class divided society, government is both democracy and dictatorship. It is democracy for one class and dictatorship for the other class. For example, the bourgeois democracy is the dictatorship of the bourgeois class over the working class; it is the dictatorship of the bourgeoisie. It is a democracy by an insignificant minority. It is democracy for the rich where the capitalist class controls not only the political institutions but also structures other institutions in such a way as to guarantee their overall control on the society.

Since it does not serve the working class interest, it has to be destroyed and replaced by a radically different form of state, by a different set of institutions to serve the proletarian interests. Regarding the socialist democracy, Lenin frankly accepts that the new socialist state established after the revolution will be an instrument of power and repression quite as much as the capitalist state. In it, the proletariat, 'organized as a ruling class creates its own appropriate apparatus of violence to enforce its class purpose on the non-proletarian and other elements'. The victory over the bourgeoisie requires a long persistent battle which can be carried through only by strong determination and use of force. During the transitional period from capitalism to communism, class struggle will continue and it will aim at the complete overthrow of the bourgeoisie. During this period, 'the state must inevitably be a state that is democratic in a new way (for the proletariat and the propertyless in general) and dictatorship in a new way (against the bourgeoisie)'. DP is also class state but with a difference. The difference consists in the fact that all hitherto existing class states have been dictatorship of an exploiting class minority over the exploited majority, whereas the dictatorship of the proletariat is the dictatorship of the exploited majority over the exploiting minority'. The twin purpose of the dictatorship of the proletariat is i) to defend the revolution and ii) to organize the new social and economic order.

These functions, according to Lenin, are carried out by the Party which is the guide and leader of all the exploited classes. Thus in the hands of Lenin, the dictatorship of the proletariat became 'the dictatorship of the Party'. He advocated that the transition from socialism to communism will be carried out by the party which will not only suppress the exploiters but also discipline the workers and the whole population. Reduced to simple terms, Lenin's argument was that any state is an instrument of class domination. Where there is dominance, there is neither freedom nor democracy. It is only in the communist society when the class struggle has ended and a classless society has been created that it will become possible to speak of freedom.

'Only then' according to Lenin 'will there become possible and realized a truly complete democracy, democracy without any exception whatever. And only then will democracy begin to wither away....Communism alone is capable of giving really complete democracy and the more complete it is, the more quickly will it become unnecessary, and wither away of itself. In other words, communism will cause even the truly complete democracy to wither away. He categorically states that 'it is constantly forgotten that the abolition of the state means also the abolition of democracy; that the withering away of the state means the withering away of democracy'.

The more complete the democracy, the nearer the moment when it begins to be unnecessary.

Thus in the context of bourgeois democracy, democracy does not exists; in the context of dictatorship of the proletariat there is more democracy than before in the sense that the proletarian majority, rules over the minority, but all the same real democracy still cannot exist; in the context of communism, democracy should not exist because it is superfluous. While for Marx democracy as such is a stateless society; for Lenin democracy is a form of state and therefore, a stateless society cannot be a democracy. With Stalin, the dictatorship of the proletariat came to be associated with autocracy and reign of terror.

A new turn was given to the theory of revolution; the party was converted into a centralized and all powerful bureaucracy. DP meant further centralization of power and greater use of repressive and arbitrary power. It became a regime in which one man had absolute power of a kind which Lenin had never imagined. Stalin used that power to the full, herding into camps millions upon millions of people and liquidation of countless others including the vast number of people who were part of the upper and uppermost layers of society.

Thus whereas Lenin reduced the DP to the dictatorship of the party; Stalin further reduced the dictatorship of the party to the dictatorship of one person. It was taken for granted that the Party and the working class formed a perfect unity and that the former represented the latter.

PLURALIST THEORY OF DEMOCRACY

Apart from Elite Theory of Democracy, modern democratic theory has another dimension which has been developed primarily by the American political scientists since the second world war. This is known as the Pluralist Theory of Democracy. The elitist and the pluralist theories of democracy are distinguished as two types of democracy but there are important inter-connections between the two and the writings of some theorists contain an amalgam of both. Both theories point to the power of groups other than people as a whole and as such both run counter to the classical-liberal democracy.

Both see democracy as consisting of plurality of power holding groups and their relationship to one another and the mass of the people. Nonetheless, there are enough differences to outline them as two separate theories. In the Elite Theory of Democracy, the concern is with the elites that control or seek to control the government. In the pluralist theory, the focus is on the groups that seek to influence rather than control the government. This is understood by distinction between political parties and pressure groups. Another difference is the different role given to the electoral process in the two types of theories.

Elite theory is centred upon elections: it is by virtue of competition for the peoples' votes that the elite model is held to be democratic. In the pluralist theory, although elections may be seen as a necessary condition for the existence of the democratic process, that process is itself constituted primarily by the inter-election activity of the groups. To a very great extent, the pluralist theory of democracy was a reaction against the non-democratic character of elitism.

The pluralist theory of democracy was formulated as part of the rejection of the elitist analysis of politics. Whereas elite theory believed that the masses were incapable of making decisions on major issues, the pluralist democracy, recognizing the inadequacies of the electoral process, called for other means of eliciting the will of the people.

MEANING OF THE CONCEPT OF PLURALISM

Although the origin of pluralism lies far back in history, it became part of the liberal creed in the twentieth century. Pluralism can be characterized by its' view that power is and ought to be decentralized and scattered among a number of groups and associations. In USA, pluralism manifested itself especially in the group theory of politics. Some writers treat 'group theory of politics and pluralism as synonymous. It was the group theory of politics associated with Bentley and Truman that provided the immediate intellectual basis for the pluralist theory of democracy. Group theory entered into pluralism in two ways.

Firstly, it provided the view that the society is basically composed of various interest groups. Such groups engage the interests of the population and act as a chain between the masses and the elites. Secondly, groups provide the foundation of what is known as the 'pressure group' theory which represent the masses in a much more meaningful way because they articulate and make effective the specific demands of the citizens. On the whole, groups provide for some real participation and they advance the perceived interests of the masses.

The modern concept of pluralism believes that in the industrial/ technological societies, power is highly fragmented; it is so amorphous, shifting and tentative that only a few are said to have more than others over a period of time. Power is broadly shared among a group of competing public and private groups; those in high places appear to have more power but in fact they are mediators among conflicting interests for whose power and support they always bargain. As Durkheim maintains: 'Collective activity is always too complex to be able to be expressed through a single and unique organ of the state...A nation can be maintained only if between the state and the individual, there is inter-related a whole series of secondary groups near enough to the individual to attract them strongly in their sphere of action and drag them in this way into the general torrent of social life'. Through their leaders, such groups mediate between individual and all organized forms of power, thereby ensuring the representation of affected interests.

They give private citizen a voice in the government and ease consensus. Even though industrial and political integration and technological demands have made power concentrated in a few hands, the competition among fewer but larger interest groups goes in favour of public interest. The competition among big business, labour and government keeps each interest from misusing its power. Though there are inequalities in wealth, education and power, the presence of associations and groups provide the broadest possible representation of private interest that make democracy viable. Pluralism insists that government is not merely the responsibility of politicians and officials but also that of individuals and social groups of any kind who have their part to play and make their influence felt in indirect ways. Modern pluralism agrees that some form of elite rule by highly educated and interested groups is the essential requirement of our system. However, pluralism exists if no single elite dominates decision-making in every substantive area. If bargaining and opposition among three or four elite groups persists, pluralism remains. Here pluralism comes near the elite theory.

PLURALISTIC THEORY OF DEMOCRACY

The pluralist theory of democracy has been supported by a number of American political scientists such as S.M. Lipset, Robert Dahl, V. Presthus, F. Hunter, R.E. Agger, etc. According to these writers, political power is divided among diverse interest groups, associations, classes and organizations in the society and the elites which lead them. These groups raise their demands directly or through the mediating agencies of political parties on the political system. Pluralist democracy means 'a political system in which policies are made by mutual consultation and exchange of opinions between various groups so that no group or elite is so powerful as to dominate the government to such an extent that it may implement all its demands completely.

The theory believes that power should be shared by all groups in the society and all organizations and groups must have their share in the policy making. No social class should really control the machinery of the government to the total exclusion of other competing classes or groups. According to Presthus, pluralist democracy is 'a socio-political system in which the power of the state is shared by a large number of private groups, interests, organizations, and individuals represented by such organization...pluralism is a system in which political power is fragmented among the branches of government, it is moreover, shared between the state and a multitude of private groups and individuals. Duverger defines it as 'a plurality of decision centres'.

According to Truman, twentieth century democracy consists of a pluralistic struggle among diversified interest groups. Writing in the context of USA, he felt that United States was a democracy by virtue of the fact that no small set of the multifarious interests controlled a dominant share of public policy decisions.' For the pluralist democracy, the behaviour of the individual citizens *per se* is not crucial since the virtues of groups would make up for the failures of individual citizens to conform to the popular democratic image. If the citizens are ignorant of the political issues that affect their interests, the relevant interest groups would protect them. If the individual citizen lacks the resources to make his wishes known, the relevant interest groups would pool their resources, aggregate their separate concerns and articulate them to the appropriate decisions makers.

The key character of this model of democracy is that no single group or minority coalition groups dominate in all important areas of political decisions.

For group theorists like Dahl, modern democracy itself could be defined as 'a process of governance by which minorities— plural—rule'. In order to effect such a rule, the theorists postulate an open political system in which all citizens have the legal opportunity and the economic resources to organize and to pursue their interests in the political arena.

Such an opportunity is vital because it provides an instrument by which support and opposition towards a proposed measure may be expressed. The pluralist theory believes that normal politics consists in the resolution of conflicts among groups. As most citizens lack the competence to govern directly, democracy works better when citizens are governed indirectly through membership of or identification with a group that supports their interests. Individuals should actively participate in and make their will felt through groups of many kinds.

The democratic quality of the pluralist theory is preserved not only by the great diversity of competing groups but also by the greater commitment to the democratic principles among the group leaders and activists. A consensus must exist on what is called 'democratic creed'. All groups must have faith in the democratic methods of voting, organizational membership and other political activities. They must believe that elections are a viable instrument of mass participation in political decisions.

In the political community there must be different centres of power, influence and competition. Also a lively competition among individual elites and groups possessing different basis of power is a critical factor in the pluralist theory of democracy. Here pluralist theory comes very near to the elite theory. As has been pointed out earlier, the line between the elitist and the pluralist democracies can become blurred or non-existent. The greater the emphasis on the importance of plurality of elites and the dispersal of power, the nearer elite theory comes to the pluralist theory. Indeed, the two have been merged by Robert Dahl in his 'pluralist-elitist' theory of democracy.

Dahl's Polyarchy

Robert Dahl has explained the theory of democracy in his books A Preface to Democratic Theory and Polyarcy. In his democratic theory, Dahl has combined the elite concept of government and the electoral competition with the pluralist stress on the dispersal of power. The plurality of elites is regarded in the same light as that of the plurality of groups. According to him, people act both through the electoral system and the group process.

In his type of democracy which he calls 'Polyarchy', there are several places where decisions are made— merchants, industrialists, trade unions, farmers' associations, consumers, politicians, voters. A number of groups and association influence policy making in the government. No one succeeds in obtaining full satisfaction of their demands. Some groups may be more influential than others, though it is difficult to measure the different degrees of this influence exactly. Moreover, the groups have greater power to resist policies which are not wanted and relatively less power to get desired policies implemented by the government. He defines the normal political process a polyarchal democracy by which he means 'a political system in which all active and legitimate groups in the population can make themselves heard at some crucial stage in the process of decisions.

Dahl argues that in polyarchal democracies, it is the minorities—plural—which rule. This argument is based on two lines of reasoning: i) even superficial observation suggests that in USA, decisions are made by endless bargaining; perhaps in no other national political system in the world is bargaining so basic a component of the political process, and ii) all groups share the political power and minorities rule'. If minorities do not exercise political influence effectively, they at least are accorded sufficient political status to prevent revolutions stemming from the disregard of their intense preferences by the majority. According to Dahl, the formulation of elites is natural in the industrial democratic societies but he rejects both the notion of the 'power elite' and the 'ruling class'.

In his book Who Governs, he came to the conclusion that the city was governed by a combination of elites in the cultural and economic fields but none of which could be described as a ruling elite. He firmly believes that the political elite in USA is a democratically competing pluralist elite leadership drawn from a large number of elites in different fields of society. The laws passed by the government are the result of a compromise between the forces of labour, capital and the organized power of other intermediatory groups. Thus although minorities rule in both democracy and dictatorship, the characteristic of polyarchy greatly extends the number, the size and diversity of minorities, whose preferences influence the outcome of government decisions.

CHARACTERISTICS OF PLURALIST THEORY OF DEMOCRACY

- It believes that democracy is a political system run by competitive minorities because only they can secure political liberty of the masses.
- No single group should dominate the decisions-making process. Power should be decentralized, shared, contested and bartered among various groups in the society.
- To keep a check on the concentration of power, there should be a system of checks and balances between legislature, executive, judiciary and administrative bureaucracy.
- The function of the government is to mediate and adjudicate among different groups.
- There should be different centres of power, influence and competition with wide resource base of different groups.
- There must be consensus among different groups on political

procedures, range of policy alternatives and legitimate scope of politics.

CRITICISM AND EVALUATION

The pluralist theory of democracy presumes that the group process and its outcome constitute the popular will and the general interest. However, as Holden points out, this is based on a general fallacy since that which results from the pursuit of particular interests may not be that which is desired by anybody. Firstly there is a mistake of supposing that the outcome of the clash of interests will necessarily bear a relevant relationship to those particular interests. For example, the result of the clash of interests among the groups of property developers, inhabitants, architects, local authorities, and the environmentalists over a policy of slum clearance might well result in that nothing is done.

This would be an outcome that nobody wants. Secondly, it is also misleading that the individuals want only what is incorporated in their various interests. Indeed what an individual wants may run counter to what is involved in the pursuit of group interests. For example, as a wage earner, many people may want higher wages, but if asked at the elections, they might well say that as individuals they want a sound economy and an end to inflation even if this may mean a wage restraint.

Critics remain unconvinced that the procedural safeguards that assure competition form an adequate foundation for democracy. For example, Micheal Mavgolis points out that the pluralist theory of democracy, inspite of assuring competition among elites, does not give a satisfactory explanation on the following grounds:

- It does not devise ways for the elected legislature, the central institution of liberal democracy, to control the huge bureaucracy;
- It does not limit military‘s control of the budgetary resources and technical information that allow it to manipulate public policy in its favour;
- It lacks the capacity to limit or control the great concentration of wealth, income and employment opportunities found in large private corporations;
- The theory does not devise ways to increase or redistribute society‘s resources so that traditionally underprivileged groups like racial minorities, women and those of lower socioeconomic status get sufficient share to allow them opportunities to participate in politics with their compatriots on a substantial footing;
- It could not devise ways to achieve all the above within the limits of natural resources available for development at reasonable economic and environ-mental cost.

Thus in order to improve upon the pluralist theory of democracy, many American political scientist have developed possible restatements of democratic theory that may meet many of the above criteria. Rober Dahl, for example, has suggested socialization of private corporations either through public ownership or public control. He has argued that the private decisions of these corporations concerning economic investment and planning have so much impact on the public sector that the public must have some say in them, if the polity is to call itself a democracy‘. On the other hand, Ithiel de Sole Pool and Duncan have stressed on the necessity of making relevant information available to responsible decision makers.

It has been suggested to enhance citizens‘ control through public access to the otherwise proprietary files of a large bureaucracy both public and private by means of a nationwide computerized information network. Such information can form the basis of direct participation by citizens in the public policy formulation. Similary, Frederich Thayer has suggested that democracy can only be achieved if the hierarchical authority to make decisions binding upon others is replaced by a cooperative network of individual decision makers. However, the task of linking principles of democratic theory to the practices of democratic governance has always been difficult and it has been rendered even more difficult in recent times by the ever expanding scope of welfare state. The pluralist-elite theorists have attempted to make a virtue out of the shortcomings of these institutions.

They supplement the presumed linkages between citizens and representatives, realized through the electoral process, with indirect linkages realized through interest groups, political parties and leadership elites. Their critics have pointed out that governments based upon such practices violate too many democratic principles. However, they have failed to develop an alternative that remains true to democratic principles.

CHARACTERISTICS OF CLASSICAL LIBERAL DEMOCRACY

We can sum up the characteristics of classical-liberal theory of democracy as follows:

- The classical liberal theory of democracy from John Locke onwards, enshrines supremacy of the people.
- It takes individual as the basic unit of democratic model, assuming that he is rational, ethical, active and self-interested. It emphasizes individual freedom and the right of the individual to pursue his own good with minimum of state interference.
- It hated the tyranny of the old regimes of monarchies and aristocracies, stressed the role of vigilance and participation in protecting the hard won rights against the sinister interests of the government. Hence participation in political life was felt necessary

not only for the protection of individual interest but also for the creation of an informed, committed and developing citizenry. Political involvement was considered essential for the development of the individual.

- Participation was deemed a virtue. Through this opportunity, it was believed that the horizon of the individual would be widened, his knowledge extended, his sympathies made less parochial, his practical intelligence developed. It would serve as a means of intellectual, emotional and moral education, leading towards the full development of the capacities of the individual.
- At institutional level, it advocated representative government with elected leadership, regular elections, secret ballot, constitutional state, independent judiciary, individual rights and civil liberties including freedom of thought, feeling, taste, discussion, publication, etc.
- It made a clean demarcation between elected representatives and the bureaucracy. The benefit of popular control and efficiency can be had only be recognizing that they have quite different functions.
- At economic level, it was built upon economic inequality and political equality. It believed in competitive market economy, private possession and control over the means of production and laissez faire economy. According to Macpherson, democracy was to maximize the liberty of citizens and above all secure their property and the working of the capitalist economy. Liberal democracy neither destroyed or weakened the state, it strengthened both the state and the capitalist society.

CRITICISM

- Inspite of being a comprehensive theory of democracy, the classical-liberal theory was vehemently criticized and found inadequate to meet the needs of highly industrialized and technological states which emerged during the inter-war period and the second world war. The main grounds of criticism are as follows: The classical theory rests on a view of man as rational, active, informed and ready to take active part in the political process. Lord Bryce, Graham Wallas and later the empirical writers maintained that man is neither as rational, as disinterested, as informed or active as it is assumed to be. The classical theory either ignores, underplays or simply condemns the role of organized groups, leaders or emotions in political affairs. As Davis writes, 'the reality of irrational mass emotions, self-interest, group egoism and the prevalence of oligarchic and hierarchical social and economic organizations need no longer be denied in the name of democratic values'.
- The classical democracy is centred around the proposition that 'the

people‘ hold a definite and rational opinion about every individual question and they give effect to this opinion by choosing their representatives who will see to it that their opinion is carried out. However, it fails to provide definition of such terms as ‘people‘ or ‘rule‘ which are obviously central to a conception of government as the rule of the people. Public opinion as the basis of government is a ‘democratic myth‘. In actual practice, public opinion does not make the government; rather it is the government which moulds the public opinion.

- The classical theory is based on the assumption that there exists a common good (such as human self-development) which is always simple to define and which every normal person can be made to see by means of rational argument. However, as was pointed out by Schempeter, there is no such thing as a uniquely determined common good on which all people could agree or be able to agree by rational argument. Common good is bound to mean different things to different people.
- Public policy is not necessarily the expression of the common good as conceived by the people alter widespread discussion, debate, consultation and consent. Such a description of policy-making is held to be dangerously naive because it overlooks the role of demagogic leadership, mass psychology, group coercion and the influence of those who control concentrated economic power. According to Walker, classical democracy is unrealistic because i) it employs concepts of the nature of man and the operation of society which are Utopian, and ii) it does not provide an adequate operational definition of its key concepts.
- With the advent of the party system, democracy has been reduced essentially to a competition among the elites rather than the masses. These elites are the driving force and they formulate issues. What we are confronted with in the analysis of the political process is not a genuine but a manufactured will, manufactured in ways similar to commercial advertising. People neither raise nor decide issues but the issues that shape their fate are normally raised or decided for them. The wishes of the electorate are not the ultimate ideas nor the electorate‘s choice flows from its initiative. Rather it is shaped by the elite.
- The classical theory takes an over-simplified view of the complex procedure and decisionmaking process in politics. It lacks a satisfactory treatment of the problems caused by simultaneous affirmation of majority rule and minority right. The complex and technical nature of the political process is beyond the understanding

of an average man who is too much engrossed in his own activities. As Davis writes, 'The highly technical and complex process of policy making is over-simplified and misunderstood (by the classical theory)'.

- The classical theory of democracy was based upon political equality (equality before law) and economic inequality. While the early liberals such as Bentham, James Mill and J.S. Mill tried to absorb the working class aspirations through limited political participation, the theorists of the first half of the twentieth century increasingly lost sight of the class character of liberal democracy and its exploitative consequences upon the working-class. The neo-liberals like Lindsay, Barker, MacIver, Dewey felt that democracy with its regulatory and welfare state could be the best way of bringing a good society. Although they were not insensitive to the concentration of economic power in a few hands, yet they did not find fundamentally anything wrong with the capitalist relations of production. They hoped that with some redistribution of rights between the classes, the democratic process could adjust the differences of various interests through peaceful and rational give and take. For example, Barker wrote that such redistribution would be 'a matter of constant adjustment and read justament, as social thought about justice grows and as the interpretation of the principles of liberty and equality broaden with its growth'. And this could be done through voluntary class cooperation aided by the state. However, as been pointed out by Macpherson, such a redistribution still remains a dilemma of liberal democracies.

Bibliography

A K Tripathi: *Comparative Politics and Political Analysis*, Murari Lal and Sons, Delhi, 2008.

Arvind K. Roy: *Comparative Politics and Political Government*, Mahaveer and Sons, Delhi, 2011.

Ashutosh Pandey: *Comparative Politics and Political Institutions*, Murari Lal and Sons, Delhi, 2010.

B.N. Ray: *Contemporary Political Thinking*, Kanishka Publication, Delhi, 2000.

Badri Narayan: *Documenting Dissent : Contesting Fables Contested Memories and Dalit Political Discourse*, IIAS, 2001.

Bhikhu Parekh: *Colonialism, Tradition and Reform : An Analysis of Gandhi's Political Discourse*, Sage Publication, Delhi, 1999.

Bhuwan Lal Joshi and Leo E Rose: *Democratic Innovations in Nepal : A Case Study of Political Acculturation*, Mandala Publications, Delhi, 2004.

Dia Da Costa: *Development Dramas: Reimagining Rural Political Action In Eastern India*, Routledge, New York, 2009.

G.K. Pagare: *Contemporary Political Thought*, Cyber Tech Publication, Delhi, 2012.

Ganesh Prasad: *Contemporary Political Science*, ABD Publishers, Delhi, 2011.

J K Chopra: *Contemporary Political Thought*, Book Enclave, Delhi, 2006.

J.C. Johari: *Contemporary Political Theory : New Dimensions Basic Concepts and Major Trends*, Sterling, Delhi, 2012.

Lal Bahadur Prasad: *Contemporary Political Thoughts*, Shree Publication, Delhi, 2006.

Meghnad Desai: *Development and Nationhood : Essays in the Political Economy of South Asia*, Oxford University Press, Delhi, 2005.

Monobina Gupta: *Didi: A Political Biography*, Harpercollins, New York, 2012.

N. Jayapalan: *Comprehensive History of Political Thought*, Atlantic Publication, Delhi, 2001.

N. Jayapalan: *Comprehensive Modern Political Analysis*, Atlantic Publication, Delhi, 2002.

N. Jayapalan: *Comprehensive Political Theory*, Atlantic Publication, Delhi, 2002.

N.K. Bhargava: *Democratization in Feudal System: A Sociological Study of Political Parties*, Himanshu Publication, Delhi, 1995.

Narayan Chandra Bandyopadhyaya: *Development of Hindu Polity and Political Theories*, Munshiram Manoharlal, Delhi, 1980.

Norris: *Democratic Phoenix: Reinventing Political Activism*, Cambridge University Press, New York, 2003.

P B Rathod: *Dimensions of Political Theory*, ABD Publication, Delhi, 2008.

P.B. Rathod: *Comparative Political Systems*, Commonwealth Publication, Delhi, 2005.

Peeyush Arora: *Dictionary of Political Science*, Sarup and Sons, Delhi, 2007.

R.C. Gettel and W.A. Dunning: *Communism : A Political Reader*, Cosmo Publication, Delhi, 2004.

Roger Eatwell and Anthony Wright: *Contemporary Political Ideologies*, Rawat Publication, Delhi, 2003.

Sanjeev Kumar Sharma: *Communication Trends and Political Behaviour : A Study of Kumaun*, Pragun Publication, Delhi, 2006.

Satish C. Seth: *Communalism : A Socio-Political Study*, Gyan Publication, Delhi, 2000.

Satya Prakash Dash: *Constitutional and Political Dynamics of India*, Sarup and Sons, Delhi, 2004.

V.K. Verma: *Comparative Political Economy of Welfare States*, Kunal Books, Delhi, 2011.

Zoya Hasan: *Congress After Indira: Policy Power Political Change (1984 -2009)*, Oxford University Press, Delhi, 2012.

Index